THESE HUMBLE UNREMEMBERED LIVES

*But of the humble cottagers, the true people of the vale
who were rooted in the soil, and flourished and died
like trees in the same place – of these no memory exists.
We only know that they lived and laboured; that when
they died, three or four a year, three or four hundred
in a century, they were buried in the little shady
churchyard, each with a green mound over him to mark
the spot. . . . Yet I would rather know the histories of
these humble, unremembered lives than of the great ones
of the vale who have left us a memory.*

W.H. Hudson, A Shepherd's Life, *chapter 13 (1910)*

THESE HUMBLE, UNREMEMBERED LIVES

Stories of Families passing through Compton Chamberlayne

from 1274 to the Early 20th Century

ELISE LANGDON-NEUNER

THE HOBNOB PRESS

First published in the United Kingdom in 2025
by The Hobnob Press,
8 Lock Warehouse, Severn Road, Gloucester GL1 2GA
www.hobnobpress.co.uk

© Elise Langdon-Neuner 2025

The Author hereby asserts her moral rights to be identified as the Author of the Work.

All rights reserved. No part of this publication may be reproduced, stored in a retrieval system, or transmitted in any form or by any means, electronic, mechanical, photocopying, recording or otherwise, without the prior permission of the publisher and copyright holder.

British Library Cataloguing in Publication Data
A catalogue record for this book is available from the British Library

ISBN 978-1-914407-98-7

Typeset in Adobe Garamond Pro, 11/14 pt
Typesetting and origination by John Chandler

For Ray Kerley (1932-2011)

I REMEMBER Ray Kerley with great affection. He was a lad of 18 working on our farm when I was born. Apart from tractor driving, he helped my mother in the garden, digging and planting. He was terrorised by a little girl, who, for reasons unknown to me, he called Lucy. She played tricks on him, such as closing the door and turning the key when he was in the hen house, or stealing his packet of cigarettes and sprinkling the contents along the lane. How did he forgive me for that? He even built a tree house for me. I tagged along every Sunday when he walked his dog on the hill. During the winter of 1962-1963, we sledged down it in heavy snowfall, and one autumn wedged a jar of nuts between branches of a tree for the squirrels. Ray knew a lot about nature and life in general, although at that time he had never travelled outside our district, let alone journeyed to London. One wise saying he imparted was, 'you have to eat a bit of dirt before you die.' This had great appeal, relieving my fear of my mother's wrath when I was messing about in the mud. Years later, I discovered the true sense of this 18th century saying: everyone has to endure something unpleasant during their lifetime. But no, he couldn't have meant me.

Contents

Acknowledgements   ix

1	A Scenic View of Compton Chamberlayne	1
2	Sheep and Corn	11
3	Land and Privilege	16
4	Compton's Manor Courts and Lords of the Manor	22
5	Skidmore alias Buttler: A Family of Villeins	26
6	How Compton Manor Controlled its Inhabitants	31
7	Lynchets/Lanchards	43
8	Compton Ways and Highwaymen	46
9	Love Lost	52
10	Salacious Rumours	63
11	Much Ado about a Cake	65
12	Feisty Joan Elliott and the Troublemaker's Wife and Daughter	70
13	The Unending Jeay-Elliott Wars	76
14	Just Williams (Elliott)	82
15	The Ubiquitous Elliotts	85
16	Jeay Slanders Joan Penruddocke	98
17	William Jeay's Children	101
18	The Penruddockes' Chaotic 17th Century	106
19	18th Century Penruddockes' Aristocratic Ways	117
20	The Elkins: A Yeoman Family	119
21	The Livelongs: A Short or Beloved Story	127
22	Nicholas Lawes and his Slave-owning Namesake	134
23	The Parkers: A Family of Contrasts	139
24	Watts: From Husbandmen to Craftsmen	145
25	Watts: From Yeomen to Cordwainers to Labourers	154
26	A Pretty Rum Lot of Watts	163
27	The Fords: Challenges of Diminishing Landholdings	166
28	The Other Fords: A Churchwarden and a Merchant	177
29	Case: Rags and Riches	181

30	Naish: Everything Came to Nothing	189
31	High/Low Church	196
32	A Co-operative of Blacksmiths, Wheelwrights, and the Cooper	199
33	The Ewences' Sad Demise	204
34	House Furnishings and Personal Effects (mid-16th to early 18th century)	211
35	The Rise and Fall of the Village's Crafts and Trades	222
36	The Plowman Stonemason Dynasty	234
37	Vicars' Records of Parishioners: Poverty in the 19th Century	238
38	The Kings and their Ironies	243
39	Oxen	251
40	The Targetts and their Enterprises	253
41	Was John Piggot the Last Survivor of the Black Hole of Calcutta?	256
42	Constantia's Husband or his Doppelganger?	260
43	George William Wyman the Thatcher	267
44	Naishes Farmyard	274
45	The Wyatts: Sawyers and Hurdle Makers	279
46	Annie Gets her Man	284
47	The Keevils: Autocrats with a Sickening End	290
48	Great-Grandfather Moves Up-Country	296
49	Great-Grandfather's Good Fortune	306
50	A Heroic Vicar Leads the Villagers' Struggle for Autonomy	313
51	Turn of the Century Madness Repeats Itself	324
52	Cruelty at the Big House	330
53	Breach of Promise: Langdon vs Keevil	335
54	The Great War Comes to Compton	344
55	The Penruddockes' Fall	356
	References	362
	Sources and Bibliography	375
	Place Name Index	381
	Personal Name index	384

Acknowledgements

I AM TRULY grateful for the help I have received, whether suppling materials or information, from Alan Clarke, Martin Ingram, Gail Lawes, Margaret Wyman, Adrienne Winchester, Mary Lovell, Mary Tomes, Anna Clayton, Anne Turner, Richard Avery, Jack Deverell, Chris Pigott, Cathy Sedgwick, my sisters Anne Phillips and Valerie Sonnenberg and cousin Jean Pickering. I also wish to sincerely thank Sue Fox for drawing the plan of Compton Chamberlayne, Sophie Kari for drawing the sketch of Naishes Farmyard and Zali Krishna for help with the Index. Further thanks are due to Helen Roberts, Map of Australia Trust; The Fovant History Interest Group; Teresa Lewis, Wiltshire Online Parish Clerks Project; Madeleine Ding, Museum of English Rural Life and members of the Wiltshire Family History Society, especially Steve Hobbs, Jerry King, Jenny Pope, Graham Warmington, and Philip Rabbetts. The Staff at the Wiltshire & Swindon Archives have been incredibly kind and helpful when responding to my numerous requests. Finally, I am greatly indebted to Kristina Bedford (https://ancestraldeeds.co.uk) for transcribing documents, drawing the family trees, editing the text and her unwavering enthusiasm which encouraged me to persist with the project.

I
A Scenic View of Compton Chamberlayne

Compton Chamberlayne is nestled in the chalk downlands of South Wiltshire. For its visitors, this village where I spent an idyllic childhood is like walking into a picture postcard. W. L., whoever he might have been, wrote a series of articles about his travels for the *Salisbury and Winchester Journal* in 1886.[1] He declared, the county 'has many a charming hamlet, but none more so than Compton Chamberlayne.' It is indeed a pretty place, with enchanting, thatched cottages built from locally quarried stone, solid farmhouses, and a sleek Big House, formerly the Manor House, which is a rare architectural survival from the late Stuart period. Yet it is some years since the community gathered to tidy and upgrade the common areas to win an award for the best kept hamlet in Wiltshire.

The Big House is Grade I listed. Ten other dwellings are Grade II listed, including Camel Cottage, with a distinctive humped thatched roof, Piggotts,

Parishioners at Compton Chamberlayne receiving an award for the best-kept hamlet in Wiltshire in 1979. © Salisbury Museum.

believed to be the oldest cottage in the village, and its neighbour, the Georgian Admiral's House, where Admiral Maxwell lived when I was a child. His wiry grey figure, genial demeanour, and wish to be buried among the graves of soldiers who died of influenza in Compton during the First World War, moulded my perception of a commander of the great British fleet.

Historically, the place was not as charming as current literature would have us believe, rather it was a microcosm of the challenges that have faced families who cultivated the land over many centuries, until none of them were left. I will lay out the stories of some of these folk, intermingled with my recollections, but first let me tell you about how I came to be born there, and what I saw when I returned.

Photograph of Naishes Farm taken from the Australia map on Anzac Day, 25 April 2019.

My great-grandfather William Langdon moved up country from Cornwall and leased Manor Farm in Compton from Charles Penruddocke in 1889. He left again in 1920. My father Willie Langdon passed his early years in Dorset and became the tenant of Naishes Farm in 1943, after the estate's ownership had transferred to George Cross. Willie gave up the farm in 1978 and bought a cottage in the village. I had left eight years earlier, in 1970. Four Langdon generations lived in the village at some point during their life.

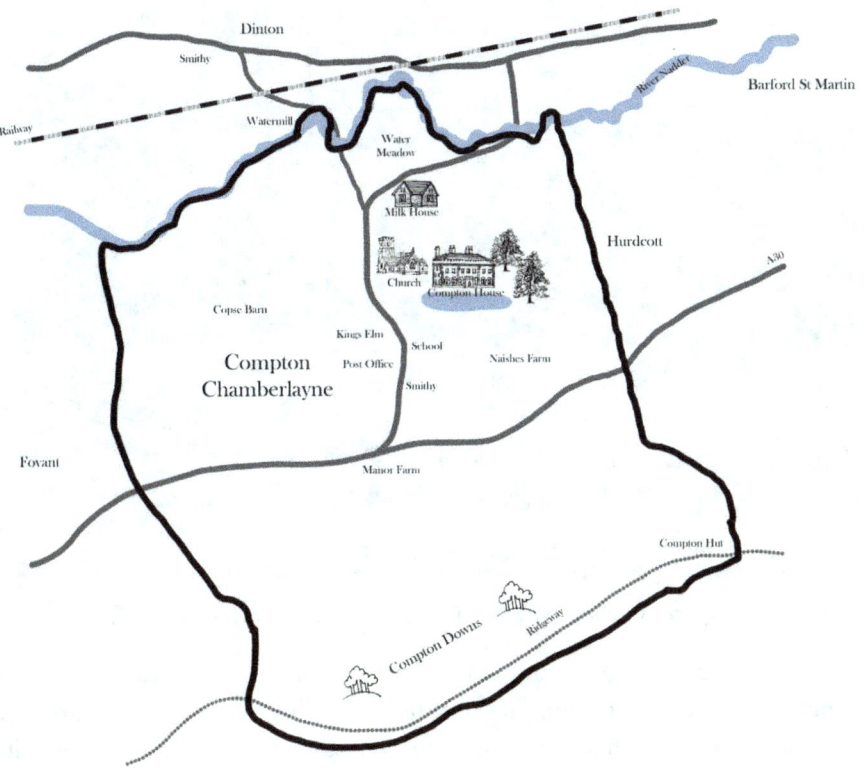

Plan of Compton Chamberlayne. Credit Sue Fox.

On 25 April 2019, I found myself standing once again at the top of Compton Downs, with Naishes Farm sitting below me. It is bathed in precarious April sunshine, calm before the next blasting of sleet, a passive pallet of garish yellow oilseed rape and deep green new season wheat. The fields are hideously gross, stripped to facilitate harvesting, with monster machines spanning the crops. Hedges have been ripped out, and there is silence where birds and rodents had once chirped and squeaked. Removing hedges does no good to Nature. The earth that their roots formerly bound together is now free to erode, and the small creatures are made homeless. 118,000 miles of hedgerows have been eradicated in England since 1950,[2] while 80 years ago Everyman's Library described its 1939 edition of W. H. Hudson's book *A Shepherd's Life* as 'the South Wiltshire scene in the early 20th century, depicting a way of life that has vanished and a landscape now scarred by the hand of modern science.'[3]

The Big House and church at Compton Chamberlayne in 1853.

A square Georgian farmhouse, and a discrete farmyard with an incongruous collection of outbuildings, puncture the yellow-green monotony. The house appears unchanged from my recollection of it, but no farmer calls it home anymore. The farmyard is different. One side used to be enclosed by a stone wall, while the other three were lined by harmonious thatched barns with walls of slatted wood. Memories slip back to the times I sat in a barn with the workmen at nammet,* when they ate their grub and teased the varmit† (me!).

If I crane my neck to the left, I can just about see the village in a crease of the wooded valley from which it took its first name, 'Compton'— coombe tun, or 'settlement in a wooded valley.' It was called Contone in the Domesday Book. The parish is more or less square, slightly elongated on its north-south axis. The River Nadder defines its northern end, and the chalk hills, where I am standing, its southern extremity. The A30 road from London to Land's End, which bisects the parish, is clearly visible from my vantage point. To the east,

---

* Lunch taken by farm labourers. Nammet is a corruption of 'no meat,' meat being too expensive for lunch.

† The men on the farm called us children varmits, especially if we did something naughty, such as trample over their freshly dug garden. Varmit is a variation of vermin, which are pests or nuisance animals that spread diseases, or destroy crops or livestock.

Burcombe huddles between Compton and Barford St Martin. Wilton is the first town along the road, followed by the city of Salisbury, nine miles from Compton. The next town to the west, after the road passes through the neighbouring village of Fovant, is Shaftesbury, twelve miles away across the border in Dorset.

From up here, a dip flanking the Nadder conceals the water meadows from view, but Dinton village beyond is clearly visible. Moving back from the river, where withy beds once provided willow shoots for weaving basket containers, a strip of woodland gives way to Compton Park. I cannot make out the Big House set in the park with its artificial lakes. The church walled within its grounds is also hidden from me.

A string of cottages lines the main street, mooching about from the hectic A30 down to the river with hardly a wiggle. At a point where it could carry straight on, only a track runs down to Dinton Mill and over the railway lines to emerge in Dinton village, opposite the old smithy shed. A metalled road shies away near the track entrance and bends sharply to the east, skirting the water meadows before turning north again over Horseshoe Bridge spanning the Nadder. The road, named Horseshoe Lane, was called the Portway in the 16th century. It reaches the Dinton road in the hamlet of Baverstock, which adjoins the Parish of Barford St Martin.

Piggotts, reputed the oldest cottage in the village.

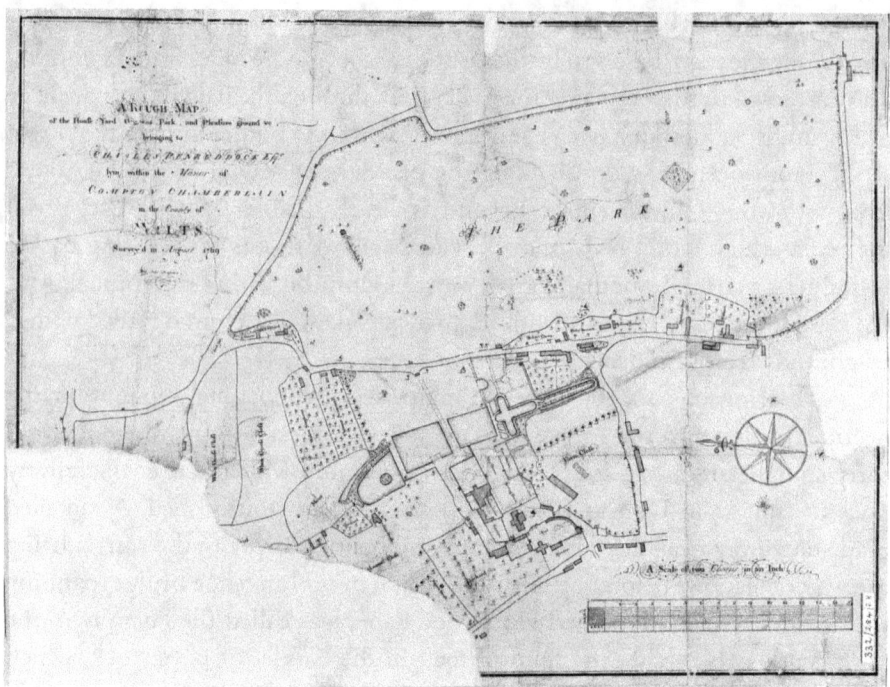

1769 estate map with kind permission of Wiltshire and Swindon History Centre (332/284/2H).

Compton is a one-street village. If I had been standing here before the Penruddockes reorganised the place, I would have seen a larger settlement with two streets, described in the survey they commissioned in 1597, shortly after acquiring the estate, as West Brook Lane and East Brook Lane. They ran in parallel. An estate map of 1769 shows East Brook Lane with dwellings alongside it. Desiring more ground for the Manor House in the late 18th century, the landowners extended the adjoining deer park, incorporating the second road and demolishing the dwellings along the way. The park was further enlarged to a peak of 150 acres in 1930, then shrank again when the field we called the Park was returned to agricultural use. This field was notable for its sprinkling of trees planted in pairs, their shade much appreciated by our dairy cows, and likewise one hollow oak used by us kids to hide in.

Apart from the Big House, Compton today has around 25 dwellings, a village hall, and a cricket pitch. Its pub, shop-cum-post office, and school are history. The hall has its own backstory, including service as a former military hut in the village's First World War camp. Three farmhouses, belonging to Naishes, Manor, and Home Farms, stand apart from the main settlement.

Less than a handful of villagers work for the estate; the rest see themselves as suave executives, rather than country bumkins. They are retired, work in Salisbury, or are weekend escapees from London. When the Domesday Book was compiled between 1085 and 1086, the village was among the largest 40% of places documented. Records spanning the last 300 years show that the population reached its zenith at 352 in 1851, with 70 houses occupied, and fell to 213 in 1911. When I was born in 1951, the population count was a mere 170 souls and is now hovering around 100. These dwindling numbers reflect the continuing devastation of a community founded on agriculture following the Industrial Revolution, which was thought to have started in 1740, and subsequent mechanisation. Recent research has revealed that over a third of male agricultural workers left the land between 1600 and 1740, suggesting the Industrial Revolution had actually begun in the 17th century.[4] Even so, before great-grandfather came to Manor Farm, his predecessor John Keevil, who had also been farming Naishes, reported — to today's ears — an astounding total of fifty workers in the 1881 census: thirty-seven men, three women, and ten boys. This number was hardly changed from thirty years earlier, when, aside from smallholders, three farmers with forty-nine farm labourers between them were recorded in Compton at the time of the 1851 census. Great-grandfather kept 19 men and boys in 1899, taking on more labour at harvesttime. He was farming 625 acres, just under half of Keevil's acreage. Less than 50 years later, when Willie started to farm 510 acres at Naishes, he employed only 4 or 5 workers at any given time to help him. Farm labourers were still leaving the land at the rate of 22,000 a year in the early 1960s.[5]

On that April day in 2019, I was alone on Compton Downs, despite 100 strangers standing next to me. Some lived in the village, but I didn't know a single one of them. I should explain what brought me back up the hill — just to be overcome with melancholic nostalgia. It was my father. During the First World War, the land I could see below was commandeered for military training and transit camps. Twelve such camps were built in the villages of Compton, Fovant, and nearby Sutton Mandeville in 1915. The one at Naishes Farm was called Hurdcott Camp, because it encompassed the neighbouring Hurdcott Farm in Baverstock. In March 1917, it was taken over by the Australian Imperial Forces to train new arrivals, and for soldiers to convalesce from their wounds. As early as 4 o'clock in the morning, volunteer privates traipsed up the mound with spades on their shoulders, intent on carving an outline of Australia across a stretch of two acres on the hillside by removing turf to reveal the underlying chalk. They needed to make a quick getaway when the clock struck seven, signalling the start of rifle practice on the ranges below, often sliding down the slope on their shovels.[6]

View of Army Camp No 11 at Naishes Farm, one of 12 camps in the parish during the First World War, as seen from the Naishes Farmhouse, and behind the huts the Map of Australia carved on the hill by Australian soldiers.

The soldiers' artistic activities did not meet with universal approval. An article published in *The Times* on 7 November 2018, entitled 'Armistice centenary: Homesick soldiers' giant map is saved,' refers to a report in *The Emu Bay Times*, Tasmania, published on 20 July of that year. It recounted that, after the War, the owner of the land sued the Commonwealth for damages. He refused an offer of £1,500, went to court, lost the case, and had to pay his own costs. The plaintiff was Charles Penruddocke.

Grass has grown over the map twice. It was allowed to reclaim the ground during the Second World War, for fear enemy aircraft would use its beacon as a location point. After the War, the Fovant Home Guard Association reinstated the map, together with regimental emblems carved on the hills in Fovant and Sutton Mandeville. A flagpole was erected on it. My father first hoisted the Australian flag at its dedication on 26 January 1951, four days before I was born. Every year after, until he retired, he carried that flag up the hill and flew it on the Queen's birthday, Australia Day, Anzac Day, and Remembrance Day. If it had rained, my two sisters and I returned home from school to find the massive canvass laid out to dry in our kitchen. It was never raised again after our family left, and regular maintenance of the map was abandoned as too costly. Grass began to take over once more. Watching it gradually fade was dispiriting, but I was not alone in this sentiment. In 2017, a group of volunteers set up the Australia Map Trust to restore it. There was a gathering on the hill on Anzac Day 2019 to hoist a new flag and dedicate the renovated map.

Looking down on Naishes, I was not only reminded of my father, but also took time to mull over the state of the farm he took on two years before the end of Second World War. Although the camp's corrugated steel Nissen

The foundations of the camp are still visible from the air. On the left on this photograph the Big House and an artificial lake are also visible. Credit Margaret McKenzie.

huts had been sold off, their concrete foundations remained. They were still visibly 'like scars' from the main road, as George Cross described them when he bought the estate in 1930.[7] One of the first things my father did was to dig up the field where they had stood to grow corn in response to the government's cry to 'Dig for Victory.' Removing them was laborious work. A searchlight close to the main road also needed to be dismantled. One field at Fovant has never been ploughed because too much concrete and brick is entombed in the earth where stables and huts once stood. By the time I came along, our field was a hunting ground for intriguing treasures. My father and I spent many an hour walking across it, collecting spent bullets, military uniform buttons, bottles with marbles used to hold in the carbonation, earthenware ink pots, and many other discards – even hand grenades – that had been turned up by the plough. The downs stood solid above us. It was over them that every morning used to brighten for me, sometimes threatening under a heavy sky, other times benign, as a dusky mirage slowly materialising beneath a grey-pink firmament.

Willie Langdon hoisting the flag on the Map of Australia on 26 January 1951.

Another memory comes bounding back as I watch the heavy traffic on the A30. 'It's time to go' my father says softly, so as not to disturb my sleep too roughly, but I have been awake anticipating his words for hours. I bounce out of bed. As I reach the bottom of the stairs, he is already on his way out to the car. A colossus in the shape of our combine harvester looms outside the barn, gently chugging. We fall in behind, lights flashing, and the small cavalcade, led by our workman Ray Kerley on his tractor, starts its slow journey. I loved the thrill of unaccustomed stillness and watching the night's mantel lift as we progressed east along the A30 on these annual outings to Wilton. There we turned onto a track that takes us onto the hill, before cutting back to our wheat and barley fields on their crest above our farm. My grandfather told me that in his time oats were grown on the hill and wheat and barley in the fields below. Earlier, the downs were used for grazing sheep, whose importance for the village's past agriculture cannot be overstated. We see not a single sheep. Daniel Defoe remarked on the hundreds and thousands he encountered when he travelled the same track over the hills from Shaftsbury to Salisbury at the beginning of the 18th century.[8]

2
SHEEP AND CORN

EARTH TERRACES OF the side of hills, known as lynchets, are ghosts of ancient times, created by the farmers who cultivated corn on the South Wiltshire chalk downs. Fertilizers only became widely available commercially from the 1850s onwards, but with their ingenuity, our forefathers came up with the brilliant idea of employing vast flocks of sheep to provide their droppings as the top dressing needed for producing optimal yields of corn. Sheep were also used as the forerunners of rollers, to trample and settle the light soil, keeping it warm and moist, and preventing newly-cast seeds from blowing to dust. Under this sheep-and-corn farming scheme, the animals were penned in folds on arable at night and driven over the downs every morning to forage.

Sheep evolution on the Wiltshire downs mirrored farming economics. During the early 17th century, the breed was hardy, able to withstand walking long distances and the daily climb to the downs, slow to fatten, and had a light fleece. As grain prices fell in the middle of the century, a larger Wiltshire horned type that produced more meat was developed by selective breeding. The Wiltshires remained dominant across Southern England during the 18th century. With the boom in the wool export trade, they were replaced by Southdowns, whose coats had more fleece. Its collapse in the 1820s led to the development of hardy Hampshire Downs, whose lambs fatten early. Sheep and corn were still vital when great-grandfather arrived in the village. In 1897, he wrote to his nephew John in Australia telling him that he had 300 ewes, intended to buy 100 more as soon as he could get the money, and believed he could very well keep 600, while tilling 200 acres of corn. He employed two shepherds to look after his Hampshire Downs. My father recalled from his youth in neighbouring Dorset: 'The most important labourer on the farm was the head shepherd and to some extent the flock of sheep ruled the farm.'

Imagine the shepherd and his dog on a typical spring morning at dawn. They rise early, and now the white throng — he in his smock, the flock bleating out before him, bells clanking against woolly necks — are making their way across the downs. Grass glistens from last night's fall of rain. Pristine

From left: Rear-Admiral Joseph Archibald Maxwell, Dorothy Clay, Dodie Maxwell, our GP Dr Richard Chaloner Cobbe Clay in costume at a Victorian picnic in Compton Chamberlayne to mark the jubilee of the village's Women's Institute in June 1965. Dr Clay is wearing a shepherd's smock. He named the carter (John) Jarvis as the last man in Fovant to wear such a smock. Jarvis is recorded at Jay's Folly as aged 75 in the 1901 census. © Salisbury Museum.

mushroom caps, fresh from earthen slumbers, catch the sun's first rays. The shepherd notices each tiny change from his trek up the hill the day before. He stands by the hedgerow, intently watching an oak leaf. Usually it flutters in the wind, sometimes with the fury of a demented witch. Today the leaf hangs quietly. The stillness is only broken by the creak of a bough or sporadic release of a rain drop lodged on a twig. A rainbow warns the shepherd there is fresh rain to come. He has his great coat with him:

The rainbow in the marnin
Gives the shepherd warnin
To car er's gurt cwoat on er's back
The rainbow at night
Is the shepherd's delight
For then no gurt ewoat will er lack

Topsoil from a fox's scratching catches his eye. The flock reaches the dew pond, where it pauses to drink while the shepherd rests on his customary stone and takes a lump of bread and cheese out of his pocket. A rabbit hops by and scurries down a burrow. From high above, he hears the poignant calls of skylarks intent on distracting passers-through away from their precious eggs, which lie bare among the flint stones. Suddenly, a wake of buzzards wheel in. Anxious lapwings announce their flight with a shrill 'pee-wit' cacophony, as the sun catches an iridescent myrtle-green glint on their dapper liveries with each wingbeat. The day has begun for the solitary shepherd on the lonely downs.

These shepherds sometimes got into trouble. Back when boundaries between manors on the downs were ill-defined, they could be reprimanded if their flocks encroached upon the one adjacent. In 1597, reports were made under oath to the surveyors of Compton that 'farmers of Broad Chalke do feed on the downs with their flock further than they ought to.'

We did not keep a flock at Naishes Farm when I was a child. Food rationing introduced during the War continued until 1954, and grassland was still being ploughed, but there had been sheep on the farm before I was born. My eldest sister Anne recalls that she had a pet lamb by the original name of Larry.* He lodged in her memory after her attempts to saddle and ride him resulted in her being dragged along the ground through a field at speed. My only encounter with sheep was on the downs in a field that great-grandfather had once farmed. I was with our farmhand Ray on one of our regular Sunday walks with his dog, when we saw a woolly bundle on its back, all fours pointed heavenward. The animal had been over-enthusiastically grazing on a clover patch and had 'blowed'† itself. Bodies of ruminates become terribly inflated with wind after consuming large quantities of nitrogen-containing plants, landing them in this predicament, unable to right themselves. The usual cure is to stick a knife into the stomach to release the air, but we were ill-prepared

---

*   As cats and Felix, Lambs were commonly called Larry.

†   Henry Fray uses the term 'they be getting blasted' in Thomas Hardy's novel *Far from the Madding Crowd*, Chapter XXI.

for such an operation. Instead, we rolled it over and stood it on its legs, which jet-propelled the hapless creature, wind hissing from its posterior, into the distance to re-join its flock.

When my father retired, his garden was in need of a lawn mower, and three sheep provided the perfect solution. He wrote about them to me in June 1981:

> I had a very official letter arrive one morning this week from the Ministry of Agriculture etc. On opening it it began 'Dear Flockmaster.' I felt very flattered, until I read it further. It was an order telling me to dip my large flock between the 15th June and the 17th July. I have been negotiating with Mummy for the loan of the bath for a day, but I have met with no success, not even when I told her an official would have to be present to test the strength of the poisonous dip [arsenic-based insecticide] I would have to use.

His trio of sheep met their unhappy fate at the end of the following summer. Their flockmaster estimated that there would not be enough grass on the land to feed them throughout the winter. He took them one-by-one to the abattoir in his car, quoting an old farmers' saying: 'A sheep's worst enemy is another sheep.'

Sheep came into their own again in Compton under the controversial European Union scheme that paid farmers to leave fields fallow. Although the project was abolished in November 2008, Compton estate still lets out grazing for them.

Hampshire Down sheep at Manor Farm, photograph from the early 20th century.

Ravens

W. H. Hudson narrates his talks with Caleb Bawcombe (a pseudonym for James Lawes of Martin, about eleven miles from Compton) in *A Shepherd's Life*. Dogs were used for hunting deer, and keepers fed them with worn-out horses that they bought and slaughtered. Their carcasses were left in the woods for the hounds to batten on the flesh, and the carrion attracted ravens. With the decline of deer hunting in the area, the number of ravens also dwindled. Only a few nesting places were left in Wiltshire by 1887, one of which was in Compton Park.

There was an old belief that ravens 'smell death.' When spotted above a flock of sheep, they were a sure sign that one of the sheep was poorly and soon to die. A similar account is given in a note in volume 40 of the *Wiltshire Archaeological and Natural History Magazine* (1942-1944):

David Watts, clerk at Baverstock, 1920, said, referring to a tombstone in the churchyard, that he and the man whose tombstone it was, were working together and one of the ravens that then (many years before) in habited [sic] Grovely Wood and nested at Compton Chamberlayne, flew over croaking. The man said 'Dave, did you hear old Jack Raven? there'll be a grave to be dug soon.' That man was buried soon afterwards. They used to say a raven's croak was a sign of death.

3
LAND AND PRIVILEGE

COMPTON CHAMBERLAYNE WAS extraordinary for stubbornly retaining elements akin to the feudal system. I cannot disentangle memories of the place from my incredulity that until 1924, when the Penruddockes sold Manor Farm, the entire village was owned by a single family. Bar this 600-acre grange, the estate was sold to one man, a London property developer, in 1930, and again acquired as a unit by an industrialist in 1974. For me, it is inconceivable that as late as the 1970s almost an entire village could still be held by one single person, and that government policy could actively encourage industrialists to use land — with which they had no previous connection — to offset against their profits. Historically, British agriculture is virtually unique for its detachment of ownership from the farming of land. This system underpins the tenacious social class system for which the country is renowned. Today, 65% of its land is owned by the aristocracy, corporations, oligarchs, and city bankers.[9]

The Chamberlayne/Chamberlain family, whose surname gave the village the second part of its double moniker, were lords of the manor in the 12th and 13th centuries. We know next to nothing about them, aside from some unsavoury characters who turned up amongst their number. The Wiltshire Court of Crown Pleas charged Roger le Chapeleyn (Chamberlayne), a clerk of Compton Chamberlayne, and another man with the murder of Walter le Rus in 1268.[10] The felons came to Walter's house, killed him, and carried away the goods they found there. Robert Chamberlain was indicted in 1303 for inciting a large mob to break into Reginald of Frome's house in Compton, where they broke his arm. The reason for this attack was probably a dispute over mortgages which Reginald held on Compton properties.

Robert Chamberlain demised a half-share of the manor to Hugh of Haversham in 1208. A century later, in 1309, the retained half was sold to Richard Grimstead. After Richard's son Thomas died in 1328, that moiety should have transferred to his son John. However, when John died in infancy the following year, his inheritance was divided between Thomas' three sisters. It then passed down through the female line, and a series of owners who were attainted and reinstated according to the changing fortunes of their allegiances throughout the War of the Roses and tumultuous Tudor reigns, until it ended up with Richard's six-times great-grandson Andrew Baynton. He sold the reversion *c* 1546 to that notorious figure of Tudor intrigue Sir Thomas Seymour.

Hugh of Haversham's half-manor descended to his great-granddaughter Matilda after her father, Nicholas of Haversham, died in 1274. She was 33 weeks old and survived. Her inheritance was administered under wardship until 1289, when an inquisition was held to prove that she was of full age and could take possession of the estate. Matilda at 16 was already married to James of the Plaunche. How was her age to be proved before the advent of parish registers? Evidence of her year of birth was given by witnesses who lived in the village, one of whom could associate her birth with the year his brother was killed. Others were present at her christening, knew or were related to the chaplain who conducted the ceremony. Yet another interviewed Robert of Compton, who carried her from the water. The baptism had been delayed for two days to await his arrival.

Inquisition Post Mortems (IPMs) were inquiries held by an escheator on the King's behalf after the death of his feudal tenants in chief, who were direct tenants of the Crown. The escheator, with the help of a jury of local men, was tasked with ascertaining the deceased's income, the rights due to the Crown, and who the next heir should be. IPMs survive from the early 1200s and continue through to the Restoration in 1660, when feudal tenure was abolished. They provide a snapshot of the usage and value of the acreages Compton landowners held, the number of its tenants, who were divided into categories according to the size of their holdings, and their worth in terms of rents paid and services provided. Some curious rents in kind come to light. While most of Haversham's ten free tenants paid a monetary sum in 1274, others made remittances ranging from a pair of gloves valued at 2 pence to be delivered at Easter to a garland of roses (whether white or red not specified) at the feast of John the Baptist. One tenant and his heirs were 'to find every night in the year a light in the mortuary in the Church of St Michael forever. And a light with 4 lamps to be burning at the celebration of each Mass.'

Next in the pecking order below free tenants came customary tenants who held virgates* of land, followed by those holding half-virgates. Each paid rent and rendered services to the lord. The lowest echelon comprised thirty cottars, one of whom, in addition to rent and work owed to the lord, was

---

* Varying measures of land, typically 30 acres, but probably much less in Compton.

obliged to give 'one cock and one hen for chersetum at the feast of St Martin, price 2d.' Chersetum, which is particularly associated with Wiltshire, is any customary offering made to the parson of the parish or to the appropriator of the benefice. Its inclusion in the *Medieval Latin Dictionary* suggests that it was a pre-Reformation Catholic custom which continued to be observed in and around Wiltshire for some time after.

During the 14th century, pepper and cumin were rare and expensive commodities. Not only were these spices sought-after status symbols in the culinary repertoire of wealthy households disposed to impress with ostentatious banquets, but they were also highly prized for their alleged medicinal qualities. It then comes as no surprise that one rent at Compton in 1274 was a pound of pepper valued at 7 pence payable at the feast of St Michael. Both pepper and cumin are found in the IPM of James of the Plaunche's wife Maud in 1329. She received 2lb of pepper and 1lb of cumin from her free tenants at Michaelmas on 29 September. Altogether, their rents in kind gifted a 'present' to the lords and ladies of the manor on every feast day. Later, in 1598, one freeholder's rent was a salmon fish, at least 2-feet long, to be delivered upon fourteen days' notice between the feasts of Pentecost and St James.

The services the tenants provided included weeding and reaping the lord's corn, mowing hay for a few days, and working throughout harvesttime, except on Sundays and feast days. Some tenants were allowed to pay in money instead of rendering their prescribed services.

After Sir Thomas Seymour was executed in 1549, Andrew Baynton sold the reversion of his half-manor to George Penruddocke, who hailed from Penruddocke in Cumberland, *c* 1557, the year before Elizabeth I ascended the throne. Two years later his widow sold the estate itself to George, who had served as the standard bearer under William, Earl of Pembrooke, commander of the English army against France and the Ottoman Empire in the Italian War of 1551-1559. George 'fought a single combat with a French nobleman of whom he had the victory for which he received great honour and advancement.'[11] He was knighted in 1568 and died in 1582, when his son Sir Edward inherited the half-manor.

Following Matilda's death during the late 1200s-early 1300s, her moiety passed through a number of convoluted family connections involving the female line, until Thomas of Lucy sold it to John Nicholas, also *c* 1557. His son Robert then sold it on to Sir Edward in 1596. Thus, Sir Edward was finally able to reunite the half-manors, and the Penruddocke family went on to reign Compton for the next 381 years.

Sir Edward immediately commissioned his brother Robert and William Bower to conduct a survey. They compiled a field book in 1597, detailing each household and parcel of land on the estate. As had been the case in the Domesday Book, arable accounted for the largest portion of agricultural land, with 846 acres farmed in common, spread over two fields. These were divided into furlongs and strips individually leased to the village's farmers. Rather than holding adjoining strips, farmers' quotas were scattered to ensure that good and poor ground was shared. The second largest portion comprised 516 acres of 'old inclosures.' Enclosure involved grouping and fencing plots to create larger parcels. The old enclosures were of meadows and land within the 'Town of Compton,' where farmsteads and cottages clustered around West Brook and East Brook Lanes. 'New inclosures' of 305 acres of pasture and 97 of arable were divided between the freeholders and principal tenants. The largest freehold, around 170 acres, was held by Robert Reade, a 'gent' who was new to the village. The demesne farm was leased to Nicholas Lawes. The common grazing land recorded comprised 34 acres designated 'common meadow,' which provided grass for sheep in the spring and hay in the winter, and 300 acres on the downs.

A heap of privileges came with the manor, in particular two watermills, where villagers were compelled to have their grain ground to flour, yielded a substantial revenue for Sir Edward. Even as late as 1819, when Charles Penruddocke held the estate, he was granting leases that obliged his tenants to grind corn at the lord's mill in Dinton. Edward ensured that he had fresh meat in winter. Animals were slaughtered during the autumn because of the scarcity of food for them in the cold months, and their meat was salted. Eating too much of it could cause skin problems. The lord had a variety of options for avoiding such an eventuality: domestic pigeons, fish from his fishponds, and game. The lord alone had the right to possess a dovecote. One had stood in the grounds of the Manor House from at least 1274.

Naturally, all rights to hunt deer, shoot birds, and trap rabbits — or coneys as they were called in Wiltshire — were exclusive to the lord. Deer were kept in the park, which was created during the late 13th or early 14th century, suggested to have been one of the earliest deer parks in England.[12] William Coffin was granted the lease of an acre at 'Foventes Leepe yate' in 1606.[13] Its gate was designed to welcome wild deer to leap into the park, while preventing domestic deer from leaping out.[14] Amusingly, another acre at Smythes Crosse in William's lease was described as 'a headache.' We know a herd of 170 fallow deer roamed the park in 1867.[15] This species, introduced by the Normans, had become the aristocrats' park animal of choice.[16]

Coney barrows were noted on waste plots on the hill in the 1597 survey. I presume the rabbits were wild and intended for trapping, rather than bred in a warren for meat and fur. Sir John Penruddocke had just such a warren in the village on Eastclose, which had been impaled by 1628, when he let the ground to Humphrey Sidley.[17] One can imagine that Coney Catch Meadow was a favoured hunting ground, although we should not jump to conclusions about the name's origins. We are in Wiltshire, where a catch meadow in the local vernacular is one where a stream of water has been diverted to fall from one level to another through carriages. What happened in Sheep Wash Meadow is clearer. As for Leporidae, Charles Sansom assisted in the capture of the last blue hare in Compton during the mid-19th century.[18] These hares, also called mountain hares, were prized for their fur, which is a blue-grey colour in summer and white in winter.

Sir Edward's Compton was typical of the chalk downland estates in South Wiltshire, where common field agriculture was practiced in the farming system based on sheep and corn, as outlined in the last chapter. The tiers of hierarchy in the village were hardly different from those described in the medieval IPMs three centuries earlier. After the lord came the freeholders, then copyholders, cottars, or those holding small tenements, the lord's servants, and landless labourers, who were less inclined to settle in one place. One such itinerant was Thomas Saunders. He had been born in far-away Warwickshire and was a day labourer in Compton in 1600.[19] The great divide between the lord's living standards and the lower ranks persisted. There was, however, little difference between everyone else. Their cottages, food, and clothes were indistinguishable, and all spoke in the Wiltshire tongue.

The Penruddockes came to Compton during a period of prosperity. Elizabethan laws had led to stability, and social measures had been drawn up in the form of Poor Laws. The Religious Settlement sought to reconcile the divide between Catholics and Protestants, and to resolve the disparities between their services and beliefs. Demand for corn increased with the rapid growth of populations in such towns as Bristol and London during the 16th and 17th centuries. While earlier crops had been grown for the subsistence of the manor and to supply local towns — Salisbury and Shaftesbury held corn markets as early as the 14th century — now corn was being sold to places further afield, and for export.

As the 17th century progressed, more and more export concessions were granted to corn growers, while duties were imposed on imported corn. Arable crops could most efficiently be produced by large-scale farming with lower proportional working costs. Consequently, landowners were eager to amalgamate strips to promote more efficient corn production and bigger yields. The increasing prosperity of farmers holding the newly-created larger plots threatened the communal sheep flock, which was essential for the subsistence of smaller farmers unable to afford a big enough herd to service their ground, or to pay for a shepherd to care for their sheep. These developments, coupled with the lord's depletion of their other common rights, squeezed the cottars out. Additionally, the Penruddockes acquired the smaller freeholds during the 17th century, and seized the opportunity to take customary tenancies in hand as they fell due during the 18th.

By 1850, the year of the Tithe Award, the main part of the parish's agricultural land was already divided between three farms: Compton Farm, later known as Manor Farm, Naishes Farm, and Copse Farm, which became Copse Barn from 1886, and is today called Home Farm. All were owned by the Penruddockes, but worked by tenant farmers. Manor and Naishes Farms are neighbours, together covering all the land at the south end of the parish, but they also include a lion's share of the water meadows flanking the River Nadder. Home Farm is situated in the west of the parish. The farmyard of a fourth, Forge Farm, where the smithy worked in great-grandfather's time, was on the main street when I lived in the village. The lady farmer at Forge Farm had a herd of Jersey* cows, whose delicate features, contrasting with our hefty Shorthorns and Frisians, were a great pleasure to encounter sauntering down the main street towards their milking parlour. Her farmhand, Ted, followed on behind them. Years later, when he died aged 80 in 2017, he was the last person in the village to speak in a broad Wiltshire dialect. My father reported a conversation with him by a cherry tree in 1995, when my mother had set her heart on protecting the fruit from the ravages of blackbirds. She wanted Ted to cover the tree with netting, which my father derided as futile because she would not be able to pick the cherries, as they would ripen at different times, and the feathered thieves would find a way under the canopy anyway. My mother turned to Ted: 'I expect you think I'm mad?' Ted considered his awkward position and proffered his unique philosophy to the couple: 'I be mad, and I do know it. You be mad, and you do know it. Willie he be mad, but he don't know it.'

---

* Our landlord George Cross was one of the pioneers of Jersey cow breeding, and his 'Penshurst' herd carried off all the big show cups. In 1925, he held the world record for milk and butter yield. Mr George Cross obituary, *The Times*, 28 March 1972.

4
Compton's Manor Courts and Lords of the Manor

VILLAGERS SUFFERED TIGHT control by the lord, who exercised his jurisdiction through Courts Baron and Leet. The lord's steward or bailiff conducted proceedings in his name, while court decisions were made by a select number of tenants, who were obliged to serve on the jury, or homage, under oath. The court's activities were recorded on pieces of parchment, sewn together to form rolls, with contemporary copies bound as books.

The principal court was the Court Baron, sometimes just called the Manorial or General Court. Its most important business concerned the transfer of land: stipulating conditions of tenure, rents, rights of transfer, inheritance of widows, and the amount a tenant had to pay to the lord for a lease, or when a new life was added to a lease. These entry fines were the lord's main source of income from the manor, while rents remained low.

A tenant wishing to give up his land first surrendered it to the lord, who then granted it to the new tenant. A tenant claiming succession by inheritance had to prove entitlement by descent or by a will, and paid a heriot, similar to our death duty, to the lord. More often than not, the heriot was one of the deceased's belongings, such as his best beast. One curious custom in Compton was the landlord's right to receive a 'deoland.' Any article or animal that had been responsible for the death of a tenant had to be surrendered to him. For instance, one William Keate of Fovant was killed in 1653 in a horrific incident. His father's horse had dragged him up and down a pasture until he died. The ground was within Compton Manor, accordingly the horse had to be forfeited as a deoland to Colonel John Penruddocke.

With every transfer, the new tenant was required to swear fealty to the lord. A copy of the court record was given to him as proof of his title. Thus, he became a copyholder. The most common tenures during the 17th and 18th centuries were for 99 years or, if longer, the lives of three named people, usually the tenant, his wife, and a child. Such tenancies provided a literal life-time security for the tenant and his dependants. The landlord had the advantage of his tenant being responsible for repairs and payment of land taxes. Other tenancies were held at the will of the lord, which allowed a tenant to live at a property without a formal agreement with him. As time progressed, rack rent tenancies held for a fixed term took over.

The Court Leet traditionally administered the customs and regulations of the manor, which were inherited or prescribed by the lord. It included, and was alternatively called, the View of Frankpledge, which was a gathering and inspection of all the men who were, or ought to be, in frankpledge. This was a system of monitoring the behaviour of the lord's underlings. Male residents over the age of twelve, including freeholders, had to appear and make their 'pledge' to keep the king's peace. Thus, they were bound together by mutual responsibility to enforce law and order — and snitch on offenders in their community.

The jury was empowered to punish those who broke the court's orders, or failed to carry out their allotted duties, with amercements, or fines, which were another source of income landing in the lord's pocket. It judged minor crimes and civil cases, particularly those involving trespass, which were settled through the mediation of appointed neighbours, or by referring to the customs of the manor and local memory. Another task was the election and swearing in of officials for the following year. These invariably included the tithingman and hayward. The tithingman was responsible for his fellows' compliance with their frankpledge. The hayward presided over agricultural activities, which included rounding up stray livestock. As late as 1889, approval was given for a new cattle pound in Home Paddock, near the stables of Compton Park.

A hayward was still being appointed at Compton in November 1896. The final page of the last available court book details the fee he was to receive for impounding stray animals: 6d for each horse, cow, or score of sheep, 1s if their owners were 'outparishers,' and, for a pig, 3d or 6d. Other officials were affeerors, who fixed and mitigated penalties dealt out by the jury, surveyors of the highway, enumerators of cattle and sheep, and policemen, whose tasks are implicit in their titles.

Until 1620, the courts in Compton's surviving records were named Courts Baron, which were General Courts not sworn on the Articles of Baron, and Courts of Survey. No court was classified as a Court Leet until the session in October 1641, designated 'Court Leet, Law Day, Court Baron,' suggesting the rolls of early Court Leets, if any were held, have not been preserved. This title is also an example of the jurisdictions of the two types of court blurring over the years, with matters previously dealt with by them at separate courts being covered in one court sitting. The session would open with the Court Leet, which was then followed by the substantially longer Court Baron, reflecting the amount of business conducted under each division.

All copyholders and freeholders owed suit of court and had to attend its sessions. Absentees provided excuses (essoins), and those who didn't attend — generally because the loss of a day's work could be more costly — were fined. These stipulations were not applicable to women, children, servants, and the poor. In the court rolls which include Views of Frankpledge, we should expect to find the names of all other male inhabitants over the age of twelve, information it would be extremely useful to have. In practice, however, the fullest account concerns those who held land by customary tenure, while sub-tenants and lodgers escaped mention unless they served on the jury, transgressed, or were named in a property conveyance. Tenants holding property in the manor with permission to live outside it might not be caught either. Freeholders are listed separately in some of Compton's rolls, but the descent of their lands, as conveyed by indenture, cannot be tracked through them because they were not governed by the manor court.

Compton's earliest surviving manorial rolls span 1576-1586, and relate to the courts of Sir Nicholas, lord of the former Haversham half-manor. A fragment from a court held on 28 March 1586 is the first following the 'purchase anew' by Edward Penruddocke, who had inherited the former Baynton half-manor. This session functioned as a survey, recapping the holdings, tenants and dates of their leases, with several new grants included. The second court after his purchase, held on 15 October of the same year, is the first of a series that runs through to 1636. It includes the court held after Edward's death in 1613 in his son Sir John's name, which was also a survey of 'formerly Baynton's.' John Nicholas had a cooperative relationship with George, which continued after Edward purchased the former Haversham half-manor from him in 1596, and included an arrangement to share heriots. Between 1597 and 1611, John Nicholas, followed by his son Robert, oversaw courts for the separate half-manors concurrently. This supervision probably continued until the two halves were finally merged into a single unit in 1636. From 1637 onward, courts were 'of,' rather than 'for,' John Penruddocke.

A two-year gap between the sessions held in April 1644 and April 1646 was probably Civil War related. Sir John died in 1648. His eldest son Colonel John was recorded as the lord at the next court in October later that year. They continued to be held in his name until 24 March 1655, when he was held prisoner in Exeter before his execution, and then in his son George's name, 'by Arundell Penruddok, his mother, & guardian of his Manor,' until 1661.

George died at the age of twenty in 1664. His brother Thomas, aged sixteen, succeeded to the estate. Three fragments of rolls, dated 1676, 1681, and 1698, remain, at which point he died, and was succeeded in 1698 by his son Thomas. Again, the records for only a few miscellaneous years have survived prior to his death in 1741. A series of sessions then run from 1740 until 1796 (with no entry for 1772), when Thomas was succeeded by his son Charles, and the manor continued to pass from father to son. Its 19th-century records, extending from 1802 until 1896, are almost complete. John Hungerford died without issue on Christmas day in 1841, after which the estate descended to his great-nephew Charles, who died in 1899, soon after the last court session was recorded.

Penruddocke Lords of the Manor of Compton Chamberlayne

Lord of Manor	Year of death	Successor
Sir George	1582	son Sir Edward
Sir Edward	1614	son Sir John
Sir John	1648	son Colonel John
Colonel John	1655	son George
George	1664	brother Thomas
Thomas	1698	son Thomas
Thomas	1741	son Charles
Charles	1769	son Charles
Charles	1788	son John Hungerford
John Hungerford	1841	great-nephew Charles*
Charles	1899	son Charles
Charles	1929	son George William
George William	1930	sold to George Cross

* Great-grandson of Charles Penruddocke (d. 1769).

5
SKIDMORE ALIAS BUTTLER: A FAMILY OF VILLEINS

COMPTON CHAMBERLAYNE'S KNOWN history begins in 1086 with the Domesday Book, while the names of its inhabitants who rendered rents and services to the lord start to emerge in the year that Edward I was crowned king of England. Among them, only Skidemore proudly endured through the centuries that followed, until it too disappeared from Compton's records with a last burial in 1632. The village's early names are detailed in Nicholas of Haversham's Inquisition Post Mortem of 1274, where the men in his half-manor were ranked as free tenants (10) and unfree customars, otherwise villeins, who were divided between those holding virgates (4) and half-virgates (21), and cottars (31). One customar was also listed as a cottar. Thus, the total number of tenants was 55, denoting an increase in the village's population from 1086, when there were 30 tenants and 2 slaves. From the poll tax records for 1377 we know that Compton then had a head (poll) count of 141, which only included the people over the age of fourteen who were liable to pay the flat rate of 4d. Johannes Skydemor is named as one of the three village representatives who delivered the groats to the collector, suggesting he was a senior figure amongst the village's elders.[20] Bouts of plague in England between 1348 and 1679 are likely to have caused fluctuations in the number of inhabitants.

Skidemore/Skydemor is a variant of Scudamore, and at the time that three men — Walter, Robert, and Richard Skidemore — were each paying 6s 8d and providing labour worth 2s 7¾d yearly to Nicholas of Haversham for their half-virgates in Compton, Peter de Scudamore was Lord of the Manor at nearby Fifield Bavant, which was then called Fifield Scudamore. The Domesday Book mentions a de Scudemer at Fifhide, as the village had been known earlier. Both the villeins at Compton and the lord of Fifield manor were probably descended from Ralph de Scudemer, a stonemason whom Edward the Confessor brought over from Normandy to help build castles along the Welsh border. More variant spellings are found in later records, most often Skydmor(e) and Skidmor(e). For simplicity, I will stick to the modern version Skidmore.

Compton's parish registers survive from 1538, wills from 1545, and manor court rolls from 1576. Taxpayers are listed in 1332, 1545, and 1576. Only five surnames from 1274 appear in the 1332 tax assessment, which suggests that the population changed almost out of recognition over a period of hardly 60 years. However, this was unlikely to have been the case. Most of the men in 1274 were villeins and cottars, whose descendants would not have been liable to pay tax in 1332, and some of the free tenants only held their land as an investment. They never lived in Compton and paid their dues elsewhere.

The parish register reveals that many of the Skidmores went under the alias of Buttler in the 16th century. Skidmore baptisms are only registered from 1539 until 1548, and Buttler baptisms from 1554 until 1574. No Buttler is recorded in the manor court rolls or as a party in a surviving property deed. But they certainly lived in the village. A Buttler's Close is recorded in the Field Book of 1597. Three Buttler baptisms within nine months point to contemporary families.

In trying to make sense of these records, I have followed the principle that the simplest is the most likely explanation. I believe the Robert who is recorded as the father of two Skidmore babies and the Robert Buttler who signed his will in 1564 are one and the same person. In the will, other children are named who used the alias Skidmore, but there are no records relating to himself as Skidmore. Nevertheless, I suspect that Robert did have two surnames. We do not know his name at birth because he was born before the keeping of parish registers, but his marriage at Compton with Margaret Osbourne is logged in 1547, curiously roundabout the same time that the baptism names switched.

Of the eight Skidmore christenings recorded, Robert's two babies were buried in infancy, and Agnes nine days after her baptism. Indeed, most of the baby Skidmores may well have died very young. A Humphry was born in 1539, with one buried in 1542, and a Richard in 1546, again shortly followed by a burial, in 1548. Perhaps as few as three survived: Joan, baptised in 1546, Julian in 1540, and James in 1542. But a James Buttler was buried in 1547. Hence, the Skidmore surname died out — if we rely on parish registers alone.

Robert Buttler was buried on 29 April 1564. In his will, signed four days before, he styled himself a husbandman, and bequeathed his most cherished possessions. Margaret received a brown ox and cow, his eldest son John ten wether (castrated male) sheep, his younger son John a brown ox, his daughter

Edith a heifer, and daughter Sybley a 'chiln' (chilver,* i.e. female) lamb. The John Buttler baptised in 1554 and Edith in 1557 were probably two of these children. Both were recorded with the alias Skidmore, John at his marriage to Ellinor Marshe in 1562, and Edith at her baptism. She in turn christened her base-born daughter Elizabeth Skidmore in 1592, and buried her as Buttler alias Skidmore seven years later in 1599. We learn from the manor court records of 1578[21] that Agnes had two brothers named John, likely making her another child of Robert, who was missed out of his will.

Richard Skidmore is noted in the burial register with the alias Buttler in 1576. In the same year, his surname appeared as Skidmore in the list of taxpayers, and likewise in his will, dated 15 March 1575. In it, he named his wife Agnes, son Thomas, and daughter Elizabeth. Agnes and Elizabeth cannot be identified elsewhere. Thomas, possibly Richard's son, was baptised as Buttler alias Skidmore in 1574. I believe that Richard was either Robert's brother or cousin. He could have been Robert's son, born before his marriage to Margaret. A Richard Skidmore was baptised in 1546, but you would then expect him to be mentioned in Robert's will. Admittedly, neither did Robert bequeath anything to his daughter Agnes. A more persuasive reason for rejecting the idea that he was Robert's son is that he, rather than 'the eldest son John,' was the taxpayer. Although a John Buttler alias Skidmore was buried at Compton in 1565 — the year after Robert died — he is unlikely to have been Robert's son as two brothers, each named John, most probably the elder and younger named in Robert's will, were recorded in the village in 1578.[22]

Why did the Skidmores use an alias? We simply don't know. The most common reason was illegitimacy, when a child initially assumed the mother's name. If she subsequently married her lover, the child might take his father's surname as well. If no marriage ensued, it would still have been possible for him to use his father's surname, even without his consent, or his father could accept paternity and include him amongst his heirs. Another possibility is that a mother was widowed when her child was young. She then remarried, and he also adopted the name of his stepfather. In any case, the Skidmore family seems not to have been over-fussed by the Church's morality teachings. Robert's daughter Sibell (Sibley) married John Pyper in 1559, nine years after the baptism of Ketterne Skidmore, otherwise Pyper, and, as already mentioned, Edith gave birth to an illegitimate daughter as well. Examples of other reasons for aliases are uncertainty during a long period of transition from the use of a single (given) name to two names, i.e. when inherited names (surnames) began

---

* 'Chilver' is from an Anglo-Saxon word, 'cilfer,' related to the word 'calf.'

to be popularised, as suggested in Chapter 20, and to identify a place of origin, another possibility mooted in Chapter 36.

The Peasants' Revolt of 1381 set in motion the end of serfdom, which is supposed to have largely died out in England by 1500. Not so at Compton, however, where the lord John Nicholas still had serfs and was keeping tabs on them. Five Skidmores were recorded as villeins at the Court Baron of the Haversham half-manor held for John in April 1576, and six at his court in April 1578.[23] The Christian name and whereabouts of the first Skidmore in 1576 are torn away from the roll. The next villein, John, is described as his brother, who was dwelling at Stockton (9 miles northwest of Compton). The third was Richard, living at Barford, and the fourth, Edith, was at Totton near Southampton. In April 1578, the homage reported that John and Richard were living within the manor, John junior was at Dinton, with Edith still in Totton. As Richard, the taxpayer, died in 1576, the villein Richard Skidmore named in 1578 must have been a second man. The fifth Skidmore, named Agnes, described as a sister of the two Johns, was living in Barford. She had illicitly scarpered off to join her husband without first obtaining the lord's licence to leave. These exoduses within a single family suggest that serfdom was finally losing its hold and there was a significant movement away from the village during the last quarter of the 16th century.

The court added William Francis' daughters Mary and Elizabeth to the reversion of a lease in the tenure of Richard Skidmore in April 1576.[24] He occupied a cottage, garden, orchard, three closes of pasture — Netherclose, Overclose and Monks — comprising two acres, some parcels of meadow, and twenty acres of arable land in the common fields, as well as the right of common pasture for eight oxen and forty sheep. This acreage was sufficient to support a good living for a husbandman and his family.

Richard was one of only twelve men in Compton whose income was high enough to fall within the tax levy, although he paid the lowest tax rate of £3 5s. The lot of unfree villeins had improved in general over the preceding three centuries. Richard, it seems, had done particularly well to become such a prominent husbandman, probably through the family's canny trading of the commodities they produced, which enabled them to acquire more land to till, and Richard to extract himself from the shackles of serfdom. If descended from Johannes Skydemor, the village elder of 1377, he could have had a better start than his kinsmen.

Both Richard and his wife Agnes had died before the next court sat in September 1577. Agnes held the tenancy for a short period during her widowhood. Hence, two heriots of 23 shillings and 4 pence each fell fortuitously due to the lord, and Mary Francis claimed the premises. There is no evidence that the Francis family, who were related to the lord, ever lived at Compton. Although he is named as a tenant there in the Field Book of 1597, a new grant to William Francis and his wife Mary had been delivered to William at Sarum in 1586.[25] The lease passed to a resident, Robert Comage, in 1604.

Sadly, Richard left none of his good luck — or, more importantly, land — for his heirs. The Skidmores who came after him were among the poorest folk at Compton. As late as 1598, Thomas Skidmore, who was probably the son mentioned in Richard's will, was described in the rolls, which are written in Latin, as a *Nativus*,[26] meaning villein — with his status emphasised by the addition of 'bond man' in English — dwelling with Francis Nicholas, gentleman. His kinswoman Edith, presumably home from Hampshire, was no better off. We learn from depositions in disputes between Joan Elliott and Mary Jeay lodged with the Bishop of Salisbury's Court in 1600 that Edith who was 40 years old, had been born at Compton and now, having no home of her own, she lodged with Joan Oakes. A comment from another witness that her sole income was derived from the 'labour of her hands'[27] paints the portrait of a pitiful spinster. She was buried at Compton in 1632, marking the end of the Skidmores in the village.

6
How Compton Manor Controlled its Inhabitants

IMAGINE THE MANOR as a self-sustaining unit, a small world providing for itself through a system of community agriculture. For the enterprise to function, everyone needed to follow rules that regulated agricultural practices, preserved common facilities, and maintained the peace and security of the village. Manorial records delight with their Middle English expressions and insight into a past way of life. While on the one hand they read like they were written in a distant country, on the other they evoke a more recent history and jog my own memories.

Where a complaint was recorded, items in the court rolls are preceded by the words 'They present.' Imposition of a regulation is signalled by 'It is ordered that.' Failure to comply put the offender under pain of a fine of a specified sum.

Many of the jury's pronouncements relate to the maintenance and repair of such common facilities as highways, gates, fences, hedges, bridges, and ditches. When the bridge at Turn Lake was in decay, those nominated as surveyors were to arrange its repair. The miller was to pay half the cost, and the inhabitants of the manor (excluding the lord) had to chip in for the residue.

> **A Tale of a Broken Bridge**
> It was winter, and my great-grandfather William had been cutting down trees. A team of horses pulled the trunks over a small bridge all week until one day, on reaching it, the horses absolutely refused to move. Both persuasion and threats failed. William gave in, believing there had to be a reason for the horses' behaviour. Lo and behold, the bridge collapsed during the following night. The horses probably sensed subtle vibrations, or heard movement beneath the ground.

Digging up soil on the highway and taking away stones were forbidden. Two characters we will encounter later, Edward Read, who comes across as the spoilt brat of his rich father, and William Jeay junior stole from the highway. Edward was ordered to set a large stone he had taken from the road back in its proper place. William was admonished for digging up soil and hiding it on his lands. Nor was it permissible to dump soil, let alone build a privy, on the roads. Two culprits were told to remove a latrine, and another to carry away a dung heap against his house and remove doorposts, as they were nuisances for the subjects of the Lord King using the highway. Notwithstanding, the practice of dumping in the streets gained in popularity, giving the jury cause in 1642 to declare that no inhabitant in future should litter them with dung. It was not long before they were at it again, and the jury was constrained to frame an order that no person or persons whatsoever were to make or lay any soil there. 100 years later, a novel obstruction was reported. Geese belonging to the miller at Dinton Mill had 'flooded' the common road. He was warned that if this happened in future, he would have to pay a 5-shilling penalty.

Roads were lined with hedgerows. Tenants who held adjoining lands had to plant thorn bushes or quick-set hedges at their boundaries. Cutting them down was naturally an offence. Edward Read had permitted hedge-breaking at Partridge Pater — a lost fieldname at Naishes Farm — to the great damage of all the tenants in 1608, and was ordered to replenish it. He also hindered the footway which by ancient usage led from his barton (Wiltshire vernacular for yard), and had to open it again.

The lake and ditches needed to be kept in good shape. In 1610, those who had ground abutting the lake were told to clean it. This, I imagine, was the lake in Compton Park where the lord's family went boating. When ditches in the droves (green roadways) were in decay for want of scouring, tenants were ordered to carry out the work. In 1767, farmer Thomas King was presented to the court for failing to clean the ditch by the side of Martin's Mead, whereby the road was much overflowed. My parents retired to a pink cottage in Martin's Meadow. It stood next to the main village street, where that self-same ditch often blocked in heavy rain, causing flooding on the main street.

Not infrequently, instructions were issued to tenants to repair their cottages and farm buildings. James Elliott was ordered to build one bay of his barn anew. Gents were not immune — Robert Nicholas had to repair his house. Immediately after Joan Ford was admitted to her husband's property during her widowhood, the jury gave her a specified day by which to repair her kitchen. Imagine a band of neighbours marching into your kitchen and ordering you to fix it. But kitchens with open fires and chimneys could be hazardous. With

Postcard from c 1924. Left: Mead Cottage, which no longer exists. Right: Martin's Meadow, my parent's home from 1978-2011.

thatched rooves and cottages being closely packed, rickety structures could cause havoc when sparks flew. Declarations of disrepair on a new taking are common in the manorial court records, suggesting the homage inspected the fabric of homesteads before a changeover, and charged the incoming tenant with making it safe. The reported alarm of all Compton's inhabitants because Walter Elliott's flue was in decay may not have been hyperbole as he was fined 20 shillings, whereas Maudlin Oake and Francis Elliott, whose chimneys were in a less dangerous state, only faced a penalty of 10 shillings each.

Subletting without licence, obtainable at a price from the lord, was an offence. Humphrey Elliott broke an ordinance by failing to remove Richard Thomas and his wife, who were inmates of his house. William Oake followed the correct procedure and was granted a licence to take over his mother's tenement. He agreed to pay her £5 a year in rent, or provide her with 'meate and drinke and cloathes att her choyse,' thus ensuring she did not become a burden on the parish.

When the pound was in disrepair, needing to be secured by a stone wall, three villagers were appointed to procure workmen and set them to work. Inhabitants had to contribute 10 shillings apiece, with no hint of any contribution from the lord. Some owners of stray livestock impounded by the hayward preferred to try to get away with a cheaper method than paying a fee to retrieve their animals. Richard Oake was a habitual offender. Robert Nicholas impounded his cattle on 16 May 1642. At about the twelfth hour at night on the same day, Oake broke into the pound and seized them against the peace. His cows were out and about again on 1 June, when George Comage put them into the pound. Richard, this time at about the first hour at night, broke into it. On both occasions he had to pay an amercement of 5 shillings.

The stocks required renovation in 1652, when those refusing to comply would also be fined 5 shillings. I wonder how often the petty criminals locked in them endured ridicule and humiliation from the good folk of Compton. Way back in the 14th century, Thomas of Grimstead's widow Joan was enriched with the unusual asset of '3 foot-irons issuing from the capitage of three fellows there at Martinmas,' as part of the third of her husband's half-manor assigned to her. In my time, one of the most dangerous criminals in Britain dropped in on Compton in 1964. Policemen searched our woods by helicopter for the serial murderer Angel Face Probyn, who had escaped from Dartmoor Prison. He had been disturbed while trying to steal a car in the village and left his boots behind in his haste. After two months of freedom, he was eventually captured in London. Only three minor offences adjudged in Compton's manorial court are recorded in the rolls, two of which highlight the unsavoury characters of two 'gentlemen:' Edward Read 'broke the head' of John Fry and caused him to bleed. He was fined 9 pence. Robert Nicholas paid the same sum for making an affray and drawing blood. Some years later, Richard Shuger assaulted and drew the blood of a member of the gentry, Thomas Nicholas, for which he had to pay a higher penalty of 5 shillings.

Throughout the period covered by the manorial records, leases specified that trees on a tenant's land were the lord's property. Tenants had to gather timber and firewood from common land, or needed to secure a licence from the lord for a fee, in order to cut timber on their own grounds. John Lynwood was granted one to take the shrowds (branches) of the trees growing on his holding at 'Chalke Hill.' Wood was scarce as a natural resource on the chalk downs, which supported few trees or bushes. Peat from the New Forest was used for fuel around Salisbury up to 1840.

In 1580, the court ordered that henceforth no one should fell or carry away nether broom, thorn, bushes, or any other form of kindling from the lord's wood or the common. The beginning of the 1590s saw a bout of cold winters in Western Europe, which could explain why William Elliott and Edith Ford were out gathering wood in 1593. William was amerced for felling young groves by the public road without licence, and Edith for cutting down trees on the lord's waste at Turn Lake.

Yet the estate was not lacking in trees. At the time of the 1597 survey, the plantation at Compton Ivers alone comprised 299 acres. But the lord saw wood as part of his revenue, with a further suspension in 1659 of the right to gather timber for fuel and carpentry on the common down coming as no surprise: 'It is agreed by the Tenants and ordered at this Court that there shall be noe furses cut on the downe for the next seven years to come. And that whosoever breaks this order shall forfeit xxs'

The surveyors who compiled the field book paid great attention to trees, noting wherever thorn, broom, hazel, and birch could be found in the withies and coppices. On the north side of the river, many great withies* were considered fit for sale or to burn in the lord's house. Elsewhere, a plot might have no trees reported, though often the total number of oaks, elms, and ashes was recorded. Oaks were assessed according to their fitness for trimming shrowds, 'ffireboot,' or felling for lumber, with ash drawing such comments as 'in a few years will be very fit for plough timber.' 'Ffireboot,' little changed from the Middle English 'ffirebote,' was the right of a tenant to take from the land occupied by him a reasonable amount of wood for fires in his and his servants' houses. I would hazard a guess that the surveyors considered 'ffirebote' the lord's right, given the number of penalties effectively charging tenants for firewood.

Places where tenants had taken wood were also duly noted in the survey. For instance, John Nicholas had acquired three closes carved out of the common where villagers had formerly taken timber for their houses and furze for heating. The surveyors' indignation resounds through their report: 'There are many trees growing on the hills with shrowds which the tenants adjoining claim and take but they are the lord's,' and 'Note that this half acre lyeth high and is among the Trees and William Elliot shrowdeth the Trees on each side the Timber whereof belongeth to the Lord.'

Two clumps of trees on Compton Down always fascinated me. I was told they had been planted in the shape of an apple and a pear. They are Scotch firs, which grow best in moist, fertile soil, rather than dry well-drained chalk. Nevertheless, they have endured for many decades. They were there in my great-grandfather's time, as well as my own. The pear-shaped clump is called Long Folly, somewhat perversely as 'folly' denotes a circular plantation of trees on a hill.

Boundaries were a constant problem. At the court session on Christmas Eve in 1594, which fell on a Tuesday, everyone was told to enclose their part of the common. The task had to be completed before Sunday next, that is, within five days. In 1660, thirteen tenants were to meet every Friday and replace the bounds which were in decay until all were set, under a pain of 10 shillings for

---

* Here, withies could mean willow trees, rather than bushes with pliable branches.

each neglecting his task or stopping before it was done, while Richard Berry was assigned a stick to make the staves (posts) of the bounds. On another occasion, eight tenants were told to begin to set the bounds of all the lands within the manor, and warned 'nott [to] give off till they have finished this necessary worke.'

Tenants were eager to covertly grab land whenever the opportunity arose, for example, when a plot fell vacant. William Jeay was the most audacious culprit, his numerous iniquities are detailed in the Chapter 16. In April 1586, the jurors reported that widow Edith Marshman had not yet restored her encroachment upon the soil of the lord at the Grove, according to an earlier ordinance. They decided to hold a view and establish a merston (boundary stone) there, in its accustomed place. Neither Edith nor the jury had acted as they should by September of that year, when the order was repeated, with the said Edith admonished that she 'do abyde their judgement.'

The jurors were dragged out in 1610 to deal with a boundary dispute between Edward Read, gentleman, and the lord. In 1636, four tenants were ordered to

> Vewethe differenc[es] in the Com[m]on ffeild[es] betweene the Landlord and the Tennant[es], and betweene Tennant and Tennant, and to measure the Land[es] and to sett out the bound[es] accordinge to their Judgement and discretion after they haue measured the same, to avoyde future quarrell, and to mayntayne peace.

Common rights were granted to copyholders for a certain number of cows and sheep. Villagers lower down the pecking order could only let out a single pig or cow, if indeed they had one, onto waste land, in the quarry, on the downs, or on the droves. We can see how these customs were slowly hacked away. Grazing stock in the quarry came to an end in 1597, when the surveyors voiced their opinion on the matter:

> The tenants claim a kind of common for their cattle and sheep but we do verily think they cannot possibly have had any rate for a certain number of cattle as they had on other commons before the enclosure besides it has never been presented at any court of survey as a common.

They reinforced their contention by stating 'neither has it been presented at any court that any of the tenants have opposed each other with a greater rate or number of cattle there than they ought to have done, which would have been many times if they had any right of common.' Their argument that complaints would be expected if tenants had a right of common is convincing, since tenants were generally known to graze more livestock than their quota. Boniface Parker had overburdened the common with cattle — which common is not specified. Robert Nicholas placed six more sheep than he should have on the common downs and fields, and had to forfeit 6 pence for each sheep. The surveyors added a telling comment to their appraisal: 'If it were enclosed it would make a pretty good close of ground as it is waste ground.'

Grazing regulations restricted when and where livestock was permitted to browse. Firstly, the homage decided that cattle should not be kept on the droves. Nevertheless, cows were happily munching along the ways to the common field and to the lord's close Courtheath in 1598, when the jury went to drive them off. From 1741 onwards, cows swiping the odd tuft of grass in the droves as they ambled towards the common mead had to be accompanied by a driver to chivvy them along.

According to ancient custom, as reiterated at court in 1606, no tenant should keep their sheep in the common droves after the Feast of the Purification until the Feast of the Nativity, a restriction which was later extended to Holy Roode Day. Sheep were therefore not allowed in the droves between 14 September and 25 December, and from 1741 they were no longer permitted in the common mead at all.

Pigs were giving the jury grief in the early 17th century. By 1615, they were banned from the droves. John Nicholas fell afoul of the ordinance, which cost him 3 shillings. William Jeay failed to keep tabs on six yearling pigs and was ordered 'to watch over them from time to time, under a pain of delinquency for whatsoever pig of 4 pence.' Despite this, his son William was still servicing his pigs in the droves fourteen years later, and was issued with a 12-pence fine. Jeay, among others, had pastured pigs in Town Mead, prompting the court to immediately ban pigs from the meadow. By 1634, the court had had enough of errant pigs, and demanded that tenants insert a ring in their noses. This measure was to preserve the grass, as rings cause pain to pigs when they root and dig. Initially, as was so often the case, little attention was paid to the court's efforts, with numerous tenants penalised for their ringless pigs in 1636.

Protecting soil and crops was imperative. An order was made in 1598 forbidding English plough cattle (oxen) from enjoying the common fields before harvest, except on the tenants' own lands. Tenants' temptation to send their sheep into the corn fields immediately after the harvest festival church service greatly occupied the court during the first decade of the 17th century.

Ordinances and a memorandum asserted that neither the farmer,* any of the tenants, nor freeholders were to break corn fields with their sheep by putting them on the stubbes (stubble) of barley until the Feast of St Michael (29 September), of oats until the Feast of All Saints (1 November), and of wheat until Martins tide (11 November). Moreover, according to ancient custom, when Christiana Nicholas' sheep were depastured in the East Field, the sheep of Francis Elliott and Edward Martin should be depastured in the West Field.

Horses were not to be led through standing corn and could not be fed in the corn fields until Whitsuntide. Tenants were ordered in 1648 to pay for preserving crops from crows and cattle. And in the same year:

> It is ordered att this Court that forsomuch as it appeareth that the gathering of weedes in the Corne feildes is a great hurt and spoyle to the Corne, and a greate greivance to the Tenantes, that no person heareafter shall gather or plucke vpp any weedes in the Corne feildes, vnlesse it be in a mans owne proper land, vpon payne to forfeite for every tyme — vs.

What prompted such an order? Weeds also meant wild herbs in Middle English and could have still been used in this sense by rural communities in the Early-Modern era. Were tenants objecting to neighbours plucking their wild herbs or were they trespassing on adjoining land and pulling up weeds to stop them spreading to their strips? A slovenly worker whose land bore a luxuriant crop of weeds was a plague to any neighbour who carefully kept his ground clean. Wild oats in particular are a problem in corn fields. I am reminded of a young man my father employed. He came to the farm with his own father, who was a tractor driver. The son was not entirely of sound mind, for instance he had a proclivity for starting fires, which limited the tasks that could be safely allocated to him. One day, my father set him to work tugging up wild oats in a corn field. There he stood amidst the corn, with hardly a muscle moving, eyes fixed on a distant void that no one but he could see.

Only the land's surface layer was let to tenants. What lay beneath belonged to the lord. Before the 1597 survey, tenants were able to collect chalk from a pit by the south-west corner of the arable fields. The surveyors had something to say about this:

> There is a chalk pit at the bottom of the downs where the tenants do fetch the

---

* The Elizabethans used the term 'farmer' to denote a bailiff who farmed the demesne land.

chalk for the manuring of their lands for the great enrichment of their grounds for the presents for which the tenants that would fetch should give somewhat to the lord for acknowledgement only for that the soil is the lords and the tenants cannot break it otherwise in time they may claim it as a right.

Thus, they spotted an opportunity for the lord to grant licences for chalk extraction. The same applied to clay in the meadow. John Edlerton of South Newton forfeited 3 shillings 4 pence for digging clay at Turn Lake without a licence.

In their search for waste ground that properly and of right belonged to the lord of the manor, the surveyors discovered a piece of good ground in the Gastons, 'where the Butts sometime stood.' Clearly, this area had been used for archery practice. The court ordered in 1621 that 'whatsoever Inhabitant for themselves, (their) children & servants will provide bows & arrows according to the form of the statute, under a pain for whatsoever default of 12 pence.'

The statute was a law passed by King Henry VIII's Parliament in 1511, just before his invasion of France the following year. It remained in force until the Victorian era, obliging all Englishmen under the age of 40 to have bows and arrows and practice archery for the defence of the realm. The upper age limit was extended to 60 years by an act in 1541, which specified that boys between 7 and 17 years had to have a bow and two shafts, and older men a bow and four arrows. They were also to cut butts and shoot at them. Non-compliance carried the stiff penalty of 6 shillings 8 pence. The felonious men of Compton were in luck with their manorial court, which only penalised them with a fine of 12 pence.

Interestingly, in Middle English 'butt' referred to an abutting strip of land, and was often associated with medieval field systems. This seems to be the sense of the word in Compton's Field Book in a section headed 'Beginning at the South Side of Townsend Hill and going South up to the Butts upon Chalk Hill,' which lists several small holdings described as, for example, 'One Butt Cout ½ acre late parcel of Bounds tenant,' and 'Robert Read two Butts.'

The court became obsessed with lynchets, spelling the word in a variety of ways, during the 1740s and 50s, when they are recorded in just about every court roll that includes ordinances. They first pop up in a memorandum in 1631. Freeholders and tenants agreed that 'none of them hereafter shall feed and depasture their horses and cattle upon any lynchardes in the corn fields, but only at their several lands, in the highways and under the down hedges without prejudice or hurt to their neighbours corn.' Lynchards next turn up in 1743. The court pronounced that no person shall plough or 'ear up' any in the

Drawing of the yew tree in front of Compton Church, initialled JWH, dating from the 1890s. The artist is unknown.

common fields. The ordinance was repeated in 1748 and in 1751 no grass was to be cut on the lynchotts.

By the 19th century, the outside world was making itself strongly felt in the small community. With nationwide common law courts and accelerating social change, the manorial courts lost their usefulness and did not play such an important part in village life as they had formerly. Officials were left with little more to do at court sessions than make pleasant speeches and drink to the health of the lord. Reports of their yearly proceedings at Compton between 1859 and 1896 are slim and repetitive. A few deaths of tenants and surrenders, and the grant of one late copyhold were noted.

A perambulation of the manor's bounds was ordered in 1864. Back in 1654, a similar order had been made that tenants and inhabitants meet together to walk the bounds along the downs between the manor and Broad Chalke, a village bordering Compton on the top of the hill, and to renew them to their ancient sites as heretofore accustomed. Before parish maps became available, the location of these boundaries was learnt on this system. Older members of the community who had memorised the bounds then passed their knowledge on to the next generation. Thus, the living record could serve as evidence in disputes, as when Humphrey Watts reported under oath that his father had told him the bounds of the coppice should run from the south of the hedge which divided the late common of Compton from Hurdcott Farm to the hedge on the south side of Salisbury Way (Ridgeway).

Richard Roberts had let his cows into the cemetery in 1881, which proved to be a misguided idea when they injured shrubs, and he was fined 5 shillings. Things could have been worse. Luckily, unlike in the churchyard, there was no poisonous yew in the cemetery. In his charming style, W. H. Hudson tells a story about Old Joe, who wandered the villages around Salisbury Plain with his team of six donkeys, delivering coal. One night, he arrived late in a village and, unable to find grazing for his neddies, secreted them in the churchyard. He promptly fell asleep among the gravestones. On waking the next morning — early, to round them up before any person discovered he had been making free with the vicar's grass — he discovered them all stone dead. They had browsed on the yew tree. Although Britain has more ancient yews (early and pre-Norman) than any other European country, for obvious reasons they are rarely to be found outside churchyards. The Ancient Yew Group classifies one of the three yews in Compton Churchyard as veteran, with an estimated age of 400-900 years. It caught the eye of JWH, who painted it in the 1890s. A younger yew was planted in 1977 to mark Queen Elizabeth II's Silver Jubilee.

The yew tree, June 2023.

A Yew Hedge for Playtime

A magnificent yew hedge protected the east end of the front garden at Naishes Farmhouse when I was a child. A branch sprung out at its side, which on misty mornings morphed into the spectre of a knight on a legless horse, wearing a jousting cloak. Almost as tall as our house, the hedge was

> dense and awkward. Only small children could force a path through its twisted lower limbs. In springtime, scented violets delicately carpeted the secret entrance, which became a front door when playing games of houses. Inside, a wonderland of cavities was adapted into pretend bedrooms, which connected to a communal area in the middle. This evergreen edifice has since been uprooted.

The only ordinance of substance made in 1896 was for all leaseholders and copyholders to keep their buildings in repair. The dangerous state of Edward Watts' cottage when it finally fell into the hands of the lord was no doubt the trigger for this reminder. The court's preoccupation with Watts' properties is related in Chapter 26.

One of the most intriguing revelations of these late records is that there were members of the jury who were illiterate, signing with their mark: six of the twelve in 1868, and still one at each court of the 1890s. Even as early as 1600, depositions at the Bishop's Court reveal that the vicar gave lessons to the village's young men.[28] A Sunday school is likely to have filled the gap until a day school, which existed from at least 1819, was established, followed by the National School. But as we learn in Chapter 51, not everyone considered education beneficial to labourers' children.

Early 20th-century postcard showing the schoolhouse set back in the centre. It became a private residence after the school closed in 1933. The first house on the right is the Admiral's House, and the thatched house is Piggott's Cottage.

7
Lynchets/Lanchards

THE SURVEYORS OF Compton divided the manor into sections in 1597, describing the route they followed in headings throughout the Field Book. Three of these routes use lanchards as a point of reference:

> 'Going south from the hill fort athwart [across, especially in an oblique direction] through the furlong called Lanchard land'
>
> 'Beginning at the East side of Sopors Wale [boundary] towards the South and thereof and going East athwards a furlong running North and South & shooting upon the Salisbury Highway coasting south'
>
> 'Beginning on the East Side of the Wale or Lanchard which boardeth up to Chalk Gapp and coasting eastward athwart the furlong called Chalk Hill'

The spelling in the manorial records of mid-18th century is lynchet, lynchard, or lynchotts. I was intrigued by these West-country words. Although their context dictates that the homage's reference is to bands of grass running between the ploughed strips of different tenants, my voyage of discovery revealed that not only the spelling, but also the meaning of the modern word lynchet had an interesting genesis. It is most often defined as ancient man-made terraces on the side of a hill. In his 1967 article 'Towards a Terminology for Strip Lynchets' in the *Agricultural History Review*, G. Wittington wrote that the original sense of the word was in fact very different. Lynchet is derived from the Anglo-Saxon word 'hlinc,' used to distinguish a particular point on boundaries, usually with reference to a ridge in the landscape: 'hafoc hlinc' — hawk's ridge; 'rahlinc' — roe's ridge; 'brom hlinc' — broom ridge.

Apparently ignorant of Compton's Field Book and manorial records, Wittington claims 'lynchet' was first documented in 1669 by J. Worlidge in his book *Systema Agriculturae*. For Worlidge, a lynchet was 'A certain line of Green-sword or Bounds, dividing Arable land in Common Fields,' concordant with its use in our court books. He believed that the word was not associated with terraces on hills until the 1790s — but the Field Book suggests he could be wrong. Thomas Hardy, writing in the late 19th century, was well aware that lynchets were terraces, describing them as such in novels set in the Blackmore Vale, located below the hilltop town of Shaftesbury.* After this hijack, 'strip lynchet' came into being in the 1920s, and according to Wikipedia this double name is now more commonly used: '[they] appear predominantly in Southern Britain, many in areas close to Iron Age forts and other earthworks, including later Roman earthworks and earlier barrows for the Neolithic and Bronze Age periods.' Confusingly, this new duo covers both hill and flat areas.

Imagine my surprise on encountering an article in the *Antiquity* journal of 1927 by my childhood GP Dr Richard Chaloner Cobbe Clay, whose surgery was located at Fovant until he died in 1970. In it, he explains the different lynchets in great detail, and refines the terminology. I had already known he was a keen amateur archaeologist who collected Stone Age artifacts, but not that he would be helping me with a lynchets conundrum in my sunset years. He distinguishes lynchets on hills, found mainly in chalk districts, from those in the valleys. The area enclosed by the hill lynchets lies on ground where the natural slope of the land has been flattened by ploughing, thus forming terraces. He pictured these lynchets as giant stairs, qualifying them as a 'flight

The lynchets above Bishopstone in Wiltshire. Credit Mike Barratt (user Mikebarratt). Transferred from en.wikipedia.org.

of strip lynchets.'

The lynchets on the hills date from a time when valleys were vast marshes covered with dense vegetation. Prehistoric man wisely lived in the hills and cultivated the land adjoining his home.

The lanchards in Compton in 1597 were sited near the Iron Age hill fort, and originated as borders formed by the farmers there exactly as Dr Clay

---

*   In *Wessex Tales*, 1888, and *Tess of the D'Urbervilles*, 1891.

describes.

The Saxons broke with the tradition of hill-top habitation and settled in the valleys. The 'strip lynchets' which were commonly found at the foot of the slopes thus date from Saxon times. Unlike the terraces, these are no longer visible to the naked eye. Out of sight, out of mind accounts for the current perception of a lynchet, or rather lack thereof. Yet, what both definitions agree on is their formation by ploughing.

Wittington observed, presumably from his readings of 17th century texts, that the word lynchet, as such, is common in Wiltshire and Dorset. Lynch or lince is used in Dorset and Hampshire, while lanchard is still to be found in Somerset. The term wall or whale is used on the Somerset-Dorset border — and in Compton. This in turn explains what William Jeay was doing in 1598 when the homage admonished him for encroaching with his plough on diverse parcels of land in the common fields, by making walls and boundaries, written in English as 'the wales and Lambshares.'[29] He was grabbing land by destroying the lynchets separating his strips of ground from those of his neighbours.

8
Compton Ways and Highwaymen

The manor court's ordinances for road repair reveal landmarks and ways unfamiliar today. I had been unaware that there was a shrine in the village before reading an order to repair the road leading towards it. Part of the track at Hollow Head was in decay in 1637, and needed to be repaired.[30] The hollow is a passage between the village and Naishes Farm, which opened into a way across the fields and continued through a line of trees at Hurdcott to the City of Sarum (Salisbury). To reach the A30, whose construction was begun in 1702, you needed instead to take a sharp right northward from the head of the hollow, and proceed down the lane I ran down to catch the bus to school. By 1778, the original route to Salisbury was no more than a path.

The Hollow. Credit: Richard Avery, CC BY-SA 4.0 <https://creativecommons.org/licenses/by-sa/4.0>, via Wikimedia Commons.

William Massey was censured for pulling down a stile and erecting a hedge on it, which obstructed His Majesty's subjects from passing.[31] It has since vanished without trace. The name of the field at the top of the hollow has been corrupted to Hollyhead, and is an example of the peril of jumping to conclusions. Before I examined the manorial records, I romantically fancied the name's origin was associated with villagers collecting holly in the woods there to decorate their homes at Christmas. Even though Queen Victoria popularised Christmas trees, my cousin tells me that apart from attending church, our family at Compton did not celebrate Christmas during the first twenty years of the 20th century.

The ridgeway track running along the top of the downs was mentioned in an Anglo-Saxon charter,[32] indicating that it has been in use from at least the early Middle Ages. It was the main route through the village from Wilton to Shaftesbury, and was turnpiked during the 18th century. On 23 October 1769, a reward of ten guineas was offered in the *Salisbury and Winchester Journal* to anyone who could give information to Nathaniel Day, Bailiff of the Manor of Compton, identifying the 'Person or Persons, [who] ... clandestinely broke the chain and Lock, being put across the Road, commonly called the Coachway, leading from Salisbury Plain to Compton Chamberlayne in this county, to prevent the Waggons from injuring the Hill, it being a private Road.'

A gate is shown opposite Chiselbury hillfort on the Andrews' and Drury's *Map of Wiltshire* of 1773. George Cross writes that an old local told him he could remember when the stagecoach ran along it daily. It was a good carriage road at that time, and stopped at the inn, Compton Hut, to pick up and set down passengers. I fear he must have been having the squire on. Although we know it was kept in good repair until at least 1839, as on 17 June the *Salisbury and Winchester Journal* published a call for tenders to repair the whole line of the hill-top turnpike road, the lower thoroughfare (now the A30) had become the official coach route in place of the ridgeway in 1787, after the gentlemen and inhabitants of the neighbourhood petitioned Parliament in 1768 to adopt the lower route. Today, the ridgeway is diminished to a track used by adjoining farmers and hikers.

Dr Clay had a passion not only for local history but also for ghosts. He told tales of his escapades while outwitting poltergeists, and of the highwaymen who in earlier times had held up stagecoaches on the turnpike road.[33] He had spoken to two men who had seen the large staple in the trunk of an oak on the edge of Gaston wood near the old turnpike, to which Cunning Dick had tethered his horse. Jack Rattenbury was another highway man who worked the road. In January 1776, the confederates Boulter and Caldwell robbed a man near Pewsey, north of Salisbury, who sent a description of the men and their horses to the local newspaper. They were arrested in Fovant and brought before Charles Penruddocke at Compton House.

Mary Sandall, a young woman of 23, also tried her luck along the ridgeway. In a scene straight out of *The Wicked Lady*, a Mrs Thring was walking along the turnpike road one spring day in 1779, minding her own business, when her travels were rudely interrupted by Mary, dressed as a man, sitting astride a horse and wielding a pistol. The story goes that Mrs Thring handed over 2 shillings and a black silk cloak, but it proved too much for her when she was told to give up

The ridgeway, June 2023.

her ring and shoe buckles. She pretended to see her husband coming, and the 'horseman' took flight. On arriving home, the gutsy lady raised a posse, which soon tracked down her assailant. Mary, stripped of her disguise, was immediately recognised as a local from Baverstock. She was found guilty, and sentenced to death at the assizes. Happily, she was granted a reprieve.

Other villains operating on the ridgeway were less fortunate. Highwaymen were customarily hanged within sight of the scene of their crime. A few miles to the west of Compton, on a promontory of the downs appropriately called Gallows Hill, Dr Clay had spotted the old hanging tree, with a long, thick branch stretched out at right angles about eight feet above the ground. He could clearly see a groove in the branch cut by the chains of the gibbet as it swung eerily in the wind. Steps carved into its trunk for the hangman to climb to fix the gibbet were also discernible.

The first plan we have of Compton Hut appears on the Ordinance Survey Map of 1811. A public house stood on the north side of the road, which included a garden, orchard, and enclosed paddock. On the south side there were outbuildings, stables, and a barn. Its proprietors are presumed to have struggled to maintain trade after the turnpike was allowed to expire. Nevertheless, from 1760 onward the premises were let to a succession of 'innkeepers:'[34] Thomas Gould, Phillip Bennett, Samuel Ingram, and Thomas Loveless, who died in debt in 1814. His wife and children renounced their rights to letters of administration, which were granted to Thomas' principal creditor William Seagrim, a Wilton brewer.

William Corp initiated a revival, with the inn described as 'new' when he was the licenced victualler in 1822-27. His efforts met with some success. Dr Clay told my father that, within his memory, it brewed some of the best beer in the district, and gave him a note which read: 'Dec. 4th., 1830. 50 labourers of the Parish on Compton Chamberlayne partook of dinner and good strong beer, provided by Mr Corp of Compton Hut, given to them by Mr. Penrudocke.' William died in 1838, and his wife Mary was named as the publican in the 1841 census. She was still listed as its occupant in the Tithe Award of 1850, but was not logged at Compton in the 1851 census. During that year, the manor court named Robert Stevens, who was a farmer at Broad Chalke, as the owner of the lease of an inn on the downs, when admonishing him for destroying a bank on the boundary with Broad Chalke. The vicar recorded that he housed agricultural workers there, as did John Keevil. * In 1865, the Hut was in hand, and in a dilapidated state.

Presumably, renovations were undertaken, since it was let to W. J. Roberts by 1876, and in 1881 to Barnett Sanger.[35] The property was described as a homestead on 4 May 1906, when Mrs Barnes placed advertisements in *The Salisbury Times* offering 'high dry and healthy' farmhouse lodgings with a good supply of farm products, beautiful views, and good accommodation for cyclists.[36] Kelly's Directories inform us that Clement Barnes let apartments 'for down air' there in 1907 and 1911, and listed it as the dowager Lady Pembroke's home for consumptives, also with an emphasis on its elevation above sea level and fresh down air, in 1915 — but no one lived there after that date. George Cross reports that it was a ruin by the time he bought the estate in 1930. The last inhabitants of the site, aside from frequent gypsy camps, arrived in 1944. For about two months, an American anti-aircraft gun was placed there to protect the troops at Dinton and Grovely Woods. Further along the track to the west, the next watering hole on the coach road, Fovant Hut, still stands today as a private residence.

A spinney that marked the plot of Compton Hut often drew me in on my Sunday walks across the hill with Ray and his dog. I would kick over

---

* Details of the Incumbents Book are given in Chapter 37.

The track leading from the Downs to the A30. It continues across the road to Naishes Farmhouse. Note the chalk pits, and the folly of trees, which is pear-shaped, on the right at the top of the hill. This photograph was taken in April 2010, when the Map of Australia had been grown over by grass.

remnants of broken bricks and the pots and pans left by the gypsies who had camped there among timeworn apple trees, daydreaming of the inn's welcome during bygone times. The lonely spot evoked a poem written by the nine-year-old me, the first line: 'As I thrust the door open, it almost seemed there.' I could hear a faint babble of convivial chatter and the crackle of a cheerful fireplace. A comforting fantasy of warm relief and safety drifted out towards me. Reality returned in the final lines of the poem:

> No, there is no cheerful fireplace, there is no door
> But just a garden to remember by
> With the tall trees touching the sky
> And snowdrops and forget-me-nots
> The sweet smell of apple blossom scents the air
> Only the rooks in their nests dwell here

An ordinance repeated at every session in the 18th-century manorial rolls reminded residents that the road down the hill from the hut and the road through the park were the private property of the lord, and no person had the right to travel, or drive cattle thereon, without his permission. By 1659, tenants had already disowned their right of ingress to the mill through the Farm Orchard, acknowledging it as a mere courtesy. The way on the hill was the very one I used to walk up with Ray. It's the one I was referring to when I warned my father that the entrance was being used by picnickers, and he told me they should enjoy it, as we were blessed with the countryside always being there for us. Nodules of iron pyrites littered the track's surface, to delight of myself as a child, and the ploughboys before me alike: 'On past the steep wall of an ancient chalk-quarry, where the ploughboys search for pyrites, and call them thunder bolts, and 'gold,' for when broken the radial metallic fibres glisten yellow.'[37] Apparently 'the vulgar' call them thunder-stones.* Now, I would no longer be allowed to walk up to the hill along the track. It's out of bounds.

---

* 'Thunder-stones, as the vulgar call them, are a pyrites; their fibres do all tend to the centre. They are found at Broad Chalke frequently.' Audrey, John. The Natural History of Wiltshire, written 1656-1691. Britton, John. ed. *Wiltshire Topographical Society.* 1847, p 40.

9
Love Lost

WE NOW MOVE on to another source of information that offers a glimpse of the characters who lived in Compton at the turn of the 17th century.

Proceedings in ecclesiastical courts were either 'ex officio,' that is, initiated by church officials responsible for alerting their authorities to moral transgressions, or 'instance' cases, where one party, the plaintiff, lodged a complaint against another, the defendant. Prevalent amongst instance cases were defamation, and matrimonial and testamentary disputes. Parties appointed proctors who prepared articles or questions for the opposing party and their witnesses. Testimony given in answer was noted down by the court clerk, who collaborated with the witness to produce the depositions endorsed by the witness' signature or mark, and filed in act books. Consequently, the depositions cannot be regarded as verbatim transcripts of the witnesses' words. Questions and answers were usually written in separate documents, rather than together, with the questions more often missing than the answers. Indeed, no questions at all have survived for cases from Compton Chamberlayne, leaving us flailing about in the dark to guess their substance. Deponents were sometimes interrogated further if new issues arose, or to challenge their credibility.

Aside from a bit of Latin, the depositions are written in Early-Modern English, the Shakespearean language spoken by the deponents. Here the spelling is changed to modern English in the quotations where words uttered by the witnesses are used. Words now rare in modern English remain as originally recorded if their meaning is easy enough to fathom otherwise, an explanation is given. Spelling of the deponents' names is inconsistent. To avoid confusion, they are reproduced throughout in their most consistent form or as their modern variant.

Love lost is a tale of missed opportunities for marital happiness and the role of two fathers, Francis Nicholas, who supported his daughter Warborow's desires, and John Nicholas, who thwarted his son Robert's future wedded bliss. You might call them 'the good' and 'the bad dad.' Both were gentlemen, related, and descended from an old Wiltshire family which is first found seated at Ryndway, otherwise Roundway, 1 mile north-east of Devizes, during the reign of Edward III (1327-1377).

Warborow and Robert were named as parties in separate suits involving betrothal that came before the Bishop of Salisbury's Consistory Court in 1586 and 1607. The depositions of the two fathers preserved in the Bishop's Book provide an insight into their different paternal approaches.

A family's heritage and legacy were of the utmost importance to the landowning class. Parents usually negotiated marriage matches to a candidate who would enhance their family's standing and wealth, while the younger generation was increasingly swayed by romantic attraction in their choice of partner. Henrietta Stafford Penruddocke of Compton (1742-1761) provides an example of when it would have been more fortuitous had the parents acceded to a daughter's choice. She is said to have 'died of love' at an early age as she was not allowed to marry the lover of her choice, who was considered 'detrimental.' His elder brother afterwards died, and he succeeded to the baronetcy and property.[38]

Express consent of both parties was necessary to make a valid marriage, and forcing a child to marry against their wishes was frowned upon. As single women could not own property and so bring assets to the union, the bride's family typically offered a dowry, consisting of a large sum of money, to their daughter's suitor.[39]

Before we proceed to the court cases themselves, a flavour of the events can be gained from considering the standing of the Nicholas family in Compton. In all, seventeen Nicholas children were baptised in Compton Chamberlayne during the 1500s, with some delightful pre-Norman given names, for instance, Ambrosse, Gryffyne, Petronell, and Gabriell. Alas, the parish register cannot be used to link these children to their parents because the parents' names are not recorded, except for Isabell, baptised in 1539, and Thomas in 1590, with both fathers named as John, although they are highly unlikely to have been the same John. The 1539 baptism is not only the first record for that family in Compton, but one of the very first in the parish register.

Where witnesses testified before a church court, a short biography is usually available at the beginning of their statement as recorded in the Bishop's Book, which provides information that is especially helpful to modern researchers when parish records are missing. It comprises the witness' name, residence, age, and most often the length of time they had lived in the parish. If not from the cradle, their place of birth is sometimes included. Their social status or occupation is also entered, or, if a woman, her marital status instead, and how long they have known the plaintiff or defendant. Hence, we know that 'good father' Francis came to Compton when he was ten. He had been born elsewhere in 1536. No deposition is available for Warborow, but it's highly likely she was the Warborow christened at Compton in 1562, making her around 24 when her suit came before the Bishop's Court in 1586. Manorial records tell us that Francis married Christiana,[40] and Warborow had a sister named Susan/Susanna,[41] who could well have been the 'Susand' baptised at Compton in 1559. Francis died in the 43rd year of Elizabeth I's reign, which ran from 17 September 1601, when his widow Christiana was ordered to deliver his best animal as a heriot to the lord.[42] Susan married Thomas Miller, who became the customary tenant of Francis' land in the right of his wife after the death of his mother-in-law in 1611.

Bad father John was born in the village *c* 1547 and baptised in the same year, together with his twin brother James. Baby James died shortly after birth. Their father John acquired one of Compton's half-manors *c* 1557, and was the lord of the manor from 1579 until 1586. An older son Robert inherited when John senior died in July 1595, and sold it a year later. John senior's inquisition post mortem[43] reveals that Robert was aged 'sixty years & more' when his father died, meaning he was born before 1535, and was twelve years older than his brother John. John senior, therefore, was probably born around 1515 and was near 80 when he died. Isabell, baptised by her father John in 1539, was likely another of Robert's and John's siblings.

The link between the Compton and Roundway families is evident from two land transactions. John junior, together with Griffin, son of Robert Nicholas of Roundway, admitted Thomas Parker as tenant of Newclose in 1583. In the same year, Griffin and good father Francis, with his daughter Warborow, took a tenancy of Porters, which included 40 acres of arable land.[44]

Bad father John married Margaret Toppe (born *c* 1557), probably around 1584, the year she first came to the village. Robert's parents are named as John and Margaret Nicholas in depositions taken in 1607.[45]

Warborow Nicholas' suit against George Worth was the first of the two complaints to come before the court. The gist of the dispute can only be gleaned from answers to questions posed to Warborow's father Francis, and George's answers to additional questions in her suit. His first replies and the questions to each of them have not survived. The case was prompted by George's change of heart after he proposed marriage to Warborow. According to Francis, before his daughter accepted him, George had asked for his blessing and consent to the nuptial. In hindsight, Francis realised that George had sought his permission 'more [to secure] his preferment and advancement in worldly wealth' than inspired by a sense of 'victory and achievement of his long-attempted enterprise in seeking and obtaining the goodwill' of his daughter. He believed George had played on his benevolence and fatherly devotion to eke out a marriage settlement 'with sufficiency of substance as to his good liking and hability.'

Francis knew his daughter had set her heart on marrying George. With her happiness uppermost in his mind, and 'wishing specially the well bestowing of his daughter to live in the world as also the satisfaction of her own fantasy, seeing the same so firmly fastened in perfect good will to George [he] did in very deed promise' a dowry, and to provide the pair and their children with a couple of geldings as long as he lived. George had appeared happy with the arrangement, and promised to take Warbarow as his wife. The contract was solemnised between them upon these conditions after George betrothed himself to Warbarow using the very words of the Book of Common Prayer. 'Solemnised' here does not infer a church ceremony, but rather a conditional contract to marry.

As deposed by Francis, not only had Worth's affection for his daughter, 'who before time he had made all men believe he loved most dearly,' subsequently faded, but he had also put about bad and evil reports of both Warborow and Francis himself. Disillusioned, Francis withdrew his offer of a dowry.

George's testimony is inconsistent, at first confessing to pursuit of Warborow in marriage, and later refuting that he wished to marry her. He admits to often meeting her when he 'wooed her goodwill in the way of marriage,' and she responded 'very forward in words and behaviour.' His answer in the affirmative to another question raises the suspicion that he slipped a cheapskate ring onto Warborow's finger, as it continues 'but whether the ring mentioned in this article was good or no he knoweth not.' George acknowledges that he met Warborow at her uncle Gawen's house, while insisting he had not 'importuned or solicited her.' On one occasion, he carried her on his horse to her father's house in Compton, though without any intent to become betrothed to her.

It seems Warborow did not have a horse of her own. By sending the gift of a mare to Francis for his daughter, whereupon Francis bought her a saddle and bridle, George might otherwise have intended to endear himself to her, however he said it had not been for her to keep, rather he had begged her father to give her a gelded colt. He declared he had neither asked Francis to buy Warborow clothes for a wedding, nor sent for her to fix a day for the nuptials.

Although he once rode with Francis and his daughter, the conversation they reported on that occasion did not take place.

We do not know whether Warborow ever married. She could have been the Warbero Nicholas buried at Compton in 1606, when, if born in 1562, she would have been aged 44. Another candidate is John's daughter Warbera, reported to have been with her sister at a dance hall in a case heard in 1601.[46*]

While Francis' deposition gives the impression of a father whose daughter's happiness in marriage was paramount, Robert had no such luck with his parents. They were determined at all costs to prevent their son from marrying the bride of his choice.

There is no record of Robert's baptism, and the depositions do not state how old he was at the time of the trial in 1607, only reporting that he was a minor. He was certainly under 21, which was 'full age,' as it was called in the Elizabethan era, for boys, while it was 16 for an unmarried woman. We know from the manorial records that Robert was a middle son. He had an older brother John, and another brother Thomas, who was only eleven in 1601 when his father was obliged to secure a licence for him to hold a tenancy.[47] There could well have been more siblings.

Robert Nicholas and Margaret Waterman were young lovers. When Margaret told Robert she was pregnant, they exchanged vows in their own words and declared themselves man and wife. Although marriage was usually thought of as an act solemnised in a church, an informal declaration between a couple was sufficient to establish a legally binding union before the law was changed by the Marriage Act of 1753. Words of betrothal had no prescribed format, neither were witnesses required. These kinds of contracts were called spousals. The law that validated them had originally been enacted to safeguard a person's freedom to choose a spouse and prevent parents from pressurising children into marrying someone selected for them against their will,[48] which is exactly what happened to Robert. His parents were against the match, and immediately arranged for him to marry their preferred bride, Alice Jeay, in a church service. Once a spousal had been asserted, orchestrating a marriage to someone else was actually forbidden.

Margaret in her despair lodged a complaint against Robert and Alice. At stake in the suit, which came before the Bishop of Salisbury's Court in 1607, was not merely the breach of Robert's promise to marry her, but whether or not they had already become husband and wife. Usually when there was conflict, the court endeavoured to broker an amicable settlement to soothe relations

---

*   See Chapter 10.

within the community. This was not an option with spousals, where a moral issue was predominant, and disciplinary steps to bring both parties into line with the Church's creed might be necessary. For these reasons, the court was obliged to investigate the relationship between the couple.[49] If satisfied that Robert had entered into a prior marriage with her as Margaret claimed, it was bound to uphold the union and annul the subsequent church marriage between Robert and Alice. In order to be valid, words in a spousal had to be spoken in the present tense. Use of the future tense constituted a promise to marry rather than a contract of marriage. This, though, should have been irrelevant here because when sexual intercourse had taken place, the church court considered the union to be immediately and irrevocably binding.[50] Such was the springboard for Shakespeare's play *Measure for Measure*, written only three years earlier in 1604, in which two of the characters are punished for illicit sexual intercourse and their failure to marry. Despite the Church's prohibition of sex before marriage, the reality that nearly one third of brides were pregnant when they wed in church could not be ignored. In theory, therefore, Robert's family faced a formidable challenge, and no doubt pinned their hopes on the emerging trend of courts favouring a solemnised marriage over a spousal.

Margaret Waterman is an enigma. No information as to where she lived, whether in Compton or a nearby village, or which could otherwise identify her, has come to light during my searches. The Nicholases' objection to her is likely to have been her lower social status. She might even have been a servant in their household. Their own choice, Alice, was the daughter of William Jeay. Although never mentioned as such in the manorial court records, he styled himself a yeoman in his will, which was still a rung below the gentry on the social ladder. He was, however, an ambitious man, who had set himself on an upward trajectory by acquiring land as it became available through enclosure. In 1576, while John Nicholas paid the most tax, Jeay's assessment was the third highest in the village. The strength of John's disapproval of Margaret was such that it outweighed his strife with Jeay. As we will learn later, Jeay was known to be an unpleasant character, frequently embroiled in disputes with his neighbours. He had earlier sued John Nicholas. We know this because in a suit heard in January 1604, when John was a witness lending support to William Elliott against Jeay, he testified that he himself had obtained a release from further prosecution by Jeay after 'having stopped his mouth … with a piece of money to buy his peace.'*

---

* See Chapter 13.

At Margaret Waterman's court hearing, it transpired that before Robert was married off to Alice, her mother had called on his father and told him her daughter was pregnant by Robert, that he was reputed in Compton to have said Margaret was his wife, and he intended to marry her. She asked for John's consent and goodwill to allow them to marry in church. Instead of showing understanding and compassion, John immediately arranged for Robert to marry Alice. Robert's mother, also named Margaret, knew that her son was still in love with his sweetheart and asked Nicholas Lawes, another member of the village's upper class, to persuade Robert to dissociate himself from her. Lawes obligingly came to the Nicholas house, where he found Robert together with his father. When he asked Robert whether he was the father of Margaret's child and what he meant to do about it, Robert willingly acknowledged his paternity, and confirmed he intended to marry Margaret. John's reaction, as related by Lawes, was harsh and uncompromising:

> [He] not liking therewith and being somewhat movid [angry] then said unto the said Robert Nicholas his ... son that if he did marry or take to wife ... Margaret Waterman, that he should never have penny or penny worth of [him] ... and therefore willed him to take heed what he did and to look to himself.

Realising that the threat of disinheritance had little effect, he upped the ante, telling his son:

> If he did marry or take to wife Margaret Waterman aforesaid and forsake Alice Jeay his said married wife ... he would hang him if there were any law in the world to hang him if that he would forsake his married wife and take another woman to wife.

John continued his rant, berating Robert for being uncourteous and uncivil to his mother, and failing to show her due respect, she having on one or more occasions said that if he married Margaret, 'she would go before a Judge of Assize and disinherit him of that land which was to come unto him by her and pass it away from him to another.'

More verbal pressure could hardly have been thrown at Robert. Martin Ingram, writing on church courts, sex and marriage in England for the period 1570-1640, suspects that Robert was flogged by his father to put him in a more obedient frame of mind,[51] while the case's depositions record that John concluded his evidence by saying Robert had been very willing to marry Alice, was not compelled to do so, but voluntarily and 'willingly yielded his consent.'

Robert might not have felt too enamoured of his father due to his pledge to have him hanged if possible, but the threat of withheld financial support alone would have left Robert with little choice. Couples among the middle and upper ranks of society usually only considered marriage when they had the resources to establish a household of their own, which was commonly provided by their parents and relations. Still Robert resisted, otherwise why was he sent away for a month? His father testified that he had lived 'soberly and quietly with his wife in very familiar and loving manner, and seemed to rejoice that he was so married,' letting it slip that this was after Robert had come home after spending a month away.

Nicholas Lawes told the court that Robert looked very sorrowful at their meeting, and after saying he would marry Margaret, implored his father to 'answer what will you have me do else?' John's misogynistic reply offers an insight into his utter contempt for women: 'why man thou art not the first that hath begotten wench with child and not married with her,' continuing 'why man, cannot a man fall into a turd but bind him to his nose as long as he liveth?'

This was too much for Lawes who, grasping John's determination to deny his son's wishes, decided to meddle no further. He agreed it was correct that in Compton Robert was commonly reported to be the father of Margaret's unborn child, and many did say they were contracted together.

John's wife Margaret had been listening in on the conversation between the men, one imagines with her ear to the keyhole. When she heard Robert answer that he thought the child was his and he meant to marry the girl, Margaret burst into floods of tears and fled down the hall. She told the court her husband would never give his consent, but she could not remember him ever using threatening words to dissuade his son. Like Lawes, she had heard people say in Compton that Robert promised he would marry Margaret, but maintained he only meant this 'if that he could obey his friends consent thereunto.' By 'friends' she was referring to the wide network of relatives and confidants who had an interest in, and influence over, who Robert took for his bride.

John Combes, who was married to Alice's sister, gave evidence assuring the court that Robert and Alice had been married during a genuine religious service. He had been present in church when they were married in Shaftesbury — notably not at Compton — on the Monday before Candlemas (29 January 1607). He believed the parties were free to marry, and Robert for his part had confirmed this during the ceremony, undertaken 'with the consent of parents and friends of both parties.' He had witnessed the discussion of the marriage settlement, which was then signed and sealed by both sides, Alice's father William delivering the bond to Robert for his daughter's portion, and Robert's father setting 'his hand to a writing concerning his said son's portion.' Thus, he knew both sets of parents consented to the marriage. As a minor, Robert would have needed his parents' consent to marry, and there should also have been a licence confirming that consent.

Combes had not seen such a licence but knew that banns were published. Mr Thomas Cooper, the vicar, had married the couple 'according to the order set down in the book of Common prayer,' and he believed Cooper was a minister, although he himself had not been present at his ordination. He testified that Robert and Alice had lived together in the same house after the ceremony, and he supposed the marriage was consummated, since he had seen them in bed together, and heard Robert acknowledge they were husband and wife.

Francis Jeay, Alice's brother, also came forward as a witness to the nuptials, and confirmed John's version of events. He assumed the couple had carnal knowledge of each other, as he too had seen them in bed together. This might seem strange to us, but, at the end of an Elizabethan wedding celebration, guests could proceed to the couple's bedchamber. Francis trusted Alice was a virgin when she married Robert.

If there had been any contract between Robert and Margaret, John Combes declared it was not made with his friends' consent. Furthermore, he thought Robert was hardly of an age to 'judge of the danger of an oath, and believed that if he knew the penalty lying upon a perjured person he would not forswear himself … [and] That he hath heard that the said Robert hath set down many untruths in his answers.'

This was not a fair reflection of Robert's own testimony. In the main, he accepted the evidence given by others, simply recasting Lawes' assessment of his father's 'somewhat movid' reaction as words spoken in an angry manner. On one important point, however, he strongly diverged. Usually, with the passage of time, defendants succumbed to their parents' constant haranguing and became unwilling to acknowledge a spousal at the trial. Robert affirmed his contract with Margaret and calmly told the court that the marriage between him and Alice had, on his part, been solemnised only to pacify his parents' anger and displeasure, and was done much against his own will.

Surely such a statement should have clinched the matter, but Margaret lost her case. Only one of the plaintiffs in the 26 spousal suits heard in Wiltshire between 1601 and 1640 was successful. Perhaps an assumption that parents knew what was in their children's 'best interests' prevailed, or it was simply a matter of wealth and status winning the day.

Margaret's baby was christened Warborowe in Compton Church on 15 May 1607. Was there an irony in giving her the same name as the unfortunate Warborow we encountered earlier? The baptism register records her as baseborn, with the surname 'Nycholas' and father Robert. Her mother's name is absent, which is extraordinary because as a rule only the mother of an illegitimate child was recorded, with the father left unidentified. Thus, there can be no doubt that Robert acknowledged Warborowe as his child. Regrettably, I have been unable to find any further records which could tell us what became of the girl.

Did Robert pine for Margaret, or settle down happily with the bride chosen for him? Robert's and Alice's son John was baptised in the same church as Warborowe, on the last day of August in the following year. He was the first of the couple's ten children, suggesting the marriage was functional in at least one respect. But if a happy man is someone who works hard to secure a healthy financial future for his family, his marital contentment could be interpreted differently.

A person's tax liability is commonly considered an indication of their financial status. Necessitated by her military commitments, Parliament granted Queen Elizabeth I a subsidy in 1576. Every subject who received income from land, including leaseholders and copyholders, was obliged to pay that tax. John Nicholas was assessed at the highest rate amongst his contemporaries in Compton. In 1641, a tax was levied to support Charles I's army, which was in peril from the Scots. It fell on individuals and corporations with moveable goods worth £3 or more, or whose income from land was 20 shillings or more. Robert's worth was overtaken in the years up to 1641.[52] He no longer ranked among the gentlemen in the village, and his liability at 5s 6d fell well below the four men named as such: John Penruddocke at £7 10s, Nicholas Lawes £1 2s, Thomas Smith £1, and Thomas Mylward 16s 6d. Robert had even fallen behind many of the yeomen, including Alice's father William Joy (Jeay), whose liability amounted to 13s 9d. Did a lacklustre life cause him to lose or squander the riches he must have inherited, even though he was not the eldest son?

Robert's and Alice's family failed to thrive. Their first son died when he was six. One of their other five sons, Edward, left a clear footprint in Compton Parish records but he probably had a small abode, with a liability under the hearth tax for only one fireplace in 1662.[53*] In 1669, at age 52, Edward married Anne Singer. She was a spinster, aged 55. Edward is described as a yeoman, with no word as to whether it was his first marriage. This would be particularly

---

* See Chapter 34 for more about the hearth tax.

interesting to know as some years before, in 1657, a Nicholas Nicholas whose father's name was Edward was baptised in Compton, suggesting that, like Robert, he had fathered an illegitimate child. Edward buried Anne in November 1684 and married widow Ann Laurence less than three weeks later. The manorial court fined one Robert for making an affray and drawing blood in 1629.[54] He could have been either Robert senior or the son he baptised in 1611, who would have been eighteen.

The miserable fates of Robert's three daughters certainly reflect a decrease in the family's fortunes. In an era when single women were looked down on, one was buried unmarried at the age of 32, and another baptised an illegitimate child in Compton in 1652. The third, Elinor, according to Peter Wilson Coldham's *Complete Book of Emigrants*, left for America aged 42 in 1660. She was bound to 'Henry R,' merchant, to serve for four years. No further explanation is given, leaving only speculation. Perhaps binding herself as a worker was the only way she could secure the wherewithal to finance her voyage to a better life in the new colonies.

Robert and Alice lived in the village until their deaths, Alice's in 1658 and Robert's in 1661. In his later years, Robert let things go. Complaints were made to the homage that both his barn and house were in decay.[55]

Robert's brothers John and Thomas were listed as gentlemen and tenants at the manorial court sessions between 1618 and 1625.[56] Both died in 1625/6. The unimaginatively named Nicholas Nicholas was the last of the family baptised in Compton. After two burials during the 1730s, the cognomen completely vanished from the parish records, and the sad stories of jilted Warborow and thwarted lovers Robert and Margaret were lost from the village's collective memory.

10
Salacious Rumours

ONLY A FEW years before Nicholas Lawes went to Margaret Nicholas' house at her bidding to dissuade her son Robert from marrying Margaret Waterman, she had sued one of his servants, John Stone, for defamation. This pleading first came before the Bishop's Court in December 1601. It seems to be a case built on Chinese whispers.

Stone had been 'a daunsinge' at Willoughbie's dance hall in Barford St Martin. On the Sunday following, he was dining in the Lawes household with Nicholas and his wife Frances, together with their other servants John Wells, Richard Goodfellow, and Thomas Antrum, plus a visitor, John Watts, all of whom supported Stone's defence. During dinner, Stone said there had been talk at the dance about William Adlam and Margaret Nicholas which he had been ashamed to hear. The Lawes, along with other witnesses, interpreted this to imply Adlam had carnal use of Margaret's body. Frances commented, 'were it her case Adlam should come no more at her house for fear lest he should be suspected to committ adultery with her.' John Wells recalled that Stone had said Margaret's two daughters Phyllis and Warbero were at the dance, 'at whom some in the Company did laugh and mock,' and he thought it was a pity because they were a couple of handsome young women. In Nicholas Lawes' judgment, Stone's words could be taken in different ways according to context, but for his part he 'Doth not think the good name of the said Margaret to be impaired' by John repeating the rumour. The other witnesses concurred.

George Fry, Edward Bacon, and Leonard Lush, who were servants in the Nicholas household, testified for Margaret at the trial. George had met John Stone in the street. They fell into conversation, during which Stone marvelled that John Nicholas 'will suffer such a knave as William Adlam to come to his house reporting so of our mistress and her two daughters ... that he ... might have his pleasure of them when he would.' Fry had also been at the dance hall when Stone had spoken in similar terms, but 'delivered so privately' to him that he thought 'no man else could hear the same words.'

John Nicholas sent Lush to call John Stone to his house. They met in the kitchen, with George, Edward, Leonard, the Nicholases, and their daughters present. Lush gave the fullest account of this occasion, reporting that his master then confronted Stone: 'So it is Stone I have sent for you about words which you should report that William Adlam should keep my wife and ... two daughters.' Stone challenged Nicholas to resort to the law if he thought he had slandered either Mr and Mrs Nicholas or William Adlam, and he would 'shuffle for himself.' On Margaret questioning him as to whether he had said Adlam should keep herself and her two daughters, Stone declared he had told no one but herself. 'No,' said she, 'you told more of my house besides myself.' Stone insisted, 'I told nobody but you and your man George.'

Contrary to the Lawes' servants' opinion, Fry and Lush believed Margaret's good name and reputation had been impaired by the words which Stone repeated, with Lush adding that this was because 'in what company soever she and her daughters do come they are laughed and jested at.'

The outcome of the case is not known.

11
Much Ado about a Cake

JOHN NICHOLAS FEATURES again in our next case. Let's imagine the scene as he, a man in his prime at 57, stood before a table in the Bishop of Salisbury's courtroom. Behind him on a raised throne sat the ecclesiastical judge. John's eyes alighted on the oak panelling, thankful that it was keeping the draft at bay on this chilly October morning in 1599. He had signed his name and was awaiting questions. John was there to lend support to John Dugmore, the vicar appointed to the parish some three years before, in his bizarre suit against Robert Ford. Reverend Dugmore was claiming his fee and a cake due to him for conducting the churching ceremony of Robert's wife, Agnes. What was bizarre? Surely, he was entitled to his fee, but the cake?

The court clerk sat opposite John, preparing to note down his testimony as he would do for all the witnesses. Later, he would write them up in a formal style for the official record. After cutting a new nib into his goose-feather quill, he placed it in a brass holder on his table, lifted his head, and idly studied the man standing before him. He was

Consistory Court, Chester Cathedral.   E. Blanche Jones.

An Antique Drawing of the Consistory Court at Chester Cathedral. While the case concerning the cake as partial payment was heard by the court at Salisbury Cathedral, it would have looked very similar.

a gentleman, that was for sure, with his leather doublet and flash of colour from his red jerkin and yellow hose, shades the lower classes were forbidden to wear under Elizabeth I's sumptuary laws.

John was somewhat perplexed by all the fuss the vicar was making over a cake, but then he knew the village well enough to understand that despite the court's desire for the parties to reach a compromise for the sake of community harmony, no conflict could be settled in a neighbourhood wrought with bitterness and rivalry. Even the procedures for arbitration and mediation by locals which the church had established were useless in Compton. The questions began. Yes, he knew Reverend Dugmore was paid £8 yearly and was entitled to a fee for performing certain obligations, but, noted the clerk, 'what the same oblations are or what is meant thereby he knoweth not.' In fact, incumbents were entitled to fees for performing services of baptism, the churching of women, marriage, and burial. What could John tell the court about the fees and customs for churching women in the parish? He had heard that after a woman in Compton had given birth, she went to the church to give thanks. She paid 6 pence, and laid a cake on the communion table.

Churching ceremonies were conducted at the end of the 40-day period traditionally allowed to a woman for recover after childbirth. She donned her best clothes, covered her head with a white veil, and presented herself in church before the congregation to give thanks for surviving the delivery. The rite was performed even if her baby was stillborn or had died unbaptised. It marked the woman's return to her domestic duties, and resumption of sexual relations with her husband. Fees and customs relating to the ceremony varied between parishes. In Compton, as John testified, the fee was 6d and a cake. According to witnesses called later, the vicar would accept tuppence and a crisome (piece of cloth) worth 4d instead of the full 6d, but — at least for Reverend Dugmore — the cake was essential. John's evidence was not contested. He had no knowledge of who was entitled to the cake, which was the main bone of contention.

William Elliott, who also supported the Reverend, was next up. He signed with his mark, and told the court he was a husbandman, aged 55, who had been born in Compton. On second thought, he had moved to the village as an infant. The court learned from William that it was customary for a cake worth 1 penny and made of flour to be 'brought to the church by the midwife … which cake was sometimes better than at other times according to the hability of the party that came to give god thanks.' Clearly, the baking skills of some Compton ladies left a little to be desired.

And who did the cake belong to? William was sure the cake belonged to the vicar. He could only relate his experience as a pupil of the former vicar

Sir Humphrey Dale. On many occasions, the minister had taken the cake, divided it amongst his scholars, and William had enjoyed a piece. After Dale's time, as he had heard, sometimes the vicar, and at other times the clerk, served the cake. He had never heard that it did not by right belong to the vicar. Since Reverend Dugmore had been appointed to the position at Compton, he had likewise received the cake, but during the past four or five years Mr Fricker, the current parish clerk, had challenged his right as vicar, asserting that it belonged to him as clerk. Osmund Fricker appears to have been joined in the action as a defendant. He was a tailor, aged 70, and had lived in the village for 48 years.

Another witness for Dugmore, William Jeay, a yeoman, aged 60, signed his name and told the court he had lived in Compton for 30 years. He had also been a pupil of Sir Humphrey Dale, and remembered that the cakes were divided amongst the scholars. Since Reverend Dale's time, his wife had given birth to nine children. At each churching, she had paid 6 pence and laid a cake on the communion table. He had heard that this was customary within the parish, but did not know if the cake was for the vicar's or the clerk's use.

Defence depositions were heard the following year, in 1600. Siding against Dugmore, John Gwilliams, the vicar of Burcombe, who had earlier been the curate at Compton for seven years, was in no doubt that the cake belonged to the clerk. When he was the curate, he had never heard anything to the contrary by common report, and according to Elizabeth Watts, the then midwife, the cake went to the clerk, although he did not know for what purpose. Gwilliams initially encountered the tradition at Dorothy Watts' churching. She was the first woman to be churched by Reverend Dugmore after he became the curate at Compton. When she laid down a piece of cloth and a cake on the communion table, he, 'being newly come into this country and not acquainted with the customs,' asked her what the cake meant. She replied it was customary at a churching for a cake to be given to the clerk. Afterwards, he had taken the cake and divided it amongst the pupils, and 'not disliking thereof but accepting,' he took the piece left over.

Arthur Beach, a tailor, aged 62, who could sign his name, had lived in the village for 32 years, and had been the clerk at Compton for 16 before Mr Fricker took over the role. When he acted as clerk and, as had been credibly reported to him, for many years before, the cake belonged by custom to the clerk to do with as he wished. Nobody had ever suggested otherwise. Nevertheless, he had been content to let Reverend Gwilliams, a good friend who 'taught his neighbours' children,' to 'break or cut the said cake and divide the same amongst his scholars.' Beach had willingly received any part that was left over, and Mr Gwilliams had never pretended that it was his to have. Things continued in the same way when Mr Fricker became the clerk, that is, until Reverend Dugmore appeared on the scene and challenged his right to the cake.

Dorothy Watts was the final witness whose deposition was recorded. She was 68, signed with a mark, and said she had lived in the village for 40 years. For seven of these, she had been the local midwife and, as such knew that the clerk had the right to dispose of the cake as he wished. What's more, her predecessor Elizabeth Watts had been of the same opinion, Sir Humphrey Dale having told her the cake belonged to the clerk. Dorothy had accompanied Agnes Ford in church to, as she said, give thanks. She explained that during her time as a midwife, she had come to the church 'with any woman to be purified,' and followed the custom as described. Interestingly, she considered that the procedure cleansed the woman's body of the impurities of childbirth. This belief was not unusual, even though misinformed. The churching of women is thought to derive from a Jewish purification rite; however, the Christian ceremony contained no comparable elements.

William Elliott was the only deponent who was sure the cake belonged to the vicar, but he appears to have been an unreliable witness. His account also diverged significantly in another respect. He testified that towards the beginning of Dugmore's suit, the defendant Ford had told him he was 'behind' with Mr Dugmore 'for the first time of his wife's churching a cake, and for her second churching 6d and a cake.' He asked William to intervene on his behalf to persuade the vicar to settle the case, which he had tried to do without success. William's testimony implied that Ford was unable to pay, but Dorothy Watts deposed that Agnes had the 6 pence with her, and the vicar refused to accept the money without the cake. Even John Nicholas believed this was the case. Both Arthur Beach and Osmund Fricker had heard the vicar 'confess' that either Agnes or the midwife had laid down the money on the communion table, but he spurned it because she had not brought a cake. Fricker added that the two women then declared they 'would leave it whether he would receive it or no … whereupon the said Mr Dugmore took the same 6d away from the said board with his hand and what afterwards became thereof he knoweth not.'

Gwilliams labelled Reverend Dugmore's witnesses as 'partial and affectionate.' Jeay was an enemy of Robert Ford, and Elliott an enemy of one Miller, who was a party 'touched' in the suit — an entirely plausible opinion given Compton's partisan community. Arthur Beach concurred that Jeay was Ford's enemy, and believed Elliott had not been truthful about his age. Gwilliams likewise mentioned Elliott's inconsistent reporting of his age. Indeed, one would have thought that Elliott, having been baptised in Compton in 1553, would have been fully aware that he was almost 9 years younger than the 55 years he admitted to. Unless, of course, he had been baptised when he was nine and confused his baptism with his birth, but he had also changed his mind about being born in the village. The reason for his unreliable testimony may not have been sinister — in other suits he is described as a poor simple country man, easily flustered when confronted by men of authority.

Again, the outcome of the case is not recorded. As time progressed, the court allowed actions to be abandoned before reaching a judgement. There might have been out-of-court negotiations leading to the vicar dropping his claim or perhaps Agnes finally baked a cake. The mystery remains as to why she arrived at her churching without one in the first place, and what bothered the vicar so much that he took the matter to court. Although the benefice at Compton was poor, Dugmore is unlikely to have been on the bread — or cake — line. The whole affair smacks of a deeper enmity between the vicar and members of his congregation, and implies that he was not above the bitterness that prevailed between his parishioners. John Dugmore remained the vicar of Compton for over 30 years, until his death in 1634. The Fords were an old, well-placed Compton family, with Robert's son Christopher succeeding Dugmore as its next vicar.

The last churching rituals in England occurred during the early 20th century. I noticed in a collection of monthly Downton & Charlton village magazines that churching of women services were still being held at St Lawrence's Church every week on Wednesday and Friday at 10am in 1890.[*]

---

[*] The magazines are bound in a book that has recently been donated to the Wiltshire Family History Society.

12
Feisty Joan Elliott and the Troublemaker's Wife and Daughter

WILLIAM JEAY CAUSED havoc in Compton Chamberlayne for around 50 years between 1570, when he arrived, and 1619, when he was buried in the churchyard. His neighbours described this disagreeable yeoman as subtle, cunning, crafty, and foul-mouthed. They had good cause to loath him. He sued gentlemen John Nicholas and Nicholas Lawes, and, amongst others, defamed Joan Penruddocke, Christopher Marshman, Robert Ford, and Richard Oake. Most predominantly, William was locked in a bitter conflict with his neighbour William Elliott, a poor husbandman with a hot temper. Their wives Joan Elliott and Mary Jeay, along with Jeay's daughter Margery, were dragged into battle with them. Amusing as the Shakespearean insults they hurled at each other are to read today, they represented serious affronts to Elizabethans that victims could only leave uncontested at their peril.

A glut of defamation cases involving sexual slander came before both the church and secular courts in and around the early 1600s, when increasing importance became attached to sexual reputation or 'credit' as a measure of respectability.[57] The Bishop of Salisbury's Consistory Court experienced a tremendous surge in the number of such cases. Whereas only twenty-two were heard in 1566, the court was handling between 50 to 60 a year *c* 1615. The plaintiff could choose between a secular court able to award monetary damages, or a church court that could order the offender to make a public apology. The latter was often the preferred recourse, not only as a way to rehabilitate the accuser, but also to enhance his or her reputation.[58] Depositions made by both the principal parties and witnesses filed in the Bishop's Book provide an insight into these suits. Unfortunately, as mentioned before, their survival condition is patchy, often requiring some creative interpretation.

Joan Elliott and Mary Jeay chose the Bishop of Salisbury's Court in April and May 1600. Mary claimed that she had been defamed by Joan, and

Joan that she had been defamed by Mary. Joan also claimed that she had been defamed by Margery, and Margery countered with the same complaint against Joan.

The wives fell out in a big way when Mary alleged that Joan had told tales about her husband to the authorities. Details emerge in a conversation which Mary had with Joan's husband William, as reported by Edith Skidmore and Richard Oake, and supplemented by Joan's denial. Richard, a lad of nineteen, lived with his widowed mother Joan Oake, who hired William to thatch the roof of her cottage. He was busy with the task on a day before Christmas in 1599, while Richard ran back and forth bringing him fresh supplies of reed and spars.

Meanwhile, Edith Skidmore was living with the Oakes and working in their house, when her interest was piqued by Mary shouting up to William on the roof, 'thy wife is an arrant [errant] jade* to misuse my husband in this kind of order.' Being nosey, which seems to have been a general characteristic of the womenfolk of Compton, she stepped into the doorway and leaned over the hatch to better catch what was going on. Richard was on his way up the ladder carrying materials for William.

Joan Elliott's version, no doubt originating with William, is that the exchange started when Mary asked her husband where Joan was, William replying that she was at home, and Mary saying then there was a jade at home, for his wife had gone to Marlborough to make an oath before the Lord Chief Justice of England alleging William Jeay wished he be hanged. According to witnesses, William had made his way through a storm from Hurdcott, arriving at Joan's house sopping wet, with torn breeches. He was presumably travelling home, since the Elliotts' holding in Hurdcott bordered on that of the Jeays' at Compton. Joan invited him in to dry himself by her fire, and offered to patch his breeches. She fetched him a drink of beer, but it was so 'small' (weak) that she thought he would not drink it, and asked him if she could buy some malt from him to make stronger beer. He replied that the Lord Chief Justice would not suffer him to buy barley, and he wished him hanged for it. Edith recalled Mary saying to William 'I would thou shouldest well know and so do all the parish know ... that my husband hath little need to come to dry himself by thy fire.' William himself said nothing, except that he did not know about Joan's trip to Marlborough, which is surprising. How could his wife's journey, which even today takes an hour by car, pass him by unnoticed?

* According to the *Merriam-Webster Dictionary* jade was first used in Middle English to mean 'a broken-down horse.' Later the word was often applied to a woman considered worthless. Nowadays, a jade more often means a disreputable woman.

Depositions were made by eight women concerning an incident on the busy thoroughfare through Farm Close on a Sunday between Christmas and Candlemas (2 February) that same year. Personal details reveal that they were a mixed company, ranging in social status from Magdalen Dugmore, aged 18, who was the cleric's daughter, to Mary Sidley, aged 50, the wife of John, a day labourer.* The other 6 were Joan Palmer, aged 20, a spinster who lived with her father 'upon his courtesy,' Edith Skidmore, Joan Oake's lodger, 40, and also a spinster, who by contrast said 'she liveth only by the labour of her hands and hath neither house or maintenance,' the wives of two husbandmen, Jane Marshman, 34, and Mary Elliott, 47, Margaret Palmer, the wife of a weaver, and Joan Oake, a widow, both aged 60.

Joan Palmer appears to have been the first to arrive at Farm Close. She saw Mary Jeay returning home from evening prayer, engrossed in conversation with her daughter Margery, and after them Joan Elliott, Edith Skidmore, and Magdalen Dugmore, who approached, 'making some straw there.' From this turn of phrase, we can guess they were tittle-tattling. Suddenly, the witness heard Joan lash out, calling Mary a jade, and she angrily retorted that Joan was a jade to call her a jade. Next, Joan said to Mary that she 'wast taken in thy barn a jadinge,' suggesting Mary had earlier had a tryst in her barn, and mocked her: 'doest [thou] want Rowley to rub thy old bones that thou mightest throw him out of thy bed.' Joan Palmer, in her father's house, had since heard Joan confess that she had spoken these words, although since the beginning of the suit she, the defendant, had denied it.

Mary Sidley also overheard the words spoken by Mary which prompted Joan's outburst. On that same Sunday evening, which she dated to after Twelfth Night (5 January), she was at her door to the street when she saw the pair standing about an acre (*c* 60 metres) distance apart. Mary yelled to Joan 'dost ... lack one to light thee a candle into the barn to guide him the right way,' followed by Joan bellowing about old Rowley. On interrogation, Mary professed she truly did not know what was meant by Mary's comment about the candle. Alleged paramour Rowley was possibly the man of that name baptised in Compton in 1545 (therefore not particularly old), whose name appeared in the list of Compton's taxpayers for the subsidy of 1576.

Richard Oake recalled that Mary had mentioned a candle and barn incident when speaking to William on the roof, though again no sense can be made of it. She said there were 'boies [boys] sitting at the door at midsummer eating of pescod [pea pods] and one came into the barn then to

* John himself gives evidence in another case I will relate later, in which he is described a husbandman.

fetch ... [a] knitch [bundle] of hay and one goodwife Lywood telling ... Joan Elliott thereof they both went into the barn with a candle lighted and could see nobody whereunto.' If these barn episodes were one and the same, Oake's account could infer that Mary's taunting of Joan painted her as too much of a coward to enter a dark barn alone, while in Sidley's narrative the words 'to guide him' imply Mary was up to no good in the barn. Either way, the two witnesses describe a colourful charade of a-jading and carrying candles in dark Elizabethan sheds.

After they had 'done' gossiping with James Elliott's wife at her house, Jane Marshman and Mary Elliott also entered Farm Close, where they saw the trio of Mary, Joan, and Margery, with others, standing by the stile. Jane heard Margery say to Joan 'thou ... art a whore to use my mother so.' A seesaw slanging match ensued, with Joan telling Margery she was a whore, and Margery answering, 'I say thou art a whore of thy tongue (garrulous, rather than unchaste),' followed by Joan's final blast 'thou ... art a whore to call me whore.' Joan immediately willed the assembled company to bear witness. Mary Elliott, Edith Skidmore, Magdalen Dugmore, Joan Oake, and Margaret Palmer all concurred with Jane's account before the court.

To prove a defamation, plaintiffs needed reputable men and women of the community to testify to their good character and reputation, depose that the words spoken were considered harmful to a person's reputation, that they had indeed diminished the plaintiff's credit, and had been uttered in the presence of others. On all counts, the present suits revolved around whether the use of the words jade and whore had defamed the plaintiff. Although calling a woman a whore or jade was not necessarily an accusation of prostitution, implying sexual immorality was very upsetting for a lady in the early 17th century. Chastity was central to her reputation in the domestic role society assigned to her. By the double standards of the day, fornication and adultery were considered a greater sin for a woman than for a man. A woman accused of loose living could find herself friendless, unmarriageable, and unable to support herself. For her, it was worth the time, effort, and expense of going to court to mend her damaged social standing, while the ecclesiastical court was tasked with restoring order to the community in which she lived.[59]

Witnesses were asked for their opinions on the effect an imputation of being a jade or a whore had on a woman. In general, they considered these words damaged her reputation, especially, as Osmund Marshman later deposed, if spoken in 'choler or maliciously.' Mary Sidley's explanation is representative of those other witnesses offered: 'to term any woman jade maliciously doth signify and import that she of whom the same is so spoken hath been and is so common that ... any man might have the use of her.' She considered jade and whore to have little difference in their meaning, both denoting crimes of incontinence, evil life, and conversation. Views differed as to whether in the given circumstances these words had in fact harmed the three plaintiffs.

Mary Sidley's deposition following the initial exchange she overheard between Mary and Joan is crossed out in the Bishop's Book, but her belief that Joan was discredited by it stands. She alone took this view. Although Richard Oake considered that Mary's words as heard when he was on the ladder defamed Joan, he confessed to being 'a young man and of little experience and therefore [one who] cannot otherwise depose hereunto' more than by referring himself to the opinion of those of better experience than himself.

Jane Marshman doubted that Margery's words at Farm Close defamed Joan. She, according to her deposition, 'is persuaded in her conscience and doth verily believe that Margery did not in calling her whore mean or intend any carnal abusing of her body but only of her tongue.' Mary Elliott thought Margery only spoke in defence of her mother, and not with intent to discredit or charge Joan with the sin of incontinence, because she had only called her a whore of her tongue. Jane believed that, if anyone, it was Margery who had been discredited, as she was an unmarried maiden and had not before been either spoken of or suspected of any loose living. Margaret Palmer agreed, saying Margery was 'greatly impaired' by the scandalous utterances, 'so much the more in respect that she hath always been reputed and taken a very honest and civil maiden and not touched or suspected of any evil behaviour.' Consequently, 'she might suffer great hindrance to her preferment of her marriage.' Joan Oake shared this conclusion. Margery therefore came out well. Her marriage prospects, if ever in danger, were clearly repaired because she found a husband soon afterwards.

There was a general consensus that Joan had defamed Mary. Joan Palmer thought Joan Elliott's words were 'of great ignominy [and] scandal,' and could not but discredit the person to whom they were spoken. Magdalen Dugmore described Joan Elliott's manner as 'angry and malicious,' and Edith Skidmore as 'very spiteful,' portraying her tirade as stemming from a 'malicious stomach.' Margaret Palmer too said Joan had spoken 'in great choler and rage.'

The witnesses were then asked about the plaintiffs' characters. Mary Sidley assessed Mary Jeay as being 'a woman of good modest sober and quiet behaviour, no brawler, no tale carrier nor inclined to speak evil of her neighbours and so commonly accompted* reputed and ... beloved of her neighbours, a

---

* Accompt is an old word used by Shakespeare in the Prologue to *Henry V*, meaning account.

small company keeper, not touched or suspected of any misdemeanour.' She knew this because she had often been in Mary's presence at her house and in other places. She answered similarly about Joan, while implying that she was quick to fly off the handle: 'while she hath known her she hath behaved ... well and honestly and hath been well thought of amongst her neighbours and not accompted a brawler or slanderer of her neighbours or desirous of troubles or brawls but when she is moved thereunto.' Edith added it was commonly said amongst Joan's neighbours that she 'doth meddle more as well in this as in other matters than she needed to have done.' Richard Oake, who also gave good character references for both Mary and Joan, mentioned that Joan 'hath been and is given to contention and will speak sometimes she careth not what and a little thing will move her to fall out with any of her neighbours.' Mary Elliott joined the others in lavishing praise on Mary Jeay. She had known Joan Elliott similarly to be an 'honest paynesfull* woman,' but could not answer for her behaviour as she had had 'small society with her other than good morowe or good een when she hath happened to meet with her.'

The hints at Joan's irascible nature contrast with Mary's 'low spirit,' as described by Jane. Joan's disposition is raised in a case before the Lord Chief Justice related in the next chapter, when John Nicholas recounts[60] that after William Jeay had caused some of her husband's cattle to be impounded, and

> having urged Joan as it seemed to anger as he chanced to ... go to the outer wall of his barton he saw Joan Elliot with her fist or hand ... strike William Jeay in the powle [head] or between the neck and shoulders his backside being towards her and he going from her and she following him and giving him three or four blows.

She was indeed a feisty lady. With this added to husband William's hot temper, we can conclude that life in the Elliott household was anything but boring.

---

* A now rare meaning of painful, which was used in the 16th century to signify painstaking, careful, or industrious.

13
The Unending Jeay-Elliott Wars

AT THE SAME time as their wives were fighting in court, William Elliott sued William Jeay for defaming him by insinuating that he was dishonest. An imputation of dishonesty was deeply serious for any man because his livelihood depended on a reputation for trustworthiness. Jeay counterclaimed against Elliott for calling him a knave, with both events having taken place in St Michael's Church. Men were slowly leaving after evening prayer on a Sunday between Candlemas and Easter. Their womenfolk appear not to have lingered so long. Osmund Marshman heard Jeay ask his neighbour John Elliott how some wood he had lost came to be in his ditch. John Dugmore, the vicar who liked cake, remembered John replying that he could not tell how. Upon hearing this, William Elliott came back through the porch and, being a 'very angry and chollerick sort,' repeatedly 'in a very vile stomachous and malicious manner' called Jeay a knave, interjecting all the flowery insulting expressions of the day — lienge (vassal), dunce, coseninge (swindler). He spoke with such vehemence that the cleric and others present 'bade him for shame to rule his tongue and hold his peace,' or get out of the church. There can be no doubt as to the level of William Elliott's fury. Marshman considered his words 'opprobrious, scandalous, and vituperous [worthy of blame],' opining that they were 'adjunct unto chiding and brawling and not usually or ordinarily spoken but upon falling out.' Thomas Saunders concurred, adding that he had subsequently met Elliott coming towards the church, where he admitted that he had sworn at Jeay. John Dugmore reported that William and his wife later confessed their fault to him, and promised 'to discharge the fees of the court that should be due.'

Our old friend John Nicholas was still in church. He had left his seat and was 'leaning' by his neighbour Nicholas Lawes, engaged in a tête-à-tête about the poor and such matters, when he was distracted by Jeay calling Elliott a 'thief and in [a] very rude uncivil and brawling sort charged him' with taking his wood, and 'farther that there was never a true man of the name.' Likewise, William Parck, a yeoman of New Sarum who was residing in Compton with

Edward Penruddocke at the time, recalled William Jeay 'using many other brawling and contemptuous speeches' to suggest that all of the Elliotts were thieves. William Elliott junior, a husbandman six years younger than William senior, heard Elliott protest that Jeay was wrong to call him a thief, and he could prove it.

John Sidley was about to leave the building when he heard William Jeay 'begin to talk of hedges and wood and such other matters, whereby thinking there would be somewhat ado [he] stood still at the end of his seat.' In his version of events, Jeay called Elliott back as he was leaving, bellowing 'thou hast stole my wood and hast carried it unto thy common close to make thy hedges there.' William Elliott swore bitterly, as deposed by others, that it was his own wood. Jeay countered that he had 'showing for it,' telling him the tithing man had fetched some of it from 'where it was hid in thy kinsman's John Elliott's ditch,' and since he lost his [guard] dog, he could keep nothing from Elliott.

Sidley was among those who advised William Elliott to depart. Afterwards, he said Jeay was left 'babbling, talking and quarrelling and continuing such his rude and uncivil terms,' reiterating that 'there was never a one of the Elliotts true.' Nicholas Lawes, the farmer,* asked whether he could prove Elliott had stolen his wood. Jeay replied, 'I have [evidence] at home to show.'

When they were alone, Sidley chided William Elliott: 'I marvel you cannot let him near knowing how he dealt with you but lately at the quarter sessions† and that there is no end with him when he is once set in a babbling.'

Following on from these suits in the Bishop's Court, William Jeay took his disputes to the Lord Chief Justice in London. Depositions survive for the allegations heard in November 1603 and in January 1603/4. They refer back to several claims William Jeay had brought against William Elliott and his wife Joan, as well as other inhabitants of Compton Chamberlayne, but they are short on details. Their main focus is on a release which Jeay had extracted from Elliott to prevent him from pursuing him further in the Consistory Court by terrorising him with a writ that alleged he and Joan had committed criminal offences.

Robert Read, the gentleman with a large freehold, deposed that on a day during Trinity term (May-July) in 1601, he met Jeay in the Middle Temple

---

* Nicholas Lawes was termed 'the farmer' because he farmed the demesne land.

† The Criminal matters that came before the quarter sessions were too grave to be dealt with summarily at the petty sessions, but less serious than those tried at the Assize Courts. The quarter sessions also had administrative authority over licensing, the highways, and offences against the poor laws.

in London, coming from the Crown Office. Jeay showed him a document containing accusations against William and Joan Elliott, signed with the marks of several men. One of them subsequently told Read that although he had agreed and endorsed the document, he 'utterly denied that [he] ever heard or knew of any misdemeanours or evil life objected against Elliott and his wife to be inserted therein or that they did subscribe to any such a thing.' The mind boggles, but alas we are not made privy to the nature of their purported evil life. While at the Crown Office, Jeay had procured a writ which bound Elliott and his wife to appear before the Lord Chief Justice. Read knew this because he was one of the securities for the Elliotts' appearance. They turned up as summonsed, and waited three-four days before they could be examined, spending all their money on food and lodging during this time. Worse still, they were threatened daily by Jeay, who told them the Lord Chief Justice could send them to prison. By this means, Jeay persuaded Elliott to supply him with a release from all claims against himself and his family.

John Nicholas deposed that at the time of the release he and Elliott travelled to London to answer a complaint of misconduct which Jeay had made against them. They appeared before the Lord Chief Justice, who ordered Mr Lea's chambers to draw up interrogatories. While this was being done, Lea put them from time to time 'to great charge and hinderance.' On telling him they were weary of it all, Lea warned that unless they 'yielded and released Jeay they were like to have no quite.' Nicholas, therefore, as we have heard before, 'stopped the mouth of Jeay with a piece of money to buy his peace [and] was set free from a [future] like arrest' without entering a bond of good behaviour. Elliott likewise agreed to a release, though much against his will.

John Nicholas described Elliott as 'a poor labouring husbandman having nothing but what he earned and a plain simple country man utterly illiterate and of soft and timid nature and such a one that may easily be urged compelled or forced,' for fear of being brought before men of authority, 'to yield to that which may much prejudice him and his estate, for such a poor simple man he is commonly reputed and taken to be.' Read confirmed that Elliott was incapable of answering for himself and feared authority. He believed Elliott would 'do anything though it be to his utter undoing' if threatened with imprisonment, and reported that Elliott had told him 'weeping and making great grief [he] wished himself dead or that his honour would hang him out of the way he had been so vexed by Jeay for six years and had been by him undone.'

Mr Lea had instructed his clerk George Marks to draft the release. Read was at his chambers when Marks was undertaking the task, and lamented that Elliott would be undone by it. Marks, who dated the day of the release more precisely as 15 June 1601, said he was only doing as he had been told, which was to draw up 'a release of all suits, quarrels and controversies whatsoever and of all charges or expenses taxed or adjudged against' William Jeay and his wife and daughter on behalf of William Elliott and his wife in the Bishop of Salisbury's Court. Read then left, returning later to find both Jeay and Elliott present. He called Elliott aside, asking him what he had done. Elliott replied that he had made Jeay a release. Read explained how he had compromised himself, because it absolved Jeay from other suits and the costs taxed by the court. Elliott, despairing, said he could not tell what he had done, pleading that Jeay had threatened him with imprisonment if he refused. Although he had signed the release, he said he would not deliver it until the Lord Chief Justice had become acquainted with it. They then set forth together for the Lord Chief Justice's Chamber, where Jeay had already arrived. On being told that the release had been delivered to Jeay, and all matters described in it had ended, Elliott fell to his knees and entreated the Lord Chief Justice to be good to him.

This unexpected reaction alerted his Lordship to Jeay's mischief. He declared 'he did not like such [an] ending,' and scolded Jeay: 'Sir, if you make me acquainted with the beginning of your matters you shall make me acquainted with the ending of them, and therefore use me so no more, I like not these matters it smells naught' — i.e., it stinks.

Read believed the writ had been issued against Elliott without any just cause, and 'was done by ... Jeay more to defraud Elliott and his wife of such charges as was adjudged ... than of good matter or cause.' Furthermore, he condemned Jeay as a man excommunicated at that time in his parish church. Later it came out that he had also been bound over to be of good behaviour in the past. Nicholas assured the Lord Chief Justice that when Elliott signed, he was not so bound, rather the couple had been and still were of good behaviour, and did not deserve any warrant to be issued against them.

Nicholas then also attested that Elliott and his wife were honest people. He described an incident, no doubt raised by Jeay, that had occurred ten years before. Some of his mother-in-law's sheep had been shorn during the night. Officers searched several abodes and found wool in Elliott's house, which they retained in custody for a fortnight. Elliott's frequent demands for its return were denied, until he brought the matter before a justice of the peace who found no proof of theft. In his deposition, he recalled seeing Joan Elliott attack Jeay with her fists.

It was inevitable that the quarrelsome William Jeay and hot-tempered William Elliott should clash, drawing quiet but resolute Mary and feisty

Joan into their affray. Jeay seems to have been literate. He could sign his depositions with his name, while Elliott was illiterate and signed with a mark. Jeay, a few years older than Elliott, was an outsider who had come to the village when he was 30. Elliott could well have seen Jeay as a threat to his standing in the community. The Elliotts were deep-rooted in Compton. More than twenty of their baptisms had been recorded in the parish registers before the first Jeay baptism of Mary, the eldest of William's and Mary's nine children, in 1573. At least six contemporary Elliott families are mentioned in the Bishop's Book, headed by William, William junior, John, Francis, James, and Christopher (Cutt). They were a clan, more than likely all related to one another.

William Jeay was a yeoman with two tenements. He held 55 acres of arable in the common fields. William Elliott was a husbandman. He ostensibly had less than ten, also renting a few unspecified acres from St John's Hospital, Wilton, and his cottage from Thomas Gawens, a free tenant. He took over his tenancy from John, his father, in 1586. This holding comprised a new building with a small backside and six scattered acres of arable, mainly in half-acre parcels. From their descriptions, the land was poor, including two on hills and two in Stoney Bottom and Flexland.

The disparity in social standing between the two Williams is also evident from their levies for Queen Elizabeth I's subsidy of 1576. John Nicholas, as already mentioned, paid the highest rate according to Compton's list of taxpayers. William Jeay's burden was half as much as that of Nicholas, and one James Elliott, possibly William's uncle, paid half as much again. As the Penruddockes enclosed land to create larger farms, small farmers lost out unless by fair means or foul they managed to benefit from the redistribution by acquiring more property, thereby rising to yeoman status. Enclosure created a dog-eat-dog village society, with William Elliott struggling to reach a higher social level. A new arrival in the village who acquired land by dubious means surely goaded him. The manorial court recorded that after Felice Elliott died, Jeay wrongfully detained three parcels belonging to her which were due to the lord,[61] and encroached on other land recently vacated by Robert Bound.[62] The 1597 survey frequently refers to Jeay ploughing further than he ought to, and occupying acreages he had no right to. A whole page is devoted to John Nicholas' evidence under oath concerning parcels which Jeay had surreptitiously seized. Jeay himself lodged complaints against other tenants for trespassing on his holding in the common fields, claiming Humphrey Watts had cultivated and harvested corn on a quarter of an acre, and one Curtys had cut down and carried away some of his oats.[63]

William Elliott had also attempted to covertly increase his holdings, although his incursions were small and not as blatant as Jeay's. He was thwarted by the keen eyes of his neighbours. In 1585, the homage ordered him to repair the damage he had done by ploughing the lord's waste soil at Gaston,[64] and in 1589 to remove a fence he had built on land in Richard Bound's tenure.[65] He was in trouble again in 1593, with penalties imposed for encroaching on the lord's land and enclosing two perches of garden in Gaston without licence.[66] Gaston and earlier Garson are probably corruptions of Gawens.

Most cases of persistent defamation brought before the Bishop's Court ended in mediation or arbitration. The final outcome of the bitter dispute between the warring Jeays and Elliotts is more intriguing — no less than Compton's very own tale of Romeo and Juliet, but with a happier ending.

In his will, which he made shortly before he died, aged 80, in September 1619, William Jeay gave his third son James 12 pence and, for James' better advancement, his recently purchased tenement at Burcombe. Three years later, in 1622, James married Eyddeith (Edith) Elliott, which must surely have caused William to turn in his grave. Edith was likely the grandchild of William Elliott's second cousin Christopher. James was 46 when he married, and Edith 20. Their union was well accepted by both families. James was not regarded as a black sheep by the Jeays. His mother Mary appointed him executor of her own will. James and Edith baptised six children in Compton between 1623 and 1633, but neither James nor Edith is recorded in the parish burial records for Compton.

The surnames Jeay and Elliott disappear completely from Compton's parish register by the end of the 17th century.

14
Just Williams (Elliott)

WILLIAM ELLIOTT WAS born in 1543/4 if he was indeed aged 55 in 1599, as he told the court during John Dugmore's suit against Robert Ford. The curate Gwilliams highlighted in his testimony that William had been inconsistent in the reporting of his age. He must, however, have been around the age he claimed because a second William Elliott, designated junior, who gave evidence in court a year later, said he was 50 and had lived in Compton for 40 years. This makes him only a few years younger than William senior, who was a named party in the suit. He was in any case between 15 and 20 years older than his 35-year-old bride Joan Watts, whom he married at Compton in 1589. She had been baptised in the village in 1564.

A family tragedy befell them in June 1604, when daughters Joan, aged four, and Frances, aged seven, were buried two days apart. I can see William standing by their small graves, eyes fixed on his empty hands, and Joan shaking her head in despair. Their children were victims of the plague, which gripped the villagers with terror. A severe local outbreak had started in Bristol in August 1603, and continued throughout 1604. It was the greatest visitation of plague ever recorded in Bristol, where at least 3000 people died.[67] In Compton, eighteen burials were recorded in 1604, whereas the annual average for the first quarter of the 17th century was logged in single figures. The entire Wells family was buried in May: Four-year-old Christian on the 7th, her father George on the 9th, and mother Edith the day after. The wealthy Read family suffered likewise, with Robert interred on the 4th of July, William on the 17th, the family's servant boy Aaron on the 29th, and Jane on the 4th of August. Another couple, Bettres and John Whityere, suffered the same fate, and were buried within three weeks of each another. Justices of the Peace at the Trinity Session of 1604 ordered the Treasurer of the Marshalsea to pay 10 shillings weekly for the duration of the infection to the overseers of the poor in each of four parishes infected with the plague: South Newton, Fisherton, Milford, and Compton Chamberlayne.[68]

The Plague of 1563

Another family, the Marshmans, suffered severe losses during an earlier visitation of the plague in 1563, when London had its worst outbreak of the 16th century. Of the seven burials in Compton during that year, three girls — Elizabeth, Joan, and Agnes, all buried on the 12 November — shared the surname Marshman. A note in the register tells us that Elizabeth and Joan were sisters. Another Marshman, Humphrey, was buried on 26 October. No baptism record has survived for Elizabeth, but the other three were teenagers, Agnes aged thirteen, Humphrey fourteen, and Joan fifteen.

William held considerably less arable land than the 20 and 30 acres belonging to his cousins, descended from his father's brothers Walter and James. As we have another William Elliott yet to come, I will call this one 'Gaston William.'

In 1609, Joan was admitted to the tenancy of a handkerchief-sized parcel of the fourth part of a rood lying in Gaston, granted for the term of the lives of her husband, herself, and their sons Martin and Emanuel.[69] It was probably her vegetable patch. She took over her husband's tenancy after William's death in 1614, but died four years later, at which point Martin was admitted to the handkerchief. He becomes a consistent presence in the manorial records after this, but any other holding he may have had is not described. In 1621 and 1622, he was in default with his rent. After 1631, he is listed as a tenant by indenture, implying a fixed non-inheritable term. His brother Emanuel has left no footprint apart from his life as recorded in his mother's 1609 tenancy admission.

Another William Elliott and his wife Joan, come to light in Compton's manor court records during the second decade of the 17th century, after his demise. This William was buried at Compton on the 29 April 1631, and his administration bond names his widow as Joan. He was probably Gaston William's first son.

The court session held in October 1631 noted that Joan's husband William had died since the last court, which was held in April of that year.[70] Joan was admitted to his tenancy during her widowhood, their property alas not described. This term ended with Joan's marriage to Christopher Harwood, when Gaston William's holding reverted to the hands of the lord. Joan must have married and died in quick succession because she was buried in February 1632. A new tenancy was granted to her widower Christopher, together with a cottage, garden, orchard, and one acre of pasture 'late enclosed' that had been occupied by Henry Lawrence.[71] The lives named in this second lease were Christopher Harwood, son of Christopher Harwood, Marion his sister, and Christopher Harwood, son of John Harwood.

Christopher Harwood junior married the vicar's daughter Jane Dugmore on the 28 April 1634 at Compton, which causes some confusion with regard to a family tree uploaded to the *Ancestry* website, in which this marriage is attributed to the older couple. Granted that the names Joan and Jane are often interchangeable, however, Christopher junior and his wife Jane baptised twins Ann and Alice in 1636, which would have been quite a feat for the then 73-year-old Joan. The Harwoods came from Fovant, where Christopher senior baptised his namesake son in 1610. Christopher Harwood junior surrendered Gaston William's holding in 1638, with a new tenancy granted to Francis Ford.[72]

As if two were not enough, a third contemporary William Elliott lived in Compton. Between the burial of Gaston William in 1614 and that of his son William in 1631, another William Elliott was interred there in 1626. His was a humble existence. In 1610, he had been granted the tenancy of a cottage, a close of one acre, and common pasture for one cow, with his father Humphrey and sister Edith.[73] A realistic identification can be made with the William Elliott junior who gave evidence at the Bishop's Court in 1600. The manorial records name 'William Elliott junior' for the first time in 1604,[74] and periodically thereafter until 1614, when two Williams, senior and junior, are both noted to be customary tenants. Gaston William's son was only about fifteen in 1604, therefore William junior was probably the second William registered in court. As we know, William senior died in 1614. Two William Elliotts, senior and junior, are again recorded at the sessions held in 1620 and 1621, by which time William's son would have been around 25.

15
THE UBIQUITOUS ELLIOTTS

IN THIS CHAPTER, I follow the Elliott family during the *c* 120 years they are recorded at Compton. Without a detailed analysis of the surviving manor court records, matching property described in the tenancies granted, and cross-referencing the lives named against those in wills and parish registers, everything would be guesswork. I cannot guarantee that all my conclusions are correct, only that they avoid some of the errors I have found in Elliott trees on the *Ancestry* website, as mentioned in the last chapter.

A few interesting facts emerge. The lords were downright greedy in their fixing of fines and heriots. Progressive enclosure to the detriment of cottagers and benefit of the lord and major tenants can be followed through the records. Often, only one son from a family inherited land that enabled him to maintain a standard of living akin to that of his parents. Thus, the other sons became cottagers, with little more than a vegetable patch and a right to graze animals on ever-decreasing common land. They sustained their existence through day labour or left the village. My analysis also revealed some interesting family situations, and answered the question as to why the Elliotts suddenly disappeared.

If you care to veer a short distance off the ridgeway above Manor Farm, you will find yourself in Chiselbury, the grassed over remains of an Iron Age univallate hillfort. I often wonder if Elliotts lived within its ramparts, fashioning the artifacts from that period since found on the downs. If they were not visibly present then, I feel certain one would have cast a greeting to anyone trudging the ridgeway in early medieval times, because both it and the Elliotts must have been there. If only the Domesday Book had recorded the names of the inhabitants of Contone.

As things stand, the family can only be traced in Compton from 1539, when the parish register tells us that Walter baptised his son Humphry and James buried his wife Joan. Clearly, the Elliotts were already ensconced in the manor. Early court entries are littered with them. Yet, their spoor runs dry after the 1660s. 'Elliott' is absent from all records relating to the village for nearly 200 years, only slowly reappearing during the mid-19th century. Imagine sitting on a train when another train passes the window, and you catch glimpses of a few passengers in the other locomotive as the two pull apart at speed. Without doubt, many more were travelling on that train. Parish registers, wills, and manorial records act as the windows onto those passing carriages. They give us flashes of the bigger picture which has been lost through lack of documentation, or because records have failed to survive. And we might not even catch such glimpses like the miller who, as a medieval saying goes, does not see everything that is carried past by the stream.

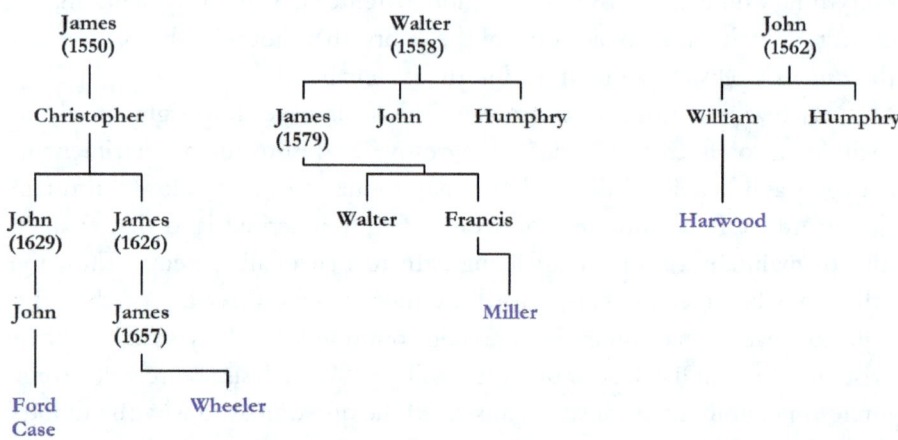

The three brothers and their heirs, with dates of wills in parentheses, and families who eventually took their land in blue

In the space of twelve years, between 1550 and 1562, three Elliotts who made wills died in Compton. They were husbandmen with copyholds. Their bequests indicate that they were brothers. James was the eldest and apparently the wealthiest, which suggests he inherited their father's holding. He made his will on 9 May 1550, and probate was granted on the 28th. He named his wife Joan and children Christopher, Alice, and Agnes, and also mentioned his grandson, Christopher's son John, his godsons James and Walter Elliott, and Robert Elliott of Burcombe. Firstly, he bequeathed a 'stocke' to each of his daughters — to the value of 12 shillings for Alice, and 6 shillings 8 pence for Agnes. We can be certain that James did not saddle them with a wooden frame used at the time for punishing felons. The word 'stocke' in the wills that

I have encountered usually refers to a colony of bees. In Middle English, a 'stock' was a trunk. Neither interpretation would usually be associated with a monetary value. 'Stock' was defined before 1700 as a range of wooden articles, crops, breeds of animal, or — the most likely way in which James used it — 'a sum of money set aside for a special purpose.'[75] Whatever the stocks were, they were held in Byrcum (Burcombe) for safekeeping, Alice's in the hands of William Hortington and Agnes' overseen by Robert Elliott. In addition, James desired that his wife Joan and son Chrystofe (Christopher) should give Alice five bushels of wheat and five of malt annually on the feast of Saint Michael the Archangel. Other gifts of lambs went to his grandson John, and to Henry and Edward, sons of Thomas and James Martin. James gave his godson James Elliott a 'chylver hogge' (a year-old female lamb*). Finally, the 'Resydew' of his estate was passed to Joan and Christopher. James' brother Walter Elliott and Thomas Martin, who were appointed overseers, were to have a wether (male) sheep for their trouble. Thomas Martin was probably James' son-in-law. He wed Elizabeth Elliott at Compton in 1541, when she was described as James' daughter.

In his will of 1559, Walter named his wife Julyanne and children James, John, Margaret, and Humphry (probably of the 1539 baptism), and his brother John. The records are silent as to the fate of Walter's copyhold after his death. However, we know it eventually passed to his son James because the manor court noted in 1586 that Margaret, James' widow, held it during her widowhood.[76]

John signed his will on Christmas Day 1562, and was buried on Boxing Day. He named his wife Joan, daughter-in-law Alice Panye, and children Joan, William, Agnes, and Humphry. We can safely assume that Joan took over her husband's tenancy during her widowhood because she was fined 40 shillings for demising her common rights against an ordinance of the court in 1577.[77]

Walter's son James made a will in 1579. He named his wife Margaret, daughter Elizabeth, and sons Walter and Francis. James' brother Humphry is also mentioned, along with a bother-in-law 'Mountigewe.'

The wills of the three brothers with six sons — Christopher, James, John, Humphry, William, and another Humphry — and three grandsons — John, Walter, and Francis — do not account for the twenty Elliott boys baptised in Compton during the 16th century. For the most part, their fathers are not recorded in the parish register, and research of Francis, named as the father of Francis junior in 1561, proved to be impossible because the only

---

* The word hog was applied to any animal of a year old.

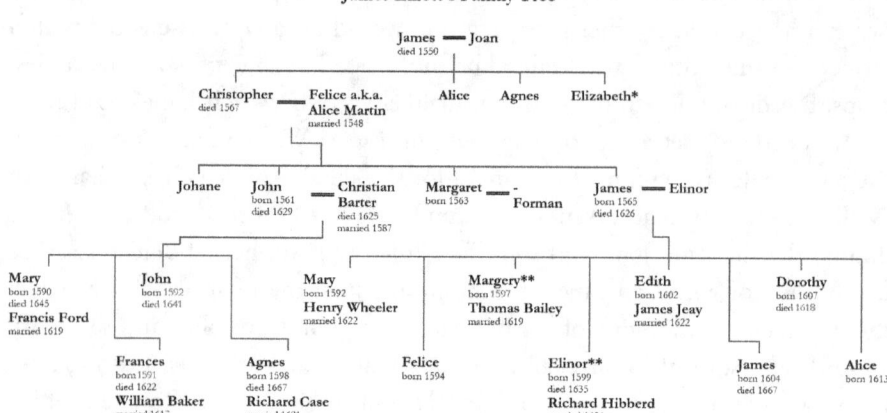

fathers of a Francis documented elsewhere are called James, John, and Walter. High infant mortality is a reason for the absence of some baby boys from later records. Others who reached adulthood moved away or fell between gaps in surviving records. Only one male descendant of each testator can be traced with confidence through the manor court rolls and Compton's parish registers: James' son Christopher, John's son William, and Walter's son James.

Christopher was buried at Compton in 1567. His probate in 1570 documents his family of two daughters, Johane and Margaret, and two sons, John and James. These children were hardly more than infants: John was six (baptised 1561), Margaret three (baptised 1564) and James two (baptised 1565). No baptism entry has survived for Johane. As Christopher's heirs were minors, they were placed under the guardianship of their mother Felice, Thomas Martin of Fovant, and William Elliott of Baverstock,[78] who were most likely their uncles. The guardians bound themselves to the Archdeacon of Salisbury's clerk to bring up the children honestly and virtuously, or cause them so to be educated, and to give them wholesome food, lodging, and clothing until they reached the age of majority. Then, they were immediately to deliver whatever their father had bequeathed to the children without fraud, guile, or deceit. These forms of guardianship bonds were called tuition bonds, which safeguarded the upbringing of boys under fourteen and girls under twelve. This particular bond raises the suspicion that Compton's vicar was unfamiliar with the name Felice and misinterpreted her as 'Alice' when he entered the marriage of Christopher Elliott to Alice Martin in the parish register in 1548.

Felice (spelt Fyllys, Phillys, Phillis, Phillidis) alone among the Elliotts is named in the early surviving manorial records that span ten years from 1576

FAMILIES PASSING THROUGH COMPTON CHAMBERLAYNE   89

Walter Elliott's Family Tree

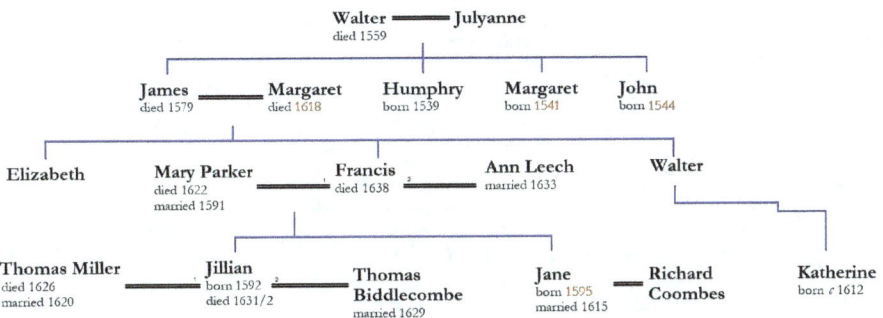

William Wattes in his will dated 19 September 1545 bequeaths sheep going with Walter "Elyat" in Compton

to 1586 and relate to the Haversham half-manor at Compton. In 1576, after Christopher's untimely death, she was admitted during her widowhood to the tenancies of two messuages known as Porters and Pryncys (Princes), with a heriot of the half-part of an ox valued at 10 shillings. Christopher had held his tenancy by copy of court roll, dated 7 June 32 Henry VIII (1541). Further details of the copyhold are not given.

The only Elliott liable to pay the tax raised in 1576 was one James. Although his assessment at £4 was considerably less than that of the lord of the manor, John Nicholas at £16, it was higher than the £3 due from the twelve low-end taxpayers. This assessment reveals a large disparity between James and the other Elliotts, who enjoyed nowhere near his means. James, as already mentioned, seems to have been older than his brothers Walter and John, but was long dead by 1576 when James, his second-born grandson, was only 11. This leaves Walter's son James as the most likely taxpayer, and presents a conundrum as to how such a reversal of financial standings between the cousins could have come about.

Either Walter had more property with no surviving documentation, for instance in the Baynton half-manor, or, as seems more likely, the affairs of Christopher's widow Felice were in turmoil. In 1578, she agreed to surrender all her interest in her estate to John Nicholas, which was then regranted to Francis Nicholas, who paid her £20. He was obliged to obtain the good will of George Penruddocke to a partition of her tenement, which suggests that part of it was sited in his Baynton half-manor. The property consisted of her copyhold of Porters and Princes, forty acres of arable land, three fardels (or virgates) in the common meadow (called Brode/Broadmead), close pastures in Princes, the Grove, and the Ham near Wyngose (Wingoose), together with common pasture for eight large cattle and forty sheep. Francis' regrant was for

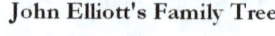

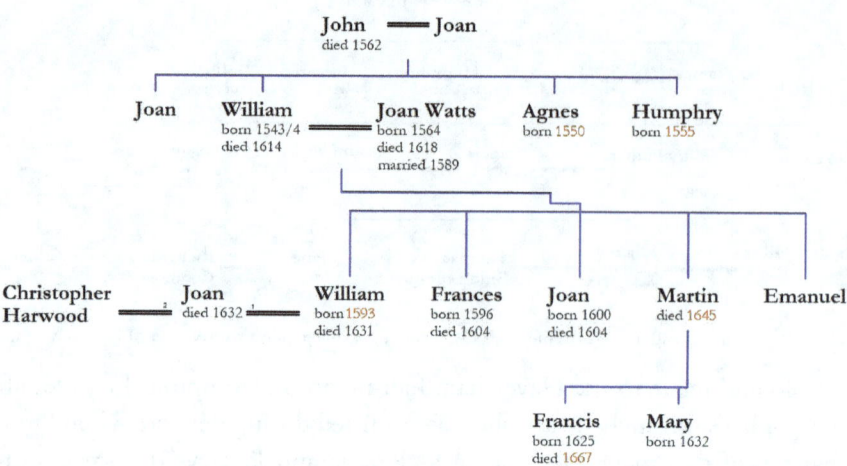

the lives of himself, his daughter Warburie (Warborow), and Griffin Nicholas, son of Robert Nicholas of Roundway.

In his turn, he surrendered a small part of Felice's holding, including half an acre of pastureland called the Grove, which was newly enclosed, in 1585. Edmund Trowbridge was in occupation at that time. A new lease was granted to Edmund, his brother Edward, and Amy Elliott successively. I have not been able to establish the relationship of Felice to Amy or the Trowbridge brothers, which disturbingly indicates that there is more to the Elliotts than meets the eye in the surviving records. This small holding eventually passed out of the James/Christopher family line to Francis, Walter's grandson.

Edward Penruddocke demanded a fine from the copyholders when he inherited the former Bayntons half-manor in 1582. His first court, held in March 1586, lists five Elliott copyholders, all of whom were descended from the testators, the dates of their wills noted in brackets as follows: James and John, the grandsons of James (1550) and sons of Christopher and Felice, Margaret the daughter-in-law of Walter (1559) and widow of his son James (1579), and William, the son of John (1562).

The largest acreage was held by James' descendants, his grandsons John and James. The youngest of the two, James, celebrated his 21st birthday in 1586. They had two copyholds totalling 50½ acres. One comprised Porters, with 20 acres of arable land in both their names. Their mother Felice had held 40 acres at Porters in the Haversham half-manor, reinforcing the theory that Porters was split between the half-manors, although there could have been a transfer made between them. Research by the Victoria County History project has concluded that the lands of each half-manor were dispersed and intermixed throughout the whole of the parish.[79]

The other parcel of 30½ acres of arable was held in the names of Felice and John, and did not form part of Felice's former Porter-Princes holding. I will call it the Homeclose tenancy because it included a messuage called Homeclose. John paid an entry fine of £20 for the first and £25 for the second holding. Each copyhold required a heriot of the tenant's best animal or 40 shillings at the lord's choice. Compared with the value of 10 shillings laid down in the 1541 copyhold, this heriot, a little over 40 years later, was huge.

James, Walter's son, died in 1579. A tenancy with 28 acres was granted anew to Margaret during her widowhood and to the couple's son Francis in 1586.[80] Their copy was delivered to Francis at Sarum. However, Francis married Mary Parker at Compton in 1591, and the year following they baptised Jollyan (Jillian/Julian), one of very few entries for the Elliott family, in which the father is named in the parish register, apart from the seven diligently recorded children of James.

In 1586, William, son of John, was granted the copyhold of a new building and six scattered acres of arable land, with two described as lying upon 'Chawlkhill,' one by Worthie gate, one in Flexlande, and half an acre upon Fowle Hill, in Stoney bottom, against Jeies (Jeay's) Headge and Gawens Bushe, the latter formerly in Francis Nicholas' tenure.[81]

Interestingly, whereas Walter's grandson Walter and John's son William were their sole heirs, James' grandsons, John and James, seemingly shared their inheritance. These brothers seized the opportunity to provide homes for their children, or to invest for their future, when Nineteenacre field next to Hurdcott was enclosed and divided into parcels in 1615.[82] John acquired five and a half acres with John and Frances and four acres with Mary* and Agnes, and James five and a half acres with James and Dorothy and four acres with Mary and Alice. Cottages were built on the plots, and at least one was sublet. We know this because in 1619 John was granted a licence — for a fine of 20 measures of oats — to sublet his cottage, late Stones, and four acres late enclosed in a close called Nineteenacres, to Francis Ford, who had married his daughter Mary.[83] There are no traces today of cottages ever having stood on the part of the manor adjoining Hurdcott — although they could be obscured by a concrete base which is all that remains of an electric power station that stood in the vicinity during the First World War.

---

*   Mary's baptism in 1590 is recorded with her father named as John.

John married Christian Barter at Fovant in 1587. His brother-in-law John Barter was granted the tenancy of a cottage and several closes in Compton successively with Jane Fricker, Osmond the tailor's daughter, and John's daughter Frances in April 1604.[84] Brothers John and James acted as pledges, but it was John Barter who paid the entry fine of £15. He made a nuncupative will on the 2 August, and was buried at Compton nine days later. Imagine the pain he must have felt on his deathbed as he told his scribes that if he had only escaped his illness, he should have married the maid Jane Fricker, their banns having already been called in church three times. His sickness was surely the plague. Perhaps he had visited William Elliott, who owed him 10 shillings, and had caught the infection from his two daughters, who had died during the epidemic that June. The main beneficiary of his estate was John Elliott. Administration was granted to his fiancée Jane. Two years later, she married Thomas Antrum, and they took over the tenancy of the cottage. Frances remained the last life surviving on the tenancy.

All three of John's daughters were married at Compton: Frances to William Baker in 1617, Mary to Francis Ford in 1619, and Agnes/Ann to Richard Case in 1621. John began to sort out his affairs in April 1626. In accordance with a licence to demise, Mary and Francis Ford together with John Case, son of Richard and Agnes, were admitted as tenants to the four acres in the Nineteenacre field.[85] John himself, his son John, and Francis Ford were admitted to the five-and-a-half-acre parcel. Francis undertook 'not to put out the said John Case vnlesse he hath a child by Mary his now wife,' and then to give John 10 shillings. John soon had to find a new place of residence. Francis baptised a daughter, Jane, in 1628.

John's son-in-law Richard Case and his son John had been admitted to the Homeclose tenancy, with two closes enclosed in the East Common added to the holding.[86] This, together with the Nineteenacre field, enclosed in 1615, and John Whitemarsh's admission to the blacksmith shop and an acre of pasture late enclosed in the West Common in 1621, shows that John Penruddocke was continuing apace with his father's project to enclose grazing land. Yet common was still available, as the right to graze twelve large cattle and sixty sheep on common pasture granted by the earlier Homeclose copyhold was retained.

Both John and James had only one son. James' son James was first named as a customary tenant by the manor court in 1601,[87] and regularly as a tenant or juror thereafter. John's son John suffered from either poor physical or psychological health. His condition was even more debilitating than that of the village 'simpleton' John Toomer, considered an idiot by the vicar three and a half centuries later in 1852. That John was able to work as a labourer at the time the 1851 census was taken. John's son, however, was incapable of caring for himself. John senior's son-in-law Richard looked after him, and promised in open court that if he was still living after John died, and John the younger was no longer living with him, he, Richard, would give 40 shillings yearly to John or any person who cared for him.[88]

John and James made their wills during the 1620s. James signed his on 14 April 1626, and was buried on the 15th, with probate granted on the next day. He appointed his wife Elinor and son James his executors, and made bequests to five daughters: Elder (Elinor), Alice, Mary, Margery, and Edith. A sixth, Dorothy, had died aged nine, predeceasing her father. A seventh, Felice, is not named in the will, but the manor court in 1613 recorded the grant of a copyhold of two tofts, a cottage, and part of a close to her with her sister Mary and their father James. Baptisms for seven of James' children are documented in the parish register: Mary in 1592, Felice in 1594, Elinor in 1599, Edith in 1602, James in 1604, Dorothie (Dorothy) in 1607, and Ales (Alice) in 1613. Margery, baptised in 1597, whose father's name the vicar failed to note, was most likely the daughter James mentioned in his will. James' holding passed to his son James.

John senior was buried at Compton on 28 May 1629. His wife Christiana had died four years before him. In his will, signed on 8 April, he tasked Richard Case with administering John junior's affairs for the term of his life and making sure his needs for subsistence were met. He also named his other son-in-law Francis Ford, granddaughter Jane Ford, grandsons John and Christopher Case, granddaughter Mary Baker, and his sister Margaret Forman.

Unlike his father, James junior did not leave making a will to the last minute. His is dated 6 April 1657, and he was buried in November 1667. In it, James does not mention either a wife or child, indicating that his male line of Elliotts, as was the case for his cousin John, died out with him. He left 5 shillings to his sisters Margery Hibberd and Edith Jeay, 1 shilling to his sister Elinor, and £5 to his niece Edith Jeay. The surviving marriage information for Margery does not square with that provided in James' will. According to the parish register at Compton, Margery Elliott wed Thomas Bailey in 1619. There are no records documenting a burial for Thomas or a second marriage for Margery. There is, however, a Sarum Marriage Licence Bond that records Ellen Elliott, a spinster, aged 27, of Compton Chamberlayne, and Richard Hibbord (Hibberd), aged 24, of South Burcombe, in 1626. Ellen must have been James' sister Elinor born in 1599. Interestingly, 'parents' consent' is written under 'bride notes.' As she was past the age of majority and considering her cousin

John's condition, mental impairment could be a reason why parents' consent would have been needed.

All James' other bequests benefitted his 'cousin' Richard Wheeler, including his ground called Quarry Close and the corn growing on it, items of furniture, pots and pans, bedding, and his wearing apparel. Richard was James' nephew rather than his cousin, the eldest son of his sister Mary. The parcel he calls Quarry Close was Porters, which had been enclosed from Quarry Close.

Mary had married Henry Wheeler at Compton in 1622, and they baptised Richard later that year. In 1674, when church attendance was both a religious obligation and a legal requirement, the churchwardens presented[*] Richard and his wife Elizabeth on the Visitation of the Bishop of Sarum for absenting themselves from divine service and sacrament, while confirming that as far as they knew they were not papists or sectaries.[89] Churchwardens were often unwilling to present neighbours for ecclesiastical offences. It is therefore telling that two of the signatories, Christopher Bailey and Richard Hibberd, were related through marriage to Richard's aunts. Perhaps the sisters were none too pleased with the will. On the same visitation, the churchwardens censured a vicar named Francis Greene for failing to go on a perambulation during Rogation week, when he should have blessed the crops. He must have been substituting for the incumbent John Martin.

An Elinor Elliott appears to have had an illegitimate son George fathered by Robert Comage (Commege/Comedge/Cumidge/Cumage). George Comage's baptism is recorded in 1607 at Compton with the alias Elliott, and without his parents' names attached. Three years earlier, in 1604, Robert had been granted the tenancy of a cottage and close, a portion of meadow, and twenty acres of arable land in the common fields along with his son, and Elinor Elliott, 'daughter of James.'[90] Elinor, one imagines, was keeping house for widower Robert and his young son David, who had only been baptised at Compton five years before, and one thing led to another. In 1609, the reversion was granted to Robert Comage and his son George. Who was Elinor? She is unlikely to have been James' and Joan's daughter. As James died in 1550, if he had had a daughter called Elinor, she would have been at least 57 when George was born in 1607. She certainly could not have been James' and Elinor's daughter Elinor who was baptised in 1599, making her only eight years old in 1607. Robert Comage was buried in 1658. The homage presented that the heriot due was forgiven 'for his horse was lost in

---

*   Churchwardens were obliged to make annual 'presentments' to the Bishop or Dean of the Diocese, reporting on the church fabric, conduct of the minister, and religious habits of the parishioners.

the wars, Mr Penruddocke promised to allow this,'[91] which probably means it was appropriated by soldiers during the Civil War. His son David entered the Church and married Elizabeth Melward (Millward/Miller) of Compton in 1634, when he was a curate at East Stour, Dorset. In the 1641 lay subsidy, David is described a clerk at Compton, while Christopher Ford was the vicar.

The manor court recorded Margaret's death in 1618.[92] Francis was admitted as tenant during his life, after handing over a gelding worth £3 to the lord as a heriot. He was immediately elected the enumerator of sheep, and continued a strong presence at the sessions as a juror.

Francis' and Mary's daughter Jillian married Thomas Mylward (Millward/Miller) in Salisbury in 1620. He was the grandson of Francis and Christiana Nicholas and brother of David Comage's wife. They baptised three children: Jane in 1621, Robert in 1622 and Francis in 1625. By April 1626, Thomas' health was failing prompting his mother Susan (née Nicholas) to secure Robert's future by adding him to her lease of a standard husbandman's holding with 34 acres in the common arable fields.[93] A month later, the family buried Thomas, at age 35. Francis surrendered his tenancy in April 1629 for a regrant to himself, his daughter Jillian Miller, a widow, and her youngest son Francis Miller, thus providing for his future.[94] The new tenancy included an additional fourteen acres of pastureland. Most, as with Richard Case's inheritance in 1626, had been recently enclosed in the East Common. The rent and heriot were the same as in 1586, but the fine paid had increased astronomically from £30 to £120. Jillian, as Julian Millard, married Thomas Biddlecombe three months after Francis' regrant. He was added to the copyhold, when a further fine of £13 fell due.

Francis had married Mary Parker at Compton in 1591. She testified in the suit Joan Elliott brought against Margery Jeay, which came before the Bishop's Court in 1600.[95] The clerk reported her clarification in answer to a question about the relationship between her own husband and Joan's husband William: they 'do call [themselves] cosens but of what Degree they are she cannot answeare.' Faced with the same problem, I have profound sympathy with this lady. Whether relations between the cousins were friendly or not is another matter. One should remember that Gwilliams, in his deposition during Reverend Dugmore's suit against Robert Ford in 1600, suspected that William Elliott's testimony was 'partial and affectionate,' which he reinforced with the quip that he was an enemy of one Miller, a party 'touched' in the suit.[96] This suggests that William was at odds with the Miller family, whom his cousin Francis had made his heirs.

Mary was buried in 1622 and Francis wed Ann Leech in 1633. Their marriage was short. Francis was buried only five years later, in 1638. In his will, he remembered his wife Ann, daughter Jane Combes, granddaughter Mary Combes, and brother Walter. Jane had married Richard Combes at Compton in 1615. Ann surrendered her husband's holding in 1643, at which time it passed to Francis' grandson Francis Miller junior.[97]

But what about the younger brothers? Two were called Humphry: James' brother (born in 1539) and William's brother (probably born in 1555). Although missing from the manorial surveys, they were still living in the village but in meagre circumstances compared with their elder brothers. The Field Book of 1597, which lists each household, includes Humphry. This name consistently appears amongst the jurors at the court sessions held between 1592 and 1617, but it is unclear whether only one or, as is more likely, two Humphrys are involved. As noted in the last chapter, Humphry was granted the tenancy of a cottage with his children William and Edith in 1610. When he died in 1628, his daughter, who had married Richard Thomas in the meantime, took over the tenancy.[98]

In the same year that Francis inherited from his father, a Walter Elliott, probably Francis' brother, took up the tenancy of a cottage with half an acre and the right of common pasture for one cow.[99] He was the Walter who was ordered to repair his badly decayed flue in 1624.[100] He surrendered his tenancy in 1629,[101] when it was regranted to himself and his daughter Katherine, who was born *c* 1612. She married Thomas Pinnell in Salisbury in 1630.

The Bishop's Court depositions also name two other Elliotts who lived in Compton. In 1600, a Robert Elliott, husbandman, testified in the vicar's cake suit that he was 30 years old and had lived in Compton for 24 years. Robert Elliott was given orders regarding the pasturing of his sheep in 1609.[102] He was not named as a tenant in the manorial records, but these are incomplete. One must remember that James Elliott mentions a Robert of Burcombe in his 1550 will, though he must have been another Robert, possibly the witness' father.

The second Elliott named in the depositions is Christopher, whom William Jeay alleged John Penruddocke kept at the Big House as a stallion for his sisters' entertainment. Cutt, as he was called, was probably the Christopher baptised in the village in 1594. Nothing is known about him or his relationship, if any, to the brothers James, John, and Walter, and their descendants.

Of the manor's twenty-five customary tenants in 1611, six were Elliotts: John, James, the widow Margaret, William senior, Humphry, and William junior. Only three Elliott householders were left in Compton in 1641. Thirty-seven Compton villagers were liable to pay tax that year.[103] Among them, James Elliott, the bachelor, paid 9s 7d, Ann, Francis' widow, 8s 3d, and Walter 1s. James was his grandfather James' heir. He had a large house with four fireplaces and was the only Elliott liable for hearth tax in 1662.[104] Francis and Walter were Walter's grandsons. The land held by the third brother John had already passed into Harwood hands.* Walter's land was subsequently taken over by the Miller family, and the Wheelers inherited James' land.

Why did such a large family as the Elliotts disappear from Compton's records after the 1660s? One explanation, when you look back, is that they had a propensity to produce daughters, and later sons without progeny. The last baptisms recorded are those of Martin's children Francis and Mary in 1625 and 1632. The last burials of Elliott men are of John in 1641, Martin in 1645 and James and Francis in 1667. John was probably the son of John Elliott, whom Francis Ford promised to support for life. James, as we know from his will, was childless, and there are no signs of any surviving sons from Francis Elliott.

Glimpses through the manor court records hint at a dissonant family dynamic. I have already mentioned that William and Francis' son-in-law Miller were adversaries, and my suspicion is that James' sisters were put out by his will. Brothers James and John farmed neighbouring strips in the common arable fields, but their heirs did not always see eye-to-eye. Friction between James' son James and John's son-in-law Francis Ford is evident from the court amercing James and Francis Elliott, with two others, for conspiring indiscriminately against Francis Ford and John Winterbourne in April 1638.[105] Another controversy that cast James Elliott and Francis Ford on opposing sides is reported at the session held in May 1656.[106] Nine members of the homage, including John's son-in-law Richard Case and James Elliott, presented Edward Penruddocke as the tenant for William Jeay's two copyhold tenements after William's death, according to the custom of the manor. Three others — Francis Ford, Robert Comage, and Francis Miller — refused to support him. Neither would they present his relict Christian Jeay during her widowhood, claiming they were altogether ignorant of the custom. In the end, Edward was admitted to the copyhold.

---

* See Chapter 14.

16

JEAY SLANDERS JOAN PENRUDDOCKE

WILLIAM JEAY CONTINUED to make trouble in Compton and, as if saving his best for last, the spiciest case came before the Bishop's Court on 14 October 1615 in the suit filed by nineteen-year-old Mistress Joan Penruddocke. Sir Edward Penruddocke had died the year before, leaving his only surviving son John as head of the household, where he lived with his mother, Lady Mary Penruddocke, and two of his four sisters, Mary and Joan.

The story begins with two gentleman, Penruddocke's steward and bailiff, namely Stephen Bowman and Nicholas Lawes, with whom we are already familiar, strolling down the road together. As they were passing Jeay's house, he called out from the doorway grumbling over some wrongs 'pretended to be offered to him' by the squire and his late father. He demanded that Bowman give him a copy of the presentation recorded in the manor court rolls that contained their complaint against him. Bowman refused, as Jeay had failed to appear at the court.

The nature of the complaint that troubled Jeay is unclear. We know that he bitterly objected to people walking on any part of his land. How many paths meandered through it is not known, but in 1590 he persuaded the homage to punish anyone who crossed his close to reach the common road.[107] In March 1598, the homage ordered that no one henceforward should drive their cattle by William's Newclose at a certain place called the 'Peck of Purtwey' (Peak of Port Way) when grain is in the fields, under a pain of a 5-shilling penalty. The last two complaints recorded against him prior to the court hearing were in March 1606[108] and June 1615.[109] At the earlier session, the homage presented that since 'tyme out of mind' there was a stile at the corner of William Jeay's Newclose on a path leading from John Dugmore's close to the Peak of Port Way. William had hedged it up and dug a ditch, thereby interrupting free passage along the path. He was ordered to open it up again and build a new stile. In June 1615, he had broken an order to erect a gate to the common meadow at the end of his land, and was to forfeit a 20-shilling penalty assessed in default at an earlier session.[110] Whether or not this was the complaint that aggravated him, he had still not dealt with the gate in October 1620, despite repeated orders by successive courts.

During his heated altercation with Bowman, Jeay suddenly espied Christopher (Cutt) Elliott walking by, and shouted that his landlord, Mr John Penruddocke, 'might be ashamed to keep such a knave as Cutt Elliott in his house to grope his sisters.' Whereupon, Bowman, who spent his time between Compton and Salisbury and was married to Penruddocke's sister Mary, demanded to know which one he meant. William named Joan, and, as Bowman testified, further declared 'that he would not say but folks did think that Cutt Elliott was kept for a stallion in the house and words to the same effect and purpose, being uttered and spoken to the hurt and discredit of the Mistress Joan Penruddocke and to the impairing of her credit and estimation being a modest maiden as he believed.' He, and later other witnesses, understood a stallion or stud to be a male horse kept to impregnate mares. Jeay's words insinuated that Joan suffered Cutt 'to have carnal use and knowledge of her body, and to live incontinently with her.' Earlier, Bowman had heard Jeay say that he warranted Elliott had touched Joan bare. Lawes recalled Jeay had also said to Bowman 'it is like he was doing with your wife too for she hit him a box under the ear.'

Bowman averred that he had never known any honest maiden to be groped, 'but other dallying gesture maybe used to maidens without offence.' It was correct that Christopher Elliott lived in Penruddocke's house and 'had his diet there.' We gather from Lawes, who wore Mr Penruddocke's livery and 'sometimes stayed at dinner or supper,' that Elliott was inclined to flirt: 'he will sometimes jest with the maidens there [in the house] pulling them by their coats.' By this, he probably meant that Cutt would tug a sleeve in jest.

Three witnesses painted the picture of an earlier idyllic parochial scene rudely disturbed by the defendant. John Penruddocke was near his house 'looking on' the hay makers, when Jeay approached demanding a copy of the said presentation, which Penruddocke refused to give him, again because he had not come to the court. Jeay responded by referring to those in attendance as whoremasters and bandying abuse about Penruddocke's father, which suggests his grievance was related to the directive to remove his hedge, made before Edward's death in 1613. On being ordered off the property, he perched himself on one of the ever-present stiles, using his vantage point to holler after Penruddocke as he was making his way towards his house: 'Do you, do you,' he stuttered, 'keep a knave in your household Cutt Elliott to go to church and grope your sisters.' This testimony was given by John Seymor, Richard Webbe, and Augustin Hickes, three of Penruddocke's house servants, who also wore their lord's livery, received wages from him, and had their 'meat and drink of him.' Augustin Hickes, who had been peacefully mowing grass at the time, said he had heard that Jeay had been very troublesome to the Chief Justice Popham during his time.

Joan, the witnesses agreed, was known as a sober, modest, and chaste maiden. They believed such an allegation would discredit her name and hinder her in her 'preferments in marriage.' Nevertheless, she married John Clarke of London at Compton four years later, in December 1619. Joan's life was sadly cut short at the age of 26: a marble plaque headed 'In and near are buried,' which lists members of the Penruddocke family, includes 'Joan wife of John Clarke Esq. May 1622.'

The deponent Austin Hickes was living in the Big House at the time. Perhaps he later offended the village toffs in some way, because in 1649 John Penruddocke and others, including William Jeay, sent a petition to the Justices of the Peace sitting at Warminster.[111] They complained that Hickes had entertained William Powell as an inmate in his house, although he was neither a parishioner nor had he been born in the village. Due to his obstinacy in refusing to evict William, they were likely to have even more impoverished people in the parish, when they were already hardly able to supply their own poor. They must have failed to rid themselves of Powell because he married Susan Millward, the daughter of — no less — a gentleman, at Compton in 1678.

17
WILLIAM JEAY'S CHILDREN

WILLIAM DECLARED IN his deposition for the cake case that he had baptised nine children in Compton. He is named as the father of only two in the parish register, James and Margery, but the stand-alone baptisms of all his children, except Alice, correspond with the children recorded in his will. William and his wife Mary named their first two progeny after themselves. Mary was baptised in 1573 and William in 1575. James in 1575 was followed by Francis in 1577, Margery in 1580, Elizabeth in 1584, Sara in 1586, and Jane in 1590.

Like their father, William's children were no strangers to the Bishop's Court. Two were parties to defamation suits recorded in the Bishop's Book. Depositions were entered in a claim which James Cordery brought against Francis Jeay in 1612. No explanation is given as to the nature of the slander. Cordery is characterised as a farmer and proprietor of the rectory of Compton. He had granted William Jeay certain tithes, being part and parcel of a lease which expired at Lammas. This festival, traditionally observed on 1 August, celebrated the first harvest of the season. Tenant farmers presented their crops to their landlords, while their wives busied themselves baking loaves of bread from the fresh wheat to be consecrated at church. The word lammas is a corruption of the Old English *hlaf,* meaning loaf, and *maesse,* meaning 'mass' or 'feast.'

Only Francis' answer in the case has survived. He stated that he had four one-yard parcels of land in the tithable places of Compton. He cut his wheat on Lammas Day and made it up into 75 sheaves, worth, he believed, tuppence apiece. A week before, he had harvested oats in a close which also fell within the tithable sites. The oats were bound into nine small packs, each worth 3s 4d. After finishing the work, Francis carried his crop away for his own use, leaving its tithe portion in place. James and William turned up on Lammas Day, when the wheat and oats were to be tithed out by Francis. They were discussing who should have them — as William was involved, no doubt in a heated manner. Francis, who was more than willing to satisfy his just tithes and free himself from further trouble, told them that whichever one had the right should carry the corn away, whereupon William declared himself the owner. Contending that his lease did not expire until the day after Lammas, he grabbed the bundles and disappeared in the direction of his barn, leaving, I imagine, a stunned and gaping Cordery dumbfounded in the close.

As we have already seen, to evade a spousal, William Jeay's daughter Alice was married off to Robert Nicholas, the son of John, who despite this supported William Elliott against her father in the suits explored in Chapter 13. Alice had inherited something of William's incendiary character. In a suit that first came before the consistory court on 30 May 1614, and three further times during the autumn and winter of that year, Edward Reade claimed that Alice had defamed him by repeating a conversation between himself and Susan Sidley, insinuating that he intended to force her, a young woman of 23 married to Humphry Sidley, to have sex with him.

Sybil Parker, aged thirteen, recalled that Susan, Edward, Alice and Robert, and Margaret Lynwood were in the parlour of her father's house on Our Lady's Day (the feast of the annunciation). Edward got wind of Susan having spoken to Alice about him. He called Susan and 'demanded of her what she could say unto Alice Nicholas in disgrace of him.' She replied, 'Why, I did say that you took the cards out of my hands and that you did take me up in your arms and throw me across ['a thwarte' in Margaret's version] the bed.' 'Nay,' said Edward, 'I did but put thee down upon the coffer.'* Susan maintained she had been flung on the bed, or whatever piece of furniture, against her will, and Edward had threatened Alice: 'look that I have no more of this matter, if I do I will trouble you or sue you.' Either then or later, Susan could not recall exactly, he had likewise warned her that if she said anything to disgrace him, he would sue herself or Alice.

Despite Edward's threat, Alice was unable to resist the temptation to pass on such juicy gossip. Magdalen Oake, who was married to Richard Oake, the young man on the ladder in Joan Elliott's suit against Mary Jeay, reported that she had overheard Alice both in her father-in-law John Nicholas' parlour and at a churching say to one of her neighbours, 'how chance you cannot keep the young man at home,' swearing, 'as god may pardon her' that she saw Edward and Susan suspiciously together on a bed. Alice meant, Magdalen was sure, that they had or intended to 'commit the sin of incontinency.' Bridget Whitemarsh was also in the parlour and concurred with Magdalen's testimony. Avis Pope, who had been sitting by the fire minding her own business, heard

---

* Actually, a wooden box or chest, often a strong box for valuables, probably with an uncomfortable rounded top.

nothing. Magdalen believed that by repeating the conversation she heard, Alice had much hurt and taken away Reade's good name, fame, credit and reputation. Bridget and Avil were of the same opinion.

The proctor for Alice's defence endeavoured to discredit Magdalen by questioning the witnesses about her honesty. Margaret testified that she had seen Magdalen sell a flitch of bacon at the Poultry Cross Market in Salisbury. Afterwards, she had picked up a hen that was pecking about at the cross and made off with it in her bag. Sybil had also heard such a thing reported. Margaret deposed that the Oakes were held to be poor, and to labour hard for their living.

Again, the outcomes of these cases are not recorded. Either the plaintiffs' reputations were restored or Alice's words, and whatever Francis had uttered as the grounds for Cordery's suit, were found not to be libellous. Certainly, Alice did not ruin Reade's already good chances in life as the son of the largest freeholder. He was appointed Sheriff of Salisbury in 1624.

William was 'sick' in October 1621, too ill to steal into the pound and collect his swine. Instead, he sent his daughter Jane, who was fined for breaking in and taking three pigs at the hour of 10 at night.[112] Notably, it was William's adversaries James Elliott and Thomas Ford who brought this crime to the manorial court's attention. His son Francis was fined for damage to the pound gate during a similar stunt.

When William died the following year, Mary officially took over his croft during her widowhood. She passed away in in 1631. Their eldest son William gave two horses at the price of £9 to the Lord as a heriot, and was admitted to two tenements.[113] The homage immediately ordered him to repair a building which was in decay, but William proved even more dilatory than his father. He was penalised in 1633 due to his pigs illicitly enjoying grass in Town Mead. In 1635, he was fined 2 shillings for refusing to lead (bring) his copy to the court of survey. He disobeyed three ordinances, costing him further fines: 3s for depasturing three horses in the grain fields, 12d for servicing his cattle in the common meadow, and another 12 for letting them out in the grain fields. The homage ordered him to repair his barn, possibly the building that had already been deteriorating four years before. The saga continues with yearly reprimands from the court. In 1636, he dug up soil in the King's Highway and hid it upon his lands;[114] in 1637, his house at East Brook was in decay; in April 1638, he was ordered under a pain of 3s 4d to repair the gate at the common meadow — the very gate his father had been told repeatedly to repair over the preceding seven years. It was still in disrepair in October, when he had to pay the fine and was threatened with double the amount if the gate was not put into good shape. In 1646, he cut down two 'Wallnutt tres' growing near his house, to the great damage of the lord, and had to pay £3 (about £350 today) in compensation. By 1648, things were getting serious with his barn, now reported to be 'greatly' in decay. He was told that failure to attend to it would be met with a penalty of 20 shillings. The following year, the homage again reminded him to put the gate at the common meadow in order, this time under a pain of 5 shillings. Two years later, he had still not got around to the task, and the penalty was increased to 10s. He had also set his bars near Horseshoe out of the ancient place where they once stood, and was told to put them back under threat of another 10-shilling penalty if he did not comply. He didn't of course, and had to forfeit the 10s, with a new order issued imposing a fine of 20s if nothing was done. In 1653, he was one of a few tenants who were directed to fix their houses, under a pain of 10 shillings. Amazingly, he was the constable in October 1652, when he reported to the court.[115] I suppose he was elected to that position on the principle that an old poacher makes the best gamekeeper.

How did it all end? Only with his interment in the churchyard two years later. His widow Christian was left to resolve matters. Faced with a fine of 40 shillings in 1658, she repaired the house, outhouses, and barns. John Penruddocke's two sons Charles and Edward were added to the reversion of William's lease in 1639, their entry in the court book set off with a hand doodle in the margin.[116] These additional lives were a legal device to ensure that the land would eventually fall into the lord's hand. The holding included 22 acres of arable land in the common fields, considerably less than the original 55 granted to William's father William in 1586.

William's younger brother Francis is described at the manorial court in 1615 as a tenant by indenture,[117] which gave him less security than a copyhold tenancy. Indentures lasted for a fixed term, and ran on until notice of termination was given by one of the parties. Their youngest brother James was a resident, which probably means he was in an even more precarious position as a subtenant. Neither of the two brothers are named in the manorial court records after 1621. Burial entries for them are missing, and no baptism entries in the parish register log Francis as a father. James' final record in the register is the baptism of his son Francis in 1626.

This, however, was not the end of the Jeays. Out of the blue, Anthony Jeay's name pops up at a court session in 1652 as a resident who owed suit and failed to attend when summonsed to serve on the jury.[118] Baptisms of four children between 1663 and 1675 are the only parish records that name Anthony and his wife Elizabeth. His relationship with William is obscure, except for a shared irascibility. He was yet another truculent Jeay. A dispute between Anthony Jeay and Edward Nicholas was reported in the Visitation of the Bishop of Sarum in 1674.[119] The pair had not received the sacrament at Easter, although not of their own volition. 'Their forbearance was occasioned from a Suit of Law maliciously prosecuted (as we all conceaved) to the Scandall, and disturbance of ye neighbourhood,' wrote the vicar, who had refused to give them communion. Despite his utmost endeavours to reconcile the warring parties, he was unable to prevail and threatened them both with suspension from the Church if they tried to receive the sacrament. Edward voluntarily offered to submit to reason regarding the differences between them, and the vicar promised to readmit him. There is no word as to whether Anthony ever redeemed himself, or, regrettably, any details to illuminate their quarrel.

18
The Penruddockes' Chaotic 17th Century

Sir Edward Penruddocke's son Sir John (1591-1648) fought for the Royalists in the English Civil War. He was appointed High Sheriff of Wiltshire by Charles I after he raised the royal standard at Nottingham in 1643, and was also a friend of the King. Incidentally, Charles rested for a night at Fyfield Manor, one of the other Penruddocke seats, on his way from Bristol to Newbury in 1644.[120] Earlier, in 1585, the Penruddockes had entertained the King of Portugal at Compton.[121] During his sojourn, Joan, the wife of Sir George's brother John, delivered their twins Anthony and Elyosa (alias Lucy), who were baptised in Salisbury, and the King was godfather to them. The Penruddockes were certainly part of the monarchy's in-crowd.

Two of Sir John's sons lost their lives fighting in the Civil War. Captain Henry Penruddocke suffered a gruesome death at the hands of Ludlow's troopers when he was staying at West Lavington in December 1644:[122]

> Finding young Mr. Penruddocke in one of the rooms where he was fallen asleep in a chair, after two nights of hard service, they pulled him by the hair, knocked him down, and broke two pistols over his head … The gentlewoman of the house and her two daughters then fell upon their knees before the soldiers, begging for the life of their guest, declaring that he was a gentleman, and whose son he was; upon which one of the troopers, who was a collier, swore that he should die for his father's sake, and putting a pistol to his belly shot him dead.

The Penruddocke family gained dubious fame in 1655, when Sir John's eldest son, Colonel John, led a rebellion against the Cromwellian Protectorate. The events leading up to this, known as the Rising, have been well documented. The enterprise was doomed from the start, with little support from local inhabitants, who were loath to upset the economic upturn and stability which followed the end of the Civil War. Only two gentlemen, a gardener, three servants and a yeoman are recorded amongst those who joined the cause from Compton.

Engraving of Colonel John Penruddock(e) (1619-1655) by George Vertue, 1713. Antique copper line engraving by Michael Van der Gucht (1660-1725), first used in A plate to Ward's History of the Rebellion. From The Universal Magazine, published by J. Hinton at the King's Arms in Newgate Street.

Colonel John Penruddocke set off with his troop from Compton Park in the cold and wet early dark hours of 11 March. Imagine him donning his red cloak and wide-brimmed black hat, complete with a bush of feathers (impractical attire for combat), his wife Arundel waving and calling 'God spede you' (God prosper you) as he galloped past the church and through the gates on his stead. Was his mood one of foreboding, or confidence that by the end of the day Charles II would be heading back to Westminster from exile? Together with Hugh Grove and Francis Jones, two other colonels commissioned by the King, he rode to Clarendon Park to meet Sir Joseph Wagstaffe, whom Charles had dispatched from the Continent to take command of the Rising. The joint force of around two hundred cavaliers reached Salisbury before dawn. Townsfolk peeped out of their houses as the royal standard was raised in the market square. They saw the rebels haul the assize judges and John Dove, the current High Sheriff of Wiltshire, from their beds, and the town's horses taken from the inns to provide mounts for prisoners released from goal. Few good citizens joined the rebels. Wagstaffe was eager to hang the judges and High Sheriff immediately as representatives of the Protectorate, but Penruddocke and others intervened to save them. Life is not fair, as we will see from the contrasting fates of Wagstaffe and Penruddocke themselves. The cavaliers, reinforced by the prisoners, proceeded westward taking Dove, still in his nightshirt, with them as a hostage. He was permitted to dress at Blandford — we are not told who provided the clothes — and was later released at Yeovil. Reinforcements failed to materialise, and many recruits turned back.

Exhausted and dispirited, the rump of the troop stopped for the night in the small town of South Molton in Devon. There, government forces, led by Captain Unton Crooke, surprised them in their quarters, taking Penruddocke, Grove, Jones, and, it is thought about 60 men, prisoner. The rest were either killed or, like the lucky Wagstaffe, succeeded in making their escape. He is believed to have jumped his horse over a churchyard wall, where to this day a gate is called the Wagstaffe gate. He fled back to the Continent.

Colonel John was tried, with others, for high treason before a jury at Exeter. Records vary as to how many prisoners were found guilty and hanged. In an act of clemency, Cromwell allowed Colonels Penruddocke and Grove to be beheaded, as an instant death. Francis Jones, who was related to Cromwell through an intricate web of marriages, appealed and was released. Nevertheless, he was forced to sell his estate at Newton Tony the following year, and his family sunk into obscurity. Seventy rebels were sold as slaves for 1550 pounds of sugar each, to work on plantations in the British colony of Barbados. John's cousin Edward Penruddocke successfully petitioned to be sent to Virginia instead, where he hoped to receive better treatment from its many Royalist colonists. His servant was hanged.* Two deportees escaped from Barbados and returned to relate their experiences, prompting a debate on slavery — but only as to whether free-born Englishmen might be enslaved. Britain had been engaged in the transatlantic slave trade for the past century, and was heading towards supremacy as the world's biggest slave-trading nation in the 1730s.

Colonel John addressed the assembled company from the scaffold set up on the green outside Exeter castle for his and Grove's execution on the 16th of May 1655:[123] 'Gentlemen, it is the common custom of all persons who come to die to give some satisfaction to the spectators.' He spoke without expressing contrition for his actions, rather proclaiming that his only crime had been loyalty. He had argued at his trial that by definition it could not have been treason, as Cromwell was not King. On that spring day, the slow clangs of the toll bell must have contrasted eerily with the feverish chorus of birdsong and insects whirring among the fine old trees that surrounded the green. After his speech, John kissed the headsman's blade and committed his soul to God. He knelt down to fit his neck into the block, stood up again, bade the audience pray for him, and told the executioner to observe his right hand. When he raised it, the man should do his office. Then he knelt for a second time.

John Penruddocke's decapitated corpse was hurriedly dragged away and transported to Compton for burial. The church accounts book records that his body was brought home at a cost of £7 and 9 shillings, and buried three days after the execution. A large coffin was uncovered in a brick vault during repairs to the floor of the Penruddocke family pew in the nave of the church in 1855. Thick pieces of wood had been screwed onto the outer side, suggesting it had been encased for travelling. The coffin contained bones, apparently of a middle-aged man, and portions of a substance supposed to be skin, with short light-coloured or red hairs on it. No part of a skull was discovered, nor any teeth found. His head, which had been exhibited on the castle gate at Exeter to deter further dissent, was afterwards lost.

An exchange of impassioned letters[124] between John and Arundel on the eve of the execution shows how the couple's close bond helped them through this wretched end. She closes her letter:

> Adieu, therefore, ten thousand times my dearest dear! and since I must never see you more, take this prayer: 'May your faith be so strengthened, that your

---

* See Chapter 20.

constancy may continue,' and then I know heaven will receive you, wither grief and love will in a short time (I hope) translate, my dear, your sad, but constant wife, even to love your ashes when dead.

He responds, addressing her lovingly:

Dearest, Best of Creatures, I had taken leave of the world when I received your's. It did at once recall my fondness for life, and enable me to resign it ... when I reflect I am going to a place where are none but such as you, I discover my courage.

He declares that he will not make a public spectacle, and asks her not to think meanly of him for giving way to grief now, in private,

when I see my sand run so fast, and within a few hours am to leave you helpless, and exposed to the merciless and insolent, that have wrongly put me to a shameless death.

The colonel stares out at us from his portrait with the reflective eyes of a mild man. His great-uncle Robert by contrast has the shifty eyes of a bullish combatant in a painting that hangs in Wilton Council Offices. Robert, later Wilton's MP, forced Thomas Errington of Great Woodford, with whom he and his brother Edward had a long-running feud, into a water-course during an affray in 1592. Errington drowned, and Robert's claim of self-defence oddly appears to have absolved him of any crime.

John studied law, and is said to have delighted in books. His marriage, probably initially one of convenience to bind together two prominent families, was loving, nonetheless. It was a widespread belief in the 17th century that love came after a wedding. Perhaps, as with Oliver Cromwell and his wife Elizabeth, who married out of prudence, the deep and enduring bond between John and Arundel had developed over the course of time. Like the gentry in general, John had led a life of pleasure, enjoying the pastimes of hunting and shooting. On one such occasion, after Christmas in 1648, he and his brother-in-law Stephen Bowman discovered the ancient stone circle at Avebury while riding with John Aubrey. Yet he was an aggrieved man, who had lost kin fighting for the King, and paid substantial fines for his family's allegiance to the crown.

Arundel and her children were forced to leave Compton. John Martin, the vicar and a good friend, took them into his home at Tisbury. He had been a student at Oxford when the Civil War broke out in 1642. Without hesitation, he joined the Royalist army, where he met Sir John Penruddocke, who promised him a living. True to his word, Sir John appointed him immediately after his ordination in 1645. Martin was arrested following Colonel John's abortive rebellion. To quote Wood's *Athenæ Oxonienses* (1691-2), he would have 'without doubt, gone to pot, could the rebels [Roundheads in this case] have found sufficient witnesses that he had been involved.' After William and Mary ascended the throne in 1689, Martin refused to take the Oath of Allegiance. He still felt bound to James II, to whom he had earlier sworn fidelity. He remained vicar of Compton throughout, possibly because he was friendly with Bishop Burnet of Salisbury, who said of him: 'Martin was pious, amiable and learned. During times of great vicissitudes his principles remained unchanged.'[125] A tablet on the north wall of Compton Church memorialises his death in 1693.

Piecemeal sequestration of the Penruddocke estate left Arundel struggling to secure her children's futures. She applied for restoration of her husband's personal effects, beseeching, among others, her uncle John Trenchard to assist her. She had miserably failed to enlist his help once before, when she had frantically tried to petition for her husband's life during the thirteen days between his arrest and execution. Now, she wrote again, telling her uncle that her husband had suffered the greatest of punishments, but asking what her seven poor children had done:[126]

> I have such a dearth of friends and plenty of enemies, some whereof (I trust) have buried their enmity to us in the blood of my husband and therefore may be the more easily reconciled to bestow on us the only good that they can do us, that mercy may leave us to eat as well as justice, having given us plenty of tears to drink.

The monarchy was restored in 1660, five years after Penruddocke's execution. At last, Arundel could return to Compton, which she commemorated by planting an elm tree in the parkland surrounding the Big House. It became known as the King's Elm. In choosing this particular species, the heartbroken widow was following a long-established tradition.[127] Elms usually grow alone, are long-lived (except when they were devastated by Dutch elm disease during the 20th century), and reach great heights, which, as folklore would have it, has imbued them with the power to impart wisdom. By virtue of their leaves growing at the top only, rather than branching off everywhere on the trunk as with other trees, they also symbolise something different and new — a fresh start. Elms were planted in times of chaos and war to engender an

Southward view of the main street in Compton Chamberlayne showing the King's Elm Inn during the 1930s.

understanding between opposing factions that would bring them together to resolve the conflict. Arundel trusted in her tree's aura to dispel the alienation she had suffered from the people around her, instil courage to never relent in her struggle for a better future, and ensure that the choices she had made would eventually lead to happiness. This did indeed come to pass.

Charles II was fearful of re-igniting hostilities, and reluctant to punish Cromwell's supporters or return their lands to their Royalist predecessors. Consequently, not everyone who had suffered for the cause recovered their properties or received compensation. The economist Eric L. Jones argues that the Rising set the course of English history for centuries to come: 'the victors and vanquished came together again as a single landed class able to circumscribe royal authority and perpetuate their own power.'[128] A placard in Compton Church proudly memorialises 'John Penruddocke beheaded at Exeter the sixteenth and buried the nineteenth of May 1655.' However, Arundel was not altogether true to the ethos of her elm tree at the time, and stridently led the widows of the men executed for their involvement in the Rising in their quest for revenge, which for her remained unrequited.

Fusion of the opposed elite factions did not help the common man, as Jones explains, since it 'established or re-established the increasingly repressive system of landed estates.' Land ownership provided status and access to political office, and could be used to suppress the dissent of those seeking equality. Colonel John's youngest son Thomas became the MP for Wilton in

Northward view of the main street in Compton Chamberlayne showing the King's Elm Inn during the early 20th century

1679.* Landowners managed to dominate their tenants until the depression of the late 19th century.

The King's Elm stood for almost two and a half centuries, before it was blown down in a storm during the early 1900s. Rounds from the trunk were cut and distributed to various people in the village, including my great-grandfather, who used his as a tabletop. It landed up on the list of his daughter Emily's effects when they were sold at auction in Salisbury following her death in 1978. My father put in an offer but was outbid. By some means unknown to me, he later managed to obtain one of the rounds. The Women's Institute planted an elm on its original site in Compton Park in 1974. Alas, after all their hard work, the ladies were unable to quench their thirst at The King's Elm Inn beerhouse, named after the symbolic tree, which had served locals from the early 19th century, as it closed in 1953.

The day of Charles I's execution, 30 January, is one I easily remembered as a child, in contrast to the many dates that floated off into oblivion during my tiresome history classes at school. I was born on that day 269 years later. My father's birthday treat for many years was a trip to London, which

---

* Curiously, George Cross thought that Thomas might have favoured the cause of the Protector, as he found a portrait of the Parliamentarian Sir Thomas Fairfax hanging amongst the Cavaliers when he bought the estate, but Fairfax, perhaps out of self-interest, later supported the Restoration.

The same view in 2024 as the one shown on page 113.

included a visit to Charles' equestrian statue in Trafalgar Square. I suspect Royalist sympathies lurked within him. Memorial wreaths and flowers were always clustered around the statue's base, placed there by monarchists on the anniversary of his death. Charles' bronze effigy faces Whitehall and gazes ghoulishly toward the Banqueting House, where its real-life model was executed. The statue was not always there — Charles' Lord High Treasurer had originally commissioned it for his garden. At the end of the Civil War, it was sold to a metalsmith who hid it, to avoid melting it down as the vendors had intended. After the Restoration, it was moved to its present position, which harmonises uncannily with a story about the Penruddocke's connection to Trafalgar Park in Wiltshire.

Maurice Buckland (Bockland) erected a touching plaque in Standlynch Church to memorialise his wife Joan, who was Colonel John Penruddocke's third daughter:

> To the Memory of his Beloved Wife Joane, the 3rd daughter of Coll. John Penrodock, of Compton, Esq. (who was beheaded for the King's Cause) who brought forth 3 sons, & 6 Daughters, and one Son abortive, of w^{ch}, and the Collic, She Dyed the 10th of Jan. 168$^{8}_{9}$.
>
> In deep sense of her Virtue, & Pious zeal for Rebuilding this Little Church, Founded in the year 1147, wth a gratefull, but sad heart, this Monument was Erected by Her Ever Loving M.B.

Joan was 34 when she died a painful death following the birth of her 'abortive' tenth child. She was 18 when she wed Maurice in 1672 at Iwerne Courtney, Dorset, her mother's home before she married the Colonel. The couple lived at Standlynch manor,* where Joan set about rebuilding the small church on their estate. Work was completed in 1677, when the building became the family's private chapel. Joan's monument is dwarfed by another on the wall opposite, dedicated to a more famous personage, Admiral Nelson, and his heirs.

The current manor house was built in 1733, and changed hands between slave-owning proprietors of West Indian plantations. After the Battle of Trafalgar, Nelson's brother Reverend William Nelson, who was created the 1st Earl Nelson, lobbied Parliament for an estate in recognition of his brother's service to the nation. The Crown bought Standlynch in 1814 and gave it, along with a pension, to Lord Nelson's heirs. Thus, it became known as Trafalgar Park in commemoration of Nelson's victory. A connection to Joan was reestablished when the earldom passed to Thomas Bolton, the son of Nelson's sister Susannah, his wife Frances, née Eyre, having descended from Maurice and Joan.

Standlynch Church. Credit British Listed Buildings (https://britishlistedbuildings.co.uk), Mark Wolstenholme (https://disqus.com/by/mark_wolstenholme/).

---

* Near Downton, and about 18 miles (29 kilometres) from Compton.

Nelson's heirs acquired additional land and enlarged the estate. Like the Penruddockes at Compton, as we shall see later, the agricultural depression caused them severe financial problems. These, together with death duties and the abolition of honorary pensions by the Labour government in 1947, forced the 5th Earl Nelson to sell Standlynch in 1948. The church has remained closed ever since. Recently the estate has changed hands again, and the manor house and church are scheduled for restoration.

19
18TH CENTURY PENRUDDOCKES' ARISTOCRATIC WAYS

COMPARED WITH THE centuries before and after, the 18th was unusually comfortable and uneventful for the Penruddockes. Two documents give us an insight into how they lived. The first hints at whoring, and the second reveals that they followed high-fashion wig coiffeur.

Colonel John Penruddocke's grandson, Thomas Penruddocke, wrote another of the family's surviving letters after one Newman tried to throw himself on Compton Parish in 1739.[129] This intriguing despatch is an attempt to persuade the addressee, one of Salisbury's justices, not to allow Newman back into Compton. Thomas had been paying Newman 3 shillings a week, which according to his account was given out of generosity because he was 'without father.' In truth, the stipend was more likely an inducement to keep Newman away from the village, as Thomas had had a tryst with his mother which left him vulnerable. The letter is intriguing, in that Thomas at the same time disowns Newman and denies his own paternity, there being hints that Newman was Penruddocke's illegitimate son. Thomas writes:

> If the villain had ten times as much [as 3 shillings] he would spend it at the alehouse, he is a lazy louse and will set his hands to nothing for a livelihood so he can live idle. He might employ himself a great many ways for a maintenance if he will but his nature bends to nothing but drunkenness and all sorts of idleness and adversaries. He could earn 4 shillings a week by knitting nets and cowls for perukes but prefers to mump about the country as a vagabond.
>
> It's hard to have such reflections renewed and brought against one in one's old age [he was 61]. I disown the villain, his mother never swore it was mine for she that will be a whore to one will be to another. If everyone had the usage as I have had, certainly whoring would be out of fashion.
>
> I hope you and the rest of the justices will favour me and send him to a house of correction where he might be put to hard labour. He has nothing of a Gentleman in him. He is a great lust and has neither honour nor courage in him.

I suspect the villain was Richard Newman, who was recorded as baseborn when his mother Mary baptised him at Compton in 1698. Richard was buried at Fovant in 1756.

Portraits of Colonel John Penruddocke present him with natural, shoulder-length dark wavy hair. Thomas Beach painted John Hungerford Penruddocke, who became lord of the manor in 1788, and his wife Maria wearing wigs made of curled white hair. Wigs were first used during the 1500s to cover sores and patchy hair loss due to syphilis, and to prevent lice infestation as they could be boiled. Balding heads had also long been unfashionable. They became especially popular in England after King Charles II returned from France in 1660 — he wore a dark one to cover his prematurely greying hair. Nevertheless, white wigs were considered the height of fashion. They were also the most expensive, drenched in powder to make them look as white as possible and convey an impression of wealth. The powder was made from finely ground starch, with a variety of scents added. A large quantity of flour was diverted to its manufacture, which increased the price of bread, a staple diet of the poor. The Hair Powder Tax Act was established in 1795 to finance government programmes, and most especially to fund the Revolutionary and Napoleonic Wars with France. It required those wishing to use wig powder to obtain an annual certificate and pay a stamp duty of one guinea per annum. Failure to do so was penalised with a fine. The Wiltshire & Swindon History Centre hold lists of certificates that were filed in the Quarter Session courts for 1796 and 1797.[130] From these, we learn that not only John Hungerford Penruddocke and his wife Maria used hair powder, but also their butler and footman, who both wore the squire's livery. On his certificate, the butler was named John Brabraham. The parish register records a nuptial between two parishioners, John Brabram and Mary Bowles, in 1789. John reported John Jerrrard for killing game at Guston (Gaston) Broad Chalke in 1799, and was buried at Baverstock, aged 62, in 1827.

Like many great houses of the time, they followed another fashion too, keeping two black servants. Constance Henrietta Lowther Penruddocke (1856-1936) collected family legends. One related to John Hungerford Penruddocke and a servant she named Bechaut. The only records in the British Isles of Bechauts that I have been able to find is the burial of a marine in 1848 and in a prison register in 1862, both held in Guernsey. Is it at all possible that the spelling could have become corrupted through memory and the passage of time? He, she wrote, married a white villager and on the arrival of an infant the squire inquired of his nieces 'is it a piebald?'[131]

20
The Elkins: A Yeoman Family

THE TALE OF two impressive Georgian tabletop tombs in Compton's churchyard begins with the wealthy and status-conscious Elkins family.

Elkins records at Compton date back to 1563, when William Elkins was granted a badger's licence at the Wiltshire Quarter Sessions,[132] which allowed him to buy corn in one place and carry it elsewhere to sell at a profit. It was issued under legislation that stipulated applicants had to be aged thirty or more, a married householder, and resident in the county for at least three years. According to the preamble of the relevant 1563 act,[133] these conditions were required because, following an earlier enactment in 1562, 'such a great number of persons seeking only to live easily and to leave their honest labour' had applied for a licence, diminishing the number of good and necessary husbandmen and being most unfit, which was 'very hurtful to the Commonwealth of the Realm.' Furthermore, some used devious means to increase the price of corn.

We encounter William again as a juror in the manorial records of 1590 and 1591. Zachariah makes his debut in the same rolls, when Nicholas Lawes, who farmed the demesne land, assigned Homeclose to Robert Penruddocke and Zachariah 'Elkin,' a yeoman.[134] Although this term was first applied to farmers in the mid-15th century, the title was not common in Compton at this early date. It places Zachariah on a social rung below the landed gentry and above husbandmen. His high standing in the village is evident from his assigned task at a court in 1586, when he delivered copies of the roll to tenants Robert Ford and Francis Nicholas.[135]

Zachariah comes across as the patriarch of Compton's Elkins clan. So much so, that a number of family members were not sure whether to call themselves Elkins or Zachariah during the late 16th and early 17th centuries. This could be a case of a late transitional shift from one name to two, i.e. from the use of just a first given name to the addition of a hereditary second name, when that second name was often still unstable. However, it was unusual in the rural south of England for anyone not to have a stable surname by 1400. The first Elkins baptism recorded at Compton is that of Alles (Alice) in 1590. Her parents were probably Zachariah and Alis (Alice), who are later named in the parish register as the parents of Agnes, baptised in 1601. Robert, baptised in 1596, twins John and William 'Zaccarye,' alias Elkins, in 1594, and Stephen, with the same alias in 1603, were likely their children as well. Zachariah is consistently named at the manor court as a juror or customary tenant until 1635. When the court listed residents in addition to customary tenants between 1620 and 1624, Robert and Stephen were also included as residents.

Zachariah was granted a copyhold of 20 acres and 1 rood of arable land in the common fields in 1597.[136] His tenancy otherwise included a messuage measuring one acre with its garden, orchard, and backside, two half-acres of meadow, one in Broadmead, the other in Courtmead, a dole (share) of meadow, as well as an entire close of pasture comprising four acres, and the right to graze forty sheep on common pasture. He surrendered his copyhold in 1624 in exchange for an indenture for the lives of himself, his wife Alice, and Robert, their son, which released him from certain constraints of the court and likely raised his title to a freehold. Alice Elkins was buried at Compton in 1626, and Zachariah, as Zachariah Elton, in January 1634/5. He was pronounced 'dead' at the manorial session held in April.[137] From then onwards, Robert became a regular presence at the court until April 1660.

He was younger than his twin brothers, and an atypical choice for Zachariah's successor. Twin John became a miller, dealing in corn like his grandfather, while William is nowhere to be found. He probably died in infancy, as so often happened with a multiple birth. Stephen was employed as Edward Penruddocke's servant, and joined Colonel John's rebellion together with his master in 1655.[138] He remained loyal to the end, and was taken prisoner in Exeter and hanged, while Edward, as already mentioned, was transported to a royalist-friendly colony.

John, with his wife Susanna, baptised Thomas at Compton in 1643, and Susanna in 1644. We know that he was a miller because he was named as such in April 1641, when the homage ordered the supervisors of the King's Highway to adequately repair the bridge at Turn Lake, next to the mill.[139] He served as a juror between 1639 and 1643, and died in his early 50s in 1648. His wife, daughter, and son were remembered in his will, signed in 1647.

Robert married Elizabeth Aldredge at Compton in 1623. They called their first son Zachariah. Sadly, he died aged eleven years. Had he done so earlier, his parents might have had the opportunity to baptise a namesake son Zachariah. As it happened, this old biblical name was not carried through to future generations. Robert was recorded as the father of four other children baptised at Compton between 1623 and 1633: Dorothie (Dorothy), Bridget,

Caterin (Katherine), and finally Robert, on 26 May 1633. Elizabeth, described in the Bishop's Transcript as 'wife of Robert,' was buried just under a month later, on 19 June. I suspect she died as a result of complications following childbirth. Robert senior took a second wife, also called Elizabeth. We know this because he named her as his wife in his will of 1674, and an Elizabeth Elkin/'Zachary,' widow of Robert alias 'Zachary,' was buried in 1676. Another Elizabeth, 'daughter of Robert,' buried in 1635, was possibly their daughter. There is no baptism record for her.

In 1649, John and Arundel Penruddocke granted Robert a lease for his life and the lives of his children William, likewise without a baptism entry, Robert, and Katherine.[140] Robert senior was buried at Compton on 19 June 1674. His will is undated, and only names his children William, Dorothy, and Bridget, who received a few pounds. The rest of his goods and chattels were given to his wife, who presumably held the tenancy during her widowhood.

A gap in the manorial records which follows between 1661 and 1703 is a nuisance, as is William's lack of both a baptism and burial entry. In any event, he left no surviving sons. With his wife Sarah, William baptised six children between 1668 and 1678. The absence of further records for the first two suggests that they died young. Burials confirm that two of the other four died aged two, one aged four, and one aged nine. One of the two-year-olds and the four-year-old died in May 1674, along with two people from other families. Six villagers, including a four-year-old child, were buried in June. Only three burials are recorded during the rest of the year, in March, August, and September. Smallpox, which had reached epidemic proportions in London, could well have been responsible for the unusual cluster of summer deaths in Compton, and a family losing its last hope of heirs. It would take another century before Edward Jenner discovered in 1796 that vaccination with cowpox conferred immunity against smallpox.

> **Objection to Vaccination is not New**
> From 1853 until its repeal in 1971, the Vaccination Act imposed compulsory vaccination against smallpox of every child within the first three months of birth, their general health permitting. Large street protests were held against the Act during the late 19th century.[141] Some participants were arrested and fined, or sent to prison. Banners were brandished proclaiming 'Better a felon's cell than a poisoned babe.' Henry Jarvis, Compton's blacksmith, was granted a certificate of exemption for his three-month-old baby at the county petty sessions in Salisbury in October 1898 on the grounds of conscientious objection.[142]

Eventually, the heir to Zachariah's land was his only surviving grandson Thomas, son of John the miller. Thomas styled himself a yeoman, donning his great-grandfather's mantle — perhaps in a literal sense, as a scarlet mantle was found in his garret after his death.* At the age of 30 in 1683, he married the widow Lucy Lacy, who was 5 years his senior. Notwithstanding this, she was to outlive him by over 20 years, passing away at the grand age of 89. Fittingly for a miller's son, Thomas' bondsman was a baker, John Goodfellow of Salisbury. Thomas is listed as a leaseholder in 1710, in the next tranche of surviving manor court records.[143] The esteem in which he was held by the community is manifested by his attendance, with Jeremiah Northeast and the churchwardens George Goodfellow and William Morgan, at Nathaniel Hancock's induction into the vicarage in 1693.[144] He is named among those required to pay the poor rate — raised to supported the poor of the parish — in 1699.[145] At the same time, he may well have been living beyond his means. Short of money, he borrowed from the yeoman Stephen Naish. Stephen demanded in his will, signed in December 1700, that the debt be paid to his son Stephen immediately after his death.

Thomas and Lucy baptised three sons: Thomas in 1683, John on Christmas Day 1685, and William in 1688. Thomas, the father, died in 1714, and was the first member of the family to be interred in the extravagant tabletop tomb. His inventory shows that he lived lavishly.* As he died intestate, Lucy made a declaration that her late husband's possessions were to pass to their eldest son Thomas, who was aged 31. After only five years, he joined his father under the tabletop. Matriarch Lucy was buried with them years later in 1737.

Following Thomas' untimely death, his brother John inherited their father's holding. John wed Mary, the daughter of Robert Ford, at Salisbury Cathedral in 1721, when he was described as a farmer. Marrying in the cathedral was a prestigious event. With cloth manufacture the main industry in the city, it comes as no surprise that their bondsman John Hibberd, who lived in Compton, was a weaver. The groom was himself the bondsman to a clothier of Burcombe, Robert Walker, at his marriage to Mary's widowed younger sister Frances at Salisbury Cathedral in 1726. On this occasion, John's rank was recorded as yeoman, like his father. John and Mary baptised six children at Compton between 1722 and 1740. Their two sons, John, baptised in 1725, and Thomas, in 1735, survived their father, as did their daughters Mary and Sarah. Two other daughters died at the respective ages of eight and eighteen days.

*   See Chapter 34.

William, Thomas' childless youngest son, signed his will on 6 November 1750, and was buried aged 72 at Compton in 1760. Monetary bequests were made to his brother John, his kinsman John Elkins, and to Sarah Elkins. Thomas Elkins was appointed executor. The will makes no reference to land held at Compton, although Mary Worth of Hale in Hampshire had conveyed a house and some pasture to William, son of Thomas Elkins, at the manor court in 1707, and William was a frequent member of the homage between 1733 and 1759.[146] He bequeathed two tenements, Cartwheel and Abbits (Abbots) at Fovant, to Thomas Hickman, and an estate in Dorset to Mary Lacy, whom he calls 'my sister.' Mary must in fact have been a half-sister, born during his mother's first marriage.

Sarah wed Edward Ewence, the blacksmith, in 1766.* Her older sister Mary married Christopher Abrey (Abree/Albrey), a cooper, in Salisbury in 1745. Their bondsman Robert Summers was a weaver in the city, while both the bride and groom lived in Compton. The marriage was short. Mary died aged 23 years in 1749, predeceasing her father. She is remembered on the side of her grandparents' tabletop tomb. The two daughters she bore, Mary and Ann, eventually married grandsons of John Hibberd, the weaver.

Following in his father Thomas' footsteps, John Elkins became prominent in Compton during the first half of the 18th century. In 1736, he was the only resident, apart from Thomas Penruddocke, to sit on the jury at the Quarter Sessions. He was also a member of the homage at almost every session of the manor court from 1740 until his death in 1773.[147] While acting as an affeeror in 1741, John was surely bursting with pride when his second son, five-year-old Thomas, appeared in court,[148] no doubt smartly dressed as a mini-adult in a skirt-coat and breeches made especially for the occasion. Picture the father chuckling to himself, thinking back to the scene in his cottage the night before when the boy's mother sat by the fire, painstakingly sewing the final stitches on his outfit by flickering candlelight. The little boy figuratively took a copy of the roll 'out of the hands of the Lord.' In reality, Thomas South, Charles Penruddocke's steward, gave it to him. By means of this ceremony, Thomas was added successively after his father and his mother Mary as a life on a copyhold dated 1724. Their lease was for one half-part of a messuage, which included twenty acres of arable in the common fields formerly held by Thomas's uncle Robert Ford. Thomas was admitted as a tenant in reversion but his fealty, pledging loyalty to the lord, was respited 'until it shall happen.'

---

* See Chapter 32.

John inherited his mother Lucy's longevity genes, and was buried at the age of 88 in May 1773. In his will, which he neatly signed two months before his death, he left his daughter Sarah £50, and granddaughters Anne and Mary Abrey one shilling piece each. John, his eldest son, received his leasehold, passed down from Zachariah, together with his cattle and goods. Consequently, after their father's death, each son held twenty acres in the common arable fields, Thomas having received the estate that had formerly been held by his maternal grandfather Robert Ford. Seemingly, the family's status had remained intact.

John junior, however, already had another job. Charles Penruddocke had appointed him gamekeeper in 1770.[149] In 1776, he reported William Weeks to the Magistrates' court for stealing fish, for which William was roundly fined £5.[150] He continued to sit on the manor court jury from 1775 until 1804, shortly before his death the following year. There are no traces of a marriage for John, and he cannot have left any surviving children, since his tenancy passed to his sister Sarah's son John Ewence.

His younger brother Thomas was married three times, first to Catherine Johnson at Barford St Martin in 1767. They baptised two daughters, Mary in 1769, and Catherine on 12 February 1774/5. Both mother and baby died. One Catherine Elkins was buried on 13 February that year, and another on 7 March the year following. Thomas next married Betty Holloway at Compton on 16 November 1775. She suffered the same fate as Thomas' first wife. They baptised three children, the last, Frances, on 6 February 1779/80. Elizabeth was buried on 18 June 1782. Baby Frances also died sometime in either 1780 or 1782 — possible burials for her are variously recorded as 15 and 19 October 1780, and 30 April and 31 August 1782.

Thomas surrendered his copyhold when he was 44 years old in 1779. His age was recorded in the manor court book, which is highly unusual.[151] The question hangs in the air, did he fall into despair after losing both wives, or did he give up his land because he was under pressure from his landlord Charles Penruddocke, ever-eager to take the last larger copyholds into his hands? Thomas was 61 when, in 1796, he married his third wife Mary Wilmot, who came from a labouring family at Compton. Mary was 19. She bore him just one child, William Norris in 1799, before Thomas died the following year. His last manor court entry lists him as a member of the homage in 1796.[152] I have found no further information about William Norris. A year after Thomas' death, Mary married Thomas Day, a labourer from Tisbury. Like herself, he was 23 years old. The Elkins brothers Thomas and John had had an annual tax assessment of 4 shillings.[153] Mary paid the same amount as Thomas until

1804, when the burden passed to Thomas Day. In 1807, his liability dropped to 2 shillings per annum. As the tax was based on income, it shows that the brothers were on a par economically, and at first Thomas' financial standing was maintained and passed on to his wife.

The Elkins family vanishes from Compton after the burials of brothers John and Thomas. As already stated, John's land passed to the Ewences, and Thomas' property was forfeited to the lord of the manor. Thus, an ambitious and literate yeoman Compton family came to a disappointing end.

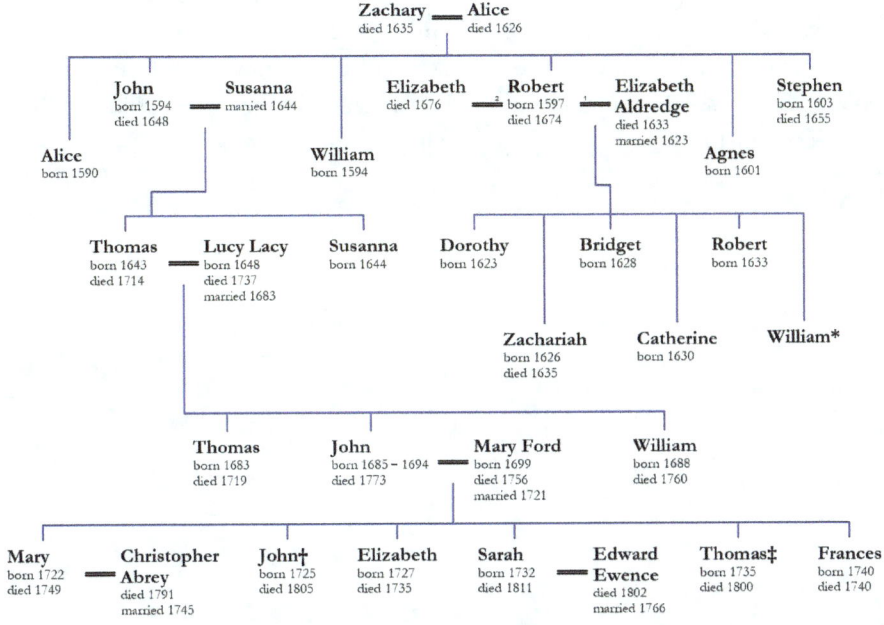

Zachary Elkin's Family Tree

* William baptised six children with his wife Sara between 1668 and 1678, all seem to have died young
† No records at Compton exist for a marriage or children for John
‡ Thomas married three times, see text

A Bondsman's Function

A man who had proposed marriage lodged an allegation with the court promising that there were no moral or legal impediments to the union, and that he would not change his mind. His bondsman, usually a relative or close friend, acted as his guarantor on a surety bond, which set a financial penalty on the prospective groom and his bondsman in case the allegation should prove to be false, or the marriage failed to take place. The penal sum was set deliberately high to deter irregular marriages. At the ceremony, the bondsman might be required to act as a witness for it to be considered valid, offer practical help with the preparations, and serve as a representative of family and friends who supported the couple, thereby reflecting the idea that marriage was not just a union between two individuals, but also between their families and communities.

Marriage bonds were no longer issued after 1823, when allegations were replaced by statements made within the marriage licence application, which were deemed sufficient to guard against illegal nuptials.

21
THE LIVELONGS: A SHORT OR BELOVED STORY

THE BYGONE NAME of a once prominent Compton Chamberlayne family is far too delightful for their story to be left untold. Carved on a second tabletop tomb in the church grounds is the distinctive cognomen Livelong, which was extremely rare elsewhere. Whoever conjured it up must have been possessed of wishful thinking — or did the Livelongs really live long?

The family's first record in Compton's parish register is the marriage of a Richard to Agnes Case on 13 February 1658/9. The second is the baptism of Thomas by his parents Richard and Anne on 18 August 1661. We can safely assume that Anne and Agnes were one and the same lady because these two given names were used interchangeably in the Case family. The couple also christened three daughters: Marie at Compton in 1663, Elizabeth at Fovant the following year, and Anne at Compton again in 1668. These girls died young. Marie was buried at Compton aged four in 1677, Elizabeth aged five in 1669, and Anne only twenty-five days after her baptism. Agnes herself was buried in 1675, and a note in the register confirms that she left Richard a widower.

The next Livelong christening in the parish register is for twins Richard and Elizabeth on 1 February 1707/8. Their parents were Richard, a labourer, and Alice. I suspect that Richard was the first son of the earlier couple, whose baptism is missing, and that he was born between their marriage and Thomas' arrival. Baby Elizabeth must have died, because they named another child Elizabeth in 1711, who may have reached adulthood. In 1763, an Elizabeth Livelong of Compton Chamberlayne wed James Taylor, a widower and parchment maker, at St Edmund's Church in Salisbury. She was aged 50 according to the marriage licence, which is a good fit. Only one burial of a Richard Livelong is recorded in Wiltshire. This Richard was interred at Compton on 4 December 1729. He is unlikely to be the first Richard, who, if he married at about 20 years of age, would have been 90 or thereabouts in 1729. His son Richard would have been about 69, and his grandson 18. Notably, this burial is the last record for a Richard Livelong, suggesting that, if not at 18, the grandson had died earlier.

The Livelong tomb.

One of the Richard Livelongs was a Quaker, and he suffered for it. He presumably joined the Religious Society of Friends in Fovant, where they first met in 1661, as there was no meeting house in Compton. This Richard was in the wrong diocese at the wrong time. The Bishop of Salisbury, Seth Ward, ferociously enforced the second Conventicle Act legislated by Charles II in 1670. The Act imposed a fine on persons who attended a conventicle, which was defined as any religious assembly held outside the Church of England. For a first offence, the fine was 5 shillings, and for the second it was 10. If the offender refused to pay, he faced imprisonment. One example of such a fate can be found in the Booke of Rigester, which recorded 'some of the material Sufferings of the People called Quakers in the Countie of Wilts, from 1635 to 1756:'[154]

> 1682. Richard Livelong of ye parish Compton Chamberlayne, was taken up by John Dorter, constable of ye said parish, with a Sessions Process, for not going to their worship, and by him brought to prison on the 8th of the 2nd month, and about the 8th of ye 3rd month to the Quarter Sessions, and for refusing to pay 3s. for 3 first days [Sundays] absence and for fees of the Court was sent back to prison, and there remains.

By this time, the older Richard had already christened his children in the Anglican Church, as his son would do later, which is surprising since Quakers rejected the established Church and its ceremonies. One possible explanation is offered by *The Oxford Companion to Local and Family History*, which in a section regarding the Quakers states that some were prepared to use the Church of England for their vital events, though the text only references burials.

In any event, the individual must have had a strong motive to spurn convention, not to mention a different one from that of the Catholic recusants in the village, who clung to the older order. He would have felt that religion and its politics had failed him. Was this due to a sense of hopelessness suffered by the older Richard after his daughters' deaths, or the despair of a younger labourer disadvantaged by enclosure?

Richard's heresy does not appear to have had a detrimental effect on Thomas, who became steward to the Lord of the Manor, Thomas Penruddocke, in 1703.[155] He had married Elizabeth Daniell at Dinton ten years before. They baptised five sons in Compton: Thomas in 1698, William in 1700, Joseph in 1704, Daniell (Daniel) in 1709, and John, who might have arrived as a surprise for the then 43-year-old Elizabeth in 1716.

Thomas, in contrast to the second Richard, was a yeoman, but he could also have seen enclosure as a writing on the wall, which would explain his insistence that his first four sons learn a trade. They all took up apprenticeships.[156] Joseph's master was a linen weaver at Silton in Dorset. In 1721, Daniel was apprenticed to Mary Forward, a weaver at Wolverton, 20 miles west of Compton and still in Wiltshire. Thomas and William stayed closer to home and learnt the craft of cordwainer from their master George Lush at Fovant. William was apprenticed in 1715, but died aged 22 in 1722, the same year he would have gained his 'freedom through servitude.'

Daniel ran into some very bad luck. Just before Christmas in 1743, he, his wife, and four young children were the subjects of a Removal Order from Dinton under the 1662 Act of Settlement.[157] They were sent to Mere, rather than Compton, to receive poor relief. For this to have happened, Daniel would have had to obtain a settlement certificate through service there before he turned sixteen.

Thomas, the father, died in August 1727. In his will, signed in February of that year, he gave his entire estate to his wife Elizabeth for her lifetime, provided she kept and maintained their youngest child John until he attained the full age of fifteen. After Elizabeth's death, the estate was to pass to Thomas, their eldest son.

John was ten years old when his father died. He remained in Compton. His brother Thomas returned, became a yeoman, and married Mary (Maria) Lodge at Salisbury Cathedral in 1738. Their marriage, which started so auspiciously, was short-lived. Possibly weakened by childbirth, Mary died in 1743. During the interim, the couple had three children: Thomas, Mary, and a second Thomas, but this is when the family's story at Compton peters out. All were buried within three months of their baptisms.

Thomas was sufficiently wealthy to lend money, even placing a notice in the *Salisbury and Winchester Journal* on 13 April 1767: 'to acquaint the public, that any person who shall have occasion for a sum of money, from 500 to 1200 l [£]. at midsummer next may be supplied therewith [by him] on a proper security.' He was buried later that year, on 21 December, in a tomb ordered in his will, which he wrote in his own hand and signed on 10 July 1764:

> It is my will that my Body be in a plain & decent man[n]er buried near as may be to the Dust of my late dec[eas]ed wife and a Table Tomb sett on us like that belonging to ffarm[er] Elkins's ffamily ...

The dark behemoth covering the Elkins' dust, which stands behind the church, bears the heavy architectural moulding which is typical of an early Georgian tabletop tomb. Thomas Livelong's mausoleum is formed of a limestone chest on a plinth, and stands in front of the church. Both tombs are Grade II listed. During the half-century separating their construction, tomb design had become more neo-classical, and the Livelongs' is an elegant example of the later period. It is inscribed with the names of Thomas and his

The Elkins tomb.

wife Maria (Mary). Was Thomas Livelong making a truly friendly gesture, aspiring to hold hands with the grandees of the village, or does this represent the zenith of a bitter rivalry between the two farming families, with Thomas intent on emulating the Elkins, who had established themselves at Compton at least 100 years before the Livelongs?

Thomas Livelong (1698-1767) and John Elkins (1694-1773), whose father lies beneath the tomb, had grown up as lads together in the village. As adults, they cultivated neighbouring strips on the Priory Field that I walked as a child.[158,159] Until 1826, the Priory of St John at Wilton still had held some acres at Compton, leased to the Penruddockes. Reading the Latin wording on Thomas' stone, which depicts Mary as a virtuous wife and Thomas as a true friend, I imagine this pair of farmers leaning on their hoes, exchanging the time of day while they worked side-by-side during the mid-1700s. But perhaps the scene was not as idyllic as I fancy, and they were instead sending each other sideways glances, anxiously watching each other's crops to check whether they were thriving better. The younger Livelong probably expected his contemporary to join his parents in the family grave. For some reason, although buried at Compton, John Elkins is not named on the tombstone.

Thomas had cause to feel bitter and defeated when he made his will. He had no surviving children to pass his estate onto, while John, who outlived him by six years, had two sons and a daughter. As it happened, the

Elkins family only endured in Compton for one more generation after the Livelongs.

Thomas Livelong appointed his brother John, who was eighteen years his junior, as sole executor of his will, signed on 10 July 1764. He left his Priory estate to him for his lifetime, if the term granted should so long continue, and after his decease to John's eldest surviving son for the remainder of the term, stipulating that he 'shall within Six Months after my decease purchase of the Prior or Lord of the said Priory and add the life of Charles Penruddock the younger of Compton afores[ai]d Gentl[eman] in my stead and exchange my sister's life now thereon for such other life as he shall think proper,' this on pain of forfeiting the estate to Thomas' nephew William Carpenter. Through this unusual proviso, Thomas shows himself to be determined that the land he held on a three-life lease from the Priory of St John of Wilton should remain in the family. If his brother failed to purchase an extension of that term with new lives substituted, the remaining years of the lease were to pass to his sister's son. John obeyed these instructions, and his homestead at the edge of the Manor House grounds appears on the estate map of 1769. Also in his will, Thomas bequeathed a suit of mourning apparel, both linen and woollen and new throughout, to his servant Hester Marchant the younger, if she was still with him at the time of his death. He mentions a mourning ring, which was an heirloom passed down through the generations of a family that had suffered recurring grief.

Strangely, no baptism entries for any of Thomas' sisters can be found in Compton's parish register, whether due to document survival, damage or decay, or the possibility that these events took place at home rather than in church. We know from his will that Thomas had a sister named Elizabeth as he bequeathed the ring to her '(the wife of John Carpenter, gentleman).' When she married the widower John Carpenter at Baverstock in 1728, she was recorded as resident in Compton and born in 1703, a date falling between her brothers William and Joseph. Her husband was a clothier in Salisbury, and his bondsman Joseph Carpenter a tailor in Compton.

Mary Livelong, who married John Shean in Compton in 1737/8, was likely another of Thomas' sisters. Both Mary and John were resident in the village. John was buried at Compton in 1755 and left his estate to Mary. There are no baptisms for Shean, or its surname spelling variants, in the parish records. In 1768, Mary was married for a second time to Christopher Abrey, none other than the widower of Mary, née Elkins. Mary, née Livelong, died at the end of 1783, and Christopher in 1793. They were childless.

The final record for a Livelong in the village is the 1769 map, which includes John's name. I have not been able to establish whether he married, and fear he was the John Livelong buried at Ringwood in Hampshire on 27 November 1778, where the parish register includes the forlorn note: 'John a stranger.' Why was he there, what was he doing? The burials of two other Livelongs are recorded at Ringwood, but the last had taken place over 50 years earlier.

Thomas' elaborate tomb represents the Compton family's swan song. Over the years, most children born into the Livelong family failed to reach adulthood. For Thomas and his father, who achieved the respective ages of 66 and 69 years, their surname was indeed fitting, bearing in mind that a person who reached 30 during the 17th and 18th centuries was expected to live for only another 20 years.

The last death record for a Livelong that I have been able to find anywhere in Britain belongs to Lucy, a long-lived spinster of 85, who was buried at Boldre near Lymington in Hampshire in 1859. She had worked as a blanket weaver, and baptised an illegitimate son George in the parish in 1806, whom she outlived. Otherwise, a William Livelong of Soho in London paid poor rates in 1896, and is named in the electoral register the following year, and a Thomas Livelong pops up amongst the wills of soldiers in Bengal in 1840. Vague hints that the name survives in the United States can be found in a couple of family trees on the *Ancestry* website which include two individuals, Goldie and Troy, credited with that surname. However, Goldie's father is an Edrington, and she has no spouse, and Troy's father is unknown. Anyone who has found evidence of alive-and-well Livelongs is welcome to contact me. In the meantime, it seems that while a few really *did* live long, their surname has, or has just about, died out. But Livelong does not mean live long at all. The 'live' in Livelong derives from lef, a Middle English word meaning 'dear or beloved.'

22
Nicholas Lawes and his Slave-owning Namesake

NICHOLAS LAWES (LAWS) and his wife Frances were examined before the Bishop of Salisbury's Consistory Court on 31 December 1601 in the suit of Margaret Nicholas vs John Stone.[160] In the Bishop's Book, Nicholas is described as a husbandman, aged 35, which translates to a birth year of *c* 1566, and Frances as 3 years younger at 32. According to their depositions, he had been born at Winterbourne Stoke, she at Coombe Bissett, and they had lived in Compton for twelve years.

Nicholas' move to Compton from Winterbourne, some 13 miles (21 kilometres) northeast of Compton, comes as no surprise when you recall that the Haversherms held a half-manor at Compton and also had property in Winterbourne. Identifying Nicholas' parents or siblings has proven elusive because Winterbourne Stoke's parish baptism records do not go as far back as the 16th century. A John Lawes married Joan Jesse at her home village of Dinton in 1562. They lived in Winterbourne Stoke, and could have been Nicholas' parents. John, or another of his sons, may have followed Nicholas to Compton, as the 1597 Field Book names a John Lawes as the tenant of a cottage and one-acre plot. Two ladies with the surname Lawes, possibly Nicholas' sisters, married at Compton during the 1590s: Margaret married Richard Mills in 1591 and Dorothie wed George Fry in 1594 or 1597 (the date in the register is unclear).

Nicholas and Frances came to Compton soon after they were married in 1588/9. Frances' father, John Matthew of Coombe Bissett, assigned the remainder of a 99-year lease to Nicholas by an indenture of the 'ancient farm'[161] at Compton in consideration of the union, for which there is no other surviving record. Thus, Nicholas became the farmer of the demesne land in Compton. Very soon after, on 13 September of the following year, the newlyweds baptised their daughter Joan in the parish church. She was their only surviving child, and might well have been named after her paternal grandmother.

In April 1624, according to a memorandum in the court roll,[162] Nicholas surrendered and delivered all his rights of title to the farm to John

Penruddocke. At the next court in October, he is referred to as a free tenant, and for the first time has 'gent' attached to his name. He still owed suit to the court, was bound by its ordinances, and his heir John Bushell was obliged to pay a relief of 56 shillings and 5 pence to the lord when he died in 1646.[163]

With this elevated rank, he became stroppy, and in 1625 he was fined 6 pence for preventing villagers from using an ancient footpath through his land at Broadclose. During the following year, the manor court recorded that he had 'given forever a certain rent charge of £36 shillings 8 pence yearly issuing from his lands to the uses & intents enrolled in a certain writing in this Court.'[164] Nicholas set up a trust, whereby this rent charge was to be paid in alternate years to two charities, the Maid's Money and the Poor's Money.[165] Remittances from the first were to be given to a poor maidservant, born in the parish, who had continued longest in service and had not been detected or impeached for whoredom, and from the second to the churchwardens and overseers to buy bedding and clothing for the poorest people in the parish. This gesture might not have been as magnanimous as it appears. Not only did Nicholas obstruct Compton's throughway by building a barn on it, but he also placed part of its wall on the lord's waste ground. The trust represented a compromise which he reached by agreement with John Penruddocke to allow him to close the footpath and keep the waste land. The court pronounced the way barred up for ever, and ordered people to use the common highway or the footpath through the ground called Cowdridge instead. A counsel's legal opinion[166] suggests that the rent charge was still valid in 1743, and a receipt[167] from Ann Grace provides evidence that at least the Maid's Money was still being paid in 1766. Ann was either John Grace's widow, who was buried the following year, or her daughter.*

In 1608, at the age of nineteen, Nicholas' daughter Joan married Thomas Bushell, who was two years her junior. Thomas' father, also called Thomas, owned the manor of Netherhaven (Netheravon). The newlyweds lived in Compton. Their first child, unsurprisingly named Thomas, died at three months in 1612. In quick succession, they baptised two more children in the village, Catherine in 1613, and John in 1614. Another child, Penelope, was baptised on the last day of February in 1615/6, which was a leap year. Her mother was buried the day after, which, given the lack of any other records for the daughter, suggests that it was a difficult birth and the baby died too. Following this tragedy, the widower's health raised concern, and on 14 October Thomas senior passed his manor to Nicholas and John, with a

---

*   See Chapter 32.

right for Thomas junior to use it during his life. He declared that he did this to establish his premises 'in the blood' of himself and his son, and 'because of the affection which he bore towards' Thomas and his grandson John.[168] Sadly, Thomas junior died in 1618, predeceasing his father, and leaving his children, aged four and five, orphans.

When Thomas senior died in 1634, his grandson and heir John was still young, although already married, his nuptials at the age of eighteen to Mary Bennet of Shaftesbury, aged sixteen, having taken place at Compton in 1632. This couple also continued to live in Compton until John's death in 1655. His sister Catherine wed Edward Pyle (Pile) in 1634. Edward hailed from Upper (Over) Wallop in Hampshire. We know from a note in the parish register that the bride was living with Nicholas, her maternal grandfather, at this time, leaving no doubt that Nicholas took in and cared for his orphaned grandchildren.

Frances was buried at Compton on 1 August 1636. No burial record survives for Nicholas. He made a will in June 1646, and it was proved in December 1647. He related that he was very impotent by reason of old age. By then, in his 80th year, he had outlived his wife, daughter, and son-in-law. He wished to be buried near his deceased wife, left his estate to his grandson John Bushell, and gave 20s each to the poor and the church. Nicholas also gifted 6 shillings 8 pence to the priest to say prayers for his soul, referring to him as his 'Ghostly father,' a now obsolete Roman Catholic term for the minister who hears your confession. The use of such vocabulary during Charles I's reign reveals his High-Church beliefs and royalist leanings, allied to those of the Penruddocke family. Margaret Nicholas claimed in her case against Stone, Nicholas' servant, that he had slandered her and her daughters. She was Nicholas' neighbour, married to John, the son of the former lord. Nicholas came to the defence of his servant. Undeterred, six years later she asked Nicholas to try to dissuade her son Robert from marrying Margaret Waterman. Nicholas told the court that Robert looked very sorrowful when asked to renege on his spousal with her. Realising that Robert 'was clearly otherwise bent' despite extreme pressure from his father, he was moved to give up his persuasive efforts and withdrew from the scene. He appeared again before the court in the suit which Penruddocke brought against William Jeay for slander in 1615. Jeay had bandied it about that John Penruddocke was keeping Christopher Elliott as a stallion for his sisters. Nicholas' evidence for the plaintiff implied that Christopher did no more than flirt with Penruddocke's sisters.

What conclusions can we draw about Nicholas? He was of the gentleman class, held the freehold of the demesne farm, and as Sir John Penruddocke's bailiff wore his lord's livery. Thus, he was the second richest man living in the village, although a long way behind the squire. His liability under the lay subsidy of 1641 was £1 and 2 shillings, while Sir John paid £7 10 shillings in tax. He gives the impression of having been a good father and grandfather. He spoke the truth in court regardless of the social standing of the parties concerned, and showed compassion towards a young man who was being forced to give up a sweetheart against his will.

Now compare him with his namesake Sir Nicholas Lawes, who was the governor of Jamaica from 1718 until 1722. He was born in England in 1652, and first went to Jamaica at the age of eleven in 1663. At 40, he returned to England and lived in Isleworth, Middlesex until 1717, when he was knighted and appointed governor of Jamaica. The *Stamford Mercury* reported on 21 November of that year that he kissed his Majesty's hand at Hampton Court before setting out to take up his position. He died on the island in 1731.

The English had invaded and seized Jamaica from the Spanish in 1655, after which they continued to import slaves from Africa to work on the island's sugar-cane plantations. Some of the Africans who had been enslaved during Spanish rule escaped and established communities of free black people, known as Jamaican Maroons, in the mountainous interior of the island.

While governor, Lawes hunted down these free slaves. He made an arrangement with the king of the Miskito Indians to send him men for this purpose, agreeing to pay them the equivalent of 40 shillings per head. An article in the *Stamford Mercury* of 12 January 1721 reports:

> The latter End of August, the Mutquito Indians to the Number of about 1500 Men, landed at Black River, the Consequence of an Agreement between their King and his Excellency Sir Nicholas Laws, our Governor, and being well armed, clothed, and supplied with Provisions, at the Expense of the Government of this Island, they began their March this day to the Windward, against the rebellious, and run-away negroes, who are scattered about the mountainous parts, and very much infest the Country. They have orders to kill and destroy them.

Lawes married five widows in succession. His first three marriages produced no surviving children. Although he had two sons by his fourth wife, most of his estate passed to the wife of his son by his fifth, Elizabeth (née Gibbons), who was sixteen years old when she married in 1720. Her husband died aged 36 in 1733. Afterwards, the merry widow became known as 'the Queen of Hell' for her 'irascible behaviour and lavish parties.'[169]

Sir Nicholas was a very rich man. In his will, made in August 1730, he named 3 plantations, amongst other properties, and had 478 slaves. He referred to himself as late of Isleworth, London, the son of honest and loyal parents who had suffered for their loyalty to the Royal Family.

One of the heraldic visitations taken between 1530 and 1668 recorded Sir Nicholas' father as Nicholas Lawes, a Wiltshire yeoman, which is cause to investigate a possible relationship between Sir Nicholas and Nicholas Lawes of Compton, although I would not be happy to find one. Sir Nicholas was likely the grandson of Henry Lawes, a musician to the Court of Charles I, who was baptised at Dinton in 1596. Henry's father is named as Thomas in the parish register. He came from a tiny village called Dinder, lying between Wells and Shepton Mallet in Somerset, and married Lucretia Shepherd at Dinton in 1594. The Dinton marriage of John, whom I suspect was our Nicholas' father, in 1562 is a little troubling. Nicholas procured the copyhold of a water grist mill called Cole Mill in Dinton for himself and his granddaughter Katherine Bushell from the Earl of Pembroke in 1631.[170] This holding included a dwelling house with three ground floor rooms, three upper rooms, a loft, and a barn, but it seems more likely that Nicholas acquired the property as security for Katherine than that he or she ever lived there. As we have seen, the parish register places her in Compton living with her grandfather Nicholas Lawes when she married in 1634. Interestingly, the name of Lawes Cottage in Dinton, a Grade II listed building dating from the mid to late 17th century, is thought to have been taken from Henry Lawes.

To sum up, Nicholas Lawes of Compton was born in 1566. His father could have been the John who married at Dinton in 1562 and lived at Winterbourne Stoke. Sir Nicholas Lawes was born in the middle of the following century, in 1652. Henry Lawes is believed to have been his grandfather. He was born at Dinton in 1596, 30 years after Nicholas of Compton. Henry's father Thomas came from Dinder in Somerset. Nicholas Lawes, born at Winterbourne Stoke, was Thomas' contemporary. A distance of 58 kilometres separated Nicholas' and Thomas' homes of origin. Time and place surely argue against an opening for Nicholas Lawes of Compton in Sir Nicholas' ancestral line.

23
The Parkers: A Family of Contrasts

THE PARKERS REPRESENT a group living in Compton during the 16th century called cottars, husbandmen, or family farmers, who disappeared from the rural scene following enclosure. Then, after an extended absence from the village, a Parker family re-established itself as artisan carpenters at the beginning of the 19th century, when furniture, farm implements, and framing for cottages and farm buildings were made locally. Its members initially flourished, but with the introduction of new materials and a trend towards bigger concerns based in towns, a number of them were forced to leave and seek work wherever it could be found. The family was dispersed far and wide. Some came back, others never returned. By the end of the 1800s, there was nothing left for them in Compton, and they vanished once again.

Three Parker baptisms are recorded at Compton in the 16th century, for the girls Warburowe in 1566, Thomison in 1575, and Kattern in 1591. The Parkers almost exclusively called their sons Thomas during the 16th and 17th centuries, and the name is again prevalent when they re-emerge in the village. Some respite from the monotonous litany of Thomases is provided by a Boniface Parker, who was an unlawful subtenant in 1581,[171] and lived in Compton until his burial in 1608.

Manor court records inform us that in 1546 a father and son, both called Thomas Parker, took the tenancy of a cottage with 20¼ acres of arable land in the common fields, about an acre of pasture at Homeclose, 1½ acres of meadow, and common grazing for 8 beasts and 40 sheep. This land lay in the half-manor owned by Sir Thomas Lucy, who sold it to John Nicholas *c* 1557. The son Thomas Parker had the life of his own son Thomas added to the lease in 1576. He also held property on John Nicholas' estate at Burton in Winterbourne Stoke, which he surrendered in 1582.[172] Thomas farmed enough land to maintain a good standard of living for a husbandman.

His holding was large enough for him to be numbered among the twelve men in the village liable for tax in 1576. By 1581, he was failing in body, as he reported in his will which appointed his wife Mary sole executrix. His bequests confirm that he was comfortably well off for the times, able to give 12 pence to the parish church and another 4 to Salisbury Cathedral. His granddaughter Thomison received a table, bedstead, and cooking utensils, including a valued sylt (salt cellar), and his godsons 4 pence each. Other possessions were divided among friends and the worthy poor. Richard Kynnett was left a pottenger,* saucer, and a little coffer. A peck each of wheat was to be distributed to four named men and to mother Banstame. His 'littell sollowe' (a plough) went to Francis Elliott. Despite, his frail condition, Thomas hung on to life for another seven years, and was buried in 1588.

Father followed by son appear variously as a tenant, juror, and affeeror in the manorial records from 1576 until 1597,[173,174] when the next Thomas Parker was buried at Compton. A sad story from that year is told in an article titled 'Glimpses of Wiltshire in Shakespeare's Time,' which the *Wiltshire and Trowbridge Advertiser* published on 10 July 1916:

> We might have expected that at the time Shakespeare was writing and all England was pulsating with new life ... every man and woman would be living in hope of still better days to come but, alas, there is abundant evidence that as many persons lived miserably and died despairingly as today...

Referring to an inquest in the 40th year of the reign of Elizabeth I (17 November 1597-18 November 1598), its author continues with an explanation and a catalogue of meagre goods:

> Thomas Parker who not having the fear of god before his eyes and moved by the instigation of the devil at Stoke Fardon" hung himself "in a great thorn bush" with his girdle. His goods remained in the hands of Alice Parker of Compton Chamberlayne, widow, and were an old flock bed, two coverlets, an old bolster, two pillows, a torn sheet, a coffer, a simple cubbard and brass pot, a skillet, a couldron, a candlestick, two platters, one pottinger, wheat, rye, oats, barley worth 20s, four stocks of bees 5s, a coat, a jerkin, and the rest of his apparel 5s, a bowl, four dishes and three spoons 6d. The total value was 55s 8d.

I suspect that 'Stoke Fardon' was the hamlet Stoke Farthing at Broad Chalke. Alice, buried shortly afterwards at Compton in 1599, was most likely Thomas' wife. In fact, two women, or a mother and child, might have been

---

* A pottenger/porringer was a small basin from which broth, soup, or porridge was eaten; often with one or two flat handles.

involved here because one Alles was buried on 23 March and another Alyce/Alis/Alyn on 22 November of that year.

Was the Thomas tempted by the devil the son of the thriving Thomas who died in 1588? The chances are less than even. We know that at least two other Thomas Parkers were living in Compton during the last years of the 16th century because two married in the 1590s, and neither of the brides was called Alice.

In any event, the reversion of the 1576 lease passed to Thomas Nicholas. A Thomas Parker is named as a resident rather than a customary tenant in the manor court rolls between 1620 and 1625. As such, he was a tenant at will, subtenant, or lodger. The family had clearly lost their land. The burial of yet another Thomas in 1629 is the last Parker entry made at Compton until 1772, after which the lineage of a further Thomas Parker can be traced up to the end of the 19th century.

This Thomas was born in 1757. At the age of fifteen, he came to Compton from Downton, a village about six miles (ten km) southeast of Salisbury, in 1772. His father, also Thomas, apprenticed him to the wheelwright and carpenter John Grace.[175] I have not found Thomas' baptism, but we know his year of birth from his burial record, remaining in the dark as to whether he was related to the Parkers who had lived in Compton almost one and a half centuries earlier.

Apprentices were not allowed to marry as long as they were bound to a master. Inevitably, the lad married as soon as he was able, wooed by the seventeen-year-old Compton lass Jane Watts (1765-1831), daughter of William the shoemaker. The ceremony was held at Barford St Martin in December 1782. John Grace had died in August that year, leaving only daughters, which placed Thomas in a position to take over the carpentry business and start a family. By April 1803, Thomas was recorded in the land tax records for Compton with a liability comparable to those ranking just below the three large farmers.[176] His property included a house his wife inherited from her father the year after her marriage.* He baptised eleven children with Jane between 1783 and 1808. Four were recorded in the village later on: Edward, James, Catherine, and John. Thomas died aged 83 in 1840. He had intended that all his children should benefit from the will neatly penned for him in November 1837. John and James were appointed co-executors to sell and divide his assets with the option of retaining his houses and gardens, which were in their respective occupations, provided they paid off their siblings. A statement, possibly in his

---

* See Chapter 25.

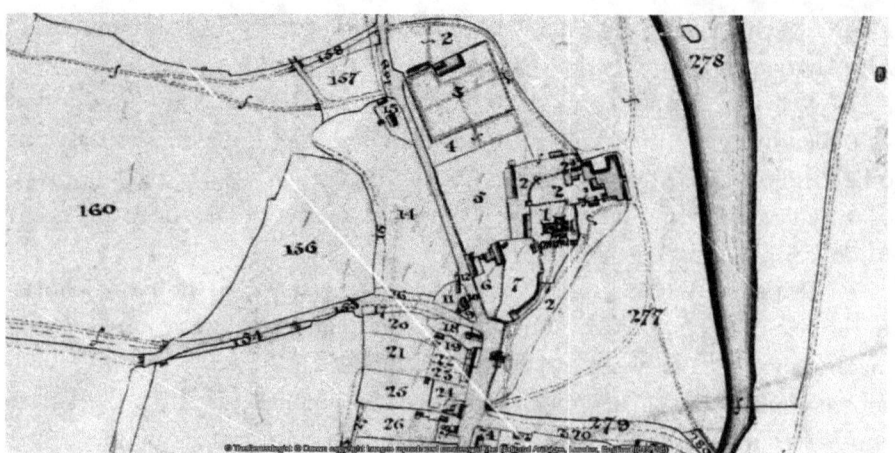

Caption: Section of the 1848 tithe map showing plots 17-20. The church is shown on plot 6. With thanks to The National Archives (ref. IR 30/38/87).

own shaky hand, written as he would have spoken, has been added at the foot of his will:

> I leaves my house that I lived in to John Parker becuase he got the Largest Familey [he had 14 children] and the other to James Parker [who had 9 children] and the orchet to be Parted between the Brothers and Sisters Every year wile the Lives do last all the frut.

John and James lived at the top of the main street near the church. The tithe awards list and accompanying map show that they inhabited the Well Cottages on plots 18 and 19 at its northern end. John's 18 with 21 perches was indeed a little larger than James' plot 19 with 19 perches. They shared the orchard on plot 20 and the adjoining waste land behind the cottages on plot 17.

Edward and James followed in their father's footsteps and became carpenters. While the younger brother stayed in the village, Edward married Anne Gillingham at Fovant in 1814 and moved to Salisbury, where he struggled to support his family. He was forced to apply for poor relief and faced a settlement examination in 1820,[177] which decided in his favour. He is recorded with Ann and six of their nine children as living in Salisbury in the 1841 census. Ann died two years later. Edward returned to Compton, where we find him living with his brother James at the time of the 1851 census. He was in Salisbury again, at Bedwin Street, and alone, in 1861.

James married Sophia Goodfellow at Burcombe in 1824. Their nine children were baptised at Compton between 1826 and 1835. Two died in infancy, as well as another baby who was not baptised. Three of the four boys, Emanuel, Thomas, and George, became carpenters. Unluckily, the demand for local carpenters had declined, and there was not enough work for them in Compton. Emmanuel joined the marines at Gosport, George was employed at the Gas Works in Portsmouth, and Thomas, though still a carpenter, lived at Broad Chalke. The fourth son, John Goodfellow, started his working life as a gentleman's servant. He moved to Hampstead, where he took up the more sedentary occupation of tailoring, and married Mary, a tailoress. The vicar reported in his Incumbent's Book that he was a 'great invalid.'

Catherine married Jeremiah Wilmot in 1830. She was 7 years his senior, and aged 44 when she died giving birth to Ellen. The vicar buried the mother and baptised the daughter on the same day, 25 March 1842. Jeremiah died in

Well Cottages on plots 18 and 19, 2023

November of that year, leaving baby Ellen an orphan before her first birthday. Her uncle James and aunt Sophia took care of her. She was still with them at the time of the 1861 census, their own children having left the household, but they died before the 1871 census was taken. Ellen, in her early twenties and single, was left without a home. She moved to Fisherton House Lunatic Asylum in Salisbury, in my time called the Old Manor, where she worked as a servant, and married in the city in 1872.

John, born in 1802, was an agricultural labourer. He was able to sign his name as a member of the jury of 'Our Sovereign Lady the Queen' at the manorial sessions between 1860 and 1864,[178] when he died. He married Sarah Elizabeth Sanger at Compton in 1823. The last of their 15 children was born when Sarah was 45 or 48. The strain may well have taken its toll on John too, as the vicar noted that he had '3 times broken blood vessel.' Their ten sons took up a variety of jobs and trades. None toiled his own land or, at least initially, provided the village with woodworking expertise. Five became agricultural labourers, three shoemakers, including Herbert who stayed in Compton, one a tailor, and one a grocer's assistant in Brighton.

Two of the labourers, Philip and Andrew Baker, worked in the squire's garden. They were both still in Compton in 1861 according to the census, which recorded Andrew Baker's wife Mary Ann (Harry Case's daughter) as a patient at the Fisherton Asylum. She was back in Compton for the 1871 census, by which time Philip and his wife Sarah had left the village. Andrew Baker and Mary Ann moved to Lanchester, where Andrew was working at the Lintz Colliery in 1881.

Two other children returned to Compton before the 1871 census. Frederick, a farm worker who had been lodging and working in South Stoneham in 1861, is listed with his widowed mother at the post office. He married Fanny (John Case's daughter) in 1873 and left Compton before the 1891 census, at which point his brother John was the only Parker left in the village.

John was living with his brother Frederick in Hampshire in 1861. Both were labouring in public works. He was recorded as a cordwainer in 1871 with his own household at Compton. He had married Diana Witt at the Independent Chapel in Fovant the previous year. He quit his old occupation by 1881, reverting to the family tradition of dealing in wood, and is also described as a woodman in the newspaper report of Frank Plowman's inquest in 1894.[179] In the 1891 census, he was logged as a wood dealer and in 1901, as a 'late wood dealer' living at South Stoneham, where there was a large community of Parkers.

The Compton Parish Register records 25 children baptised with the surname Parker between 1783 and 1835. The vicar's notes spanning 1847 to 1876 lists 31 children who had been born in the village, not including those who died in childhood. The Parkers whose presence had been so solid in Compton became — by necessity — a wandering tribe, ready to take on any employment. By the 20th century, none were left.

24
Watts: From husbandmen to Craftsmen

My interest in the Watts family was piqued by a drawing I acquired from a fine art gallery in Bath with 'Edward Watt's cottage — Compton May 25 1890 JWH' written on the bottom. The gallery was unable to identify the artist, but deduced a connection to the Penruddocke family due to another drawing in its small series, signed JHW, which features Dolforgan Hall. After Richard Penruddocke Long, a relation of the Compton Penruddockes, married in London in 1853, the bridal pair left for Compton House before proceeding to Richard's home at the Hall in Montgomeryshire. Richard can't have liked the place much, as he promptly sold the estate after inheriting it from his brother Walter fourteen years later.

Edward Watts' cottage, 1890.

A modern estate agent featuring this drawing in his window would probably add a blurb along the lines of 'a charming L-shaped cottage, perfect — perhaps requiring a little renovation — for a London weekender.' A prospective purchaser viewing the display would see a neat porch sheltering the main entrance, poky paned windows huddling under a thatched roof, two prominent chimneys, and a second door standing ajar which, taken together with the small windows on either side, convey the impression that if you were to enter the building by this door, you would find yourself inside no more than a semidetached cubbyhole crammed with tools and junk. The viewer would certainly conclude that a substantial investment would be needed to put the building into shape. When first built, all of Compton's cottages were thatched, and their walls were constructed from local limestone and the rubble of greensand which lies beneath the village's main settlement.*

Despite clear signs of dilapidation in 1890, Watts cottage, with its garden and orchard, had been a substantial enough leasehold for Edward's enfranchisement under the Second Reform Act of 1867, which granted voting rights to agricultural tenants who held small pieces of land. His name appeared in Compton's voters list for the first time in 1871, along with two Penruddockes, four farmers, and a carrier. His brother Robert next door was not permitted to vote.

The scene which held such a romantic appeal for the artist was considered an eyesore by Charles Penruddocke at the Big House. Edward and his brother Robert, two old men in their 80s, were living in separate parts of the cottage. With Robert's death in 1894, the last life recorded in the family's 99-year lease came to an end, allowing Charles to finally repossess it. The jurors at the manor court in 1896 declared that it had been left in a dangerous state, and ordered the executors to repair it forthwith to the satisfaction of the lord.[180]

The cottage had passed down to Edward through his grandfather William and father Isaac. They had worked as cordwainers in succession between the mid-18th and mid-19th centuries. The term shoemaker encompasses both cordwainers and cobblers. Cordwainers made shoes from new leather, while cobblers repaired shoes, and were only allowed to make footwear using old leather. Officially at least, cordwainers were forbidden from working with old and cobblers with new leather.

Isaac appointed Edward as executor of his will, signing with his mark, on 12 January 1849. The will conveys an impression of the size of Watts cottage, identifying at least some of its rooms. It was then in split occupation and,

---

*   Greensand is an ideal substrate for giant red wood (Sequoiadendron), and the red wood with the biggest girth in Great Britain (22m) stands in Compton Park.

according to the tithe file of 1850, stood on plot 65, which today is the site of Holmfield Cottage. Isaac also owned and occupied a garden and carthouse on plot 66 and an orchard on plot 70, altogether amounting to ¾ of an acre. Isaac bequeathed the several parts of this his last home to his two sons, Edward and Robert, and granddaughter Ann Read. Edward received the portion in which he resided, which consisted of the kitchen, a bedroom above, and the garden in front, with the woodhouse belonging to it — perhaps the semidetached shed in the drawing. Isaac also left him the parlour and the bedroom above. This part was to be assigned to Ann when she turned eighteen. Robert was gifted with the remainder of the house and garden. The whole of the orchard went to Edward for as many years as should be required to pay off the debts due, or to become due, by Isaac to Edward at the time of his father's death. As and when the debt was discharged, the orchard was to be divided by a fence in equal portions for Edward and Robert, with a right of way for them and for the granddaughter to the well, which would have been the only source of water on the property. Edward claimed two-thirds and Robert one-third of the cottage at the manor court in 1850.[181]

The first men in the Watts family known to have made shoes were two brothers: Roger and William. They too became old men. Roger's marriage licence of 1693 and the memorial of his death in 1738 tell us that he was born in 1657 and died at the age of 82 years. William's memorial states that he died on 14 January 1742, aged 78, which translates to a birth year of 1663/4.

It is credible that these two brothers were forefathers of Isaac, the last of a line of Watts shoemakers at Compton, and that this branch of the large family furnished villagers with their footwear for at least two centuries. As with all parish craftsmen, they kept animals and grew crops for their own use. The Watts, however, were already present in Compton in Tudor times, when Henry VIII established the Church of England, and in 1538 directed the clergy to keep parish registers. Were they also forefathers, and could some of them have been shoemakers as well?

The first Watts burial recorded is that of William Watts on 1 October 1545, and the first baptism entry is for Humpfrye (Humphry) Wattes on 15 October 1546. In the years which followed, spanning centuries, a succession of vicars splashed water onto the foreheads of Watts babes, and wrote their names in the parish register. Watts, Wattes or Watt is entered in the registers more than any other surname: no less than 180 times up to 1837, when civil registration was introduced. Vicars continued to log the Watts' ceremonial events at Compton until 1872. Wattes and Watts copiously litter Compton's manor court records between 1576 and 1661, which describe them as husbandmen at best, never reaching the lofty status of 'gent' or even 'yeoman.'

William distributed his goods and the land he held from the lord in his will dated 19 September 1545. First, he gave and bequeathed his soul to almighty god and our blessed lady, and all the blessed company in heaven, and desired to be buried in the church of Compton Chamberlayne. Somewhat excessively, he wished to have six priests and a curate at his funeral. Preliminaries now out of the way, his attention turned to his most prized and numerous possessions — sheep. A hundred apiece were bequeathed to his daughters Phylyppe (Phillipa) and Agnes, to be given to them on their marriage, possibly as a dowry. Each of his godchildren were to receive a sheep on the first anniversary of William's death. His flock was dispersed between a home contingent and those running with Walter Elliott's flock in Compton and Palmer's at Ditchampton, a tything in Wilton and Burcombe parishes.

From the house, Phillipa received a long chest standing in the outer chamber, and Agnes a new cupboard standing in the inner chamber. William's daughter Syble Mayow (Mayhew) and her husband Walter were given the feather bed that William lay on, with its linen and blankets. The marriage of Syble 'daughter of William' to Walter Mayhew in June 1539 is the first Watts marriage in Compton's parish register. William left part of his leasehold land and the residue of his goods, moveable and unmoveable, to his wife Alis (Alice) and son John. His other son, Humphry, whom we can safely surmise was the younger of the two,* ended up with no more than a folding board, which was probably a long tabletop with hinges, standing in the hall. From the locations of these bequeathed items, I imagine that the cottage was a single-storey dwelling and had three rooms. The hall was used as a kitchen and living room, and the other two rooms, the inner and outer chambers, were sleeping and storage quarters. The Christian parishioners found themselves in luck because, on Passion Sunday every year henceforth, everyone was to be given a loaf of bread and a spiced cake courtesy of William. That luck ran out before I lived in the village.

William's widow Alice made her will in 1558, and was buried later that year. She too wished to be interred inside the church. A donation which she made towards maintenance of the bells was perhaps meant to ensure that her wish would come true. While in 1561, William Bounde, a yeoman, generously made arrangements for three new bell ropes to be donated to the three men who shall ring for him at his burial and all the months following.[182] The bells

---

*   None of the baptisms in the parish register fit with what we know of either Humphry or John.

were causing great concern at the time. Three documented in the tower in 1553 were replaced by four new ones in 1614 and 1616. I fancy that, like myself, Alice and William loved to hear them peel 'who'll help we,' as Compton folklore would have it. The remainder of her will primarily deals with her livestock. She liberally distributed a sheep here and there, as well as her bees. Her bequest of 'my part of a Kowe bullock that ye be teyxt Rychard Sopar & me' to her godson Robert Sopar disposed of half the cow she co-owned with Richard. Humphry received her half of the cow she shared with him, enriching him with a whole cow. She willed John to give his brother half a quarter of wheat and a sack of barley to sow, suggesting that she sympathised with her younger son, whom primogeniture had treated unkindly. In contrast to her husband, she stipulated that the residue of her estate was to be shared equally between the brothers John and Humphry.

A John Watts, who could well have been William's and Alice's son, married Christian Allman in November 1539. He buried Christian in May 1559, and wed Elizabeth Mattyne (Martin) after a decent interval of six months, in November. The manor court elected John as hayward for the year 1586.[183] He must have died before the court's session in October 1589, because Elizabeth, having sublet without licence, was ordered to remove her tenants, which might just have been a blessing for them. At the next session that year, her house was forfeited for being decayed,[184] and she disappeared from the manorial records, suggesting that she had passed away.

A Humphry Watts married Dorothy Vincente at Compton in 1558. They are prominent in the surviving 16th-century Compton documents. Humphry was not the boy baptised in 1546, unless christened as an adult, which would have been highly unusual. Neither is he likely to have been William's and Alice's second son, since he was the only Watts to reach the taxation threshold in 1576. This would mean he had overtaken his brother John, who essentially inherited William's entire estate. While fathers' names were almost never included in the early baptism register, we know that at least three sets of Watts parents lived in the village in 1564, because a Joan was baptised in January, William in February, and John in April. John and Elizabeth, and Humphry and Dorothy were contemporaries despite being born a generation apart, and candidates for the children of two sets of parents. Dorothy testified at the Bishop's Court in 1600 that she had taken over Elizabeth's role of midwife and delivered the village's babies for seven of the forty years she had lived in Compton. The two women might have been related in-law.

Caution is required when making assumptions about such a large family as the Watts, but we can safely conclude from the manor court rolls that the only members who were husbandmen, tilling their own land during the last years of the 16th century, were the copyholders Humphry and John. The Field Book of 1597 records Humphry, John, and George Watts as customary tenants. This John is a newcomer for us. We know that at least two John Wattses were living in the village in 1578 as Thomas Ford made a bequest in his will that year to John Watts 'the younger.' He was probably the John who married Maud (Matilda) Parker at Compton in 1593, and was a juror at the manor court in April 1605.[185] He died in November of the same year, a wave of plague having swept into Compton in 1604. His tenancy passed to his wife Matilda.

In contrast to the husbandmen Humphry and John, the third tenant listed in the Field Book, George, only had a cottage. He had married Annis Estmeed at Compton in 1579, and is the first of the Watts fathers named in the parish register. The baptism, in 1600, was a sad affair, with the baby known to be near death, leaving no time for naming. The infant is simply described as 'Xpian,' meaning 'a Christian.' These are the only records surviving for George. He does not even feature at the manor court. Was he a day labourer, or could he have been making shoes in his cottage? Although villagers had many skills to provide for their own needs, craftsmen are documented in Compton at the turn of the 16th century: a tailor, Osmund Fricker, weaver John Palmer, blacksmith William Rawlings.* Surely there was need for a cobbler to mend worn-out boots too.

Humphry made a nuncupative will leaving all he had to his son Thomas, who was probably the Thomas baptised in 1576, eighteen years after Humphry had married Dorothy. They could have lost sons born in the meantime. Three baptisms of Watts boys during the interval between their marriage and Thomas' arrival were closely followed by the burials of boys with the same name. A note in the burial register pointing to one such pair of events concerning a Robert who was baptised in September 1560, informs us that the Robert interred in January 1560/1 was indeed Humphry's son. A John was baptised on 14 April and buried on 18 April 1564. The register counterintuitively describes him as a widower, but it is somewhat suspicious that, with only one exception, all of the deceased among the twenty-five buried in 1564 were recorded as widowed. One possible explanation is the vicar became overloaded by additional ceremonial duties and caring for parishioners. Compton was ravaged by the 1564-1565 plague, which resulted in an excessive number of burials, contrasting with only four entered during the following year.

---

*   See Chapters 11 (Fricker), 35 (Palmer) and 32 (Rawlings).

Humphry was buried on Boxing Day in 1604. He too could have died from the plague. His tenancy passed to Dorothy, to hold during her widowhood. The two widows, Dorothy and Matilda, were the only Watts tenants recorded at the manor court for the next few years. Dorothy farmed for herself. The homage enforced an ancient custom in 1606, ordering her to pasture her sheep in the West Field, and, in 1609, to her keep her sheep in the Copes and on the Downs. She also had trouble with her cows that year, when she was fined for driving them from Martin's corner — at the turning into the village from today's A30— to Hollowhead, then on the main route to Salisbury against the rules.[186] Perhaps she was taking them to Salisbury market, which has existed since 1219.

One of those cows passed to the lord as a heriot when the old lady died in her 80s in 1620. The tenancy, however, went to Osmund Marshman and his daughter Frances, who had been added to the reversion as lives in 1609. Immediately after Osmund took possession, the homage declared the cottage to be in decay. Matilda's lease was transferred to John Armory after her death in 1637.[187] Thus, the holdings of both widows passed out of Watts' hands. Dorothy's was the larger holding, with 22¼ acres of arable land in the common fields, as compared to Matilda's 4 acres.

Although Dorothy's son Thomas did not inherit his father's land, he appears in the manorial records as a customary tenant and juror after his mother's death, alas, without any information about the property he actually held. He might have just had a cottage, enough land to grow vegetables for his household, and the right for a cow to graze on the common. He married Suzanne (Susan) Webb at Compton on 23 June 1611, and they named their first daughter Dorothy, after her grandmother, at her christening in February 1612. Perhaps they also named a son after his grandfather as, according to his marriage licence bond, a Humphry Watts was born in 1611. He was buried only five years after the wedding, as a young man in 1639. Thomas and Susan baptised three more daughters between 1616 and 1621 and a son, William, in 1626.

Thomas was buried at Compton on 13 March 1638. His administration bond, dated 8 May, names his wife Suzanna. The inventory compiled after his death suggests that he was a carpenter or, perhaps, a shoemaker, rather than a husbandman. The appraisers found some interesting items in his 'shoppe:'

Two Covells, one Rowtinge axe
two hookes, one hatchett, one search
& one picke with a few small things besides

The Covells and Rowtinge axe could be tools used by either a woodman or shoemaker, depending on how the spelling of the words is interpreted. A Rowtinger axe was an attachment mounted on felling axes used for rounding or facing the foot of a tree before it was cut down with a felling saw, and a cove is a term for a moulding plane.[188] Rowting was also dialect for a routing axe used by shoemakers to gouge out a furrow in wood or metal.[189] A covell could be a corruption of a shoemaker's awl for making holes in leather or wood. I have had no luck with finding a plausible explanation for 'search.' In any case, during the 1600s shoemakers could well have required wood-working tools for making wooden-soled shoes.

Whether a carpenter or a shoemaker, Thomas was not a rich man. At his death, he owed money to his stepson John Webb, his daughter Dorothy Watts, Christopher Harwood, and John Elkins. He was, nevertheless, a churchwarden,[190] and a respected member of the community who obeyed the law. He and Christopher Harwood were the only men in Compton to provide themselves and their servants with bows and arrows in 1621,[191] as required by an act passed by King Henry VIII's Parliament in 1511.[192]

Thomas' widow Susan died in 1652, and her son from an earlier relationship, John Webb, was admitted as the next tenant in succession of her cottage and its appurtenances.[193] John was a husbandman. He had been granted the copyhold of a 2-acre close of pasture in East Common, late in the possession of Richard Berry, for 99 years in 1635, if he, William Watts, and Thomas' daughter Jane so long lived.[194] Unlike Jane, William's relationship to Thomas is not stated. Chances are he was Thomas' then nine-year-old son. It would be interesting to ascertain his later occupation, bearing in mind that a William Watts was named as a juror at the manorial court in April 1648, when he could not have been a husbandman since he is missing from the list of those who held copyholds or indentures at that session.[195] Was he a craftsman like his father?

Christenings of Watts' children cannot be found in Compton for the 35 years between those of Humphry's and Dorothy's son Thomas in 1576 and Thomas' daughter Dorothy in 1612. However, baptisms are entirely missing from the parish register for the years 1582, 1583, 1585 and 1587. This accounts for the absence of the John Watts who told the Bishop of Salisbury's Court in December 1601 that he was sixteen and had been born in Compton,[196] but even the baptism records that have survived do not catch all the births in the village. We only know from marriage licences that Walter was born in 1599 and Humphry in 1611. Mercifully, the records of Watts baptisms are steady from 1612 onward, with six entered between 1657 and 1664, when we should expect to find those of the shoemakers Roger and William. Their absence extinguished my hopes of establishing an unbroken line of descent connecting Roger and William to the Watts families who had lived in Compton during the 1500s. It seems instead that the pair descended from a Thomas Watts of yeoman stock, whose first footprint in Compton is to be found in 1648.* This does not negate the possibility that William and Roger, when choosing their trade, were following an earlier tradition of shoemaking within the wider Watts family.

Midwives in the 16th Century

Elizabeth and Dorothy Watts could only have been certified as midwives after they had married and given birth themselves. A midwife also required a licence to practice from the diocesan bishop. She first gained the requisite knowledge and experience by working with an incumbent midwife. The aspirant had to pay a significant fee on lodging her licence application, which had to be supported by testimonials from local medical practitioners, clergymen, and mothers of babies she had delivered. She then presented herself to the bishop or his chancellor for examination, accompanied by the women who had provided her references. For the Church, it was imperative that she demonstrated her ability to use the correct liturgy to baptise a baby who was ailing and in danger of dying before a clergyman could attend. Any error made during the rite risked delivering the baby's soul into the hands of the devil. Entrusting women with baptism was not a practice which escaped detractors. James I declared that he would rather his child was baptised by an ape as by a woman. His grounds were a suspicion that witches under the cover of midwifery could steal a dead baby for satanic rituals. Despite its abolition under Anglican doctrine, fear that an infant's soul might end up in limbo was still prevalent among common folk. Therefore, the Church's prime concern was to ensure baptisms were performed strictly in accordance with the sacrament of the Anglican Church, with no surreptitious Papist deviance. If the midwife's licence application met with approval, she swore an oath promising good practice and loyalty to the parish.

---

* See Chapter 25.

25
WATTS: FROM YEOMEN TO CORDWAINERS TO LABOURERS

My theory is that Isaac's great-grandfather William the shoemaker of Compton was the same William who was baptised by Thomas and Martha at Ebbesbourne on the 21st of June 1663. Ebbesbourne lies on the other side of Compton downs, an easy walk, six and a half miles (ten km) away by road nowadays. There is a Roger with no surviving baptism record, but we know from his marriage licences that he was born *c* 1657, and his will tells us that he had a brother called William.

We first come across Roger in December 1675, when at the age of eighteen he moved from Compton to Salisbury, where the City's Register of Strangers reports that he lived above the Kings Arms, had been in the service of John Porter at Compton, and was retained by Elizabeth Smith in Salisbury.[197] His next records are for two marriages in Salisbury, the first in 1693 and the second in 1695, which disclose that on both occasions his bondsman William Watts was a cordwainer of Compton Chamberlayne. Roger is described as a shoemaker, resident in the Cathedral Close — today a prestigious location — at the time of his first marriage to Barbara Atwaters, a widow, and an

Uncle Roger's gravestone.

innholder at his second marriage to Mary Pinnel. The brides were both older than Roger, Barbara by ten and Mary by eight years. On the face of it, this would not seem remarkable, were it not for a later analysis of 1851 census data from a village in the West Country which found that a quarter of married craftsmen were younger than their wives!

Roger's headstone stands in the graveyard by Compton Church, and bears the epitaph: 'A Uncle dear lyeth here.' The explanation for this is evident from his will, signed with his name in 1738. Roger left his four tenements in smelly Tanner Street (shortly afterwards gentrified, and accorded the more appealing name of St Anne's Street) in Salisbury to 'his loving' brother William, describing him as a cordwainer at Compton. In the event that William should predecease him, the tenements were to pass to William's wife for as long as she remained a widow. Alas, he does not make us privy to her name, which would have been most helpful. After her demise, two tenements each were to pass to William's sons John and William. Roger also gave a house in Winchester Street, Salisbury, to William, who only survived him by four years. He does not mention any property in Compton, although he might have been the Roger Watts named in a list of tenants paying rent to Compton Manor in 1694[198] on a messuage that by 1741 had passed to William Watts.

William's marriage to Mary has slipped the net of the parish records, but they are named as the parents of John, baptised in 1699, when William was identified as a shoemaker. The couple are not named as the parents of any other children in the register. However, Roger's will informs us that his nephew John had a brother called William, and a lease to William, cordwainer, in 1695 not only names his wife Mary, but also his son William, as additional lives.[199] John wed a Rebecca, the details of their marriage likewise absent. They baptised a son named William in 1732. He was appointed administrator at the probate of John Watts, formerly of Compton Chamberlayne, in 1784, when he was specified to be John's son.

This William, also a cordwainer, married a Compton lass, Eleanor, in February 1757. She had been christened by Richard and Ann Hibberd in March 1734. Seven months after their marriage, the newlyweds baptised their first child Roger, no doubt to please his successful 77-year-old great-uncle in Salisbury, with nine more children to follow during the next eighteen years. One died in infancy. Isaac was the second to last child, baptised on 7 May 1773.

That same year, his father started to amass houses for his children. On 1 June, Charles Penruddocke granted him a lease of three cottages, two lately erected, as well as a barn, outhouses, garden, and a pasture called Croft,

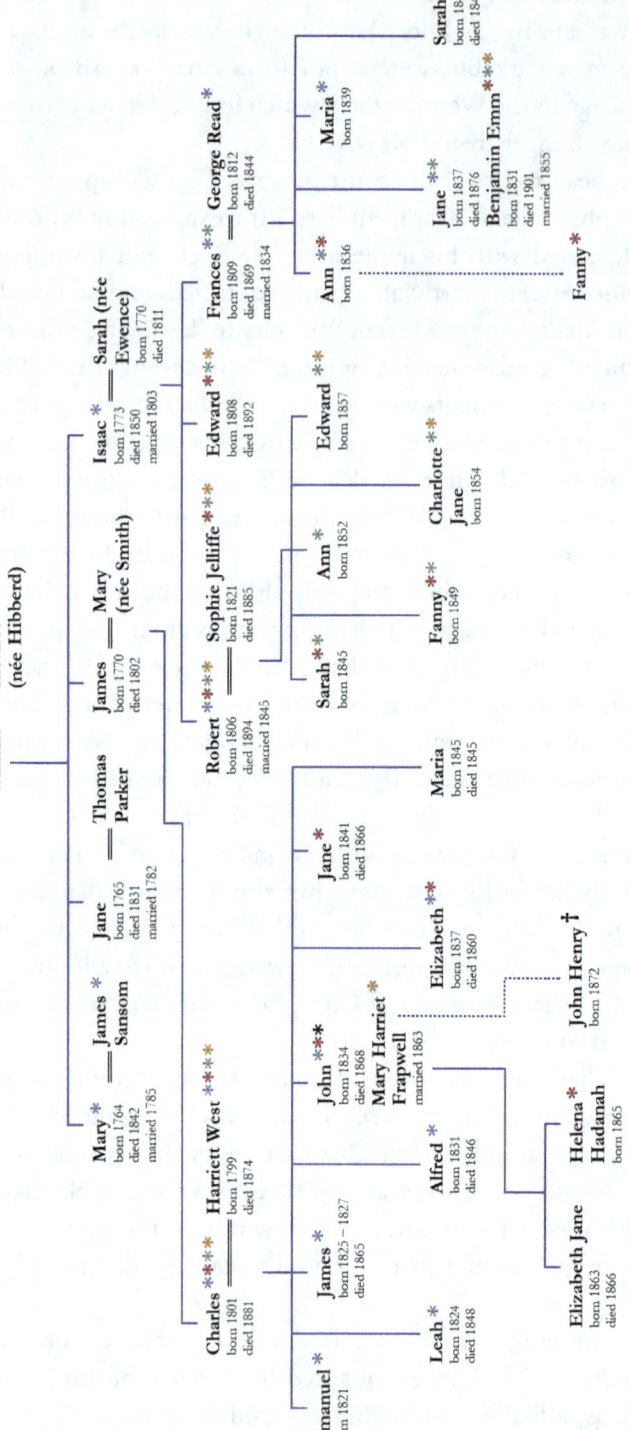

measuring two acres.²⁰⁰ The lease was for 99 years or the lives of his sons Roger, aged 15, Charles, 12, and James, 2. Two years later, in 1775, Charles' son John Hungerford Penruddocke granted William the lease of a plot for 99 years or the lives of his children Mary, aged 11½, Jane, 9½, and Isaac, 2½.²⁰¹ This plot was waste land measuring four lugs,* fit for building a cottage. William's land tax liability was 4 shillings in 1780, ranking him among the likes of the farmers John and Thomas Elkins.²⁰² He took the opportunity to buy his last property in 1791,²⁰³ after John Turner passed away. Thomas Penruddocke had leased the property, which included a meadow plot in Town Close, then called Rumballs, to John's father Christopher Turner, a maltster, in 1731. Charles Penruddocke afterwards leased the same holding to John in 1765.²⁰⁴ In his will, made shortly before his death in 1783, John bequeathed the holding to his nephews, when, by his own account, a shop also stood on its grounds. John, like William, was a cordwainer. They may well have been in business together. Shoemakers invariably worked in shops as a team, each with a designated individual task. The nephews must have given up their lease, as John Hungerford Penruddocke granted its tenancy to William in 1791, which we only know from a recital dated 1812, contained in a mortgage to shopkeeper Hester Marchant as security for her loan of £40 to Isaac.²⁰⁵

William is named in the manorial records from 1740 until 1791.²⁰⁶ Eleanor died in 1779. William's will, signed in his neat hand in 1792 — in contrast to the mark at the bottom of his son Isaac's will — provides a catalogue of his properties. After bequeathing a cottage to his second wife Jane, he gave the two houses passed down from his great-uncle Roger to his eldest son Roger, and a house each in Compton to his children James, Mary Sansom, and Jane Parker. Mary married James Sansom in Salisbury in 1785, and Jane wed Thomas Parker at Barford St Martin in 1782.† Isaac was given the house and malthouse, grounds, and orchard, formerly Turner's Farm. William speaks sorrowfully of one child: 'If my son Charles shall be alive and chance to come home again he is to have the house I left to my wife on her death or when she alters her name.' Charles may have joined the British forces and been away fighting in the French Wars. His other children who survived infancy, John, William and Betty, are not mentioned, suggesting that they predeceased their father. For reasons unknown, William added a codicil in 1798, leaving all the Compton houses to Roger for his son's use, permitting him to dispose of them

---

* A lug is equivalent to about 40 square metres.

† See Chapter 23.

by sale. William was buried at Compton in 1799, after which Roger, a yeoman at Fovant, was granted probate the following year.

Despite the codicil, William's son James took over his largest property in Compton after his death, and is recorded with a tax liability of 4 shillings in 1800, while only 2 shillings were payable on the land where Isaac was listed as proprietor and Roger as occupier.[207] There are, however, no parish or other records for Roger at either Compton or Fovant after 1800. James was likely the James Watts buried at Compton in 1802. By 1803, Isaac was the only Watts entered in the tax list.

Isaac married Sarah Ewence, daughter of Edward and Sarah, at Fisherton Anger, Salisbury, in the same year. Theirs was to be a short marriage. Isaac buried his wife at Compton eight years later, in 1811. He was left with three children between the ages of two and five. Edward was the middle child, born in 1808, between Robert, two years older, and Frances, known as Fanny, one year younger. Isaac needed a mother for his children, and married Mary Hawkins of Fovant soon after Sarah's death, in 1812.

Isaac and his progeny were born, lived, and died in Compton, but his sons were agricultural labourers. Neither became a shoemaker. We can follow them through their lives using census records, newspaper reports, and the 1847-1876 Incumbent's Visiting Book. A new vicar, George Masters, came to Compton in 1849. He was greatly troubled by Isaac and his malthouse. Other malthouses are listed in village deeds, but as a previous owner had been a maltster by occupation, I imagine this one was particularly prominent. The vicar expressed his concern about Isaac in the Incumbents Book: 'Jobless & I fear Beerhouse keeper. Must keep a look put on him when I get into residence being next door to the Vicarage I shall have good opportunity of so doing.' For him, Isaac's 70-odd years were no excuse to rest from his labours and enjoy the occasional swig of beer. The 1848 Tithe Map shows that the vicarage on plot 68 was indeed surrounded by the plots belonging to Isaac: 65, 66, and 70.

Censuses were taken on a specified day in England every ten years from 1801. Unfortunately however, most before 1841, including those covering Compton, have been destroyed. Four Watts households are recorded in the village at the time of the 1841 census, with two of William's descendants, Isaac and his nephew Charles, son of his older brother James, listed as the heads of two households. The other family hailed from Fovant. Its households were headed by Charles and his son Henry, who feature in the next chapter. Although likely, I have not found a link between these two lines. Both struggled and slid down the social ladder. Edward, who never married, seems to have

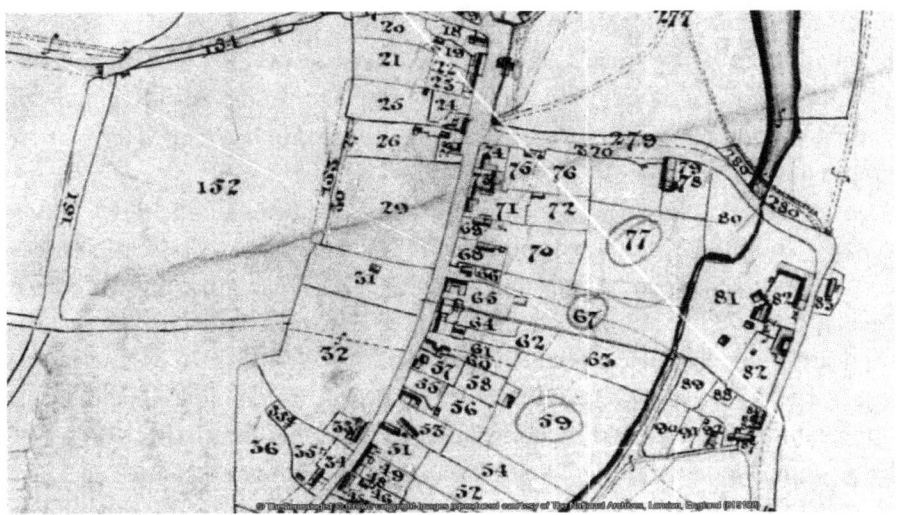

Section of tithe map showing Isaac's plots — 65, 66, and 70 — and plot 68, where the vicarage stood. With thanks to The National Archives (ref. IR 30/38/87).

been an anchor for his siblings, and I suspect for his father too, as it is clear from Isaac's will that Edward helped him out financially.

Isaac, his son Robert, daughter Fanny, and her husband George Read, together with their three young daughters, were living in the Edward Watts' cottage described in the last chapter. Edward must have resided with them, but was somehow missed off the household list. George died in 1844, leaving Fanny with four daughters aged between eight and two: Ann, Jane, Maria, and Sarah. Fanny is recorded a widow and head of her household in the 1851 census, when she and her three daughters were living together as paupers. The oldest, Ann, aged fifteen, was one of farmer William Rowden's two live-in house servants at Manor Farm.

Space was also cramped in 1841 in a smaller cottage at the base of the hollow leading to Naishes Farm, occupied by Isaac's nephew Charles, his wife Harriet, and their six children. Charles had married Harriet West, judged by the vicar to be moody. She had good reasons to be. She was 22 when she gave birth to her first child, and 46 when the last was born. A lifetime of childbirth was not unusual for a woman, but she lived to see all of her eight children, bar one or possibly two, die one after another. Emanuel, the firstborn, was a survivor. He was baptised at Fovant in 1821, and was living with his wife at Dinton at the censuses taken between 1851 and 1881. Jane was in service at Aldershot and married, aged 26, in 1866, after which I lose track of her. Alfred died aged 15 at Christmas 1846, his youngest sister Maria before her second birthday the following year, and his eldest sister Leah at the age of 23 in 1848. Elizabeth died in 1860 aged 22, James in 1865 at 38, and John in 1868 at 36. During their curtailed lives, James was a serjeant in the 29th Regiment of Foot, and John a labourer employed by the squire. He married Mary Harriet Frapwell in 1863.

Isaac died on 4 July 1850. He was the last life listed on the leases of two cottages and orchards granted to his father William, and the lease of another cottage occupied by John Sansom, Isaac's nephew. Isaac must therefore have been added as a life on the leases of the three cottages granted in 1773. With his death, these fell into the hands of the lord.[208]

The Compton Watts family then began to dwindle, opening up opportunities for Charles Penruddocke to take their leases into his hands. His bailiff John Dodds appropriated a cottage opposite the dog kennels in 1852 as no rent had been paid for many years.[209] The lease was held by the life of Stephen Watts, then aged 64. He was James' and Mary's eldest son and, like Charles, was Isaac's nephew. He lived at Baverstock, where he was buried in 1857.

Isaac's son Robert married Sophia Jelliffe, who already had a four-year-old daughter, in 1845. According to the vicar, they initially lived with Sophia's father. At the time of the 1851 census, they were recorded with two daughters, as well as Sophia's child, as dwelling in part of Isaac's cottage. Edward occupied another part, and was living on his own. Robert became overwhelmed. He deserted his family and was sentenced to six weeks hard labour in 1857.[210] After he returned, two more babies arrived, an only son, Edward, and a daughter who died before her second birthday.

Charles and Harriett enjoyed more space in 1851, when only their three youngest children were living with them. John at sixteen was a farm labourer, and his sisters were still at school. By the time the 1861 census was taken, the number of Wattses in Compton had become meagre in comparison with earlier counts. Robert and Sophia had four children with them, and Charles and Harriett were alone. Edward, who had been living by himself in 1851, now had a lodger, Sarah Read. She, of course, was his niece, one of Fanny's four daughters. Fanny is listed elsewhere as head of her own household, with her daughter Jane, whose married name was Emm. Jane had wed Benjamin Emm in 1855. They were affinal relatives. Jane was Isaac's granddaughter, and Benjamin his wife Sarah's great nephew. It was an unhappy and childless union. Benjamin was staying with his mother Charlotte and half-sister Sarah Ewence in 1861, and still recorded with his mother in 1871 and 1881. Charlotte's tumultuous early adult life, described in the Ewence story,* seemingly had a detrimental effect on Benjamin. Jane had left her husband and Compton, and was a servant at a woman's boarding house in Harley Street in 1871.

Another of Fanny's daughters, Maria, was also a servant in London. I have not been able to locate the eldest of the four, Ann, before 1871, when she and her illegitimate child, also called Fanny, replaced her sister Sarah in Edward's cottage. Grandmother Fanny died in 1869, by which time, according to the vicar, she was almost blind.

Charles and Harriett were still in the village in 1871, joined by their son John's widow Mary Harriett and granddaughter Helena Hadanah, whose older sister Elizabeth Jane had died before her third birthday. Mary Harriett gave birth to another child, John Henry Watts, in June 1872. Like Fanny junior, he was also illegitimate, the vicar having buried Mary Harriett's husband over three years before in November 1868. She later married John Lily of Bowerchalke, interestingly a shoemaker, in 1880.

Robert and Sophia were, as ever, on the other side of the wall from Edward at the time of the 1871 census, along with their daughter Jane and son Edward. They only had their son Edward with them in 1881, when his uncle Edward, aged 73, was alone again. Sophia died in 1885, aged 67. Robert and his son Edward, still single at 33, were recorded in their part of the cottage in the next census. Edward senior, aged 83, was once more giving refuge to his sister's family, his niece Maria, and great niece Frances (Fanny). Edward died in 1892 and Robert in 1894, leaving Edward junior homeless. According to the 1901 census, he was a lodger at the Kings Elm Inn. His status had been elevated to 'carter,' and he had the company of two other carters lodging with him. Edward married Catherine Elizabeth Major, a widow, at Tisbury in 1904. In 1911, they were living at Teffont Magna, where the adaptable Edward worked as a shepherd, thus ending the Watts' era at Compton.

Between 1850 and 1881, the men of the Watts family served on the jury at several sessions of the manor court.[211,212] They were among the few required to sign the court book who were illiterate, Charles senior, Charles junior, John, Robert, and Edward all signing with a mark. Isaac likewise signed his will with a mark. This family clearly spurned the education which the village school had provided for everyone since 1819.[213] Usually, caution needs to be exercised when pronouncing someone illiterate based on an 'x' appearing on a document. A mark does not necessarily indicate an inability to write. People who had learned to write had probably done so using a slate and chalk,

---

* See Chapter 33.

not a pen and ink, so they would not have been familiar with handling a pen and dipping it into an inkwell. Nevertheless, as Isaac's father William and great uncle Roger were able to sign their wills with their names, as were the witnesses of William's will, William and John Watts and John Sansom, I am confident that the choice to forego learning was theirs. Were they then the authors of their own doom?

In conclusion, the two branches of the Watts family I have traced originally toiled the land. The men of the older Compton branch were husbandmen who became craftsmen — possibly shoemakers — before they disappeared from the village's records during the last quarter of the 1600s. The other branch descended from a yeoman, whose first footstep in Compton was recorded in 1651. They became cordwainers, but descended into illiteracy in their last generations, and were recorded as labourers from the mid-1800s.

26
A Pretty Rum Lot of Watts

CHARLES PENRUDDOCKE APPOINTED a William Watts his gamekeeper for Compton and Baverstock in 1778.[214] William had wed Frances Goodfellow at Fovant in April 1752. They baptised a daughter Mary there in December, and four children at Compton between 1755 and 1774, including John in 1755, Jesse (Joseph*) in 1774, and Henry in 1793. John married Mary Sanger at Compton in 1782.

John leased property formerly occupied by William Watts from John Hungerford Penruddocke in 1804, adding the life of his son Henry, aged 11.[215] The recital in the lease states that the dwelling house, barton, and about 1 acre of land had been granted to William Watts in 1783 for 99 years, or the lives of his sons John and Joseph.

John became a taxpayer when the threshold on taxable land was lowered in 1807.[216] He was replaced after his death in 1815 by Mary, with Henry listed as an occupant. Henry had married Elizabeth Green, also of Compton, in 1811. They produced eleven children, among them some pretty dodgy ones. Here, with their baptismal years in parentheses, are those we will encounter later: James (1812), George (1818), Charles (1820), William (1822), Thomas (1824), Mary (1831), and Frederick (1834).

Henry and his wife Elizabeth, along with six of their children, are listed in the same household in the 1841 census. Their 21-year-old newly married son Charles, his wife Hannah, and their baby comprised another household. Henry died in 1846, a year after his wife Elizabeth. Two of their children, William and Mary, remained in their cottage for a while. A railway worker called Henry, born in 1835 according to the vicar's notes, lived with them. The vicar assumed his surname was Watts and that he was a sibling, writing: 'All brothers & sister, do not understand the family at all, doubt as to morality & etc.' There is no traceable baptism record for a Henry who was the son of Henry and Elizabeth — although it is feasible that Henry would give his name

---

*   Jesse is a pet form of the Middle English name Jessup, a variant of Joseph.

to a son — nor is he recorded with them in the 1841 census. William enlisted in 1847. All three had left Compton by 1851.

Charles and Hannah were still in the village at that time, and had two children with them, Sarah Jane, baptised in 1840, and George in 1842. Interestingly, George's occupation was shoemaker at the time of the 1861 census, when he was living at Fovant in a shoemaker's household. He had married and was continuing his dwindling trade at Southampton in 1881.

By 1911, George had fallen on hard times, logging himself as a brewer's labourer in the census. Soon after, his firm pensioned him off. Only his 39-year-old son Morris, a plumber's labourer, was living still with him. He suffered from epileptic fits and was deemed not responsible for his actions. One Friday in August 1914, George left his house and made his way to Wilton. The next day, he bought three-pennyworths of spirits of salt, a dangerous poison used for household cleaning, at a chemist's shop there. Later that evening, a policeman found the old man lying by the side of the Shaftesbury Road at Ugford, between Wilton and Burcombe. He had ingested two teaspoons of the toxin and was spasming in pain from a charred throat and stomach. George died the following evening at the Workhouse infirmary in Wilton. The saddest part of his story is the answer he gave to the doctor when asked why he had set off in the direction of Ugford. He said that his people had lived at Compton Chamberlayne. The poor man, tired of his life and burdened with sole responsibility for his son, as well as anxiety about the war, was desperate to return to the supportive community he had known in his youth.[217] Yet, like himself, his entire family had left the village.

Returning to earlier times, the vicar added another occupant to Charles' cottage, Thomas, giving no details other than 'very bad reputation.' Thomas was Charles' younger brother, convicted twice of poaching offences at Compton in 1844,[218] and sentenced to seven years' transportation for stealing a watch from William Raymond's house in 1846.[219] After that term, he was back in court again, where he was sentenced to twenty-one days' imprisonment for gross misbehaviour in the Wilton Workhouse in 1853.[220] Charles' youngest brother Frederick was residing in the same workhouse when he died in 1878.

Charles himself was the subject of a bastardy suit heard on 6 April 1857.[221] Hannah had died the year before, aged 37. Jane Ewence claimed that he was the father of her son, whom she named George Ewence after her father, at his christening in Compton on 27 April. She testified that Charles pursued her and wanted her to live with him. Her sister Priscilla said that Jane was going to-and-fro to attend Charles after his wife's death. Jane's father was a blacksmith, and according to the vicar's notes 'well to do.' The case was dismissed on Charles agreeing to keep the peace for twelve months. Having failed to catch Jane, or any other woman, following Hannah's demise, he was recorded alone in the 1861 census.

One of the two Charles Wattses in the village — I think we can guess which one — was convicted of assaulting Benjamin Emms (Emm) with a gun loaded with shot on 13 May 1867.[222] He was working together with Benjamin and another man named Middlewick in their gardens. It was thirsty work, and during the course of the day Benjamin had given his companions some cider. Suddenly, rain came down heavily, and the three men scuttled into Charles' cottage. Benjamin asked Charles to give them some more cider. Charles pretended not to hear, whereupon the other two risked the downfall and went into the garden, where there was a way into his cellar and cider store. When they returned, Charles came out of his cottage with a gun. Benjamin testified that he was in a passion and pointed it at him, threatening to blow his brains out. He bravely pushed the barrel aside, but the gun went off, tearing a hole in his coat. The defence argued there was no proof it was loaded, or that it hadn't gone off accidentally. In Middlewick's opinion, the gun was not pointed at anyone, nor was Charles in a passion as Benjamin had deposed. What's more, Benjamin's coat was ragged and full of holes to begin with. The judge asked Benjamin whether he was afraid of Charles. He wasn't, as long as Charles had nothing in his hand. Charles was remanded for sentencing.

In 1862, the manor court ordered James Watts, Henry's eldest son, to produce evidence of the lives, if any, on a leasehold property comprised of a cottage, garden, and orchard.[223] James does not appear in the 1861 census, but he was buried at Compton in 1865. The following year, the court demanded that the life of George Watts, Henry's second son, be proved. The homage presented in 1867 that George was 'now living.' This clearly failed to settle the matter, as two years later the court wanted proof on 'good authority.' Finally, in 1870, it concluded that George's continued presence in the world could not be proved, and the lord was at liberty to repossess the lease granted for his life. The chances are that George was still alive. A George Watts was an inmate of the Uxbridge Union Workhouse at the time of the 1891 census. He was entered as 76, married, and his place of birth was Compton Chamberlayne. Thus, he completed the trio of Henry's and Elizabeth's sons who ended up in a workhouse.

I imagine that Charles had been living in the cottage and was then left homeless, though not destitute. He was recorded in Salisbury with a new wife, Ann, in the 1871 census. I can find no evidence of their alleged marriage.

27
The Fords: Challenges of Diminishing Landholdings

A CONTINUOUS LINE of Fords, fathers and their sons, farmed at Compton for at least two centuries. How this wealthy family continued to be prominent farmers can be explained by the custom of primogeniture, whereby the eldest son inherited his father's entire estate in preference to inheritance divided amongst siblings. While this avoided slicing land into ever diminishing portions, it created an uneven distribution of wealth between their heirs which trickled down through the generations that followed. The intrinsic unfairness of primogeniture became increasingly apparent. When facing this successional challenge, my great-grandfather sold his small farm in Cornwall to rent a bigger one in Compton.* Later, when land prices fell after World War I, rather than passing the holding to his sons, he bought and leased other farms for them. He wrote to his nephew in Australia, 'you will think I am wild in my time of life buying land.' His purchases were ill conceived, and left his sons a breath away from bankruptcy during the Great Depression that followed.

The Fords also exemplify the expedience of extending family research beyond parish registers to consult manorial records, deeds, and wills to build a family tree. Only in this way was I able to identify the man who was honoured with burial under the precincts of the church: he was a farmer, not his vicar's namesake, as might have been expected.

Thomas Ford married Johane Marcheman (Joan Marshman) in 1538. The first record of a Ford baptism, including any of the surname's spelling variants — Forde, Foord(e), Fowrde, Foard — is for an Elizabeth in 1542, with her father named as Thomas. It is the only record that identifies the parent of a Ford baby in Compton's parish register during the 16th century. A second girl, Sibill (Syble), baptised in 1548, was also his daughter, as revealed by her grandmother Joan Marshman's will of 1557. As we shall see, the manor court sessions record Robert and William as their sons. Robert was likely the boy

---

* See Chapter 48.

Thomas Ford's Family Tree

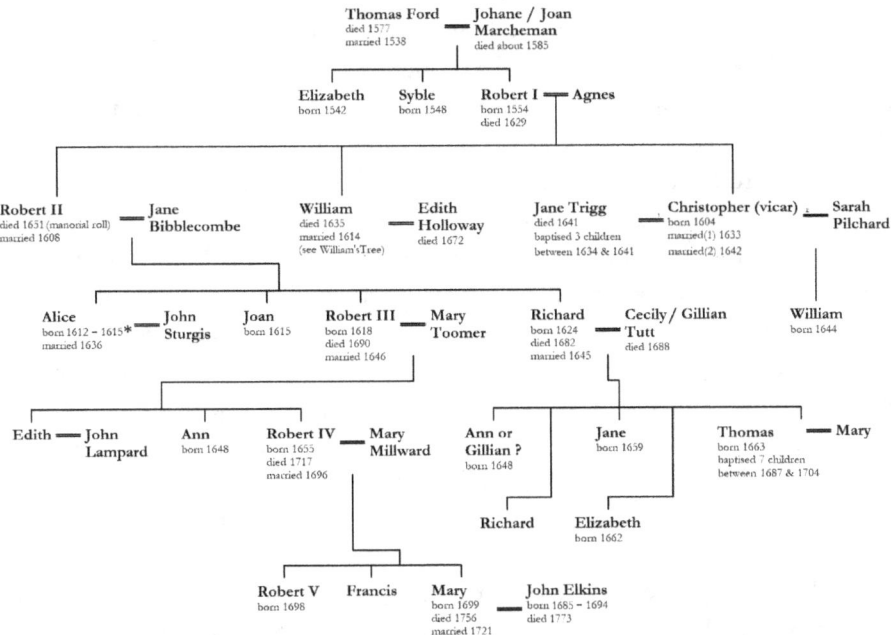

* Alice was baptised in 1612, but was recorded as age 21 in her marriage licence, translating to a birth year of 1615.

christened in 1554. Another two baptisms could well have related to Thomas' and Joan's children: Humferie (Humphry) in 1544, and John in July 1551. They probably had fleeting lives. A Humphry was buried in 1546, and a John in December 1551. Three more male Ford baptisms pop up beyond Joan's childbearing years: Fraunces (Frances/is) in 1591, John in 1595, and Thomas in 1598.

Thomas was granted a tenancy in 1561, as detailed in the survey of the copyholds held by the Haversham half-manor in 1598,[224] when his is by far the largest, comprised of 80 acres of arable land, 3 of meadow in Brodemead and Courtemead, 2 doles in the common mead, and 5 pasture closes of unstated size named Simmes, Wingoose, Overclose, Netherclose, and Broadclose. He was also given a right of common pasture for his livestock. His annual rent was 25 shillings.

In accordance with custom, after Thomas died in 1577 the land passed to Thomas' wife Joan to hold during her widowhood. John Nicholas granted the reversion of her tenure to John Cuddrington (Codrington), a freeholder and gentleman, in 1581, with the terms including a heriot of 20 shillings or the price of a horse.[225] Cuddrington was forcibly removed from the village nine years later, as we shall see in the next chapter.

Until 1585, the manor courts' juries, numbering between two and five tenants, included widows.[226] Joan was the last recorded as a juror. Her son Robert took on this role from 1586, which coincided with the first court held for Edward Penruddocke after his father George died in 1582, and his apparent change of policy to men-only juries.[227] Widows who held land continued to be documented as such, but not in any other category. Joan was buried in 1588.

Edward Penruddocke leased three parcels of land anew to Joan, her son Robert, and his son Robert successively, in 1585.[228] The first holding matched the one she had inherited from her husband, with the addition of half an acre of common arable land in the eastern field, and only one acre instead of three in Brodemead and Courtemead. Four of the five closes, measuring four acres, were retained (Netherclose, renamed as Northeclose). The second parcel comprised the fifth close, Broadclose (Brookes or Brodeclose), containing four acres, let at the annual rent of 4s 8d, with an obligation to cart or plough for the lord on three days in every year. This task may have been commuted to a monetary payment. The third parcel was a small garden, at the annual rent of 4 shillings.[229]

Robert's property transactions identify his two sons, William and Robert, whom I will call Robert II. I suspect that Robert's spouse was the Agnes Foorde who was buried on 25 March 1604, and logged as the wife of Robert in the parish register. 'Crystofer' Foorde was christened the following day. It's a safe assumption that he was the couple's third son, and his mother was a casualty of his birth.

The court's session in October 1618 is reported in the first surviving roll designated a View of Frankpledge and Baron Court. It categorises tenants by indenture and lumps residents and customary tenants together, with Robert and his son William both named.[230] This suggests that William, rather than Robert II, was the eldest son, although he married six years after Robert did. Francis, Thomas, and John Ford are also named. They were probably the three boys baptised during the 1590s. The next chapter focuses on Francis and Thomas – John is not recorded later in Compton.

Robert senior is named in every surviving manor court roll between 1606 and 1629, the year in which he died. The holding that had been granted to his father Thomas in 1561 was surrendered and divided between his sons Robert II and William shortly before his death.[231] The last son, Christopher, was fated to become a clergyman, as was often the case for the youngest male child. Robert's transaction forged the fortunes of his family's future generations. The northern half, plus a homestead, were granted to Robert II and his sons Robert III and Richard as lives in succession, and the southern part, also with a homestead, to William and his sons John and Christopher. Broadclose was split between them. Robert II retained Wingoose and two other unnamed closes. William likewise received two unnamed closes, along with Home Close and Turn Lake, for which there are no records surviving to show whether or not they had been in Ford hands earlier. Each new grant comprised only 20 acres of arable land in the common fields, leaving one with the impression that 40 acres had been lost in translation, and demonstrating frustrating voids in the document chain. The surviving manor court proceedings are incomplete, and the court in any case was only concerned with copyholds changings hands, meaning that the passage of indentures cannot be traced through its records. Fortunately, a few indentures have survived.

The new grants of 1629 each included a hop yard. Beer is made with barley, hops, yeast, and water. Replacing the traditional herbs and spices used in medieval brewing with hops revolutionised beer making by allowing the beverage to stay fresh longer, while adding today's popular bitter taste to counterbalance the sweet, fermented barley. Beer rather than water would have been the Fords' daily drink, since water sourced from wells, streams, or village pumps was polluted and apt to cause illnesses when imbibed.

William married Edith Holloway at Compton in 1614, where they baptised Bettris, John, and Christopher. He was the first of Robert I's sons to pass away, dying just before Christmas in 1635. In his will, he wished to be buried in the churchyard at Compton, and gave 12 pence to the church. He made bequests in the same sum to his brother Christopher, Francis Ford, and Richard Case. This presented a possible opportunity to expand the family, but sadly he did not state how or if he was related to Francis. Bettris was to receive £30 on her twentieth birthday. She married George Elliott, alias Comage, Elinor Elliott's illegitimate son, at Compton in 1642. John was left out of the will. Although no burial is recorded — and it is always possible in such a case that the inheritance was gifted earlier — the absence of any further records relating to him strongly suggests that he predeceased his father.

After William's death, his land passed to Edith to hold during her widowhood. Either the relationship between himself and his siblings had been toxic, or his death presented an opening to regulate matters between the families. According to a memorandum recorded at the court session on 7 April 1636, Robert was to make a drove for a cartway in Broadclose to allow Edith's cattle access to her part of the close.[232] He agreed to make a cross hedge between their grounds and maintain the hedges of the drove in future. Each of the parties was to be responsible for maintaining their part of a new hedge dividing their arable grounds in the West Common. Furthermore, they should

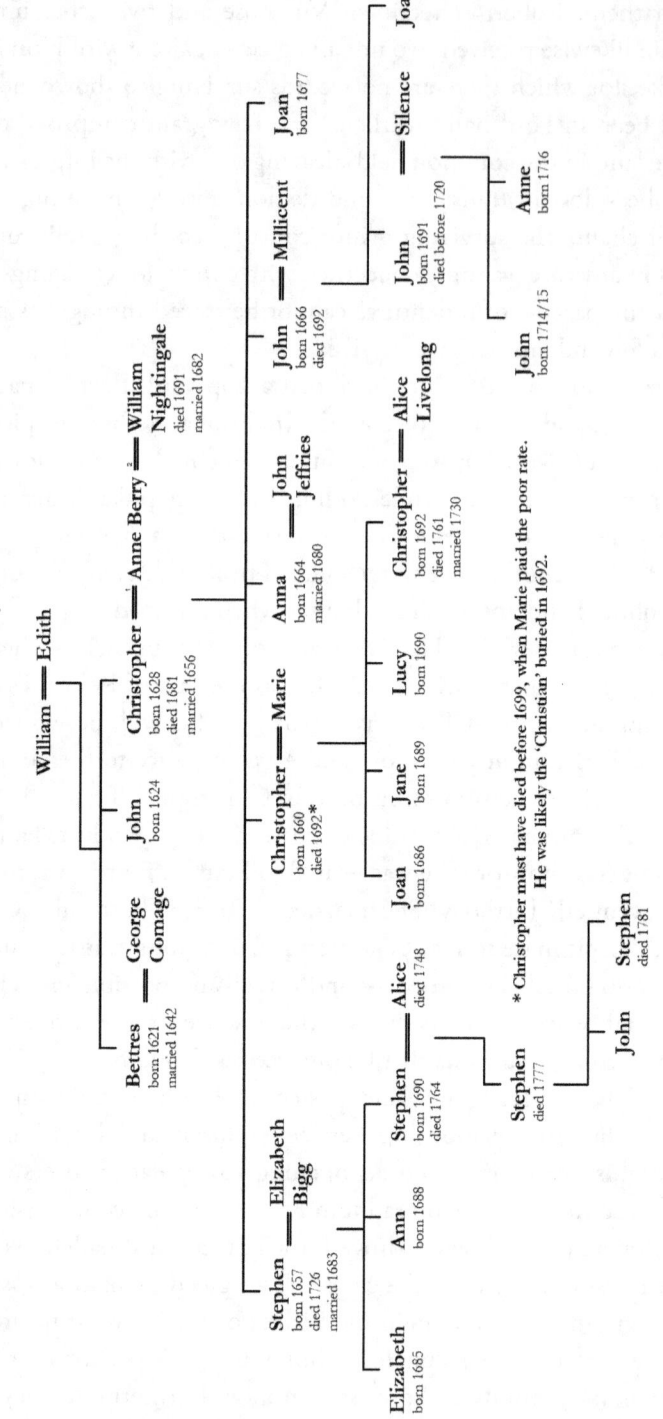

share the three carting days due to the lord, each providing one and a half days yearly.

Robert II wed Jane Bibblecombe in 1608. The Bibblecombes were another well-off Compton family. John 'Bedlecomb' paid tax in the amount of 20 shillings in 1545, which was the highest rate levied amongst the four inhabitants liable for the lay subsidy raised by Henry VIII to pay for his wars with Scotland and France. Robert and Jane baptised a son, Robert (III), and two daughters, Alice and Joan.

Robert senior died in 1651, when his lease passed to Robert III, who had wed Mary Tomer in 1646. Baptism records survive for two of their children, Robert (IV) and Ann. Thirty-nine years later, in 1690, after Robert III had died, his brother Richard should by rights have become the tenant as the last life named in their father's lease, but he was already dead.

Richard had married 'Scicly' Tutt at Compton in 1645. Together with her (recorded as Cecily in the parish register), Richard baptised Jane in 1659, Elizabeth in 1662, and Thomas in 1663. Richard is also named on his own as the father of Ann at her baptism in 1648.

Facing the inevitability of death, Richard signed his will three days before his burial in 1682. Like many others of his era, he might have felt that setting out his wishes earlier would have been tempting fate. He made bequests to his children, including Richard, who has no associated baptism record, leaving out Ann, and adding Gillian, whose christening has also not come to light. Perhaps they were one and the same girl. Richard left all his goods and chattels, including the tenement he held by 'ye lives of Robert Fford ye older and Robert Fford ye of younger of ye parrish,' to his wife, naming her as Gillian, presumably how she was commonly known. In official documents, she is Cecily, and is characterised as such — the widow of Richard, to whom freeholder Sir James Hayes granted a lease in 1683.[233] The lives in the lease were listed as Robert Ford senior and Robert Ford junior, and the property described as Cooves Farm, with ten acres of arable land and eighteen of meadow in the common fields, which shows that Richard's father held yet another copyhold.

Meanwhile, Robert III surrendered his half of Brookclose/Broadclose in 1691.[234] He was then granted an indenture for 6 acres for 99 years, or the lives of himself, his son Robert, and daughter Edith, who has no surviving baptism record. This parcel included a close of pasture or arable at Town's end called the Craft (Croft), containing one and a half acres, Wingoose, containing four acres, and a half acre of meadow in the common meadow. Robert IV wed Mary Millward in 1696, and they baptised children Robert and Mary.

The Cooves lease came to an end in 1688, following Cecily's death. Her son Thomas took a new lease[235] for the lives of himself, his wife Mary, and daughter Mary, who was their eldest child, born in 1687. They baptised six more, Thomas, Richard, Robert, Elizabeth, Ann, and Jeremiah, between 1688 and 1704/5. Thomas is recorded as a labourer at the time of the last baptism, signalling that he must have surrendered Cooves to the lord sometime during the intervening sixteen years.

Richard's other son, Richard, was probably the younger of the two. He might have been the Richard who, with wife Hannah, baptised a daughter named Hannah at Compton on 5 June 1681. The mother was buried on 13 June, and her baby on 29 July. Richard then married Jane Burden at Compton in November of the same year. They baptised five girls between 1684 and 1693. A son, whom they naturally called Richard, was finally granted to them in 1696. No later records can be associated with him.

Robert IV made his will in 1717, the year he died, leaving his land to his wife during her lifetime, and after her death to their daughters, Mary, who later married John Elkins in 1721, and Frances, whose baptism has escaped mention in the register. She was to inherit the property occupied by his mother-in-law Mary Millward. Robert gave his sister Edith, the wife of John Lampard, 40 shillings. His son Robert is not named — subject to the caveats noted above for William's son John, he most probably predeceased his father.

The ultimate fate of Robert's land is apparent from the lord's undated comment relating to around 40 acres, which included his wish to change the lease, and if Robert does not agree 'let the Tenement fall in hand the Brother and sister [Edith] both troublesome Tenants.'[236]

Returning to William's successors, his widow Edith was buried in 1672. Her holding was destined to pass to their eldest son John, but, as mentioned above, it appears he was no longer living. However, their youngest son Christopher, who was first recorded as a juror in 1650 and elected tithingman in 1676, was certainly the tenant of his father's land in October 1681. He had married Ann Berry, daughter of the wealthy couple Richard and Ursula, at Compton in 1656. Ursula, née Nicholas, was probably the daughter of John and Margaret, and granddaughter of John Nicholas, the former lord of the manor. They baptised five children in the village between 1657 and 1677: Stephen, Christopher, Ann, John, and Joan.

In 1673, Thomas Penruddocke leased a 'capital messuage,' the demesne at the time,* commonly called the Farm House, with outhouses and 295½ acres, including 180 in the common arable fields, to Christopher senior for a term of four years.[237] Compliance with its covenants was secured by a tenant's bond in the hefty sum of £300. We have no information as to whether or not this prestigious lease was extended, but there is no doubt that, of all the Fords, Christopher became the most prominent member of the village community. Looking back to the hearth tax records of 1662,[238] his father-in-law Richard Berry had seven fireplaces, his mother Edith five, while Francis and Richard had two and one, respectively. Robert is not catalogued — but the list is incomplete.

Christopher died on 14 December 1681, and lies under the nave of St Michael's Church. I have found no record of a burial for his uncle Christopher, the vicar who served the village from 1635 until 1645. He last appears in the parish register at the baptism of his son William, together with his second wife Sarah, in 1644. Christopher, the yeoman, surrendered his copyhold on the lives of himself and his sons Stephen and Christopher for a regrant to himself and his sons Stephen and John at the manor court session on 25 October 1681[239] and signed his will on the same day. He named all his children and specified that he held two copyholds, one for his life and those of his sons Stephen and John, and the other for his life and those of his sons Christopher and John. Christopher willed that the older two brothers were to pay John £40 when he attained the age of 21, and that John should yield up his claims to the copyholds, whereupon his brothers were to pay him a further £20. After the surrender, Stephen and Christopher should contract with the lord of the manor for a further estate of the copyholds. Christopher gave his daughter Joan £50, to be paid on the day of her marriage or her 21st birthday. During the interim, she was to receive £3 a year in maintenance. She was also the recipient of a porsnett (Middle English for saucepan or small pot) and his great brass pan. His other daughter, Anne, married to John Jeffries of Hinton St Mary, was given 20 shillings, and Christopher and John items of furniture. Christopher's widow Ann wed William Nightingale, a yeoman of Fovant, at Compton in October 1682. The following year, Stephen married Elizabeth Bigg at Durnford. They christened their son Stephen in 1690.

* The farms changed shape over time as parcels were shifted between holdings and waste land became cultivated. Names also changed. Here, what I believe to be the demesne is called Farm House. Other deeds refer to the Ancient Farm and the Old Farm. During the early 20th century, Manor Farm had the largest acreage, while Home Farm was probably the rump of the original demesne.

Christopher's second son Christopher wed Marie. There is no surviving record of their marriage, but they baptised children together in the village between 1686 and 1692. The last, Christopher, was their only son, and he married Alice Livelong at Berwick St John in 1730. Both were resident in Compton at the time.

Christopher's third son, John, had slipped down the social ranks to the status of husbandman according to his testament, which he made before he died in 1692. He was then only 26, married, with two children. Although he does not name his wife in his will, she was evidently the Millicent with whom John baptised a son named John in 1691. He made bequests of £30 to John and £5 to daughter Joan, to be paid when they attained the age of 21. Likewise, he gave £5 to Ann Nightingale, who had been widowed for a second time. Why, as the youngest, he should have been the one providing for his mother is perplexing. Everything else was left to his unnamed wife, his sole executrix. She was to put his legacies into the hands of Thomas Penruddocke, who should receive the same at the interest of 5% per annum, disbursing portions of Ann Nightingale's legacy to her at such times as appeared to be most useful to her. It seems that Thomas had a sideline acting as an investment banker.

John junior and his wife Silence baptised their son John in 1714/15 and daughter Ann in 1716. Although there is no record of his death, Silence's marriage to Thomas Snook at Fovant in 1720 implies that John died young, like his father. We know nothing more about John's son John. Charles Penruddocke granted the 99-year lease of a dwelling house and garden at Sandhill adjoining Richard Hibberd's house* to Ann in July 1741, 'In consideration of the many good services of the said Ann Forde hath done and performed.'[240] Presumably, she was a servant and more amendable to the squire's biddings than her troublesome distant cousins Robert and Edith. The lives in the lease were John, her brother, and Thomas Snook's son Stephen.

The manor court book spanning 1703 to 1858 is bound with a list of tenants dated 1694, in which annotations were made in 1741, and a list of the tenants paying the poor rate in 1699 added.[241] The 1694 list provides a useful survey of the Ford family's lands, and is summarised in the table opposite.

The division of Thomas' holdings between his two grandsons William and Robert in 1629 is reflected in the twenty acres of arable land held by his two-times-great-grandsons Robert and Christopher. Despite impressions from the hearth tax list of 1662, the acreage held by the two lines is comparable.

---

*   Stephen Snook is recorded as the occupier in the 1769 estate map.

Leaseholder	Copyhold/ indenture	Date	Acres in common arable fields	Total acres
Robert	copyhold	blank	20	34
Robert	indenture	1691	-	6
Thomas	indenture	1688	10	14½
Christopher	indenture	1691	20	30
Stephen	copyhold	1728	20	31½

The land held by the Ford family

Parsing the total acreages held, Robert had 40 acres, while Thomas, descended from his father's younger brother Richard, only had 14½. William's youngest son John is missing from the table. He was completely excluded from inheritance of land by his father's will, but clearly managed to secure some for himself, given that his will tells us that he was a husbandman. William's grandson Christopher held 30 acres before he died in 1692, which went to his brother Stephen, who paid the poor rate levied on it in 1699.[242] The other Fords liable were Robert, his mother Mary, who held land in her own right which was passed to John Grace in 1740, and Thomas. Stephen was buried in 1726, and his son Stephen was granted a copyhold of 31½ acres in 1728.[243]

Cousins Christopher and Stephen, each named after his father, were members of the homage from 1733 until 1760. Christopher died childless in 1761, and Stephen three years later. His son Stephen was admitted to his 1728 tenancy in 1764.[244] He died in 1777, which we only know because his sons John and Stephen, who have no associated baptism records, came to court to claim the tenancy.[245] The last Ford burial recorded in the parish register is for their great-uncle Christopher in 1761. The final manor court mention of a Ford is the lease of a cottage described as part of Stephen Ford deceased's copyhold, granted to Nicholas Plowman in 1781.[246]

In conclusion, Robert I had a large holding which was substantial enough to be divided to support his two eldest sons, Robert and William, and he added his third son in succession to one of the leases. His fourth son became a clergyman. Robert II's land passed down through the eldest son of each generation. William's only surviving son Christopher inherited his holding. Christopher instructed his eldest two sons to pay out the youngest. The two farmed the land together. Each had one son, and these cousins also farmed jointly. They had one son between them, who was sole beneficiary, and the land passed to his two sons, after which the trail ends. Even though Christopher tried to provide security for his youngest son, younger sons became casualties of the system in both branches of the family.

The value of the estates recorded in the inventories of the Fords who had moveable property worth over £5, demonstrating their relative financial and social standings:

Deceased	Inventory year	Value £-s-d	social status
Francis	1669	6 16 4	husbandman
Christopher senior	1681	148 13 4	yeoman
Richard	1682	65 10 7	husbandman
John	1692	84 19 6	husbandman
Christopher	1692	37 04 6	yeoman
Robert (IV)	1717	144 17 0	yeoman

We will encounter Francis in the next chapter. Christopher senior and Robert were the heirs of brothers Robert and William. Richard and John, likewise descendants, were disadvantaged by their birth order. Richard was Robert III's younger brother, and John was the youngest son who was to be paid out as prescribed in Christopher senior's will. The Christopher with an inventory year of 1692 was Christopher's son. His older brother Stephen was his father's heir. He survived Christopher by 34 years, but no inventory is available for him. During Christopher's lifetime, the brothers farmed together. Thus, despite Christopher junior's meagre inventory value, he still considered himself a yeoman.

28
THE OTHER FORDS: A CHURCHWARDEN AND A MERCHANT

UP IN THE tower of Compton Church, a bell imprinted with the year 1656 and the surname Ford whiles away the time. Down on the floor of the nave another Ford is honoured as he slumbers beneath a stone engraved 1681. A third Ford conducted services in the church between 1635 and 1645, when he was the vicar of Compton. Yet without any apparent ripple in the family's demeanour, the man who donated the bell left his estate to his grandson, who was a Catholic recusant.

His bell represents one of today's six, and is inscribed with the names of two church wardens, John Porter and Francis Ford, and the initials GPR, which stand for George Penruddocke Rector. John was a gentleman, and his son Thomas a goldsmith at Compton. 'Rector' here means patron of the living, i.e. the rectory/vicarage, as George was only eight years old. Francis' bell was rung thanks to the contributions of high-ranking donors.

I have not been able to discover Francis' parents. He was most likely the 'Fraunces' baptised at Compton in 1591, which could position him as son to Robert II, but then his absence from Robert's property transactions would be extremely strange. Yet Robert's brother William made a bequest to Francis in his will, suggesting that he was a member of the village's foremost Ford family. A further connection with William is to be found in the lease that had been held by William Elliott and was granted to Francis, his daughter Jane, and Christopher, the son of William Ford, deceased, in 1638.[247]

Another possibility is an affiliation with Edward Ford. In 1590, Edward and John Nicholas held the tenure of land at Compton which had been sequestrated from John Codrington because he was a Catholic recusant. After its seizure, the Crown leased the property to Edward Penruddocke's brother Robert.[248] Punishment for contravening the Elizabethan Settlement laws depended on the nature of the resistance, and could result in a fine, imprisonment or, as in this case, the confiscation of property. John could have been related to the Codringtons of Sutton Mandeville, who became a prominent recusant family during the 17th century. No further information about Edward or his lineage has emerged. However, his mention in recusant rolls provides evidence of another Ford family holding land in Compton. The dissenting connection is intriguing, as some time later Francis Ford's grandson, Thomas Watts of Ebbesbourne Wake, was also named in the rolls. Could both Edward and Francis have had strong Catholic leanings themselves?

Religious controversy was intense during Francis' lifetime. The Interregnum (1649-1660) gave way to a strongly Anglican parliament juxtaposed with a king who had Catholic sympathies. Nobody knew whether the Elizabethan settlement would remain permanent. Indeed, Charles II issued his Declaration of Indulgence, suspending all laws punishing Roman Catholics and other religious dissenters, in 1672. In the meantime, communal and blood ties often protected recusants from punishment, and the religious beliefs people presented publicly did not in any case necessarily reflect their private beliefs.[249] Compton was certainly High-Church Anglican, with the Penruddockes, like the king, wishing they could be Catholic. Although no recusants are specifically recorded at Compton during the 17th century, the curate David Comage, who had earlier lived in Compton with his father Robert, was listed in Fovant's recusant rolls of 1641-42, and he was buried at Compton in 1684 in accordance with a wish expressed in his will.

There is no doubt that the Fords took their religion seriously. As we have already learnt, Robert I's fourth son Christopher followed the common path for the youngest in well-to-do families, and entered the Church. He was a curate during John Dugmore's incumbency, before being appointed to the living. He married Jane Trig in 1633. She was buried in 1641, weakened by the birth of their child, born six months before. A note in the parish register informs us that she was the wife of 'Christopher minister.' He married Sarah Pilchard the following year.

Francis married John Elliott's daughter Mary, and they baptised their only child Jane in 1628. As we learnt in Chapter 15, John Elliott had Francis added to the leases of both his four-acre and five-and-a-half-acre closes enclosed from the Nineteenacre field in 1626. Next, in 1633, Francis surrendered the lease of the four-acre parcel for a regrant to himself, his wife, and their daughter Jane.[250] At the same court session, Jane was added as the tenant in reversion to the other parcel enclosed from Nineteenacres. Five years later in 1638, Francis extended his holdings again by acquiring the lease of a homestead, an acre of pasture-land, and six acres in the common fields, which Christopher Harwood had surrendered after inheriting it from William Elliott, and added Jane in succession.[251]

Piecing together scraps from the records left to us, Jane appears to have married Thomas Watts of Ebbesbourne Wake, who was the son of Thomas, a yeoman. Jane Watts, wife of Thomas, was buried at Compton in April 1648, when she would have been only twenty years old. Thomas was a member of the jury at the manor court during that year. In the meantime, the couple appear to have had a son, also called Thomas.

In July 1651, Francis surrendered the 1638 lease held on his own and Christopher Ford's life, along with the 1633 leases of his two holdings extracted from the Nineteenacres close.[252] A new lease for the holdings was granted and the lives associated with it were Francis, Thomas Watts, son of Thomas Watts of Ebbesbourne, yeoman, and Christopher Ford, son of William Ford, deceased. The lease was granted at Compton's manor by delivery of the rod. Throughout the records of the families I have researched, this is the only time the rod surfaces, providing an insight into the procedures of the court. The rod was a symbol of transfer, marking the official handing over of property at a public ceremony. The steward of the manor passed the rod to new tenants, in this case Francis Ford and Thomas, who paid a fine of £35.

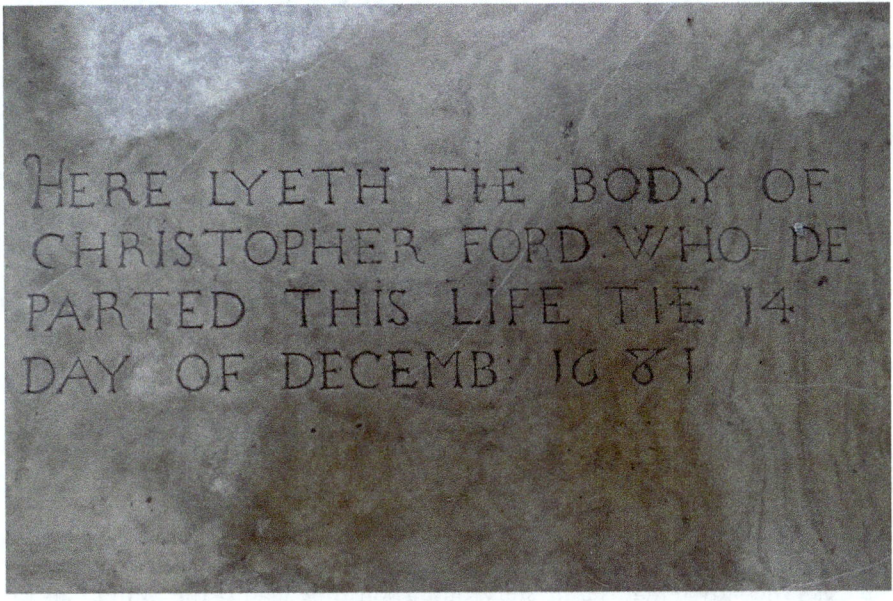

Gravestone of Christopher Ford embedded in the nave of St Michael's Church. It can also be seen in front of the lectern on the photograph of the church interior in Chapter 31.

Francis died in December 1669. His wife Mary had been buried at Compton in 1645. About four years before his death, Francis made a nuncupative will declaring in a number of people's hearing that all his real and personal property should pass to his grandchild Thomas Watts.

Thomas Watts, who was in all probability Jane's and Thomas' son, married Martha Penne at Bishopstone near Salisbury in 1662. They baptised two children at Ebbesbourne: William in 1663, and Martha in 1665. I presented my belief that William became a cordwainer at Compton in Chapter 25. Thomas was listed at Ebbesbourne in the Recusant Rolls of 1661-1662, along with Henry, Joseph, and David Watts,[253] but could paradoxically also have been the Thomas Watts named in the Glebe terriers as an occupier of Church land in Compton's common fields in 1672.[254]

Remaining with the Thomases, a Thomas Ford is logged in the manorial records, mostly essoined, under the heading 'residents' until 1625, and as a juror during every year between 1633 and April 1641. His family affiliation is obscure. He was almost certainly the Thomas who married Margaret Levet at Salisbury in 1624, and could well have been the Thomas baptised at Compton in 1598. He was the father named at the christening of a son named Thomas in Compton in 1628 and, with Margaret at their children's baptisms between 1635 and 1639. He was a tradesman, described as a merchant providing cargo when the homage complained that he had ridden across the common meadow and made a road against the ancient ordinance.[255] Not that they could do much about it, as the lord had given him permission to take this route to the mill. Apparently he kept pigs too, as he was numbered among those who were pasturing their pigs in the Townmead when the jury put an end to the practice.[256] Thomas was buried in September 1641. His son was probably the Thomas who married Jane Rawlings at Compton in 1653, and the father named at the baptism of a third Thomas in 1654, as well as John in 1662.

Apart from Mary's marriage to John Elkins, only Ford burials are recorded in Compton's parish register during the 18th century, the last, as already mentioned, pertaining to Christopher in 1761.

The manor court names yet another Ford within its pronouncement in 1648 that the common road leading towards Katherine Ford was in decay.[257] Who was Katherine Ford? Today, a road in Fovant leading to Dinton is called Catherine Ford Hill. I have found no further mention of her in any of these villages. The lady remains a mystery, and a warning against the limitations of trying to stitch together patchy records. However, her contribution to our story is the confirmation of yet more Fords in the village who are lost to memory.

29
Case: Rags and Riches

While other families are documented earlier in Compton, the surname Case endures the longest over the centuries. Percy Case was our dairyman, though I struggle to remember his features. He remains with me only as a vague gestalt, tall and wiry, but perhaps he was not so tall. I was small at the time. I cannot recreate a single sentence he spoke or call up a smile. Only an impression of grouchiness lingers. He was there with the cows in the milking parlour fixing the machine to their teats, scrubbing down the floor at the end of an early morning milking session, or writing up their names, Doris, Bluebell, Bella, Daisy, Buttercup, on a blackboard. My older sisters were not overhelpful in jogging my memory: 'They had one daughter. When Mrs Case was carrying her, she was so modest that no one ever saw her.' That would be par for the course. A friend from the village told me that when she was pregnant her mother refused to walk through the village with her, but this was later, and she was not married. Nevertheless, it brought to mind a story dating to around 1860, recounted by Dr Clay.[258] A young woman did not dare to walk through the village with her illegitimate child, and instead tackled the old road along the downs. Both died of exposure, and were found not far from Fovant Hut, where the parishes of Ebbesbourne Wake, Fifield Bavant and Fovant meet. Eventually, following an argument amongst the parishes about which should bear the cost of her burial, the overseers of Compton, where the woman had started her journey, were persuaded to take responsibility. It is hard to fathom how the villagers could have been such a sanctimonious bunch.

Percy's family vividly illustrates the plight of the rural poor in Victorian England. His great-grandfather John (1767-1841) and great-grandmother Jane, née Strong (1776-1848), married at Fovant in 1798. They had been born in Homington, a village sitting between Compton and Salisbury. Their three sons were christened there: John in 1806, George in 1809, and Henry, who was Percy's grandfather, in 1813. He was variously called Harry and Henry thereafter. John and his sons were shepherds. The family moved to Compton before the 1841 census, when they were recorded in three households headed by John senior, John junior, and Henry.

John and Jane shared a house with George and his wife Harriette. John died two months after the census was taken, and Jane in 1848. By 1845, George and Harriette had a cottage of their own, which the vicar tells us was rent-free. George was Rowden's shepherd, earning a weekly wage of 2s 6d. The vicar considered the couple 'very nice people,' but they left Compton before the 1851 census.

John junior and his wife Elizabeth, along with their daughters Ann and Fanny, were living with Elizabeth's parents James and Mary Sansom at the time of the 1841 census. Both parents died in the two years that followed. Anne and Fanny were christened during the 1830s, and a son George in 1842. Later, the vicar described them as so poor that they had 'No hut,' and lived with two other families in a house with only two sets of rooms. Intolerably crowded cottages were not unusual. Many labourers and their large families shared their living space with related families as well as lodgers. They did not have the luxury of piped water and rarely had a bath. When they did, a metal tub was set up near the fire. Water closets and baths were only installed after George Cross bought the estate in 1930 and modernised the cottages. Overcrowded and unhygienic conditions fostered lice, vermin, and disease: two of Robert and Emma Toomer's sons, aged five and four, were taken by one such disease, diphtheria, two days apart in 1865. Percy and two of his siblings were among several school children who suffered from the infection in 1897[259] and fortunately survived.

In particular, the milieu of John's and Elizabeth's daughter Anne* was one of despair and hopelessness. She married James Fry, alias Newman, in 1846. He had been baptised in the spring of 1823 by his mother Maria Newman, who wed a servant, John Fry, a couple of months later. John's first wife, who was also called Anne, died in February 1822, possibly as a consequence of complications following childbirth as, after Elizabeth in 1816 and Jane in 1819, they baptised a child John in September 1821. John senior's life ended tragically when he hung himself on a nut tree near his house on 16 February 1845:[260] 'On that night…he got out of bed, and escaped into the adjoining fields, where he was followed by his wife, his son and a neighbour, but were too late to prevent his self-destruction.' Testimony at his inquest revealed that he had for some years been afflicted with bouts of insanity, and was very depressed for six weeks before his death but thought to be recovering. The coroner

---

*   The vicar records her name as Mary Ann in the Incumbent's Book.

FAMILIES PASSING THROUGH COMPTON CHAMBERLAYNE

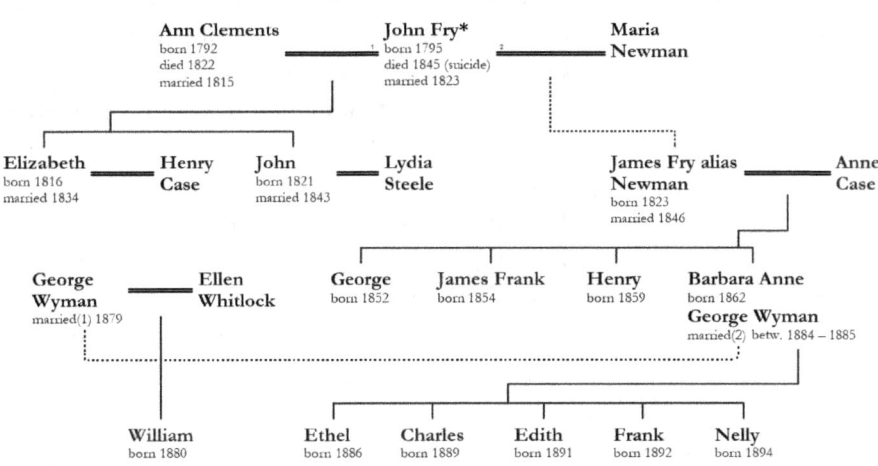

Anne Case's Relationship to the Fry & Wyman Families (see Chapter 43)

*John had three children with Ann and eight with Maria.

concluded he had acted while temporarily insane. Maria was left a pauper with her youngest child Thomas, aged seven, still at school. Only three years after her father-in-law took his own life, Anne's mother threw herself down a well.

Reverend Edward Collett, vicar of Bower Chalke, over the hill from Compton, collected information on his village for his *Collett's Farthing Newspaper* between 1878 and 1924.[261] In it, he lamented that the incidence of mental instability in Wiltshire was particularly high. This dismal statistic is confirmed by Dr Clay's recollection of many more suicides occurring when he took over the practice of his father Dr Chaloner Clay at Fovant in 1916 than was the case at the time he was writing in 1969.[262]

John's and Elizabeth's second daughter Fanny went into service near Aldershot, while their son George was already working as a farm labourer when he was nine years old in 1851. Later, he served in the marine artillery in the West Indies for four years. He was recorded in the 1861 census as unmarried and an invalid Royal Marine soldier living with his uncle John Welch at Portsea.

Harry, the last of the three Case brothers who came to Compton from Homington with their parents, married Elizabeth Fry, John Fry junior's* sister, in 1834. The 1841 census was taken on 6 June, by which time Harry and his wife Elizabeth, who were both in their mid-twenties, already had four children. Their dates of birth are given here in brackets: Emmanuel (1836), Mary Ann

---

*   For more about John junior, see Chapter 37.

(1837), Henry (1839), and Eliza (1840). Two old ladies were also lodging with them. The next child to be born was christened Elizabeth on 18 June 1842. Her mother was buried, aged 25, 4 days later, and baby Elizabeth on 9 August.

The vicar's notes tell us that after both mother and son lost their spouses, Jane kept house for Harry. She earned 2 shillings and 6 pence in wages from the parish, and Harry 6s from his employer William Targett at Naishes Farm. They were on a tight budget, with a rent of £1 10s per annum, and had to rely on income from other members of the household. Emanuel also worked for William Targett, earning 5s a week. At the time of the 1851 census, when he was sixteen, he was employed as a footboy in Salisbury.

Jane died in 1848, and Harry married his second wife Louisa Jelliffe in 1855. She was the widowed daughter of James Steel and sister of Lydia, Harry's deceased wife's sister-in-law married to John Fry junior.* Lousia's first husband William had been killed by the kick of a horse — again information from the vicar's visiting notes. I have found no official record of these events, but farm accidents were common. The Coroners' Bills relating to Compton for the short period between 1752-1796 include a man killed by an overturning cart in 1763, another by a cartwheel running over him the following year, and a death by suffocation caused by a falling rick in 1780.[263] William Plowman, a lad between eight and nine years old, was taken to Salisbury Infirmary with a fractured thigh after being run over by a hay waggon at Compton in 1862[264] and likewise George Read, aged eleven, with a wound over his temple caused by a kick from a horse in 1873.[265] Ten years later, his sister Eliza died at age twelve of pneumonia, after only a few hours' illness. John Hunt, again aged only eight years, suffered a fatal accident in 1886. His father was employed as a dairyman on John Keevil's farm and the boy was often about the farm, doing occasional jobs. He was riding a horse one day in the harvest school holidays that had been to drink water and was returning it to be harnessed to a reaping machine, when it stumbled and threw the boy over its head. Dr Chaloner Clay, who happened to be passing, said at the inquest that he did not think it proper to allow small boys to ride horses in that manner. The coroner remarked that it was the second such case they had had that week.[266] These children were not just playing around on farms but working to earn a few pennies.

Harry and Louisa had only one child, Frank, Percy's father, who was born in 1856. The vicar relates that Harry's and Elizabeth's eldest daughter Mary Ann married Andrew Parker, while Emanuel and Eliza went to the Cape

---

*   For more about Lydia, see Chapter 37.

of Good Hope, where Eliza married, and Henry was a footman. Clearly, Henry took on work wherever he could find it. When he wed Anna Maria Hayter at Salisbury in 1864, he was employed as a waiter. His 1871 census entry logs him as an indoor servant.

Frank married Alice Louisa Ball at the beginning of 1887, and the couple continued to live in Compton with their seven children. The girls, Beatrice Louisa (1892-1964) and Ellen Dorothy (1899-1977), eventually left, while all the boys worked on the farms at Compton: Percy Harry (1890-1979), Hector Charles (1897-1976), Arthur Cyril (1902-1986), Ernest Harold (1888-1915), and Herbert George (1894-1915).

By 1911 they were living at Turnpike Cottage, which was divided into two dwellings. Three shepherds — two Wymans and James Fry — along with Edith Wyman, lived in the second half. Frank was a labourer, Ernest and Percy horsemen, George a cowman, and Arthur, aged thirteen, simply a boy on a farm. Ernest is remembered on the Le Touret Memorial in France, and Herbert on the Helles Memorial to those who perished at Gallipoli. Their names are also inscribed on the tablet in Compton's church which honours the six soldiers from the village who died in the First World War. The remaining young Case men remained in the village.

According to the 1921 census, Frank and his three sons Hector, Percy, and Arthur, who were all still unmarried, worked for George Thomas Alyward, the farmer at Naishes Farm. Frank was an agricultural labourer, Percy a carter, Hector a cowman, and Arthur a milker. Percy had also worked for Alyward's predecessor, Tommy Rivers, who held the farm from 1905 until 1914. My parents took Tommy's daughter Kathleen with them to visit Percy on his 84th birthday in 1974. She brought a bottle of spirits with her because her father had always given him a bottle of rum or whiskey as a birthday present.

In 1976, my father told me in a letter that he had met Mr Lush, a solicitor, in Salisbury. He said that when he began at the firm one of the partners was a Mr Aylward, whose brother owned Naishes Farm from about 1915 until 1930. Mr Lush also said nothing could induce the Aylward solicitor to come into the office on Saturdays, because that was the day he spent with his brother at Naishes. Percy Danford Aylward was listed at Aldesbury (Alderbury) as single, his occupation solicitor, in the 1939 Register. Edwin Blake, my father's immediate predecessor, took over the farm in 1934.

According to the same register, Percy Case's brother Hector was the farmer at Piggott's Farm. He left Piggotts in 1947. Mary Lovell told me when I visited Compton in 2023 that his departure was prompted by a dispute with George Cross. Both Percy and Arthur were agricultural labourers in 1939, living in cottages at Naishes Farm. The Cases' association with Compton ended with Percy's death in 1976.

The sad plight of this family during the 19th century stands in stark contrast to the Cases' social standing when Richard, a yeoman, had been enticed to Compton by the charms of Ann (Agnes) Elliott, daughter of John. They married in 1621. Agnes had been baptised in the village in 1598. Richard's antecedents are obscure. The couple baptised four children at Compton: John in 1625, Christopher in 1628/9, Mary in 1631, and Annis (Agnes/Anne) in 1634. Another child called Richard, who was probably their oldest son, has no baptism record. He was substituted for Richard senior as tithingman at the manor court in 1660 because his father had become lame. Until then, between 1620 and 1661, Richard senior was regularly listed as a juror or customary tenant. His sons John and Christopher were only named once, in 1654.[267] As residents in default, they were fined 2 pence each.

A game of musical chairs seems to have been played at the 1626 court, when John Elliott's son was living with Richard, and Richard's son with Francis and Mary Ford.[268] Richard was not only connected to the Elliott family through his wife, but also enjoyed a close friendship with the Ford family. Recapping events related in Chapter 15, Richard promised his father-in-law John in open court that if John junior was not living with him when John died, he would give him, or anyone taking care of him, a yearly allowance of 40 shillings. At the same court, John Elliott senior surrendered his four acres which had been enclosed from the Nineteenacre field, and Richard's son John was granted a new lease of the same acres along with the married couple Francis and Mary Ford. Francis undertook not to put John Case out unless Mary had a child, at which time he would give John 10 shillings.

Richard was one of the wealthier inhabitants of the village, and numbered among the thirty-seven who were liable to pay the lay subsidy tax raised in 1641.[269] Discounting Compton's squire and its three gentlemen, Thomas Baylie (Bailey) paid the highest rate at 19 shillings 3 pence, followed by Robert Ford's 16s 6d, and William Joy's 13s 9d. Richard Case and James Elliott were the next most highly taxed occupiers of land at 9s 7d each. The other 26 paid less than 6 shillings. Richard's and James' standing is also reflected in the hearth tax of 1662, when Richard was logged with three and James with four fireplaces. Most taxpayers in the village had one or two.

In 1661, Richard and Agnes surrendered the reversion of a cottage which Edith Antrum had occupied during her widowhood.[270] Agnes held the copyhold in her own right, and was examined alone and privately to ensure that her surrender of the reversion was made of her own free will rather than under duress by her husband. This cottage was amongst the more desirable abodes in the village, and passed to the gentleman Richard Corderoy.

The year 1667 was one of mourning for the Case family. On 9 February they buried Christopher at the age of 39, and in November his mother Agnes. Richard himself died in July the following year. In his will, signed on 13 March, he styled himself a yeoman, although he is never referred to as such in the manor court records. Only his two daughters and son John are named in it. We can safely assume that, like Christopher, Richard junior predeceased his father. Richard left his daughters Mary Millward and Agnes Livelong 1 shilling each. Mary was married to Francis Millward, after whose death in 1696 she wed Robert Ford. Agnes married Richard Livelong at Compton in 1659. She also received her father's bed with its accoutrements. Richard gave his six-year-old grandchild Thomas Livelong financial security by bequeathing his 'lease of Gasen' for ten years to 'whomsoeuer shall keep him and after wards vnto his Mother duringe her life.' All his remaining goods and chattels passed to his son John Case.

The inventory accompanying Richard's will provides further evidence of his comparative wealth, with his 'goodes and Chattells' valued at £116, 6 shillings, and 8 pence. They comprised 30 acres of corn, 5 rudder beasties (horned cattle), 33 sheep, '2 pigges and a sow and pigges,' 3 horses, 'two Cartes and other plow stufe,' 2 leases, his furniture and household effects, and his wearing apparel. The most valuable of these items were the corn (£30), leases (£20), brass and pewter (£10), cattle (£10), and horses (£10), priced at three times more than the two carts and plough stuff.

Richard's and Ann's son John married Dorothy, which we know from the baptismal entry for their daughter Agnes at Compton in 1674. He assumed his father's yeoman status, and made his own will shortly before his death in 1693. He held a lease of 46 acres of arable and meadow land. The value of his estate was £264 and 8 shillings; the family's fortunes had doubled in the 25 years following his father's death. Richard left his estate to Thomas North, his son-in-law. There is no marriage entry for Agnes in Compton's parish registers, no baptisms of siblings, and I have likewise been unable to find a baptism for North there.

A John Case was living in the village during the 1700s, but village records fail to shed any light on his ancestry. As a bachelor, he married Mary Bailey, a widow, at Compton in 1791. Both were of the parish. They appear to have been childless. James Case, another mystery man, was named as the occupier of a cottage in the 1850 Tithe Award Register, but he is not listed in the village by any census.

I have been unable to uncover any documents that could connect Richard, who came to the village in the early 17th century, with John and his family, who arrived during the first half of the 19th. While a lineal descent from the prosperous 17th-century Cases to the 19th-century labouring family is conceivable, it remains unprovable.

30
Naish: Everything Came to Nothing

WAR WAS STILL raging across Europe in 1943 when my father took the tenancy of Naishes Farm. The surname Naish had stuck to the farm for over 300 years, longer than any other family name has been associated with a property in the village. Ash (and oak) trees were meeting places in ancient times: 'I'll meet you at the ash tree,' or in Middle English 'atten asche.' This phrase was shortened to 'ate Assh,' then 'Tash,' then 'Na(y)sh.' Finally, it solidified as Naish.[271] The surname is therefore topographical, meaning taken from a feature in the landscape. It is a fairly unusual name that originated chiefly in Wiltshire and Somerset.

Who was the man who pinned his moniker to the farm? The first record relating to Naishes Farm is a lease of 142 acres with the right to graze 200 sheep and 24 horned cattle in the common fields which Richard Naish secured from Thomas Penruddocke in 1698.[272] He also held the 'Old Farm' and demesnes of Penruddocke with his brother Stephen,[273] and became the wealthiest yeoman in Compton.

Richard was born in 1668 to parents Nicholas and Mary, who had married at Compton in 1640. I have not found his baptism entry, but Nicholas and Mary christened his sister Marie in the village in 1642. She married Anthony Jerrard in 1660, when Richard wasn't even a twinkle in his father's eye. Although theoretically two people could marry young, with the legal minimum age of 12 for women and 14 for men, the average age of newlyweds in England during the 17th century was about 25. Even assuming Mary married at 18, she would have been 46 and more than a little surprised when Richard suddenly appeared on the scene. She also gave birth to at least one other child, Stephen. The 1698 lease was granted for 99 years, or the lives of Richard's wife Alice and his brother Stephen. As with Richard, no baptism record exists for Stephen either, or any information as to when he was born.

Let's start with Nicholas, their father. Charles I was still tenaciously clinging on to the English throne when he married Mary Jonsson. Civil war was looming. Sir John Penruddocke was lord of the manor, and would be followed by his son Colonel John and grandsons George and Thomas during Nicholas Naish's lifetime. Enclosure was progressing piecemeal.

When he married, Nicholas held diverse strips, each measuring less than an acre, scattered between the furlongs in Compton's two common arable fields. In total, they probably amounted to the customary 30 acres. He also had common rights to graze stock in the meadows. After lots had been drawn during the spring, Nicholas could erect hurdles in the section of meadow he had won. Once the grass was high enough, he set about mowing. The hurdles were removed when the hay had been gathered, making way for common grazing.

Nicholas was chosen as the yearly hayward at the Court held on 20 March 1655,[274] only months before Colonel John lost his head after leading a rebellion against Cromwell. His recompense was a peck of wheat from the owners of every yard land in the two large arable fields. As a hayward, he was tasked with leading the sowing and harvesting, and seeing that all hedging and temporary fencing around the hay meadows were in proper repair. As if that were not enough, in addition to his usual work cultivating his own land, he had to be up early in the morning to check the corn fields and meadows for stray cattle, his main job being to protect the village's crops from stray livestock, and to impound animals found running at large. For this purpose, he had a horn to sound a warning when mischievous invaders headed towards forbidden fodder. The nursery rhyme character Little Boy Blue was a hayward:

> Little Boy Blue, come blow your horn,
> The sheep's in the meadow, the cow's in the corn.
> Where is that boy who looks after the sheep?
> He's under a haystack, fast asleep.
> Will you wake him? Oh no, not I,
> For if I do, he'll surely cry.

This boy had probably collapsed with exhaustion after a morning spent battling the villagers who had allowed their animals to stray. Nicholas would have fared no better if Richard Oake's antics, described earlier,* are anything to go by.

Mary Naish was buried at Compton in 1675 and Nicholas in 1684, when Richard was only sixteen years old. He was 30 when he married Alser†

---

* See Chapter 6.

† Alser is the Wiltshire vernacular pronunciation of Alice.

(Alice) Brassier,* a 28-year-old Wilton spinster, at Burcombe in July 1698. John Hibberd, a weaver of Wilton, was their bondsman.

We can imagine it was his father's hard work and determination for his son to succeed in life, as well as Richard's own ambition, which allowed him to secure his lease from the squire that same year. Richard benefitted from the huge advances in agriculture made between 1575 and 1675. Improved practices produced higher yields of corn and profits soared.

The Penruddockes' gradual dismantling of communal farming would ultimately leave Richard's Naishes Farm as one of only 3 large farms on the estate at the time of the tithe awards in 1850, when it had expanded to 500 acres. Sadly, Richard's and Alice's two sons, Richard baptised in 1699 and Stephen in 1701, were not destined to inherit and build a Naish dynasty along with the farm.

A new 99-year lease was granted to Richard in 1706, when his brother's life was exchanged for the life of Walter, Alice's cousin, the son of George Bignall of Wilton. Richard died in 1715, and Walter Bignall 'of Trowbridge' took over the farm the following year.[275] He mortgaged it to John Thresher, also of Trowbridge, to secure a loan of £400 in 1732. Walter was still listed as its leaseholder on the manorial records of 1740.[276] In 1742, Ellen Thresher assigned the leasehold estate in trust to Wadham Wyndham,[277] who was related through marriage to the Penruddockes.

The farmhouse is recorded as 'Newhouse' in the 1698 lease granted to Richard. It had formerly been occupied by Reverend Nathan Hancock, and before him by Reverend John Martin.† This suggests that the Penruddockes were allocating new houses suitable for tenants of the large farms they were creating. The current farmhouse at Naishes is not shown on the 1848 Tithe Map. William Targett, who was then farming Naishes, was awarded a house on plot 82, at the bottom of the Hollow.

Richard's death fell within a period when executors were required to appoint local men as appraisers to value the deceased's personal estate, and provide a full inventory to the church-administered probate court. The inventory taken after Richard Naish's death provides a window onto his large house, and displays his considerable wealth. After valuing his 'Wearing apparel' and ready money at £30 each, the three appraisers, Stephen Pearce, Christopher Bailey, and John Moore, walked through the farmhouse, which comprised three floors and a cellar, cataloguing and pricing the contents of each room.

---

* Some doubt surrounds Alice's surname. In Boyd's Marriage Indexes it is Breasher, and she names a brother Bignall in her will.

† It is named 'the Parsonage' in later deeds.

They found two areas furnished for dining. In the parlour, there were fourteen cane chairs set around two table boards, and in the hall, a long table, six joined stools, and three chairs. Presumably the family and the most highly ranked members of its household ate in the parlour, warmed by an open fireplace equipped, as listed, with andirons, a pair of dogs, a fire shovel, tongs, and a brush. The servants would have eaten in the hall, which was also where Richard kept his great bible.

Not only the quantity of chairs, but also the number of utensils in the kitchen, tell us he kept a large number of servants and labourers. Imagine the tumult when meals were being prepared. The appraisers counted nineteen pewter dishes, five brass pots, one bell metal pot, four 'kittles' (open cooking pans with semi-circular handles on each side, to suspend them over the fire), a dozen and a half plates, skillets, porringers, candle sticks, a mortar and pestle, as well as spits, skewers, wracks, tongs, and dripping pans. The most valuable items consisted of a dozen and a half patty pans priced at £10. A warming pan for cosy night times, a pewter chamber pot to save a trip down the garden in the dark, and a coffee pot were together valued at only 7 shillings.

The three appraisers proceeded to the first floor, noting a handsome clock hanging 'in the Staire Case'. What might it have looked like? Did it have gears and weights, or was it of the pendulum type first invented by Christiaan Huygens in 1656? Was there a single or two hands on its face, as minute hands only started to be a common feature after 1700? This luxury item was assessed at £5, as opposed to the £6 10s later estimated for a collection of six pairs of carts and six pairs of plough harnesses stored amongst the farm equipment. The men also spied several bibles and other books, worth £1, on shelves lining the walls here.

After undoubtedly spending some minutes admiring the time piece, they continued their work in the three bedrooms situated above the hall, kitchen, and parlour, along with a closet chamber. A fourposter feather bed with curtains stood in each of the hall and kitchen chambers. The hall chamber with a fireplace must have been the main bedroom. The parlour and closet chambers were probably servants' rooms. A simple 'bedstead' was recorded in the first, suggesting this was merely a sleeping pallet, and an 'ordinary' bed in the second. A sidesaddle and pillions* here hint that it was used for storage, while also providing space for a servant to sleep. Another of Richard's retainers bedded down in the stable. On the top floor, the garret was where Richard threw his old iron and disused furnace (a pan for cooking

---

* A pillion was a woman's light saddle, or a cushion attached to the back of a saddle, on which a second person could ride.

beef), storing six barrels and items of lumber in the cellar.

Four houses that stood in the yard at the homestead were used for preparing farm produce and storage. Unsurprisingly, beer was brewed in the beerhouse. A cider mill and press stood in the well house. Cheese and butter were made in the dairy house. Milkmaids milked Richard's thirty-seven cows twice a day by hand. There would have been a number of them: the average time needed to milk a cow is 20 minutes. Wool from the farm's 365 sheep was stored in 'Ye Dayry chamber,' above the dairy. The last house was a buttery, where food and drink were stored. Four large casks of liquor, or hogsheads, were kept here. Outside, cart houses stood in the orchard next to a little Gurnett house on stavell (staddle) stones, used for grain storage. Naishes Farm was not Richard's only holding. He had two other leaseholds, one in Barford St Martin and the other in Baverstock. He also rented two acres of church land in Compton.

After her husband's death, Alice moved back to Wilton, but in her will, signed in 1726, she expressed a wish to be buried next to her husband and children at Compton, where there is no trace of the children's burials in the parish registers. Her requests reveal how the farm came to pass to her cousin. Poignantly, Alice bequeathed two silver spoons 'that was my childrens' to another cousin. The spoons were no doubt christening gifts from their godparents. They were probably apostle spoons, with a figure of the saint after whom the child had been named — in this instance St Richard and St Stephen — engraved at the top of their handles. Silver was currency, considered to be a good investment for a child. The tradition of gifting such spoons dates from Tudor times, and could account for the saying 'born with a silver spoon in your mouth,' which implies a person was born into wealth. Alternatively, the maxim has been explained as an echo from the early Middle Ages, when parents encouraged their children to suck on a silver spoon to ward off the plague. The antibacterial effects of silver have long been known, and perhaps thanks to these, richer children — aside from Richard and Stephen — survived. Two other silver spoons and a silver tankard featured among her bequests.

Another legacy in Alice's will tells us that she ascribed to High-Church Anglicanism. She gave *The whole duty of Man* to her brother Bignall. This book was published anonymously in 1658, but was probably authored by Richard Allestree, who fought for Charles I. It is credited to Allestree in the *Oxford Dictionary of National Biography*'s appraisal: 'This best-selling manual's prescription of morality and effort was balanced by an emphasis on divine grace and devotional practice: the result was sober, orthodox, common-sense advice pitched at the level of ordinary Anglican parishioners.' The tome was popular during the early 18th century and was doubtless, along with her husband's bibles, a treasured possession.

Although Richard was the one and only Naish to farm at Naishes, if just for the short period of seventeen years, he was not the only farmer with that surname in Compton. Stephen Naish senior, a yeoman, made a will in October 1700, and his inventory after death was taken in December of that year. He left his wife Mary £15 per annum plus her wearing apparel, jewellery, and their household goods and implements for her use during her lifetime. As was the case for everything a wife 'possessed,' her clothes actually belonged to her husband. They were only hers on loan, to be returned to his executors following her death. The will names two sons called — according to family tradition — Stephen and Richard. He gave Stephen the debts owed to him, amounting to £210, together with a lump sum of £203. The residue of his estate was to be split between the two sons. Stephen had managed to accumulate wealth and status in life, but his net worth of £504 at death was meagre compared to Richard's only thirteen years later, which totalled £2,394.

I had initially assumed that this Stephen was Richard's brother, but he was probably the Stephen Naish who wed Mary Andrews at Devizes in 1648, eight years after Richard's parents had married. It was theoretically possible for a couple to become engaged at the age of seven but, as explained above, marriage at eight was out of the question. Furthermore, Richard was granted a lease together with the Stephen, who was most likely his brother, of the 'old farm' in 1703.[278] An account book details the Penruddocke's demesne, which included the old farm held by Stephen in 1705.[279] The holding comprised 366 acres. A receipt for the tithes signed by Reverend Nathaniel Hancoke (Handcock) on behalf of Thomas Penruddocke was found in the parish church chest: The parish register offers no help in identifying Stephen senior. During the timeframe in question, it only records the three baptisms, three marriages, and three burials I have mentioned above.

February y 11th Anno Dni (Stylo Angliæ) 1705. Rec.d from Thomas Penrodoke Esq.r by ye hands of his Tenant Stephen Naish the Sume of Twenty pounds lawfull English money; Being for the Tythes of my Vicaridge in Compton Chamberlaine for One whole year; Due & ended at Our Lady-Day last past I say Received the said Sume as afores.d By me Nath: Hancoke.

The receipt date, Anno 1705, was calculated under the old Julian Calendar. The year became 1706 under the Gregorian Calendar introduced in 1752. My father obtained a photograph of the document in 1977. Unfortunately, the location of the original is unknown to me.

The next reference to Naishes Farm following Walter Bignall's tenure is in an insurance policy relating to the Penruddocke estate dated 1770. This informs us that William Mathey (Massey/Maffeys) was in possession of a farmhouse called 'Nash's' Farm.* He had taken a lease of 422 acres in 1759,[280] considerably more than the 141 acres held by Bignall. He may well have been related to the Penruddockes, as Sir Edward's wife Mary was a Massey before she married.

---

* Possibly Richard Naish's Newhouse and/or the house occupied by William Targett in 1848, and certainly not the farmhouse standing on Naishes Farm today. See Chapter 40.

31
High/Low Church

The discovery of Alice's bequest has left me wondering how and when services at St Michael's switched from a High to a Low Church mass. The original building had been erected in the late 13th century, and may have replaced an earlier church. A period of religious conflict in the village is likewise conceivable. Iconoclasts may have attacked its fabric either during the Reformation or Interregnum. It is feasible that the plain glass of the large tracery windows replaced smashed stained glass, and a preaching cross was likely destroyed, leaving only the base that today rests next to the porch entrance.

Compton was certainly High Church during the mid-17th century. Sir John Penruddocke appointed John Martin, a High Churchman, as vicar of Compton Chamberlayne in 1645,[281] and the village also accommodated recusants.

Postcard showing rear view of St Michael's Church in Compton, as seen from the Big House. The photograph was probably taken during the 1960s.

The front view of St Michael's Church, with sunlight catching the Livelong tomb on the right, against the church wall. Photographed in December 2017.

Alex Craven, author of the Victoria County History project's series for Compton, presumes that the closed nature of the village, controlled by the Penruddockes and their appointment of clerics with whom they had close family ties during the first third of the 19th century, accounts for the dominance of Anglicanism.[282] But can we safely assume that they continued to adhere to High-Church Anglicanism?

Unlike neighbouring Fovant or Broad Chalke, there was never a nonconformist chapel or meeting place in Compton. We know, however, that Richard Livelong was a Quaker in 1682. Dramatic swings away from Catholic influences are seen within some families. For instance, Jone (Joan) Marchman's will, which she made during Mary I's reign in 1557, was witnessed by Humphrey Dale, to whom, like Nicholas Lawes, she attached the Roman Catholic title 'Ghostly father.' Three generations later in 1638, the family chose to christen a daughter with the puritan name Repentance.

Nonconformists are evident in the village during the 19th century. The Targetts, who came to the village mid-century, were nonconformists, and George Ingram's parents baptised him at the Independent Chapel, Birdbush, Donhead St. Mary in 1897. My great-grandfather had attended a Bible Christian Sunday school as a child, and christened my grandfather into this religion

The altar with a cross in St Micheal's Church. Photograph taken in 2023.

in Cornwall in 1883. Both later became Anglican churchwardens.

At least during Reverend Dudley Digges' incumbency, which began in 1884, we can imagine that, given his liberal leanings, he rejected rituals and religious icons. When I was a child, St Michael's was extremely Low Church. The Cromwellian communion table was bare until one day a cross was placed upon it unannounced. My mother, who was of Norwegian Lutheran stock and took her turn on the flower rota, was so incensed that she swore she would never attend services there again — and she never did. Instead, she and I went to the delightful church in Fifield Bavant.*

Stone beside the entrance to St Micheal's Church, believed to be the base of a preaching cross, is a grade II listed building. Photograph taken in 2023.

* See Chapter 45.

32
A Co-operative of Blacksmiths, Wheelwrights, and the Cooper

CLINK, CLINK, IRON on anvil ringing throughout Compton's daylight hours, was a familiar refrain for my great-grandfather. The echoes far and wide from its busy forge, mingling through the trees with the tinkling of sheep bells, is one of Hilda Kerley's contemporary recollections. She described the community as my great-grandfather William would have known it. When I was a child, she lived in a cottage at Naishes Farm. Some of her sons worked for Willie. After she died in 1979, Ray, her youngest, asked my father to type out her memoirs. She had come to Compton in 1906, when she was six years old, and painted a picture of village life as she remembered it in 1913. The blacksmith had long since shut up shop when I lived in the village. Only the name Forge Farm reminded me of a past village skill. My father took his broken farm implements to be mended at a brick shed on the main road in Dinton. As ever, I tagged along. The furious white-hot furnace burns in my memory — 'stand back' — I shrink away and watch the Godzilla leather-clad blacksmith shoeing a hack by the open doors. His strong hands clasp a hoof through a slit in his apron. Perspiration runs down his ruddy face, and his eyes smart from smoke and sulphurous fumes. These men suffered with bad backs. Iron dust damaged their lungs. Alternating between extreme heat and cold left them with aching muscles, and burns were a constant occupational hazard.

Back in the 18th century, this was the way of life that Edward Ewence (or Ewens) chose to follow in Compton. He shoed its numerous heavy horses, made windows and door accessories, pots and pans, metal components for furniture, plough shears, and a host of other essential iron farm implements. He mended and improvised. No one could imagine village life without him. His own children and members of their wider family worked in his bustling team as hammer or bellow boys and strikers, who swung large sledgehammers during heavy forging operations. Some sporadically peeped through the records labelled 'blacksmith' in later generations. The skill was passed down from father to son with aptitude. Those who were disinclined, or forced to seek other employment as the demand for local smiths fell, moved into agriculture, brewing, or went to sea. The girls entered service, or became seamstresses or milliners.

Edward married Sarah Elkins, a member of an old Compton family which had resided there since the 1500s. She had been baptised by her parents John and Sarah in the village in 1732. The Ewences, it seems, arrived in force during the 18th century. While there is no marriage entry for them, records of their children's baptisms at Compton are present in the parish register: John in 1767, Robert in 1769, and Sarah in 1770. Two other Ewence couples baptised children in the village around the middle of the century: James and Margaret between 1743 and 1747, and John and Christian between 1755 and 1762. The mothers were sisters from the Gosney family, which was prominent in Compton during the 18th century. Perhaps the fathers were siblings too. James' and Margaret's son Moses, with his wife Martha, christened children between 1762 and 1782, and John's and Christian's son Edward, with his wife Christian, between 1781 and 1796. This younger Edward, who was born in 1759, became a blacksmith. The vicar helpfully tells us in the Incumbent's Book that he was not related to the older Edward. Two more couples, James and Elizabeth, and Thomas and Elizabeth, were recorded as parents in the parish register during the 1790s and early 1800s, likely the next generation after Moses and Martha, and appear to have been otherwise occupied. John Lampard, a tailor, bequeathed his estate to James Ewence, son of Moses, deceased, in 1810.

We first learn that the older Edward was a blacksmith from the lease of a cottage and blacksmith's shop which he was granted by Charles Penruddocke in 1771.[283] Its location, near a pond at the south end of the village, is south of the forge my grandfather knew, remembered in the farm's name. Edward held a term of 99 years or the lives of himself, aged 37, and his sons John, aged 3, and Robert, who was then 1 year old. In 1775, he took on another lease for a cottage, garden, and orchard comprising 40 lugges, formerly occupied by Stephen Snook, for 99 years or the lives of himself, aged 32, and his sons John, 9, and Robert, 7.[284] Edward's sons' ages on this lease are correct. We know when they were baptised, but no early records survive for Edward. According to these leases, he had a remarkable capacity for growing younger, which seems to stem from a dyslexic reversal of dates: if he was 37 in 1771, his birth year would have been 1734, and if 32 in 1775, it would have been 1743. Either date could be correct. The two leases were destined to pass to John when Edward died in 1801.

Edward's smithy was not the first in Compton. Two centuries earlier, in 1576, the manor court ordered William Rawlyns (Rawlings) to repair the roof of his forge.[285] He failed to comply within the time specified and was fined 2 shillings. At the same session, John Layne (Lane) and his son John were admitted as tenants to one cottage late of new building, and the moiety of a smithy called a 'Smyth Shoppe.' After John's death in 1617, his wife Matilda held the tenancy of his cottage and 'an iron-office called a symthes shop' for two years during her widowhood,[286] until she too, as Mable, was buried. John, their son, was next in the copyhold's line of succession. Perhaps he was not cut out for smithing, because he surrendered his tenancy the following year, which marks the last record for Lanes at Compton until the second half of the 19th century.

John Armony the elder was granted the lease of a smith's shop and forge at Townsend, with 15 feet at the south end of the shop to build upon, in 1652.[287] He and his children Anthony and Jane were named as lives on the 99-year lease. The manor court granted a licence for him to extend his shop by ten feet upon the waste. John signed his will shortly before his death in 1666, and made bequests of money to his wife Suffrain, daughter Jane Grace, and William Grace the younger. Jane Armonell (Armony) had married William Grace, a blacksmith, at Compton in 1655. They had a son, whom they naturally called William. His occupation is not listed in surviving records. In the baptism register of 1689, he and his wife Joan were entered as the parents of John, who became a carpenter and wheelwright. 'Wright' derives from the Old English word 'wryhta,' meaning a worker or shaper of wood. Wheelwrights were indispensable when carts were used for carrying goods. John married Anne Sanger of Dinton in 1721. They christened their first son John the following year and first daughter Anne in 1724.

John followed in his father's footsteps. He was contemporary with Edward Ewence, each of them taking on an apprentice in 1772.[288] Blacksmiths provided the metal fittings a wheelwright needed to construct and repair carts and wooden implements. It was therefore expedient for Edward to be on hand for John, especially when he was making cartwheels. The technique developed for their assembly during the mid-18th century was to fit the iron band around the circumference while the iron was hot, which held the wooden spokes together as the iron cooled. Edward would also have collaborated with Christopher Abrey, the village cooper. Christopher had been born at Wylye, a village lying next to Dinton, and his father William was a wheelwright. Coopers made a multitude of wooden staved vessels also held together by metal bands, including barrels, butter churns, hogsheads, buckets, butts, vats, and troughs.

The shops of all three men, if not adjoining, had to be within easy distance of each other.

Business prospered for the trio of craftsmen in this vibrant hub, at least for a while. Edward Ewence, John Grace, and Christopher Abrey are listed in a series of Compton's land tax returns between 1780 and 1821.[289] The premises occupied by Edward and John were assessed at an annual tax of 2 shilling 8 pence. Both men were logged as taxpayers until 1784. After John died in 1782, his widow Elizabeth took over his levy, while their son John continued to work as a wheelwright. Elizabeth died in 1796. Unfortunately, no burial record can be clearly identified with her son John. Her tax liability was assumed by John Anderson from 1797. He was most likely a yeoman. His son Robert was appointed gamekeeper in 1804,[290] and later moved to Gloucestershire, where he was described as a yeoman.[291]

Christopher Abrey paid 4 shillings tax. He had married Mary Elkins at Salisbury in 1745. As related before, the couple's daughters Mary and Ann married brothers James and Charles Hibberd, sons of Richard and Ann. This family exemplifies the switchover of crafts caused by the decline of the cottage weaving industry. Richard was born at Burcombe in 1706 to parents John and Mary (who had the same surname at birth, Hibberd). Both his father and older brother John (born 1703) were weavers. After the family moved to Compton, John apprenticed Richard to John Knott, carpenter of Shaston (Shaftesbury), in 1721.[292] Richard styled himself a millwright in his will of 1777. He distributed his three leaseholds amongst his four youngest children (Charles, James, Mary Frampton, and Ann), missing out the eldest two: Eleanor, who married William Watts the cordwainer and survived her father by two years, and John, whose fate I have not been able to establish. One of Richard's properties is marked on the 1769 estate map, adjoining Stephen Snook's land at Sandhill.

Christopher in his will dated 1790 left his grandson, John Hibberd, who was Ann's and Charles' son, his house and malthouse, and John continued to pay tax at the rate of 4 shillings. Christopher's widowed daughter Mary Hibberd received his property called Culverhays, which had previously been held by a yeoman, William Grace. William had come to the manor court in 1762 to claim his succession to the lease, dated 1727, when the life of his son William, baptised in 1751, was added to it.[293] Four years later, William surrendered the lease at the court and added Christopher to the succession, with William Grace junior the second life named. I have not been able to establish a connection between Christopher and William, who was baptised by William and Jane at Compton in 1725. His parents could not have been the

William and Jane (née Armony) who married in 1655. If a direct descendant at all, he could only have been a grandson or great-grandson. In any event, this William was at least linked to a craftsman through marriage. He wed Jane Turner at Fovant in 1749. Her brother John was the master cordwainer who worked with William Watts. As we have established, Watts acquired the Turner property after John's death.

Although almost every village still had a wheelwright during the 19th century, when carts were essential for the transportation of goods, this occupation was no longer recorded in Compton. Nor have I been able to find mention of a cooper in the archives. The co-operative of masters — blacksmith, cooper, wheelwright, and carpenter — who combined their expertise at Compton, fizzled out at the close of the 18th century. Only the blacksmith and carpenter endured to welcome in the new century.

33
THE EWENCES' SAD DEMISE

AT THE DAWN of the 19th century, all three of Edward's children were named in the will he made shortly before his death in 1802. John, the eldest, inherited his father's shop and a hoard of tools, such as hammers, chisels, punches, drift pins, and tongs. He also received a clock from the kitchen, doubtless a prized possession, and a table board. Sarah was given Edward's bed, best chest of drawers, and £20, while Robert was only left £10. He and his family lived in Great Wishford. Sarah married Isaac Watts in 1803.

After his death, Edward's widow Sarah became responsible for his tax payments until 1811,[294] when she too passed away. John worked as a blacksmith with his mother, who, I fancy, wielded power as a matriarch, and possibly as a blacksmith herself. Sarah had been listed with her husband as a master in the apprentice register in 1786.[295] John also inherited land from his maternal grandfather John Elkins in 1805, which bumped up his capital, as reflected in his tax liability of 4 shillings per annum. A pew list surviving from 1811, when seats could be either leased or purchased, records that John also occupied the church pew held by the late John Elkins' house.[296] He was still described as a blacksmith when he renewed the 1780 lease of John Elkins' former dwellinghouse, orchard, and barton in 1835.[297]

He seems to have remained an eligible bachelor until, at the age 71 years in 1838, he married Charlotte Ames (Emm) in Berkshire. Their daughter Sarah, named after her grandmother, was baptised at Compton the following year on 1 December, the same day her father was buried in the churchyard. A few facts can conjure up a romantic fairy

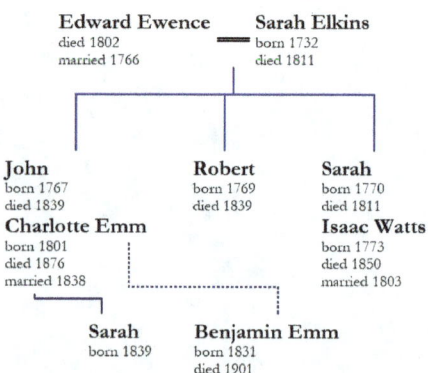

tale. Charlotte was a local girl from Fifield Bavant, over the hill from Compton. She had baptised an illegitimate child, Benjamin, there in 1831. His residence in the baptism register was entered as Woodlands, Dorset, where Charlotte was presumably living and working at the time. Had John set his sights on her at a time when marriage was out of the question? Were there regrets? Did he seek out his sweetheart after she moved to Berkshire to finally make her his wife for little more than a year of happiness? Charlotte's second marriage, we learn later, was a far from happy union.

Meanwhile, on 7 April 1817, a notice appeared in the *Salisbury and Winchester Journal* announcing the auction of a blacksmith's shop in Compton. The occupant of the shop was the younger Edward Ewence, baptised in 1759 by John and Christian, contemporaries of Edward and Sarah. This Edward joined Sarah on the tax register in 1805. Like her, he paid 2s 8d per annum, but unlike Sarah, he was merely an occupier of the property on which the tax was raised. The owner was Robert Anderson, son of the John who succeeded Elizabeth Grace on the tax list, suggesting the premises in question had been John Grace's carpentry and wheelwrighting workshop. Edward died after the auction in 1820. The surviving tax series ended in that year, and shows John still assessed at the same high rate.

The vicar identifies the next Ewence blacksmith, George, in the Incumbent's Visiting Book, which covers the period between 1847 and 1876. He was Edward the younger's son, baptised at Compton in 1788. George was living in Donhead when he married Fanny, a servant, in the village. They baptised Morgan there in 1811, and Martha in 1814. The second baptism's entry records George's occupation as 'blacksmith.' The little girl died of smallpox, aged 4 years. She had stood little chance of survival. Over 80% of infected children died of the disease during the 19th century.[298] George returned to his home in Compton around the time his father's smithy was put up for auction. There, he and Fanny baptised Jane in 1817, Priscilla in 1822, Edward in 1825, and Henry in 1828. They were well off according to the vicar, signifying that his business was thriving.

Following the Ewence archival footprint left for us, we can see how this scenario changed over time. More information about local occupations is available in the 10-yearly censuses from 1841 onwards, and the vicar's notes are punctilious on this subject. Confirming the census data, he described George as heading the only Ewence family left in Compton employed as blacksmiths. George and Fanny are listed in the 1841 census with their sons Edward, aged sixteen, and Henry, eleven, and daughter Priscilla, aged twenty, plus her illegitimate child Martha, aged three. Martha in turn gave birth to

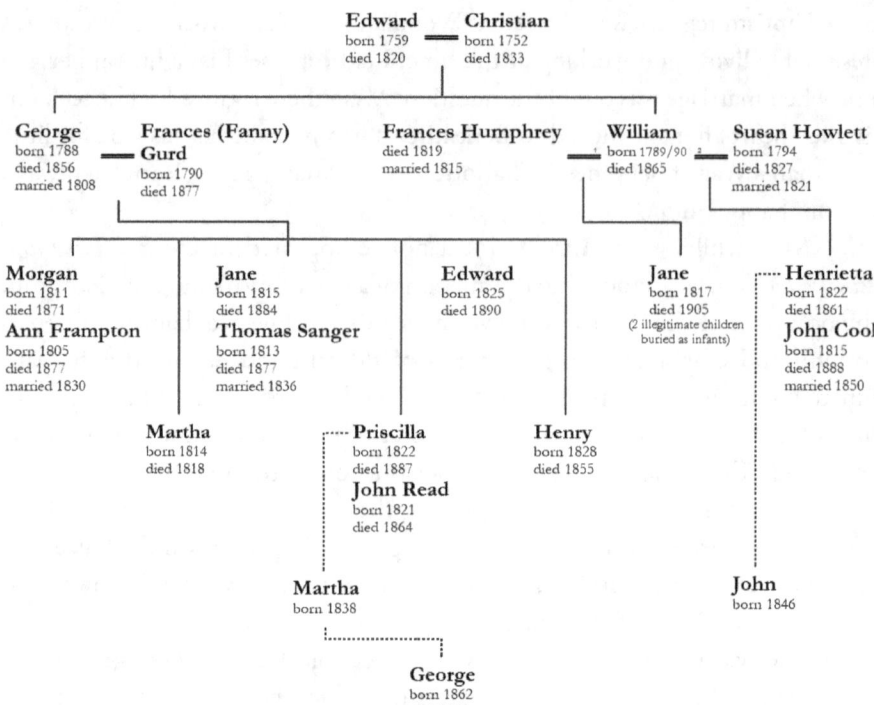

an illegitimate son in 1862, who only lived for six months. Priscilla married John Read, the squire's gardener. Despite his ill health, they had five children together.

George's and Fanny's eldest two children Morgan and Jane had married and left home to live in their own cottages in Compton, Morgan with his wife Ann, née Frampton, and Jane with her husband Thomas Sanger. Nevertheless, George's cottage was crowded with his widowed brother William and his daughter Henrietta, as well as two boys named Maidment. At the time of the 1851 census, George had Henry, his wife Caroline, and baby Edward living with him. Fanny was then a live-in servant with a local spinster, Susan Smith.

Initially, Morgan and Henry worked with their father. His third son Edward joined the navy. Henry and Caroline moved to Chicksgrove in Tisbury, where Henry was employed as a drayman at Tisbury brewery, and their son Edward eventually became a cellarman at the same establishment.

George died in 1856. Fanny had moved in with their daughter Priscilla and son-in-law John Read by 1861. She died aged 87 in 1877. Morgan persevered, but his business was going downhill. He got into trouble with the police for stealing a copper tea kettle in 1856, for which he served six weeks' hard labour in prison, and iron in 1857, punished with a sentence of three months.[299] Supposedly, his intention was to cut costs by re-working his ill-gotten gains. In the same year as his second conviction, he surrendered the lease of his blacksmith's shop for a monetary consideration. The entry of 'blacksmith' as his occupation in the 1871 census was wishful thinking. It is clear from the vicar's notes that Morgan was working at the time as a roadman. He met a sad end by his own hand in 1871.[300] His wife returned to their cottage from her laundry employment one Wednesday in October to the shock discovery of Morgan hanging from a beam in their kitchen. He had been behaving noticeably strangely after suffering from sunstroke the previous August. More than once, he had lamented that he was a broken-down man, and hoped he should not do away with himself. Ann died six years later. The couple were childless. Stephen Roberts was entered as the village blacksmith in the 1861 census.

Tracing the Ewences beyond their blacksmithing activities reveals their precarious life. Unlike George, his younger brother William never worked with iron. He married Frances Humphrey in 1815, and was a 'servant' when they baptised William at Compton in 1816. Their first and only son, he died as an infant. Daughter Jane was christened the following year, by which time William was employed as a labourer. Frances died in 1819. Two years later, William married Susanna Howlett, who was buried at Compton in 1827. Their only daughter, Henriette, born in 1822, gave birth to an illegitimate child in 1846, and later married John Cool, a carter, at Compton in 1850. Her half-sister Jane is an especially sad case. We first encounter her aged twenty in the 1841 census as a servant in James King's household. Jane never married, but bore a son named William Edward in Wilton Workhouse in 1844, and another at Compton thirteen years later, whom she buried at the age of thirteen months.*

William had his own cottage according to the 1851 census. Henrietta, her husband John Cool, their new-born son Henry, Henrietta's illegitimate son John, and Jane's illegitimate son William Edward were living with him. They were all still residing together at the time of the next census, with John Cool named as head of the household. After Henrietta died in 1861 and William in 1865, John Cool only had Henrietta's son John and her unfortunate half-sister Jane with him in 1871. Meanwhile, Jane had been listed as a servant at Broad

---

*   From 1904, workhouses were no longer recorded on birth certificates. Instead, the place of birth was entered as an ordinary street address, which could be either a real or fictitious one.

Chalke in 1851. I have been unable to locate her in the 1861 census, but we know that she was at the workhouse in Wilton in 1857.

As well as brothers William and George, another, as the vicar describes them, unrelated Ewence family, headed by a John Ewence, was recorded at Compton in the 1841 census. John was the son James and Elizabeth, baptised in the village in 1796.* At the age of seventeen, John was a labourer employed on Thomas King's farm. Either the work or his employer did not suit him, and he decided to leave. This turned out not to have been such a good idea, as King prosecuted him, and John landed up in Fisherton Anger prison for three months in 1812.[301] Later, again according to the vicar, he was employed by farmer Charles Foster, who with any luck would be more to John's liking.

John married Susanna Plowman in 1823. She was Priscilla's sister,† her junior by nine years, but both married in November of that year. The sisters had very different lives. Priscilla's was shorter, dying at only 48 as against Susanna's 64 years, but it was one of comparative luxury, her husband James King enjoying yeoman status, whereas Susanna's husband was an agricultural labourer. James and Priscilla had one child, who became a fund manager. John and Susanna baptised eight children at Compton between 1824 and 1839. The vicar depicts a poor state of affairs. Two of the daughters, Jane and Priscilla, were 'invalid,' and John himself 'v old, bad cough 21 yrs.' He must have meant that the cough was very old, because John himself was only 55 at the time. Susanna's father Nicholas Plowman lived with them, and he was certainly very old. He died aged 92 in 1850. Only the invalid daughters remained at home, until their deaths aged 24 and 32, while the other children scattered. Mary became a lady's maid in Dorsetshire. William, who was a servant in the Big House at the age of twelve, died in London. The other sons were agricultural labourers. Robert went to Holt, Henry to Chilmark, John to Bemerton, and Charles to Baverstock. According to the 1901 census, John junior had improved his lot and was a sexton and thatcher. Susanna was buried in 1860, and John in 1864, aged 68.

Charlotte, the widow of blacksmith/farmer John, was recorded in Compton with her two children in the 1841 census. She married John Wilkins, also a widower, in 1844. Without the vicar's notes detailing his household, this convoluted family unit would have been nearly impossible to disentangle.

---

*   His grandparents were either James and Margaret, who baptised their son James in 1747, or Moses and Martha, who also christened a son named James in 1765. Most likely the latter, as the vicar notes that John was unrelated to William.

†   See Chapter 38.

Wilkins John, 55, wage 7s, employer Rowden, own cottage but pay 15s 6d P rates, excellent cottage & garden, very invalid, bad breast & thumbs (this comment might apply to his wife)

Charlotte, 49. (Ewence), m Jul 20 1844. Charlotte Ames m John Ewence Jul 28 1838

Children – James b 1830, wages 3s 6d, employer ~~Rowden~~, London. His son by former wife

Ames (Emm) Benjamin, b 1830, wages 3s, employer ~~Rowden~~, Squire. Her illegitimate son, m Jane Read Oct 25 1855

Ewense (Ewence) Sarah, b 1839, ~~at home.~~ Her daughter by former husband.

According to the vicar, John was a farm labourer with an excellent cottage and garden, but unfortunately was disabled. He and Charlotte were living together in Compton in 1851. By the next census, the unhappy couple had worked out an interesting marital arrangement. As though their marriage no longer existed, John, 'a widower,' was listed as living in his son's household at Baverstock, and Charlotte, 'a widow,' in Compton with her two children. The vicar noted that John remained in Baverstock until 1869, while Charlotte continued in Compton. John's and Charlotte's daughter Sarah later went into service in Southampton, and gave birth to a daughter in 1869 before she married.

Charlotte Wilkins was entered as a widow in the 1861 census, the head of a household in Compton. Two other people were listed as living with her: Benjamin Emm (Ames), 'married,' and Sarah Ewence, 'daughter.' Benjamin was Charlotte's illegitimate son. He had married Jane Read in 1855, but they were living separately in 1861. Benjamin cohabited with his mother. Jane Emm, 'married,' was likewise recorded in her mother Fanny's household in Compton. The vicar tells us that she went into service in London. In 1871, she was a servant in Harley Street, while Benjamin was still living with his mother, with whom he continued to reside in 1881, by which time he was a widower, Jane having died in 1876. Benjamin was recorded in all of Compton's censuses through 1891.

Priscilla Read moved to Fovant before the 1881 census was taken. Her brother Edward, who went to sea, returned to Compton as a Greenwich pensioner, and was recorded there with his wife Mary Ann in the same year. Their two unemployed teenage sons, Jesse (a billiards marker) and Joseph, were living with them. Both had been born on the Isle of White, where Edward himself died in 1890.

The Ewence family's sojourn in Compton finally ended with George's daughter Jane, the eternal spinster who had given birth in Wilton Workhouse. She was the only Ewence left in Compton by the time of the 1901 census. Her nephew Henry Cool, one of her late sister Henriette's sons, was cohabiting with her. He was an unmarried pensioner, late of the Royal Marines.

34
House Furnishings and Personal Effects (mid-16th to early 18th century)

Until 1858, church courts were responsible for proving wills and granting letters of administration. Three acts passed in 1529 imposed a duty on executors and administrators to ensure that they provided an inventory of the deceased's moveable property for all estates worth over £5. Establishing the value of their assets was intended to facilitate the settlement of any dispute that might arise amongst the beneficiaries. Although bonds of obligation were issued from 1530 until 1782, inventories in the Wiltshire and Swindon Archive's collection of Compton wills and probate are first seen during the 1560s and disappear after 1735. Local men, invariably three from Compton, conducted the appraisal, or valuation. Of course, its subjective nature could lead to over- or underestimations. Items of little value or already bequeathed did not need to be included. Fixed furnishings, such as bench seating, cupboards, and shelving, were likewise excluded for the most part. Other caveats to be remembered when relying on an analysis of inventories are that the deceased may have retired from active farming or disposed of some of his possessions before his death.

I looked at seven Compton wills which include bequests and nine inventories of husbandmen and yeomen dated between 1545 and 1726, to form an idea of its local husbandry practices, changes brought about by enclosure, and the villagers' living conditions. My analysis reveals the practical effects of gradual enclosure and the dismantling of communal farming from the 16th through 18th centuries.

Dates and names on wills and inventories

Date	Name	Occupation	Value	Comment
1545	William Watts	husbandman	-	will
1550	John Elyat	husbandman	-	will
1558	Alyes Watts	husbandman	-	will, William's widow
1563	John Elliott	husbandman	£10 14s	inventory
1579	James Elliott	husbandman	-	will
1605	Humpfrey Watts	husbandman	-	will, William's son
1619	William Jaye	yeoman	-	will
1626	James Elliott senior	husbandman	£102 5s	inventory
1648	Thomas Bayley	yeoman	£25	inventory
1667	James Elliott	-	£24 12s 4d	inventory
1668	Richard Case	yeoman	£116 6s 8d	inventory
1693	John Case	yeoman	£264 8s	Inventory, Richard's son
1700	Stephen Naish	yeoman	£504 5s	inventory
1715	Thomas Elkins	yeoman	£427 18s 8d	Inventory
1715	Richard Naish	yeoman	£2,394 14s 10d	inventory
1726	Thomas Livelong	yeoman	-	will

Names are written in this list as in the original documents. In the main text, they are spelt as most commonly recorded in contemporary documents, or as today. The people named in the first five lines of its second column lived during the Tudor era. Elizabeth I ascended the throne in the year Alice Watts made her will. George I's reign was nearing its end when Thomas Livelong signed his will.

The 16th century items examined were all wills with the exception of John Elliott's inventory, which highlights the importance of common rights. His assemblage of four cows, thirty-eight sheep, six pigs, an ox, and four horses grazed on common pasture in 1563. At the beginning of the 17th century, the lots of husbandmen were not greatly different to those of yeomen. The lines between the minor landed gentry and wealthier yeomen, as well as between wealthier husbandmen and the poorer yeomen, were blurred. Indeed, the most costly inventory, valued at £102 5s, is for husbandman James Elliott in 1626, which is only surpassed towards the close of the century by that of yeoman John Case at £264 8s in 1693. Unfortunately, there is no surviving inventory for the first yeoman in my series, William Jeay, who made his will in 1619.

Rents were stagnant for about 100 years from the middle of the 1600s. At the same time, the expansion of towns was fuelling a growing demand for corn. As the century progressed, tenant farmers who acquired larger parcels of arable and enclosed pasture became increasingly prosperous. A case in point is provided by the Bailey family. Thomas was a yeoman, and the inventory taken after his death in 1648 was valued at £25. His son Christopher accumulated substantial wealth during his lifetime, having assets worth £220 10s in 1690. While yeomen prospered, husbandmen, who were unable to survive without common pasture, were forced to give up their arable land. They were either driven out or reduced to subsisting on wage earnings. Yeomen dominate husbandmen by a ratio of sixteen to four in the 18th century wills and inventories from Compton held by Wiltshire archives. Overall, only three husbandman-testators are left in the village archives, the last dating to 1770.

The four inventories from this period which I examined were all for yeomen, and even within this class a large gap in capital is displayed by Richard Naish's valuation of £2394 14s 10d, double the sum of the other three inventories combined. Yet he still grew wheat and barley on common land in 1715. Enclosure was only finally completed *c* 1795.

Looking at the assets recorded in these wills and inventories in detail, we find, as expected, that sheep are prominent throughout, second only to corn in value. Cows were kept to supply homes with milk, butter, and cheese. James Elliott owned a brown one in 1579, and Humphrey Watts likewise had only one in 1605. A later James Elliott boasted eight 'rother beastes' (horned animals) in 1626, while Richard Case only owned five in 1668, as did Thomas Elkins in 1715, when his contemporary John Case had two cows.

The thirty-seven milking cows which Richard Naish kept are comparable to our dairy at Naishes Farm. They were his third most highly valued asset but, unlike my great-grandfather at the turn of the 20th century, he did not sell milk on a commercial scale. He processed it in his dairy house, where a collection of cheese vats and butter churns were found. Thomas Elkins stored a butter churn and cheese press in his brewhouse. Such cheese was of poor quality and intended for immediate consumption. My father recalls manual butter-making in his memoirs. Milk was left to stand in a pan to let the cream rise to the top, which was then skimmed off into a barrel and churned. The task, he laments, required strong arms and stamina. It was one of the most tiresome chores he was set as a child, standing in the dairy, which was always very cold, spending many weary hours turning and praying for the butter to 'come.' We made our own butter at Naishes using electricity.

Generally, a pig or two gets a mention in the inventories. As with so many other items, Richard Naish owned the most, seven 'great' pigs and eleven 'little ones.' These were lumped in with the poultry, worth too little to be valued separately. Flitches of bacon were a common item. The value of a side of bacon increased nearly six-fold over 63 years. Humphrey Watts' trio were worth 8 shillings in 1605, Thomas Bailey's eight £5 in 1648, and Richard Case's two £1 10 shillings in 1668.

Bees were always kept on farms for honey and wax. Their low value excluded them from inventories, but they are encountered in wills. For instance, Thomas Livelong bequeathed his wife her bees as well as her wearing apparel and rings. Before the Married Women's Property Acts of 1870 and 1882 allowed a married woman to retain her own possessions, they belonged to her husband for as long as he was alive. My father also kept bees, and told a story about them when he moved to Naishes during World War II. He brought a heavy suitcase with him, which sorely puzzled the removal team as to what it could contain. He thought it better to keep mum because it was stuffed full with packets of sugar, which was rationed. They had been purchased under perfectly legal war regulations for the feeding of his bees in winter. Much as he loved them, sadly, his beekeeping days came to an unhappy end when my eldest sister was stung, and my overprotective mother persuaded him to banish the colony. Even the victim felt bad about it.

Crop development is vital for increasing yields. Legumes were already sown during the Middle Ages to enhance the quantity of nitrogen in the soil needed by cereal crops. Rye, the most frequently sown grass, was used to control weeds, and to improve soil structure and drainage. John Elliott was cultivating rye and peas in addition to wheat, barley, and oats in 1563. He had a malt mill, which is a common item in the inventories, used to malt barley for beer-making.

From the mid-17th century onward, farmers began to grow clover to enrich the soil with nitrogen, which improved crop rotation and led to dramatic increases in cereal yields. Vetch (or tares), a member of the pea family found in John Case's 1693 inventory, also makes excellent hay and boosts sheep husbandry. As well as 129 acres of wheat, 122 of barley, and 8 of oats, Richard Naish's inventory listed 49 acres of peas, vetch, and clover, and 23 of grass, in 1715.

Turnips, like clover, augment the soil with nitrogen. They proved to be an incredible advance when introduced by Viscount Charles 'Turnip' Townshend. As a fallow crop, they can be used for feeding sheep in winter, solving the age-old problem of how to provide sustenance during the cold months. They are absent from the inventories, which might be dated too early, as this new method was popularised in England during the 1730s, or because soil in chalky areas is often too thin for supporting turnips, although they are documented at Burcombe in 1752.

Floating of the water meadows turned out to be the greatest advance in overcoming the winter hunger gap in South Wiltshire. Richard and Stephen Naish's lease of farms and demesnes in 1703 included three large water meadows, lately improved by 'watering.'[302] According to this method, meadows were covered in flowing water during the early spring to incubate the grass and carry nutrients from the river onto the land. This early grass then provided fodder for sheep after supplies of the previous year's hay crop had run out. As a result, sheep numbers could be increased, which in turn led to greater corn harvests.

Farm equipment was heavy and clumsy. Weight was needed for the wooden ploughs to cut through the soil. Alice Watts held half-shares in a plough and cart in 1558. Her son Humphry had three harrows, which were made of wood, with iron or ash wood teeth. Ninety years later, in addition to a plough and four harrows, Thomas Bailey owned a cart and dung pot. Such paniers were strapped to a horse's back. The dung was then spread onto the fields through an opening released at the bottom of the pot — with an arduous grooming task awaiting the horseman at the end of the day. Yet again, Richard Naish had more of everything — six waggons, five ploughs, twelve harrows, and two dung pots — but they were no more advanced than the implements used 100 years earlier.

The early inventories include tools, hatchets, rakes, picks, and forks, which are not mentioned later, presumably because of their comparatively low value. John Elliott had a scythe for cutting hay. His reaping hooks and corn fork evoke a tableau of harvesttime in the mid-16th century, when it represented a no less gruelling labour than in the vivid picture painted by Richard Jeffries in 1889:[303]

> I used to wonder how these men and woman could stand it, for the summer day is long ... The edge of the reap-hook had to be driven by force through the stout stalks like a sword, blow after blow, minute after minute, hour after hour; the back stooping, and the broad sun throwing its fiery rays from a full disc on the head and neck. I think some of them used to put handkerchiefs doubled up under their hats.

That a handkerchief could lend itself to improvisation did not escape my father either. I see him at harvesttime about to take his turn driving the combine. The sun beats down as it always did, and modernisation has more likely increased than reduced the dust. He wears his handkerchief restyled to fit atop his billowing white hair with a knot at each corner.

An intriguing ladder of great length — worth 10 pence — is also itemised. Chances are, John did a bit of thatching for his neighbours like his kinsman William, whom we learn from the Bishop Court depositions thatched Joan Oake's cottage some years later.

Spinning wool was a common sideline for husbandmen to earn extra income. Although several testators who lived in Compton during the 17th and 18th centuries identified themselves as weavers, only two of their inventories provide evidence of wool processing. Several members of the Elliott family were clothiers in Salisbury at this time. Items in John Elliott's 1563 inventory lead one to wonder whether they are coincidental or a prophecy for the future of one of its Compton branches. His pair of 'wollen cardes' were hand cards for the loosening and untangling of woollen locks to produce individual fibres ready for spinning. His 'turnes to spynne in' translates as a spinning wheel. Aside from wool, he had ten and a half pounds of yarn, which was spun thread used for weaving. Curiously, the twelve and a half pounds of 'blacke woll' valued at 10 shillings — the same as fifteen pounds of ordinary wool and yarn at 12 shillings — suggests that the wool was indeed black in colour, rather than of poor quality. Black wool is considered commercially undesirable because it cannot be dyed, but it is flame resistant, evaporating and absorbing moisture, thus keeping the wearer dry. John's appraisers listed sheep shears and a branding iron as well as three sheepskins. Yeoman Thomas Bailey also had a 'turne' in his kitchen in 1648, probably used by his son Richard who worked as a weaver until his death in 1708.

These wills and inventories of the 16th and 17th centuries clearly show that cottages were scantily furnished. John Elliott in 1563 owned an old 'flocke'* bed and two bedsteads, one cupboard, three chests, two old chests, two coffers, another without a lid, and a table-board supported by trestles. Stools and chairs are missing. His family either sat on fixed benches or blocks of wood. Humphry Watts only had a table-board and form, one cupboard, two coffers, and two bedsteads in 1605. Later inventories display a greater variety of goods and chattels. John Case owned six stools in 1693. Richard Naish had twenty-two chairs, six joined stools, and a settle in 1715.

---

*   A mattress filled with pieces of wool (flock).

Tablecloths and napkins, though expensive, are frequently mentioned. Despite his sparse furniture, John Elliott had two of each worth 10 shillings, equal in value to a collection of two latten 'basons' and six candlesticks. Beeswax candles represented a considerable advance on the rushlights used by poorer villagers, which were made by dipping the pith of a rush in mutton fat (tallow), and only emitted a meagre flame to see by after sunset.

Beds were often bequeathed in wills. Even Thomas Livelong left his daughter Elizabeth 'ye Bed, Bedstead and Bedding she usually lies on.' Prickly canvas-covered straw pallets were by now a thing of the past. Pillows had already replaced logs. An array of bedclothes is catalogued in the inventories, including coverleds (coverlids/bedspreads), bolsters (long pillows), and blankets or, more delightfully, 'plonkets,' as Humphry's appraisers called them. Husbandmen and yeomen alike slept between canvas sheets on feather beds. Throughout the period in question, they represented important status items. William Watts gave his feather bed and bedclothes to Walter and Syble Mayow (Mayhew) in 1545. Some household members were less fortunate. Richard Case owned both a flock bed and a dust bed, as well as one stuffed with feathers. Further improvement is evident twenty-five years later, when three feather beds were recorded in his son's home. By 1715, Richard Naish and Thomas Elkins had four-poster beds, hung with home-spun woollen curtains which provided both privacy and protection from cold draughts. These were luxuries primarily enjoyed by the master of the house and his wife.

Thomas' best bedroom was lavishly furnished. Its centrepiece was a bed with decorative villain-fringed curtains and two comfy feather pillows, a quilt, and a pair of blankets. A round table-board and eight leather chairs suggest that the room doubled as a dining or reception room area, while a pair of oak drawers, curtains on the windows, and rug on the floor radiate an impression of opulence. There were feather beds in the hall chamber and the garret chamber over the hall, but only an ordinary one in a second garret chamber. Tablecloths, napkins, and pillow ties were stored here, in what was surely a servant's room.

The early inventories set out household goods in a continuous list, rather than separating them according to the rooms in which the appraisers found them. John Elliott's inventory of 1563 is an exception, revealing a typical husbandman's cottage comprised of two rooms, described as a chamber and hall, and a kitchen where the malt mill stood. A chamber usually meant a bedroom. The hall was the focal point of domestic life, used for eating, for cooking if there was no kitchen, and often sleeping as well.

Three rooms are mentioned in William Watts' will,* and three are detailed in James Elliott's 1667 inventory, the lodging chamber where he died, the kitchen, and hall. James, however, had been liable to pay hearth tax on four fireplaces in 1662.

The hearth tax, levied in England between 1662 and 1689 on all householders except those paying rent of less than 20 shillings per annum, conveys an impression of the size of their homes. Records for Compton listing the number of its chargeable hearths are available for 1662. Of the total 75, only 60 are itemised, two of these lack their householders' names, and one is completely indecipherable. Richard Berry had the most fireplaces, numbering seven. Arundel Penruddocke was not named, implying that her hearths are among the fifteen missing from the list. Three had five, two four, and four three, while six and eight had two or one, respectively, indicating that the majority lived in small cottages with one or two fireplaces.

We might expect that the value of inventories taken on the death of householders soon after 1662 would be higher for those with more fireplaces. It is therefore surprising that Richard Case's is worth more than four times that of James Elliott's, as he was taxed for three and James for four. The tax rate was hefty at 2 shillings per hearth per year, equivalent to a day's pay for a skilled tradesman.[304] Richard could have avoided tax by blocking up some of his hearths. More likely though, as his son John probably had only three rooms (see below), James disposed of most of his possessions prior to his death, which, as already mentioned, would lower the value of his inventory. Notably, no hearth implements such as andirons, spits, pot hooks, or hangers are listed in his account.

Thomas Bailey's inventory is the first to portray a typical yeoman's house. He had four rooms: a hall and kitchen on the ground floor, with two chambers above. Within the hall, there was a chamber where a feather bed and flock bed stood. A looking glass and brush suggest that the lady of the house slept here with her maid. Possibly, she did not fancy sharing the hall, which was filled with two feather beds, a flock bed, four bedsteads, and two pallets. This unpleasant overcrowding was exacerbated by other things we might not like to find in our own bedrooms today: six sacks, seven barrels, weights and scales, baskets, not to mention four pig troughs. The space could potentially have been subdivided by fabric partitions to provide some privacy at night, at least for family members. The kitchen chamber was merely used for storage. The vicarage was also a four-room abode in the

---

* See Chapter 24.

early 17th century, with a barn of six rooms, house for hay, and stable of four rooms belonging to it.[305]

John Case's domestic possessions were divided into three sets of items, suggestive of a three-room cottage. The first contained three feather beds with bedclothes, two chests, three coffers, and some lumber, probably all located in a chamber shared by John and members of his household. The second, prefaced 'in the hall,' catalogued a table-board and six joined stools, but also andirons, a pair of spits, two pairs of pot hooks and hangers, and various cooking utensils, signifying that it was also the kitchen. The third was stuffed with a jumble of three bedsteads, four barrels, a cheese press, measuring vat, and lumber — likely a bedroom-come-storeroom, where junior inhabitants or servants slept.

Later, in 1715, Thomas Elkins' house had even more rooms spread over two floors, and a garret. Below the four on the second storey described above, its main area was the hall, containing a table-board, three joined stools, and four chairs, with no hint of a separate kitchen. He had a parlour, but from its contents — a 'bad' table-board, four new barrels, and some lumber — it could not have been anything special. Rather, as surmised above, his best bedroom was used to receive and entertain guests. He also had a buttery and a brewhouse. A buttery was a cool room used for food storage. We have already taken a tour* of the three-storey house newly built in the late 17th century occupied by Richard Naish, the richest yeoman in the village.

Home-made barley bread, skimmed milk cheese, milk porridge, beef broth, potatoes, peas, and bacon were the staple diet. Beer and tea were thirst quenchers, drunk out of a bowl. Richard Naish's assortment of kitchenalia extended to a cider press, and even a coffee pot for indulging in the devil's drink.† According to Samuel Pepys, the first coffee house in England was established only sixty-five years before Richard's death. Treen (wooden) vessels had already given way to brass and pewter. John Case's late 17th-century inventory includes a large selection of kitchen equipment: three bell metal pots, one bell metal skillet, one brass skillet, two kettles, one brass pan, one furnace, nine pewter dishes, two pewter porringers, one spice mortar and pestle, two pewter Lot saltcellars, two warming pans, a pair of andirons, two

---

* See Chapter 30.

† Coffee was outlawed by the Catholic Church until Pope Clement VIII sampled it and declared: 'This devil's drink is so delicious … we should cheat the devil by baptising it!' Online at https://www.catholiccoffee.com/coffee-and-pope-clement-viii-devils-drink/

spits, two pairs of pot hooks, two pairs of pot hangers, an iron shovel, a pair of tongs, a basting ladle, one pewter flagon, and two mugs, which represented an advance on drinking bowls.

Salt cellars are also listed in other later inventories. Thomas Parker, however, had bequeathed a sejlt (salt cellar) to his granddaughter earlier, in 1581. The historian Michael Clayton sums up the significance of the salt cellar: 'The comparative rarity and absolute need for salt [to preserve food] during the Middle Ages assured a place for it on the table, and the receptacle soon attained a social importance, giving it a size far larger than required in comparison to the quantity of salt it contained.'[306] Ergo, the salt cellar was a status symbol. Salt was used as currency, and its necessity, as well as the difficulty and expense of producing it though extraction from seawater and evaporation over a fire, lies at the root of the expression 'worth one's salt,' dating from the first century A.D. Early salt cellars tended to be plain and geometric in form. Later, they became more decorative. We can picture such items in the form of John Case's two fancily named 'Lot saultsellers,' one with its head turned back, sitting in pride of place on his board, decked with a tablecloth.

Lest we should assume these men were primitive yokels, note that books were found amongst their possessions. James Elliot's inventory of 1626 includes a bible priced at 5 shillings, equal in value to half of one of his three pigs. John Case owned two bibles in 1693, and Richard Naish had a 'great' bible in 1715. They were not separately valued. However, Richard also had several other bibles, which, together with his good books, was worth £1.

Clothes were passed on and gratefully received. James Elliott gave his best jerkin and leather doublet to his brother Humphry. Thomas Parker bequeathed his coat to John Snow the elder, a pair of hose to John Watts the elder, and his lockerom (coarse linen) shirt to his father-in-law. John Elliott's 1563 inventory shows that he possessed a change of clothes: two cloaks, two coats, two doublets, two jerkins, and two pairs of hose. The most remarkable item is to be found amongst the bed linen in Thomas Elkins' lesser garret chamber, and it sounds gorgeous: a scarlet mantle with a lace of silver and gold. Less than a century before, the Sumptuary Laws allowed only the highest nobility in the land to wear such a coat.

Values of the deceased's wearing apparel are given in seven of the inventories. How much a person chose to spend on clothes is naturally a matter of preference as much as an indication of wealth. John Elliott wore garments priced at 4 shillings 4 pence in 1563. Humphrey Watts' were worth half as much again in 1605. James Elliott, who was prepared to spend £3 on his clothes in 1626, must have been a snazzy dresser, while John Case saw no reason to expend more than £3 some 67 years later. His father 25 years before had left apparel worth £5. The prosperous Richard Naish was decidedly posh in his £10 attire in 1715, as compared with his scruffy kinsman Stephen, clad in £5's worth five years before.

Value of Wearing Apparel in Inventories

Date	deceased	Value
1563	John Elliott	4s 4d
1605	Humfrey Watts	6s 8d
1626	James Elliott	£3
1668	Richard Case	£5
1693	John Case	£3
1700	Stephen Naish	£5
1715	Richard Naish	£10

Finally we come to money: Richard Naish had an astounding £30 of ready cash, equivalent to over £6,000 today, lying about his house, while half of Stephen Naish's total worth of £504 was comprised of money due on bonds and 'other ways.'

35
THE RISE AND FALL OF THE VILLAGE'S CRAFTS AND TRADES

VILLAGERS WERE ESSENTIALLY self-sufficient during Tudor times. They had a patch of land to cultivate crops and grazed livestock on the common, while their chickens pecked about all over the place. They looked after bees, brewed beer, baked bread, and made their own clothes, or bartered within the community. Husbandmen fashioned tools, furniture, and fences, and built their own barns and cottages with neighbourly help. A case in point is recorded at the Court Baron held at Compton in 1585.[307] John Sidling was admitted as the tenant of a small cottage on East Brook Lane. The traditional entry fine was waved in consideration of his having built the cottage at his own cost.

Later, ostensibly unassuming parish records, court depositions, apprenticeship registrations, and land taxes, supplemented by wills, combine to build a colourful picture of Compton's hive of craftsmen activity during the 17th and 18th centuries. These fortuitously preserved documents filmically dissolve into a visual feast of weavers at their looms, tailors sewing new and darning well-worn clothes, masons chipping on stone, blacksmiths hammering metal, shoemakers cutting leather, and wheelwrights, carpenters, and coopers sawing and hewing their raw materials. They were highly skilled, intimately acquainted with local materials, and expert in how best to shape them to satisfy the needs and tastes of their neighbours. All shared the goal of providing the necessary resources for their agricultural community, and supported one another by supplying different parts for their end products, as described in Chapter 32.

The Plantagenet King of England Edward III raised a tax at the start of his War in Scotland (1332-1336). His 1332 subsidy roll is the first surviving record of the taxations levied between the 12th and 17th centuries. It was on movable property, principally the value of crops and stock, rather than land, and the roll provides personal information, whereas those between 1334 and 1524 only list village totals.

Notably, the names on the tax list were mostly Norman-French, which had replaced Anglo-Saxon ones. Some in Compton depict characteristics: John Jelous, John Escu de Mor (the moral shield), Alice de la Escheqiere (poor lady, escheqiere is derived from the Latin to ignore), Walter le Sterke (the strength), and Roger and John le Moneke (monks or individuals wishing to be known for their piety). My favourite, for which only a wild imagination can offer an explanation, is William Peckepuse. There are monikers useful for identifying occupations. A mill is recorded at Compton in the Domesday Book. Powered by the river Nadder, it was essential for grinding corn to flour, and, sure enough, Thomas atte Mulle is among the taxpayers in 1332, as is a carter named Richard le Cartere and tailor Robert le Taillour. He was not even the first tailor to be recorded at Compton. Gilbert le Tailur was listed in Nicolas of Haversham's IPM of 1274 as a free tenant holding one virgate of land. Several centuries later, Osmund Fricker, aged 70, deposed that he was a tailor when he testified at the Bishop's Court in 1600. James Northeast, also a tailor, married Joan Miles at Compton in 1624. James' son Jerome did not follow in his father's footsteps, possibly due to competition within the trade. Instead, he thrived as a husbandman, leaving goods valued at £130 13s in the inventory taken after he died in 1667. His son Jeremiah became the parish clerk. In 1699, he had a special seat according to the vicar's note in the parish register, as quoted in *Gleanings from Wiltshire Parish Registers*:[308]

> The little seat, or reading pew, standing on the right hand of the entrance into the south aisle of the church was by me, Nathaniel Hancock, vicar, caused to be erected at my own charge for the use of Jeremiah Northeast, the present parish clerk, so long as he shall continue to do and perform the offices and service of a parish clerk there.

A tailor from the village, John Carpenter, acted as bondsman at a wedding in 1728. A father and son team of tailors named John Lampard made wills in 1779 and 1810. No further tailors were recorded in the village, though women took up commercial dressmaking later in the century. The Wyatt girls were recorded as such in the 1881 census, and Hilda Kerley recalled seeing ladies from other villages coming and going in their carriages to visit a seamstress, who would have been Louisa Mason, recorded in the 1911 census.

As we learnt in Chapters 32 and 33, the village had housed a succession of blacksmiths from its early days, culminating in the large interwoven family of Ewences which dominated smithing during the 18th century.

The occupations of cordwainer, mason, and weaver began to be recorded in deeds and testators' wills at Compton during the 17th century. Long before the Watts clan reigned, John Venice, a cobbler, entered into a bond in 1683 to give up his tenement when requested,[309] and Francis Millward was identified as a cordwainer in his will of 1695. Likewise, parish records and wills unveil a 100-year-long line of masons in the Lawrence family between 1656 and 1752, followed by the Plowmans, who worked at Compton into the second half of the 19th century.*

The wills of John Ambrose in 1678 and Richard Bailey in 1707 categorise the testators as weavers. Analysis of John Elliott's inventory suggests that he was also weaving at his cottage before he died in 1562. Joan Palmer affirmed that she was the wife of a weaver at the Bishop's Court in 1600. Clusters of Hibberd weavers worked in Burcombe, Barford St Martin, Wilton and Compton during the late 17th and early 18th centuries. Evidence for the last two locations is provided by marriage licence bonds. John Hibberd, weaver of Wilton is recorded as a bondsman at Richard Naish's wedding at Burcombe in July 1698. A John Hibberd of Compton Chamberlayne is likewise logged at the marriages of Prudence Hibberd to George Bowles at Dinton in 1717, and Robert Ford's ceremony at Salisbury Cathedral in 1721.

Weavers, however, were the first of the artisan class to disappear from the village. During the last quarter of the 1700s, increasing mechanisation began to toll the death knell of the cottage weaving industry. We learnt earlier that the weaver Daniel Livelong fell on hard times when he was the subject of a Removal Order in 1743.† By 1793, spinning-jennies were in general use in Wiltshire, initially in the putting-out system. Before long, they were concentrated in factories. Carding engines were likewise invented during the late 1700s. Thus, the two processes, spinning and carding, which had sustained cottage spinning in the sheep-and-corn regions, were taken over by industrial units.

Apprentice registrations are a positive treasure trove for locating craftsmen who prospered in Compton. A law in force from 1710 until 1811 required a master of trade to pay stamp duty when taking on an apprentice. For the Board of Inland Revenue's benefit, the amount paid, master's name, trade, and apprentice were recorded in a register. Traditionally, the term was seven years. The indenture of one apprentice bound to a cordwainer in Keevil, Wiltshire, exhibited in a Chancery suit, sets out the obligations and duties

*   See Chapter 36.

†   See Chapter 21.

agreed on between apprentice and master.[310] The apprentice had to serve faithfully, keep his master's secrets, neither waste nor damage his goods, gladly follow commands, shun ale-houses and playing unlawful dice or card games. He was not to absent himself either by night or day from his master, and was not allowed to marry. In return, the master taught him his craft, supplied him with food and lodging and, in this particular example, had to provide the apprentice with a new suit at the end of the term. Legal recourse was available against a master who employed another's apprentice, as threatened by a shoemaker in Silver Street, Salisbury, who appealed through the *Salisbury and Winchester Journal* on 5 September 1782 to his apprentice, a lad of about sixteen years, who had run away 'without any provocation whatsoever,' informing him 'that if he will return he will be kindly received; if not whosoever employs him will be proceeded against as the law directs.'

John Grace, a carpenter and wheelwright, registered James Coole in 1741,[311] and John's son John engaged John Johnson in 1765[312] and Thomas Parker in 1772.[313] Another master wheelwright, Jeremiah Mead, took on an apprentice in 1786.[314] Blacksmith Edward Ewence started training James Gray in his smithy in 1772[315] and later, in 1786, Edward and Sarah Ewence were recorded in the role of master on John Essence's registration.[316] Cooper Christopher Abrey took on John King in 1749.[317]

With the progress of mechanisation, not only the weaver but also the wheelwright and cooper vanished into the ether. Other crafts persisted into the 19th century. The Ewences, who gradually faded away during the 19th century, were succeeded by Stephen Roberts, who came from Breamore near Downton, followed by Benjamin and Henry Jarvis, who were the blacksmiths in my great-grandfather's time. The shoemaker Isaac Watts was last recorded in the 1841 census, followed by John Weeks in 1851, James Petty in 1861, John Parker and Thomas Raymond in 1871, and John Bailey in 1891. Additionally, the Post office Directory lists John and Sarah Parker's son Herbert in 1849, shortly before his untimely death at 26 in 1850; Kelly's Directory lists his brother Alfred in 1855, and Jessie Coombs, a boot repairer, as late as 1920. Alfred left and is recorded at Fovant in the 1861 census. A poor choice of spouse might well be associated with James Petty's departure. At the age of twenty, he wed Mary Long, who was eighteen years old and came from Ireland. The marriage was a double ceremony with Mary Petty of Barford St Martin and Alfred Bartlett at the Catholic Church in Fisherton Anger, Salisbury on 2 February 1861. Within six months, on 8 July, James declared in the *Wiltshire County Mirror*, 'I hereby give notice — That I will not be answerable for any debts contracted by my Wife Mary Petty, after

Occupations at Compton Chamberlayne Extracted from Kelly's Directories, Supplemented by Censuses

	1841	1849	1851	1855	1859	1867	1875	1880	1898	1920
Shopkeeper	Lot Plowman	Lot Plowman	John & Robert Plowman	Thom. Abram Lot Plowman	Thom. Abram Lot Plowman	Fran. Abram Lot Plowman	Fran. Abram Jemima Plowman	Fran. Abram	John Robert[3] *grocer*	Frank Johnson *village stores*
Carrier	Lot Plowman				Lot Plowman	Lot Plowman Jas. Sansom	Jas. Sansom George Raymond	Jas. Sansom	Jas. Sansom[3] Eli Rose	Ed. Bracher Ed. Churchill
Beer retailer	Mary Corp *Publican until 1850*						Jemima Plowman	John Roberts	John Robert[3] Arthur Roberts	Valentine Lovell
Mason	Wm., John, & Robert Plowman			John Plowman	Wm. Plowman	Joseph Plowman[1]				
Farmer	James King Charles Foster Wm. Rowden	Charles Foster Wm. Rowden Wm. Targett Wm. Sanger	Charles Foster Wm. Rowden Wm. Targett	Wm. Targett Thom. Galpin	Wm. Targett Thom. Galpin	Wm. Targett John Keevil	Wm. Targett John Keevil	Wm. Targett John Keevil	Walter Keevil Wm Langdon Eli Rose	Geog. Aylward Douglas Main Ed. Bracher
Shoemaker	Isaac Watts Herbert Parker	Herbert Parker	John Weeks	Alfred Parker	James Petry	Thom. Raymond	Thom. Raymond		John Bailey[3]	Jessie Coombs *boot repairer*
Blacksmith	Morgan & Geog. Ewence		Morgan & Geog. Ewence	Geog. Ewence	Ste. Roberts	Ste. Roberts	Ste. Roberts	Ste. Roberts	Benjamin Jarvis	Henry Jarvis
Sawyer	Jas. Sansom Jas. Parker		Jas. Sansom							
Carpenter				Wm. Wilkins	Wm. Wilkins	George Flexen	George Flexen[2]	George Flexen		
Hurdle maker								Alec Dunn[3]	John Wyatt	John Wyatt

1 In the 1871 census, 2 in the 1881 census, 3 in the 1891 census.
Kelly's Directories for 1903 and 1911 are missed out of this table.
The 1903 Directory is the same as the 1898 Directory, except for the absence of John & Arthur Roberts, and Frederick Henry Cole is a beer retailer; John Samson is also absent; Henry Jarvis has replaced Benjamin; there is no shoemaker.
The 1911 Directory is the same as the 1903 Directory, bar Thomas Rivers being the farmer at Naishes Farm; Eli Rose is absent, and Edward Bracher is a carrier; Samuel Southern is a grocer at the Stores; John Mason is a market gardener at the Willows.
Additions in 1920: Edward Waterman, hairdresser; Jesse Wild, plumber; C. H. Avery, Shaftesbury Lodge Garage; John Mason, market gardener.
At the county petty sessions on 31 May 1870, Frances Abram was fined for keeping an illicit beer house.

this date.' Mary registered the birth of her first child John at Chelsea in 1862. James had moved to Grovely by 1868, where a report in the *Salisbury and Winchester Journal* on 10 October of that year informs us that he was employed by the Earl of Pembroke as a gamekeeper. He was accused of assaulting Mary Ford in the woods when he shook acorns out of her apron. His lawyer pointed out that she was trespassing, and he had merely used such violence as was necessary to compel her to give up the acorns, which should be left in the woods as food for game. The defence was accepted and the case dismissed. James and his wife must have reconciled, as in 1869 Mary gave birth to a second child, who was born at the Penruddocke Arms, Grovely, according to the family's 1871 census record.

Thomas Parker, John Grace's apprentice, became the first in a series of Parker carpenters,* who gave way to William Wilkins, listed in Kelly's Directory in 1855 and 1859, as was George Flexen from 1867 to 1880. The vicar records that he came to Compton as the squire's carpenter in 1863.

An overall impression of occupations in the village at any one time is first provided by the 1841 census. Most men were classified as agricultural labourers — although many had special skills which were concealed under the collective term 'labourer.' Otherwise, it recorded the shoemaker Isaac Watts, a carrier named Lot Plowman, carpenter Harry West, four masons who were also members of the Plowman family, two blacksmiths, George and Morgan Ewence, two sawyers, John Samson and James Parker, and a further shoemaker in the form of Herbert Parker. There was a lady publican, Mary Corp at Compton Hut, and, naturally, a gamekeeper, James Barrett, employed by the squire John Hungerford Penruddocke. The squire's land was worked by William Rowden at Manor Farm, which boasted the largest acreage in the village. He styled himself a farmer, while James King at Naishes Farm and Charles Read Foster at Home Farm still identified themselves as yeoman.

Farmers William Rowden, William Targett, Charles Foster, and Barnett Sanger were listed in the Post Office Directory of 1849. Was Barnett really a farmer? The house and orchards in his tithe award of 1850 covered less than an acre of land. Barnett was the baby of Silas' and Elizabeth's family, baptised at Stapleford in 1774. Before him, they had christened Elizabeth at Longparish, Hampshire, in 1759, and, at Berwick St James, Mary in 1762 and James in 1768. The family probably came to Compton together, but their first documented residence there was at the time of Mary's marriage to John

---

* See Chapter 23.

Watts in 1782, followed by James' appearance as a juror at the manor court in 1804 and 1805, with Silas likewise recorded in 1807 and 1809.[318] Barnett is named in the pew list of 1811, having the right to sit in St Michael's Church on account of his two houses on the hill.[319] The Sanger surname itself was not completely new to the village. Richard Sanger baptised children there between 1623 and 1633, and William Ford listed him as one of the poor to whom he gifted 4d in his will of 1635.

Silas was buried at Compton in 1819. Three of the younger generation were recorded with their spouses there in the 1841 census: Elizabeth with Henry Watts, James with Sarah (née Baker), and Barnett with Charlotte (née Rowden). Elizabeth and her husband passed away before the 1851 census. The brothers were still at Compton, although 'enjoying' very different circumstances. Barnett styled himself a gentleman, while his elder brother was a pauper living with his son Frederick. They were buried at Compton within the following two years, James in 1852 and Barnett in 1853.

Barnett married late, at the age of 45, and we do not know how he spent his earlier adult years. Perhaps it was during this time that he established a sound financial standing through service to a lord, or otherwise. Another possibility that might account for his good fortune is his marriage into the Rowden family. He wed Charlotte at Walcott St Swithin, Somerset in 1819. If she was related to William Rowden of Compton, this would have represented a marriage into wealth for Barnett, as William held 746 acres in the village at the time. However, I have been unable to find a link between Charlotte and William. Barnett appointed William as an executor of his will, and made a bequest referring to him as his friend rather than relative-in-law. Moreover, although the father of each was called Joel, Charlotte and William were not siblings.

Barnett made his will nine months before his death, stating that he had no occupation, and was formerly a 'servingman.' Unlike the servingman in *Romeo and Juliet*, Barnett was certainly literate. He signed with his name and had read and understood his testament. As he had no children, he distributed £10 each to his nephews and nieces, James' children Thomas, Frederick, and Elizabeth, who had married John Parker in 1823, and to the children of his late nephew Henry Watts. He left his wife his freehold tenements in Salisbury, cottages in West Grimstead, and two leasehold cottages in Compton, occupied by himself and by Morgan Ewence, whose sister Jane was Thomas' wife. These properties were all to pass to Thomas and Frederick after Charlotte's death. She died in 1860, and by 1865 and 1866 these nephews were indeed qualified to vote by virtue of their freehold properties, Thomas' at Green Croft Street in

Salisbury, and Frederick's at West Grimstead. Nevertheless, at the time of the 1871 census they were both still agricultural labourers.

Apart from the farmers, only three tradesmen — the shoemaker Herbert Parker, mason John Plowman, and shopkeeper Lot Plowman — were listed in the Post Office Directory of 1849. Increasingly, more reliance was placed on independent local craftsmen to provide necessary services. Family businesses were prominent in the 1851 census, with sons having joined forces with their fathers. Henry Ewence now worked with his brother Morgan and father George. John Plowman with his son Henry, and Robert with his son Herbert, were masons. John Weeks made and repaired the villagers' shoes. Amongst Compton's other craftsmen, those who felled trees, sawed them up, and fashioned them into tools, wagons, or building materials, were in the majority. A team of four unmarried timber hewers with the surname Golden, who ranged in age between 15 and 45 years old, lodging in different households, attest to a phase of logging in the woods. Three sawyers, John Samson and his two sons, cut up timber into manageable planks for carpenters James Parker and his son George, together with Harry West, to make their end products. From 1861 onwards, 'agricultural labourers' began to declare their individual skills in the censuses, describing themselves as carters, shepherds, dairymen, plough boys, engine drivers, or one of a variety of woodcraftsmen — carpenter, sawyer, crib maker, hurdle maker, woodman. When a woman worked outside the home, her occupation in the censuses is more often than not entered as 'servant.' Housekeepers, who were usually family members when the householder was a bachelor or widower, are also listed. A laundress and a school mistress were recorded in 1851, and in subsequent censuses.

General stores were well established in many English villages by the 18th century. They sold groceries (most notably sugar), thread, ribbons, candles, cleaning products, brushes, tableware, gunpowder and shot, and a variety of hardware. Before this time, William Elkins was a badger at Compton in 1563, dealing in grain for food, and pedlars trudged the ridgeway to hawk their goods. It is possible that Richard Rumball, a yeoman who took on a shop from the lord at a Court Baron in 1703, supplied the villagers with general goods alongside his agricultural undertakings. The earliest positive evidence that I have been able to discover of a shopkeeper at Compton is the recital in a mortgage to Hester Marchant, named as such, in 1812. Hester had been born in the village in 1739. She died in 1826, when the parish burial record immortalised her as a servant to the Penruddocke family. I picture this shrewd spinster of 87 years shuffling around in her shop

Postcard showing the Post Office and village shop in the early twentieth century. The post box in the wall is still there today.

to her dying day. Had she trod the flagstones in the same cottage store in the centre of the village that I knew during my childhood? Could it have had such a long history in retailing? Passing through the village in 1886, W. L. noted that 'June 1616' was carved into its stonework.[320]

However, only 'smiths' shops are listed in the 1850 tithe awards, one occupied by George and another by Morgan Ewence. The village boasted two grocery stores during the late 1850s, Thomas Abraham (Abram), who had been the squire's groom at the time of the 1851 census, and Lot Plowman, a dealer, were named as shopkeepers in Kelly's 1859 directory. If they were still living in the same places named in their 1850 tithe awards, their shops were located almost opposite each other at the northern end of the village. Lot succeeded his father-in-law William Foster, who was a grocer and shopkeeper at Compton, when he made his will in 1827. He gifted his horse and cart, and all his grocery goods, to his daughter Mary, who had married Lot in 1818, and his house and cider mill to his son Thomas, who was recorded as a manservant (butler) in the Penruddocke household in the 1841 census, and as an annuitant in 1851. As the tithe awards granted the year before placed him in the house later known as the King's Elm Inn, he might have already been serving liquor on the premises. He died at Ansty in 1853, and left his estate to his son Charles Read Foster, a yeoman at Compton.

The two shops were still operating at the time of the 1871 census, run by widows Frances Abraham and Jemima (Lot's second wife), who were both likewise listed in Kelly's Directory of 1875. Only one store was recorded in the 1881 census. John Roberts had abandoned his career as a blacksmith, realising that a better future for himself lay in shopkeeping and retailing beer. His father Stephen was listed as a blacksmith in the 1881 and 1891 censuses, but was enfranchised in the 1882-1886 voter list through his occupancy of Compton Hut,* and his premises on Compton Street. John changed direction for a second time, taking on Hale Farm in Fordingbridge, where we find him in the 1901 census. His younger brother Arthur George, who had also been working as a blacksmith in Compton, took over the King's Elm, which according to the 1911 census had eight rooms, and was listed as its proprietor in Kelly's 1898 directory, while his son-in-law Eli Rose was a carrier and farmer. Thus, this blacksmith family abandoned their trade.

Uniform Penny Postage, introduced in 1840, provided the impetus for establishing post offices in villages to handle an increased volume of mail. Fovant had a post office by 1846,[321] but for Compton, the 1849 Post Office Directory only reports 'letters sent through Wilton.' Under the heading 'Post Office,' Kelly's Directory of 1855 records that Frederick Sanger received letters and dispatched them twice daily. He was an agricultural worker who lived with his father at the time of the 1851 census as already mentioned, and with his own household at the Post Office in 1861. His hours must have been extremely long, delivering the mail before labouring for the full day. In addition, he served as the village clerk. In the 1871 census, Frederick's address is specified to be the Post Office on Shaftesbury Road, where he and his wife Lydia had four children still living with them at home. The eldest was a servant, and the second eldest, Charles, who was sixteen, reported 'Sorr out of employ' in his entry. Kelly's consistently names Frederick as the sub-postmaster and village clerk between 1867 and 1875. By 1891, aged 80, he was 'retired.' His niece's husband Edward Purver succeeded him as sub-postmaster, and was likewise listed at Shaftesbury Road in the 1901 census. Within a few years, the post office had moved to the location in the village shop where I knew it, on the main street.

Eleven servants lived and worked at the Big House in 1881: a housekeeper, a lady's maid, young lady's maid, housemaid, kitchen maid, dairy maid, schoolroom maid, laundress, butler, footman, and governess. Barnett Sanger, Hester Marchant, Thomas Abram, and Thomas Foster exemplify that

---

* It was let to W.J. Roberts in 1876, who might have been related to Stephen.

Post Office and village shop with bow window in the early 1960s.

Former Post Office and village shop in 2008. The red telephone box is type K6, produced from 1936 onwards, and still has a working payphone.

a period in service could be a stepping stone to independence. It is also notable that many of the agricultural workers who broke out of that mould were interconnected through birth or marriage.

36
The Plowman Stonemason Dynasty

THE OCCUPATIONAL SURNAME Plowman, from the Old English 'ploh,' a plough, and 'mann,' a skilled man, was originally given to one who ploughed fields, the paramount medieval agricultural worker. It was also applied to men who made and repaired ploughs, that is to say, a plowwright.[322] The earliest parish record I have found for a Plowman who worked as a stonemason is dated 1728, when Nicholas Plowman, mason, acted as the bondsman at Sarah Plowman's marriage to Thomas Meadan, a tailor, at Berwick St John. The couple and their bondsman lived in Tisbury.

Archelaus, a master mason at Tisbury, apprenticed Henry Goodman in 1774 and Charles Frampton in 1775.[323] On the first occasion, the master was described as Plowman & Co, which might well have encompassed Robert, baptised in 1727, and Hercules, who fittingly lived to the herculean age of 90 years (1738-1828). What better name could there be for a builder than Hercules! I fancy he and Archelaus were brothers, with parents well-versed in Greek mythology. Archelaus married Alice Imber at Tisbury in 1739. They baptised their firstborn William in the same year. Twelve more children followed, half of them sons.

A stonemason named William Plowman, who could have been their son, and his wife Sarah christened Martha at Tisbury in 1813. At the next baptism, in 1814, their daughter's name was entered as Louisa Plowman Hazeling, her parents entered as William Plowman and Sarah Hazeling, suggesting that they were not married. Subsequent baptism records are even more curious. Thomas Hazlen Plowman's parents in 1818 were recorded as William Hazlen Plowman and Sarah, and George William Plowman's parents in 1822 as William Hazlen and Sarah. Perhaps the couple never tied the knot, and their unconventional domestic arrangements thoroughly confused the vicar. Another possible explanation is that the Hazeling/Hazlen moniker identified his place of origin, which could well have been Hazeldon in Tisbury.

Archelaus opened a green stone (limestone) quarry at Hurdcott on the estate belonging to Sir Alexander Powell in 1775. Its announcement in the

Salisbury and Winchester Journal on 19 June stated that the stone was 'to be sold cheap.' This quarry was probably where William 'Haslen,' when excavating for stone, died under a fall of soil in May 1836.[324]

Archelaus' son Archelaus, and Hercules, likely the son of Hercules, established a dynasty of Plowman masons at Barford St Martin, while Archelaus' youngest son Nicholas set up a building outfit at Compton. Nicholas married Susanna Davage. Their marriage details have not survived, but they baptised five sons together at Compton between 1784 and 1804: John, James, Lot, William, and Robert. In 1781, Nicholas was granted the lease of a messuage, garden, and orchard, part of a copyhold formerly held by Stephen Ford, deceased, for the term of his own life and that of his son John, aged one, and William, son of Nicholas Plowman of Barford, aged fourteen. After this, William died, and Nicholas' son William was added to the lease.[325]

At least three of Nicholas' five sons became masons. Lot was initially a carrier, and later added dealer and grocer to his services. No information about James' occupation is available as he was buried in 1836, before the 1841 census.

The next generation carried on the family's building trade. Robert's only son Herbert was listed as a mason along with his father at Compton in the 1851 census. Later, Robert moved to Fovant. He was probably the Robert Plowman who was repairing masonry on Wilton Church in 1866, when a ladder slipped out from under him, causing him to fall and injure his spine.[326] He was rushed to Salisbury Infirmary. Herbert had moved to Barford by the time of the 1871 census.

John's son Henry was working with his father in Compton in 1851, while his two older sons, Emmanuel and Thomas, were journeymen masons in London. A journeyman is a craftsman who has completed his apprenticeship and charges a fee for each day's work. The word 'journey' is derived from the French *journée*, meaning 'whole day.' Unlike a master, he was not allowed to employ others. He could live where he wanted, unlike an apprentice who had to live in his master's household.

William was recorded as an agricultural labourer in every census until 1861. He married Hannah Watts, James' daughter, and died in 1866. His son Joseph was also an agricultural labourer at Compton until the 1871 census, by which time his occupation had become mason's labourer. However, Kelly's Directory lists John as a mason at Compton in 1855, the year he died, likewise William in 1859 and Joseph in 1867, marking the last of three generations of Plowman masons recorded in the village.

Tithe awards were made to Nicholas, Lot, and William in February 1850. Nicholas died later that year at the age of 92, emulating Hercules. John then took over his father's lease as the next tenant in reversion. When he died, William was admitted as tenant, and had his son George added as a life. In 1857, the family surrendered their holding to Charles Penruddocke for a consideration of £50.[327] After John Hungerford Penruddocke's death in 1841, manor courts were held on behalf of his trustees until his heir Charles came of age in 1850, when the first session was held in his name. Minutes for the 1857 court reveal that this young lord of the manor was keen to take in hand as many of Compton's 99-year tenancies as possible. He not only paid to redeem the Plowman lease, but also that of Morgan Ewence's blacksmith's shop, and the premises held by William Rowden, then occupied by Edward Raymond.

The Plowmans maintained their trade longer at Barford. Archelaus, more than likely the grandson of Archelaus of Tisbury, was born at Barford in 1785/6 and died there in 1858. He employed eight men in 1851, and his three sons Archelaus, James, and William were journeymen masons.

Two other Plowman households which descended from Hercules were headed by masons at Barford according to the same census: Henry, Hercules' son born in 1793, a master bricklayer employing one man, whose own son George, a journeyman mason, lived with him, and Solomon, Hercules' grandson born in 1811, who was also a journeyman mason.

The Plowmans' enterprise had greatly expanded at Barford by 1871. As mentioned above, Robert's son Herbert had moved there from Compton. From Hercules' family, Solomon and his son Frederick and Henry's son George, who employed three men, four labourers, and a boy, were recorded as stonemasons. Archelaus, son of the Archelaus who had died in 1858, and his son Archelaus were masons who also lived together. His eldest son James described his occupation as 'Railway employing 30 men.' Business was booming. On 26 July 1871, the *Salisbury and Winchester Journal* reported that a builder, Mr Plowman — probably James — treated 40 of his workmen and friends to a substantial dinner. James was employing only four men at the time of the next census, and suddenly went into liquidation soon after, in August 1882.[328]

He suffered another, even heavier, blow in 1894, when newspapers reported that the mutilated remains of his son Frank had been found on the rails at Dinton near the Penruddocke Arms inn.[329] His suicide did not come out of the blue. That morning, he told his mother he would not be coming home again. Frank had returned from a stint in the army in India, where he contracted a severe illness which Dr Chaloner Clay believed could have been the cause of his melancholia, referring to it as *delirium tremens*, a term more often used to denote a severe form of alcohol withdrawal. Frank had had a good deal of trouble with money matters, and during a love affair with a girl he was courting at Compton. Shortly before he placed himself in the path of the 6pm train from Exeter, he had sat in the kitchen at the Penruddocke Arms for some time, and had tea with the ostler Albert Hunt. Before making his way to the inn, he had already stood by the railway tracks contemplating suicide, and told the ostler 'I cannot say I am well, as my head is sometimes dreadful, and I am not accountable for my actions; I had a good mind to stop the train at Baverstock Lane,' meaning he intended to step in front of it. John Parker of Compton was also at the inn, and testified that Frank had told him he did not think he should be about those parts for long. John advised him not to do away with himself. He walked out with Frank and left him at the crossroads, close to where his remains were found.

Only Archelaus, aged 88, and his unmarried son Archelaus, the third generation of Archelauses at Barford, were still working as masons in the village in 1911. Afterwards, I lose track of their younger namesake, born in 1857. He just disappears into thin air, which shouldn't be the case at this late date. I have not found him in civil death records, directories, electoral rolls, the census, or on the war memorial in Barford Church. Emigration is one possibility, but ships' manifests of the time are cryptic, and only list the potential passenger as A Plowman.

As well as their five sons, Nicholas and Susanna baptised four daughters at Compton between 1786 and 1801: Priscilla, Elizabeth, Susanna, and Catherine. Priscilla's story is told in Chapter 38. Elizabeth married James Thompson at Compton in 1821. They were living at Wilton in 1851, when she was a laundress and he a coachman. Catherine was buried as a child in 1804. Susanna married John Ewence, a labourer, in 1823, and her story is told in Chapter 33. According to the 1841 census, Nicholas was living in his own cottage next door to Susanna's family. He was recorded as aged 80 (he was actually between 82 and 84), and his occupation was still mason. The vicar noted him to be living in the same cottage as his daughter, and receiving a pension of 2s, before he died and was buried at Compton nine years later.

This family of masons may have been even more extensive in their time. Other masters with the name Plowman who appear in the official records of apprentices kept in England from 1710 until 1811 are Lott at Osmington, Dorset in 1786,[330] and William at Cranfield, Bedfordshire in 1776[331] and 1778.[332] In the Nadder Valley, their monopoly is unquestionable from the 18th through to the 20th centuries.

37
Vicars' Records of Parishioners: Poverty in the 19th Century

THE VICARS OF Compton left a gold mine for future generations interested in village life during the Victorian era. For nearly thirty years, from 1847 until 1876, one after the other kept an incumbent's visiting book. Reverend Frederick Gutters, who was appointed to the living in 1847, must have been the one who was inspired to start this book, which was taken over in succession by Reverends John Browne, George Masters, John R. Wood, and Arthur W. Phelps. The vicars used it as an aide-memoire for the dates of birth, baptism, marriage, and burial of parishioners, as well as their occupations, employers, and income. Family relationships and movements in and out of the parish were noted, and candid comments occasionally added. As we have seen, when it came to the Watts clan these were less than flattering, certainly nothing approaching his praise of the Lampards as 'very nice respectable people.' The fact that they were regular communicants might well have influenced him, as George Case and Frederick Sanger were also considered to be 'very nice people.' Information is not recorded in chronological order, and the text can be confusing with its multiple crossings out, and no indication of exactly when entries were made, but it is nevertheless of invaluable help in sorting out family relationships and household living conditions.

The book lists 196 family units. Some were sharing a cottage. Not all lived in the village at the same time. A line struck through their employer's name indicates that farm workers switched over between the village's farmers. Presumably, they then moved cottage, although the book does not tell us of such changes. I wonder if this caused friction between their bosses. The Keevils seem to have had a particularly rapid turnover of labour. For instance, William Hart, their engine driver, arrived in October 1868 and departed in September the following year. Another engine driver, Charles Major, was in Compton at the time of the 1871 census, but also left according to the vicar. Eli Barnett appeared in April 1876 and then went on to Dinton. It is probable that the five shepherds employed by the Keevils were not working at Manor Farm simultaneously, providing yet another example of comings and goings. Before the Keevils, the Rowdens only engaged one shepherd at Manor Farm, and the Targetts two at Naishes Farm.

Estate papers list 43 poor people in 1764, a disproportionate number of whom were widows.[333] They were given loaves of bread, meat, and £2 2s each in May during that year. The number of inhabitants receiving out-relief and occasional relief increased sharply over a period of just 10 years, from 33 in 1803 to 106 in 1813. This trend continued, reaching 120 in 1814, before gradually declining.[334] Steps were taken to pursue men who shirked their responsibilities. In 1837, an award of two guineas was offered to anyone giving information leading to the apprehension of Samuel Jefferys, who had run away and left his wife and family chargeable to the parish. His wearing apparel was described as a round frock, corduroy breeches, quarter boots and a cap.[335] A curious development taking place between censuses is illustrated by the seven paupers, including four widows, listed in 1851, with only one entered in 1861. However, poverty in Compton did not end after that year. It pervades the pages of the Incumbent's Book. Twenty-one houses were 'behabited by Poor People.' The vicar wrote that John Penny, John Keevil's shepherd, who lived at Compton Hut, was 'badly off.' His daughter Matilda, 'a little girl,' was summonsed in 1860 for stealing part of a hurdle.[336] Aged only eleven, she was ordered to pay its full value and costs or face imprisonment for seven days. John Johnson was also 'very poor.' He worked for the railway, had 'no hut,' and lived with his wife, seven children, and two other relatives in a single room. By contrast, Charles and Flora Penruddocke had nineteen bed and dressing rooms, and twelve inhouse servants providing them and their six children with a comfortable lifestyle.

The wages paid by local farmers were lower than the national average. For example, the Incumbent's Book informs us that John Fry, who was a shepherd at Manor Farm, earnt 7 shillings a week as compared with the 11-shilling average.[337] His was the normal rate for the area in 1853, when labourers in the Nadder Valley went on strike, demanding a rise to 9 shillings. Twenty years later, wages were finally increased, partly as a result of Joseph Arch visiting Wiltshire, but they were still inadequate. Thomas Harvey, fifteen years old, was employed to frighten birds in 1879, when the rifle he was carrying went off accidently and he was admitted to Salisbury Infirmary with a gunshot wound.[338] His health was to suffer for the rest of his life. Undeterred and freshly married in 1884, he learnt that his brother James' children were in the workhouse in Slough and lodged a request to take his niece Sarah under his care. This was refused because the location of the father or whether he was legally married to the mother could not be established.[339] Thomas was a patient at a convalescent Home in Christchurch in 1891. Four years later, he came before the magistrate as his daughter was not attending school.[340] He deposed in court that he had ten dependents to keep on only 10 shillings a week. The case was dismissed on the father promising to send his child to school. By 1899, Thomas' ill health left him with no alternative but to rely on parish relief for his family.[341] George Brownsey, another labourer, applied for bankruptcy in 1908.[342] His debts amounted to £15 4s 5d, while his earnings were a mere 12 shillings a week. The Salisbury County Court heard a case brought by a labourer against a Wiltshire farmer for wages due, including during six weeks' illness, in 1900. We learn from Walter Keevil, who gave evident in support of the defendant, that it was not normal practice to pay wages during illness in Compton. The judge gave judgement for the plaintiff, explaining he did so because the evidence of the defence was insufficient to prove that the general custom was not to pay farm labourers wages during illness.[343]

John Fry was the son of John senior, who hung himself from a tree, as we learnt in Chapter 29. He married Lydia Steel in 1843. Her household was overcrowded with four or five families. John deserted Lydia and their three children in 1848, and was sentenced to a month in Devizes Prison.[344] Between 1851 and 1861, they had seven more children. All except the last died in infancy, and their daughter born in 1848 was buried when she was two years old. John is recorded as residing with his wife in the censuses between 1851 and 1881 but, according to the vicar, he lived with his stepmother Maria — not because there was no room for him with Lydia: the vicar called them 'Cat & Dog: He wont give his wife anything.'

Stephen Young was employed by John Keevil. He arrived in Compton with his wife and three of their seven children at Michaelmas in 1874. Shortly before, as the vicar reports, their son George had been killed by a fall from a wagon a few days after his fourteenth birthday. Their twin daughters were in service in Salisbury, and their eldest son was in Derbyshire. Later, at the time of the 1891 census, when Stephen was 59, he, his wife, and grandchild were 'living on poor relief.'

Three brothers from the Bailey family were classified as paupers when they were admitted to Roundway Asylum between 1881 and 1918.[*] The Wilton Workhouse, built in 1837, also took in destitute persons from Compton.

---

[*] See Chapter 46.

Vicars recorded parishioners suffering from blindness, deafness, and rheumatism. Five were invalid or very invalid. We know of the two fatal cases of diphtheria in 1865, detailed in Chapter 29, from the Incumbent's Book. Two of Thomas Harvey's children suffered from the outbreak in 1897.[345]

The National Insurance Act passed in 1911 greatly improved the lot of the poor. Before this, most villages operated a slate club in the early 20th century. Members saved money by making weekly subscriptions into a common fund to meet unexpected outlays, such as doctors' fees and funeral expenses. *The Western Gazette* reported Compton's anniversary celebration of the King's Elm Slate Club on 20 May 1905. The weather was beautiful. Members marched in procession to the fete field at Compton House — also used annually for a church fete during my childhood — accompanied by the Fovant brass band.* A capital dinner was served in a huge marquee. Mr C. Penruddocke, the president, presided, supported by Master T. Penruddocke, Reverend Dudley Digges, and others. W. Langdon gave 'The Bishop and Clergy, and Ministers of all Denominations' toast, which was followed by a plethora of speeches, including one in which Mr C. Penruddocke explained that the name of the Club was derived from the tree planted when Charles II was restored to the throne, and he trusted the Club, like the elm, would flourish for many years to come. Mr Jarvis, the secretary, said they had 52 members, and had paid out £8 3s 6d pence, but still retained a balance of £8 15s 2d. The dinner was followed by dancing and sports.

Only a couple of emigrations are recorded in the Incumbent's Book. Josiah Legg, born in 1854, went to New Zealand, two of Harry Case's children to the Cape of Good Hope, and Charles Foster left to join his son-in-law in Australia in 1869. Reverend Edward Collett of Broad Chalke wrote in his Farthing Newspaper:[346]

> Long-term stability was common in country districts. In South Wiltshire there was little urban development to attract them [labourers] elsewhere. Occasionally young sons would be drawn to the colonies or the army but generally the only significant movement was the Michaelmas Flitchings in October when farm labour was replaced or re-hired in preparation for the new cycle of agricultural activity.

---

*   Compton's brass band, reported by *The Dorset County Chronicle* to have played in Shaftesbury at the annual meeting of the Dorset Friendly Society on 12 September 1854, must have disbanded in the meantime.

Nine young men from Compton joined the marines, while another was 'at sea.' One marine died in the Chinese Opium wars. Two are noted as serving in the Artillery, and one with the 29th Regiment. All five sons of the impoverished John Johnson joined the military. Two died in service. Charles Moxon signed up to the 62nd Regiment and fought in the Crimean War. He died in the trenches before Sebastopol during the siege of 1854-5.

38

The Kings and their Ironies

KING IS A common surname. Parish registers for the villages around Compton abound with Kings. They frequently moved between locations, giving me a headache when trying to trace any particular family before census information became available from 1841.

Two Kinges were baptised in Compton in the 1500s. No Kinges or Kings were recorded in the registers during the 1600s. They reappear in registries and deeds in the 1700s, predominantly branching out from a family nucleus based in Sutton Mandeville. Nearly all were farmers. One exception is John King, who took up an apprenticeship with the master cooper Christopher Abrey in 1749.[347] He came from Broad Chalke, suggesting he descended from a different line. Compton Kings rarely married on their own turf: Mary wed at Broad Chalke in 1737, Richard at Wilton in 1750, and Thomas at Downton in 1771. Just one King marriage is registered in Compton: Joseph, a yeoman, to Mary Ovens in 1793.

Charles Penruddocke leased the 'Ancient Farm' (Home Farm) to Thomas King in 1743.[348] He and his wife Margaret baptised two children at Sutton Mandeville, Mary in 1741, and Thomas in 1743, although he was born in Compton. *The Gentleman's Magazine* announced that Mary, whose father farmed in Compton, married Henry Foote, a woolstapler,[*] at Alvediston[†] in 1762.

Thomas junior, who styled himself a gentleman, and his wife Alice baptised three sons in the village between 1773 and 1777: Thomas, Henry, and Charles. He, his wife, and their eldest son followed his sister Mary to Alvediston, where there is a memorial dedicated to all three. Charles moved to the New Forest, where he was described as a landowner in the 1851 census. Henry married Sarah Martha Rebecca Pinchard at Shapwick, Dorset in 1796.

---

* A person who buys wool from a producer, grades it, and sells it on to a manufacturer.

† Alvediston lies to the west of Ebbesbourne Wake.

During the last decade that the Thomases, father and son, were cultivating Home Farm, John King waltzed into the village. He had married Mary Larkham at Sutton Mandeville in 1767. Both were resident there at the time, and had been born in that parish. They moved to Tisbury, where they baptised five children: Mary in 1767, John in 1774, Arnold in 1777, Henry in 1778, and John in 1779. Despite appearances, this last John was not named after a dead brother. The elder John survived childhood and died, aged 49, in 1823. John and Mary had two more children whose baptism entries are missing. Both are candidates for a christening in 1779. Arundel was 52 years old when she died in 1831, translating to a birth year of c 1779, and James 70 when he died in 1850, meaning he was born in 1780 or thereabouts. The registration of 'John' in 1779 is therefore likely a case of the vicar confusing a child's name with that of their father.

Charles Penruddocke's son Charles leased Naishes Farm to John King, described as a yeoman of Hasseldon (Hazeldon in Tisbury), for twelve years in 1782.[349] This lease, with some additional land, was renewed for fourteen years in 1793, and later extended again.[350] John's wife Mary was buried at Sutton Mandeville on 26 January 1820. A year later, on 1 January, the *Salisbury*

King family plaque in Sutton Mandeville Church. Credit Jack Deverell.

and Winchester Journal reported that John King of Compton Chamberlayne had died 'after a long and painful illness, greatly lamented by his family and numerous friends, Mr John King, ... aged 80 years [born *c* 1741]. He was a most worthy and honest man, and a friend to the distressed.'

John remembered all his children, bar Arnold, in his long-winded will — one wonders how the family tolerated his garrulous company during his lifetime, or had the scribe merely exploited the convention of payment by the word? Arnold could have been the 'child of John King' buried at St Martins, Salisbury in 1793 — a significant year, as corresponding with the lease extension and the marriage of Joseph, who was probably a relative. James, Henry, and Arundel were single, still living at home and running the farm. Henry is named as a farmer in a newspaper report in 1819. Henry Heasman (Haseman), a butcher in Wilton, had stolen six pigs from him, and was duly transported for fourteen years.[351] John's two eldest children were married. Mary lived with her husband William Dryer at Kingston Deverill, near Mere. John was working Search Farm in the same vicinity at Stourton, part of the Stourhead Estate on the border of Wiltshire and Somerset, where a William King had farmed a substantial holding during the first quarter of the 18th century.[352] John also made bequests to five grandchildren, who were his son John's offspring.

The will contains an intriguing proviso. Any future sons of James, his youngest son, were to inherit his share of property at Sutton Mandeville as long as they were born of the body of any wife he married except a daughter of Nicholas Plowman, mason. It would be fascinating to know the grounds for the grudge John senior bore against Nicholas. Both had lived in Tisbury before they moved to Compton. John was sixteen years older than Nicholas. One member of the Plowman family at Tisbury, William, might have sired children out of wedlock, but Nicholas was as solid as his masonry. He was a successful craftsman, a regular churchgoer, and had his own pew in the church[353] where he married Susanna and baptised their children.

Joseph King of Hazeldon was also named in John's will, which doesn't provide any clue as to their relationship. He must surely have been the Joseph who married at Compton in 1793, and may have been a brother who followed John to Compton and then left again. According to his marriage licence, he was born in 1747, making him six years younger than John. They both lie in Sutton Mandeville churchyard, where Joseph was buried in 1813.

John's eldest son John married Ann Long at Stourton in December 1806, where they baptised their boys and girls, three of each, between 1810 and 1821. One son was buried before his second birthday in 1814 and another, aged nine,

King family plaque in Compton Church.

two years later. Ann, Mary Arundel, William Francis, and Sarah Jane survived into adulthood. Their last child, Sarah Jane, was baptised on 26 April 1821. Her mother Ann, although named in the register, had died 8 months before. Turmoil engulfed the family. Both of John's parents had passed away the year before he lost his wife. One of the rare pre-1841 censuses that has survived was taken at Stourton in 1821. John's household was a meagre one, comprised of himself, his eighteen-month-old daughter, and Maria Larkham from his mother's family, who was doubtless caring for the baby and supervising their four household servants. John had sent his son William Francis and older daughters away to relatives or friends. Tragically, John followed his wife to the grave on 17 November 1823, prompting his younger siblings Henry and Arundel to leave Compton and take over Search Farm. Both were unmarried and resident at Stourton when they died during the 1830s.

Exactly four days after the burial, James defied his late father's wishes and wed Priscilla Plowman, Nicholas' daughter. The report of his marriage marvelled that it had taken place 'after a courtship of 20 years.'[354] I wonder if James was jolted into action by his brother's untimely death. Earlier on the 6th of the same month, Priscilla's sister had married John Ewence, the very labourer Thomas King sued in 1812 for leaving his employment.[355]

Two marble plaques of identical design stationed on the inside wall of Sutton Mandeville Church commemorate the family. John senior, his wife

Mary, and their children Arundel and Henry, are named on one of them. The other is dedicated to young John, his wife, and their sons John and William Dyer, who pre-deceased them.

Of the 36 Kings buried in the churchyard at Sutton Mandeville between 1680 and 1850, many were living elsewhere when they died. Like homing pigeons, coffins travelled to their final destination from Compton, Swallowcliffe, Bower Chalke, Mere, Fovant, Ansty and, in particular, from Stourton and Tisbury. Winifred Johnson, who lived near the church, recalls the funerals at Sutton before World War I, allowing us to picture how the Kings were laid to rest:[356]

> When there was a funeral all the blinds were drawn, and the children had to stay in the house until the service was over and all the mourners dispersed. One bell in the tower was rung denoting a death and if you counted the number of times the bell tolled, you would know the age of the deceased.

John's and Ann's daughter Mary Arundel remained single, and was living at Kingston Deverill until her burial, aged twenty, in 1831. Her interment there implies that she lived with her aunt and uncle. Ann and Sarah Jane both married at Stourton. William Francis eventually took over Search Farm. On 11 September 1847, when he was about to leave the farm, a notice of its sale in the *Salisbury and Winchester Journal* listed his stock as up for auction. He had a prize flock of 939 Southdown sheep, ten capital carthorses, four of which were — noteworthily — 'chestnuts.'* There was a very choice Devon cow, four working oxen, and a capital grey stallion horse 'Young Blaze.' He had 'served upwards of one hundred mares on average for the last five years and ... proved himself a good stock-getter.'

While his brother and sister left Compton to take over Search Farm, James stayed behind. He farmed at Naishes, giving up the homestead in 1845, according to an auction announcement published in the *Salisbury and Winchester Journal* on 23 August of that year. The list of his goods to be sold included a malt mill, cider mill, and press, and equipment for cheese making. What I find amazing, though, is that he had sold over 1000 sheep the year before and William Rowden at Manor Farm sold 1600 in 1852. Had Daniel Defoe been travelling during the mid-19th century, he would have seen the same vast flocks of sheep on the downs as he observed 150 years earlier. Fifty

---

* My efforts to find out why chestnuts might be special led me solely to the Cavalluna website at https://www.cavalluna.com, which stated that they are in fact not desirable!

years after these sales, numbers were in stark decline, with great-grandfather having a flock of only 700 at Manor Farm in 1899. We do not know how long farmers at Compton continued to make beer, cider, and cheese. William Targett at Naishes advertised for a single man to manage a dairy of about 50 cows, specifying that he must be a good cheese maker in the *Salisbury and Winchester Journal* on 1 February 1868. Great-grandmother was clearly pining for the cider of her native Devon, when she lamented that apples were scare around Compton in a letter home in 1909. However, my grandfather was still making cider at Ashmore during the 1930s.

The tithe awards were published in February 1850, by which time William Targett had become the lessee at Naishes. James was then the owner of a substantial house, Priory Barn, now known as the Dower House, an orchard, and four cottages occupied by tenants. He died during the autumn, and is immortalized with his wife Priscilla on a plaque fixed to the inside wall of Compton Church that is practically identical to those in Sutton Mandeville. The Compton plaque merely records that Priscilla died on Boxing Day 1833 in her 48th year, and James in August 1850, aged 70. A second memorial to the couple is embedded in the church floor. Under Priscilla's name, an epitaph celebrating enduring love reads:

> Kind Angels guard her sleeping dust
> Till Jesus comes to call the just
> Then may she wake with sweet surprise
> And in her Savior's Image rise

Under James' name, his inscription flatters him as 'A highly respected inhabitant of this Parish.'

Despite the proviso included in John's will, James' only child, Henry John, benefitted from his grandfather's estate. The Tisbury tithe awards in 1839 reveal that he, then aged 14, was the owner and occupier of woodland, holding a number of parcels of land where four members of his grandmother's family, the Larkhams, lived.

At 26, he was a fund manager and railway proprietor living at Alderbury according to the 1851 census. Two female servants resided in his household, sisters Ann and Mary Sansom, whose father John was a sawyer in Compton Chamberlayne. Ann had baptised an illegitimate son, Robert John, at Compton in 1846. He was living with his grandparents at the time of the same census, and listed as their son. At the 1861 census, aged fourteen, he was still recorded in John Sansom's household, correctly described as his grandson, and had followed John in working as a sawyer. Robert was not recorded again at Compton and later the vicar wrote in the Incumbents Book that Robert, a sawyer, was with his uncle King, adding, 'I fancy an illegitimate child of Ann's.' Obviously, an enterprising chap, he was employed at Portsea as a bicycle maker in 1881, and as an electrical fitter and tobacconist in 1891. Finally, he became a biscuit machinery fitter at Willesden, London, in 1901.

The dynamics of Henry John's household are titillating, to say the least. By the 1861 census, he had chosen the younger sister Mary for his wife. Their four children, ranging from less than one to five years of age, were living with them — as well as Ann. The entire family, including Ann, moved to Ditchampton House in Burcombe, their address in 1871. Recent sales particulars describe it as a handsome and classically proportioned Grade II listed house with charming gardens.

Henry John's date of death, 11 July 1873, and age of 48 years are engraved on the wall plaque at Compton Church under Priscilla's inscription. After the master of the house passed away, the two sisters continued to reside at Burcombe with Mary's three daughters. Ann eventually moved away, dying at Alderbury in 1886. Mary was still in Burcombe when she passed on in 1892, and was interred in the cemetery at Wilton.

Returning to the 1841 census, James' household, comprised of his sixteen-year-old son John Henry and five servants, was not the only King ménage in the village. Just four years younger than James, John King's impoverished circumstances as a labourer present a stark contrast to his own. John probably hailed from Dinton, and was most likely the rogue punished with three months hard labour in 1826 for abandoning his first family.[357] He, his second wife Mary, and three children from their earlier marriages, Jane King, Emma and William Lampard, lived in a cottage on the main street. The vicar commented in his visiting

Memorial to Pricilla and James King imbedded in the floor of Compton Church.

book that William, who was fourteen years old, 'finds his own food,' whatever that might have entailed.

Only a couple of years before the census, two of Mary's sons from her first marriage to John Lampard, John aged 19 and Henry 25, had been found drowned in the Nadder. They had been drinking at the French Horn. While the *Salisbury and Winchester Journal* reported that they had certainly not been intoxicated, it suggested that alcohol had elevated their spirits and induced them to attempt something they knew to be dangerous, as they could not swim, adding: 'The circumstances that both the drinking and accident occurred during the time of the morning service in the parish church makes the event still more to be deplored.'[358] The article called for inspections, then lacking in country districts, to ensure beerhouses adhered to licencing hours.

John King died before the next census, which lists his widow as a pauper living with William and his wife. To misquote Charles Dickens: 'It was the best of times *for some*, it was the worst of times *for others*.'

39
Oxen

ALTHOUGH WRITING ABOUT Cornwall, A. K. Hamilton Jenkin provides an enlightening general account of oxen.[359] They ploughed in a straight line, directed by word of command. During the midday meal, their yokes were removed to allow them to graze, and afterwards they returned to be re-yoked at the calling of their names. The same pairs always ploughed together, and were given matching 'handles,' such as Brisk and Lively, Goodluck and Speedwell, Lad and Virgin. Horses, however, were cheaper to keep, could plough faster, with two being able do the work of four oxen, and one man could manoeuvre them on his own, whereas both a man and a boy were needed to drive bullocks. Teams of two draught oxen were the rule for ploughing lighter soil, and four for heavier and steep land in Wiltshire. Horses began to replace them during the early 16th century, before overtaking them at an escalating pace after the Napoleonic Wars.

As I noted a degree of late usage in Wiltshire, I was curious to discover how long oxen were employed at Compton. The Haversham half-manor boasted sixteen in 1306. Draught animals were costly, and were often shared between husbandmen as a result. James Elliott owed an outstanding debt for an ox in 1579. John Elliott owned one in 1563, which made up a team with one or more from a neighbour. Wealthier tenants, who enjoyed better resources, could afford more oxen and shire horses. In 1581, Edith Marshman had the right to pasture twenty 'oxen/farmhorses,' and John Codrington thirty-two.[360] Moving forward to 1606, a decline in their importance can be gleaned from their placement after horses when tenants were ordered not to keep 'farmhorses/oxen' in the Corne Markes* after the 1st of May.[361] Two years later, a tenancy was granted with the right of common of pasture for two farm horses or oxen. No further footprint for such bovines can be found afterwards, either in manorial records or wills and inventories. Thus, I initially concluded

---

* A mark in medieval England was 'a tract of land held in common by a community:' https://www.etymonline.com/word/mark

that oxen were not employed as draught animals at Compton after the first decade of the 17th century.

A later discovery proved this deduction to be entirely false. Salisbury Museum includes amongst its collections a somewhat odd item: a pair of hooves from the last oxen used for ploughing at Compton Chamberlayne (Item SBYWM:1971.162). They were donated by Dr Clay, date from the 19th century, and have small holes drilled around their edges. These were applied to enable the attachment of ox shoes, known as cues. Bovines have a split hoof which requires two crescent-shaped iron plates, fastened with nails onto each foot. Like horseshoes, cues improve traction and protect hooves from injury and wear.

In the late 1830s, prizes were still awarded at matches held by the Wiltshire Society for the Encouragement of Agriculture to the boy aged under eighteen years who ploughed four hours in the best manner with two oxen and without a driver. The sale already detailed offering implements and stock from the Kings' Search Farm at Stourton in 1847 included four working oxen. The fact that the same family was at Naishes Farm in Compton at the same time leads me to think they must have owned the ox who plodded along on the museum's hooves. I can picture the ploughboy singing the names of his team in a lazy drawl there to keep them happy, accompanied on cold days by the tinkling of frozen urine clinging to their tails, as they slowly trudged the long way up and then down each acre — the measure that could be ploughed by two oxen in a single day. The last farm auction of working oxen in the vicinity that I have been able to find was advertised in 1905.[362] Two 'fresh' pairs were to be sold at Manor Farm, Codford St. Mary, eleven miles northwest of Compton.

40
The Targetts and their Enterprises

THE TARGETT FAMILY passed through Compton during the 19th century. Two generations, William and his son William, farmed Naishes for around 70 years with one foot in the village and the other in Barford St Martin/Baverstock, where they were proprietors of the French Horn Inn, later renamed the Penruddocke Arms. A fleeting mention of Henry Targett in the list of the poor of Compton estate, compiled in 1764,[363] tells us that the family had ventured into the village before.

According to non-conformist records of births and baptisms, William senior was born on 25 February 1787 to parents William and Mary at the British Lying-In Hospital at Endell Street in Holborn and baptised there on 8 March. The maternity hospital provided for in-patients only. It was a women's preserve, almost exclusively staffed by female midwives. A long bedrest, 'lying-in,' was prescribed at the hospital after postpartum confinement and Mary was discharged on 20 March. She gave birth there to another baby, Sarah, on 19 May 1790, who was likewise baptised at the hospital. William's occupation on the hospital register was recorded as 'stonemason' at the first and 'sawyer' at the second birth. On both occasions, the parents' 'settlement' was Tisbury.

In 1814, when William was 26, he married Elizabeth Goffe, a Barford girl. The ceremony was held in Compton, William's residence. He was recorded at the manor court in 1846,[364] and named on the tithe award. Although the award logged the farmyard where it stands today, there was no farmhouse nearby as today. William's house on the tithe map of 1848 lay at the village end of the hollow way leading up to the farm.

Elizabeth was buried at Barford in 1822. The couple appears to have been childless. William married his second wife, Sophia King, at her resident parish of Dinton in 1828, when he was described as a widower of Barford. I have been unable to find a record of William junior's baptism, possibly because of the family's non-conformist beliefs. According to the 1851 census, he was born at Dinton in 1829. His seven siblings were baptised at Barford between 1832 and 1845, when their parents' address was entered as the French Horn Inn.

William and Sophia were living at Salisbury Turnpike, Barford at the time of the 1841 census, along with the six children who had been born before that year. The vicar also supplied an address for them in Milford Street, Salisbury in the Incumbent's Book. William seems to have been extremely mobile, and open to running different enterprises. By the next census in 1851, the couple was split between their farm and the hostelry. William was recorded at Compton with 400 acres of land and 15 labourers. Four of his children resided with him. Sophia was listed at the French Horn with the occupation of 'Innkeeper's wife'; William junior, aged 22, and another son, aged 7, lived with her. They buried two daughters between the two censuses, one aged two years and the other ten months.

Naishes Farmhouse in the late 1950s/early 1960s. Note the yew hedge on the right.

The *Salisbury and Winchester Journal* reported a sudden turn of events on 21 May 1853. William, aged 64 years, was found dead in his bedroom at Compton. The coroner concluded the cause to have been a stroke. The newspaper described him as of Compton Chamberlayne, formerly of The French Horn at Barford St Martin, and much respected.

William Targett junior married Sarah Jeffery from Donhead St Mary at Tisbury in 1859. They baptised their first two sons at Barford in 1860. William, his mother, and sisters continued to juggle farming at Naishes with running the now renamed Penruddocke Arms. He and Sarah were at Naishes Farm with their six children at the time of the 1871 census. They left during the first months of 1881. William's name appears in Compton's 1881 electoral register, but he is recorded at Idmiston, farming 800 acres, in the census taken on 3 April. One son living with them was an undergraduate at Oxford, and another a medical student. William Cull, John Keevil's bailiff, was living at 'Targets Farm' according to the same census. The current farmhouse at Naishes was first documented in the 1884 edition of the Ordnance Survey map. Therefore, it must have been built either during the Targetts' tenancy after 1848, or for John Keevil after he took over the farm.

William's handwritten farm books came into the possession of his grandson's widow, who donated them to the Museum of English Rural Life in 1972.[365] The first entries are dated 1866, when William was at Naishes Farm. Some fascinating recipes for use in agriculture are included:

Foot-rot mixture
   1 pound blue vitrol
      1 pound sugar of lead
      1 pound Verdigris
      4 oz alum

Ointment for Horses heels
    Olive Oil & goulard 1 oz
    Spirits of Wine & Camphor ½ oz
    Mix and put into a tin for use

Water proofing for Boots
   3 oz Bees Wax
   1 oz Pitch
   1 oz Rosin
   4 oz Horse grease
   4 oz Beef marrow
   ½ pint unboiled Linseed Oil
   Simmer the whole in an earthen pot
      It is ready for use

For the Mange – Horse
Train Oil 1 pint
Oil of Turpentine ½ pint
powdered ginger ¼ tbs
Gunpowder (fine) ½ oz

Lord Radnor's receipt [sic] for Lumbago
1 pint raw Linseed Oil
½ oz oil of Orignum
2 oz oil of Opodeldoc
½ oz Powdered Salmoniac (Sal ammoniac)
1 oz Powdered Camphor
1 oz Laudanum
1 oz Ammonia
Mix well together

To preserve foxes heads and brushes you should dissolve corrosive sublimate in naptha (naphtha)

Other intriguing ingredients are powdered rhubarb, used in a distemper mixture, and liquorice in a condition powder for dogs.

41
WAS JOHN PIGOTT THE LAST SURVIVOR OF THE BLACK HOLE OF CALCUTTA?

IN HIS BOOK *Nadder tales of a Wiltshire Valley* first published in 1995, Rex Sawyer claims that the namesake of Piggott's Farm, John Pigott, was reputedly the last survivor of the Black Hole of Calcutta, and his tombstone can be found near the path leading to St Michael's Church.[366] This notion sprang from his interviews with Compton residents while researching his book. But is there any truth in the claim?

John died aged 58, and a notice of his death in the *Gentleman's Magazine* in June 1788 supports Sawyer's assertion:

> Lately, Captain Pigott, of Compton Chamberlain [sic], Wiltshire; one of the 23 persons who providentially escaped the fate of their fellow prisoners suffocated in the Black Hole of Calcutta in 1756, of whom, except Governor Holwell, he has not, we believe, left a survivor.

The source of this information is not given. When John's daughter Elizabeth died in 1816, an announcement in *The Bristol Mirror* on 31 August proudly depicted her as the 'daughter of Captain John Pigott, of the Royal Invalids, survivor of the Black Hole of Calcutta.'

Chris Piggot's blog of his extensive study of the Pigott family is an invaluable source of information about John.[367] Although John was English, Chris believes he had probably been born in Ireland around 1730. In 1750/1, while still in Ireland, he joined Colonel John Aldecron's Regiment of Foot, which shortly afterwards became the 39th (or Dorset) Regiment of Foot. It was stationed in Calcutta at the time of the Black Hole incident. John certainly sailed with his company on the Primus of India from Kinsale in Ireland in March 1754 to join a fleet of six ships bound for the East Indies. The vessels carried Crown troops to bolster the East India Company's forces.

The EIC had grown from a small group of investors who sought to capitalise on new trading opportunities during the 1600s into a concern that dominated the global textile trade. Along the way, it amassed a military force to protect its interests. In the early 1700s, the company maintained tenuous truces with the 'Nawabs,' or viceroys, who ruled the princely states of the Mughal Empire.

The company built Fort William in Calcutta, Bengal, to defend its factory in the city. Similar corporations from other European countries were also expanding in the region. Perceiving a threat from French business undertakings, the EIC began to build up the city's fortifications. Siraj ud-Daulah, the local Nawab, feared an encroachment on Indian sovereignty and cautioned both the French and British to cease their activities. While the French complied, the British ignored his warning. Siraj reacted by marching on Calcutta with a large army, 50 canons, and 500 elephants. What a magnificent sight that must have been! Unsurprisingly, British staff at the fort did not see it that way. They were terrified, and scuttled off to the company's ships in the harbour. John Holwell, who was employed by the East India Company to collect taxes, took command of a token force that stayed behind to guard the fort. He had no military experience, and his troop was soon forced to surrender. They were rounded up and imprisoned in its small dungeon, the infamous 'black hole,' on the night of 20 June 1756. The room was only intended to hold two or three criminals. Historians believe that 64 prisoners were incarcerated there. It became so tightly packed that the door was difficult to close. After a night of suffocation and trampling to reach a barred window for air and handouts of water, heat exhaustion had killed about 46. The exact number of survivors cannot be established because the Indians neither took a head count nor listed the soldiers who surrendered at the fort. Not all the prisoners had been registered as members of the garrison either, and many escaped between capitulation and confinement.

Researchers excluded John from a list of the British Army survivors as he was not named among the officers who accompanied the most senior of their number, who died at Calcutta following his voyage out to India. Chris Piggot suggests that John's name was missing because not long after the Calcutta incident, on 21 September 1757, he was promoted to lieutenant and transferred to the 36th (or 2nd Battalion, Wiltshire) Regiment of Foot at Madras. Chris has found a recent comment in Chelsea Hospital Records which supports his contention.

John is likely to have come to Compton after he joined the Wiltshire Regiment. He married Jane Bennett in February 1764, at which time both were living in the village. His military career progressed further in December

Path leading to the entrance of St Micheal's Church. Pigott's headstone is the first shown on the right.

1778 with his promotion to Captain in the 12th Regiment of Foot. Finally, in February 1780, he transferred to the Independent Regiment of Invalids, Portsmouth.

He was buried at Fovant on 23 May 1788. His memorial confirms that he was a captain of the Royal Invalids and the husband of Jane. Sixteen years his junior, she was buried at Fovant six years later. Both were living in Compton when they died.

What about the Pigott tombstone that truly stands next to the path in Compton graveyard? The names 'Robert Pigott' and 'John Pigott' are barely discernible through the labyrinth of lichens that has eaten into the stone. Volunteers transcribed gravestones and memorials in Wiltshire during a county-wide survey in the 1980s. The Wiltshire Memorial Inscription Index reference 93144 claims that the stone at Compton Chamberlayne bears the names of three of John's and Jane's seven children: 'Robert Pigott 10 Dec 1831, John Pigott 4 Jan 1841 and Constantia Maria King 24 Sep 1837 age 62 sister.'

Five of the siblings — John, Robert, Elizabeth, Frances and Constantia Maria — continued to live in Compton after their mother died. Elizabeth, the eldest, took over the household. She was the first to pass away, aged 50, in 1816, and was interred with her parents at Fovant. She mentioned five by name in her will, missing out her youngest brother Joseph. I have not been able to discover what happened to him. If he travelled, like his father, as a member of the military, he could have been the Joseph Puget buried at Madras in 1833. Of the other siblings, only Constantia Maria and Sophia married, and only Sophia, who left the village, had a child — Frances Sophia Newland, who lived in Luton.

Caption: Pigott's headstone.

The burials of Robert, John, and Constantia are recorded in the Compton parish register. Frances died on 25 February 1841, just over a month after John. Strangely, she is not included on the gravestone. It is possible that her name sunk below ground as the stone settled. The deaths of these five siblings marked the end of the Pigotts' sojourn in Compton and Fovant.

The assertion in Rex Sawyer's book is therefore half-true. John Pigott of Compton was most likely the last survivor of the Black Hole of Calcutta, but he was buried at Fovant.

42
Constantia's Husband or his Doppelganger?

CONSTANTIA MARIA PIGOTT wed Edmund King, a yeoman of Swaythling, North Stoneham in Hampshire, at Compton on 2 July 1819. At least four news outlets announced the marriage, including *The Gentleman's Magazine* on 2 July 1819, which described Constantia as the third daughter of the late Captain Pigott. There is no record of a baptism ceremony in Hampshire that could relate to Edmund. James and Sarah King of Swathing are the most likely candidates for his parents.

The age gap between the nuptial couple was ten years, if their Sarum Marriage Licence Bond is to be believed. The declarations recorded in the licence are very clear: Constantia's stated age is 34, indicating a birth year of 1785, and the groom's is 24, suggesting 1795. According to the transcription of Compton's parish records, Constantia was baptised in 1775, which, if correct, means that she was in fact 44 years old in 1819 — not 10, but 20 years older than Edmund. Her death details also tally with a 1775 birth. She was buried in 1837, when her age was entered in the burial register as 62, agreeing with her death certificate and gravestone inscription. However, a lease granted to her brother Robert in 1806 supports a birth date nearer to what is implied by the marriage licence.[368] She was named in the lease as a life, aged 25, which would mean she was born *c* 1781. The order of her names varies within the different parish records: Constantia Maria at her baptism, and Maria Constantia at her marriage. In the lease, her burial entry, and death certificate she is just Maria, while the inscription on her gravestone reads Constantia Maria. All of these documents certainly refer to the same lady. Unfortunately, the discrepancy in her age remains an indeterminable conundrum. One bizarre explanation might be that she was mentally or physically impaired: though she had indeed been born in 1775, whenever convenient, such as upon marriage or the grant of a lease, she could be passed off as considerably younger than her true age. However, the bondsman Hatton Figes of Romsey would have risked a significant fine of £100 (over £10,000 today) for reporting an untruth in his declaration. Even if the nuptial wasn't a sham, it proved to be a disappointment, with no sign of children born to the couple, and Constantia remaining in the village, where Edmund left only a limited footprint — concerning a hedge at the manor court in 1821, and as a member of the homage in 1823[369] — before fading away completely.

Was it Edmund or his doppelganger who was convicted of forgery at the Old Bailey on 17 August 1835? Remarkable parallels including their names, childhood homes, and occupations suggest that they were one and the same man. Furthermore, the defendant told the court he had served in the Royal Regiment of Horse Guards, which would account for Constantia's name on the British Army pension awards register for the period 1815-1827. Yet the age of 33 years which the defendant gave at his trial, supported by his statements in subsequent convict reports, suggests a different person to Constantia's Edmund, as it would bring his birth year forward to around 1802, widening their age gap still further to 27 years.

Newspaper reports of the trial[370] describe Edmund as a respectable looking man who said he was a farmer in Hampshire possessed of considerable property, and had come to London to settle the affairs of his recently deceased father. The court heard that he had been staying for some time at the Mitre and Dove Public House in Westminster, where he gave the landlord, Mr Gilpin, a cheque for £10 in the name of Thomas Smith, receiving £5 back in change. During its deposit, the bank's cashier failed to recognise the signature and refused to accept the cheque. King claimed that Thomas Smith was a solicitor practising at number 14 Lincoln's Inn Fields, whom he had employed to dispose of some land. The police were unable to locate a man going by this name at the given address. A Thomas Smith, tanner, did have an account with the branch, and was called to give evidence. He testified that the handwriting on the cheque was not his own, and he did not know the accused.

King presented his own defence. In his version of events, he was on his way to the Inner Temple to see a lawyer, Mr Hill, and met Mr Smith instead, who told him Hill had left the address. Smith also told King he was a lawyer and would help him. King explained that he was entitled to some funds and wanted advice on selling the stock, whereupon Smith produced a power of attorney which King signed for him to take to a stockbroker with whom King's family had previously done business. Afterwards, the defendant went to the Royal Regiment of Horse Guards Barracks at Knightsbridge for the night.

King was convicted and sentenced to deportation to Australia for life. On arrival aboard the convict ship *IEC Henry Porcher* in Hobart Town, Tasmania in November 1836, he maintained that he was a widower with one child, and was worth between £8,000 and £9,000,[371] begging the question of why he had not employed a professional lawyer to defend him at his trial. If he was Contantia's husband, he lied, since she died just under a year later, in September 1837, and there is no record of any child. The convict report describes his appearance and his identification of seven siblings: 'one Brother is Captain George King now Port Officer V.D. Land, William, Frederick, Augustus, Charles, 1 at Chesterfield, a Tanner, 1 at America, 1 on Sea Coast Station, 1 sister at Cape Town, 1 sister died at V.D. Land was married to Mr Hammond.'[372] It also states that he was born at Portchester, which lies within the borough of Fareham, and is located sixteen miles south of Stoneham. Evidently, George King was less than thrilled at the prospect of encountering his convict brother, and arrangements were hastily made for Edmund to serve the term of his transportation at New South Wales. He left for Sydney nine days after his arrival.

George's parents, James and Sarah, baptised George and his brother James on 15 April 1804, when, according to the Fareham parish register, George was fourteen and James thirteen years old. Their specified birth years are 1790 and 1791. Possibly, in George's case, the rationale for the baptism was to facilitate his naval career, as two weeks later he joined the Navy as a midshipman.[373] Although a baptism certificate was not required, he may well have been an ambitious young lad looking to his future. After serving for six years, he would have qualified to sit the lieutenant's examination, for which he did need to present a baptism certificate attesting to his age. He was indeed later promoted to lieutenant, and finally attained the rank of commander. In the absence of any other George King recorded in naval documents at this time, it is virtually certain that he was the port officer at Hobart. He was aged 65 when he died there in 1858, which is a suitable fit for a birth year of 1790.

There can be little doubt that George was Edmund's brother, but was Edmund Contantia's husband? George's parents were most likely the James and Sarah (née Porter) who married and died at Swaythling. James was a tanner and farmer. He signed his will on 7 July 1822, leaving his entire estate to his wife. It was proved in January 1829 by his daughters, Sarah Ann Fowler, wife of Matthias Fowler, and Rachael King, a spinster. A Sarah Ann King was one of the witnesses at Edmund's and Constantia's marriage, and a Sarah Ann King married Matthias Fowler at North Stoneham in 1824. Matthias, an innkeeper, was declared bankrupt in 1837.[374] Census returns inform us that Sarah Ann was born at Portchester in 1797/8. She died at Guildford in 1856, when she was reported by the *West Surrey Times* on 19 July to be 'the wife of Mr Matthias Fowler, formerly of the Star Inn, Guildford,' and by the *Hampshire Advertiser* on the same date as the 'daughter of the late James and

Sarah King of Swaythling, aged 58.' No baptism entry for her has come to light. Likewise for Rachel, who was buried at South Stoneham in 1875, with a stated birth year of 1810. She was linked with Sarah Ann as a petitionary creditor to her bankrupt brother-in-law Matthias.

Neither Sarah Ann nor Rachel was named among the siblings listed in Edmund's convict report, though two of those who were can potentially be identified as their own siblings. In May 1831, Sarah Ann Fowler, formerly Sarah Ann King, gave her consent as the sister and guardian of Charles King, a minor, aged 20, to his marriage to Mary Deller, who was 30 years old. The sister Edmund declared to be in Cape Town was probably the Miss M. King who prosecuted a postman for embezzlement. In October 1835, he had intercepted an envelope containing a £10 note sent to her by Mrs Fowler, the wife of Mathias Fowler, of the Angel Inn, Lymington.[375]

Edmund reported that he had been born at Portchester. George and James were born in the same borough. Ticking off possibilities for the other brothers and sisters on Edmund's list, Augustus could have been the son James and Sarah baptised at Bishop's Waltham (nine and a half miles north of Porchester) in 1801. Like his father, he was a tanner according to the 1841 census. No baptism can be found that places a William King in this clan, but there is a record for a labourer, aged 21, born at Portchester, who joined a Welsh Regiment in June 1817. Nor is there a baptism entry for a Frederick King with parents named James and Sarah in Hampshire, and I have been unable to find any other clues linking him to the family. With no identifiable baptism entry for Edmund, Sarah Ann, Rachel, and Eliza — or, indeed, Frederick and Charles — one possible conclusion is that James and Sarah did not christen their children unless and until there was a good reason to do so, though one could not marry without having first been christened. Other explanations for missing parish records have already been detailed in Chapter 24. Family trees on the *Ancestry* website claim that some baptisms relate to these children, but they are all problematic, for instance because the mother was not named Sarah, or the child was born after Sarah had died. An Edmund was christened by a James and Sarah King in Holborn, London on 21 February 1796, and the same couple probably baptised Amelia at Holborn in 1798, but why would a farming family rooted in Hampshire christen only two of their numerous children in London?

There is, however, good evidence that the sister who married a Hammond was Eliza. She wed James Meers Hammond of London, merchant, in 1823. A notice in the *Salisbury and Winchester Journal* on 9 June states that she was the second daughter of Mr James King, tanner, of Swaythling. Eliza had a miserable life, which is worth relating in order to appreciate the darker side to successful venturing families of the early 19th century. Again, Chris Pigott's blog provides the details.

She and her husband arrived at Hobart in April 1824. She probably gave birth to her daughter on the voyage, and returned to England eighteen months later. Her second child was born in September 1825. Both of Eliza's parents died during her sojourn at home, as did her two children, who were buried at Brixton on 25 February 1829. Her husband chartered the ship *Sarah* in February 1828 to transport goods and some passengers from England to Tasmania. It was commanded by his bother-in-law Captain George King, and anchored at Hobart in June 1828. It set sail again, bound for England, in February 1829. Eliza and James with their daughter Maria, born in England in 1827, returned to Hobart in January the following year,[376] when Eliza gave birth to her fourth child Eliza onboard five days before reaching land.[377] James returned from England in December 1829 and, 'very much indisposed with the effects of a fever taken at St Jago, from which he never recovered,' died six months later, aged 26.[378] Baby Eliza died on 23 April 1831, aged 15 months, and her mother followed her to the grave 3 weeks later, on 16 June, at the age of 31. Thus, between 1829 and 1831, the entire family was wiped out, save for the orphaned four-year-old Maria.

The circumstances of Eliza's death are strange to say the least, as revealed by reports of her inquest in *The Tasmanian* on 18 June 1831 and *Sydney Gazette* on the 28th. It was held 'to investigate the circumstances attending the premature and distressing death of Eliza Hammond.' A clergyman, Reverend Richard Yaldwyn, had removed Eliza from her residence in Hobart against doctor's orders, taking her to New Norfolk two days before her death. The reverend gentleman was the brother of George King's wife Harriet. He had become Eliza's lodger shortly after his arrival in Hobart three months before.

Three years later, in 1834, the case of Underwood vs King concerning his will came before the Supreme Court in Hobart. Newspaper reports, for example in *Trumpeter General* (Hobart) on 19 December 1834, explain that he had made one — but had not signed it —immediately before his death, which left all his property to 'Mrs Maria Underwood, a stranger, and passing by his own relatives.' A Mr J. C. Underwood had announced his intention to sell Eliza's residence by auction on 6 October 1830. The particulars of this sale described the property as one of the few residences in town suitable for a respectable family. Newspaper reports do not identify the defendant in the case, but we can safely surmise that it was George. His wife and the deceased were two of Richard Yaldwyn's nine children, mentioned in his will with codicil proved in February 1808. Richard had been the squire of the Blackdown estate in Lodsworth Sussex, and had lived with Martha Searle, the daughter of one of his tenants, for some years before he married her in London in 1797. Clergyman Richard, their eldest son, was born before the wedding, and Squire Richard named his youngest son, born after the couple married, as his heir. However, like the other children, Richard senior did receive £2000 under his father's will.

Edmund King obtained a Ticket of Leave[379] in February 1845 on condition that he remain in the District of Port Macquarie. It was cancelled in November 1850 due to his absence from the region, and on 2 May 1851 *The New South Wales Government Gazette* reported him as illegally at large. Details of his place of birth, age, and the ship he arrived on are consistent with earlier information. However, he is described as five feet eight inches, of a fair complexion, with light brown hair, light blue eyes, the top of his forehead bald, forehead high, nose long. By contrast, his description at the time of his arrival in Hobart in 1836 was five feet eleven and three-quarter inches, dark complexion, and dark hazel eyes. Only the long nose and high forehead, bald at the top, of 1851 match his depiction in 1836.

The transported Edmund King's story now potentially becomes even more bizarre. An Edmund King testified at a coroner's inquest into the death of one Mary Sadler, a widow, in January 1849.[380] She had been engaged to him, but failed to appear at the wedding because she was murdered by the man he had sent to fetch her. Edmund deposed that he was George Wyndham's superintendent at Glendon Brook, which is in Hunter Valley. A credible link to our Edmund is George's birthplace at Dinton, neighbouring Compton. He was baptised there by his parents William and Latitia of Dinton House in 1804. George emigrated to Australia in 1827, and founded a vineyard in Hunter Valley.

Whether the convict Edmund King was Constantia Maria's husband hangs in the balance. I can only present the known consistencies and discrepancies for you, the reader, to form your own opinion.

Constantia Maria's epitaph is likewise steeped in contradiction. She succumbed to dropsy — an example of contemporary doctors' tendency to report a primary symptom rather than the cause, as they did not then have the means to diagnose the underlying reason. Also called oedema, it denoted water retention and consequent swelling. She most likely died from cardiac dropsy, today known as congestive heart failure. Frances informed the registrar of her sister's death at Compton in 1837. On the death certificate, Constantia's name appears as Maria King, and her age as 62 years. These details accord with her burial record. However, a second entry in the Wiltshire Memorial Inscription Index, with the reference 93141, names her as Constantia Maria Pigott. Such reference numbers refer to a single stone or memorial. Therefore, two reference numbers would usually indicate two separate headstones or inscriptions, but in this case there is a double entry for a single one inscribed with different surnames. Reference 93144 includes Constantia's age and identifies her as a sister of the other people memorialised on the same stone, suggesting that this entry with the surname King represents the correct transcription.

I am indebted to and thank Chris Pigott for information gleaned from his blog at https://pigott-gorrie.blogspot.com/search?q=Compton+Chamberlayne, email exchanges with him, and through our co-operative research.

43
George William Wyman the Thatcher

Parents turning up at your school was decidedly not the norm during the early 1960s. Angst-ridden parent-teacher evenings belonged to the future. In any case, on this unprecedented visit, they came in the morning. I had been on what today is called a sleepover with a classmate. My parents had wanted to forewarn me, worried I might hear on the bus home that 'the farm' had burnt down. They told me that one of our barns had been destroyed by lightning during the night, but the other barns, farmhouse, and animals were all safe.

I learnt what I know about that night from my sister Valerie. She and our parents had been woken up by a storm. Piercing thunder had frightened our mother, and they gathered in the kitchen. Suddenly, Brindle, our boxer dog, leapt from the floor in front of the Aga, as if in pain. She must have felt a shock from the lightning strike on the barn, which also brought the telephone lines down. As flames triggered their destruction, my father drove the two miles to Barford St Martin and raised a friend to call the fire brigade. Five engines arrived. Forty men fought all night to quell the blaze. My mother gave them breakfast in our kitchen, where they left sooty silhouettes on the walls they leaned against.

Only the day before, the village thatcher, George William Wyman, had finished refurbishing the roof of the barn. One day, he stood back and admired its neat golden crown with the pride of an expert craftsman, and the next, he wept at its disintegration into a heap of black straw and twisted collapsed beams. This memory tugged at my heart strings and prompted my curiosity about thatching in the village, as I wondered how George William became the last man in Compton to be skilled in this artisan craft.

Thatch, with its varieties of long straw, water reed, and combed wheat reed, was the only roofing material available in most of the English countryside until the late 1800s, when tiles and slate began to provide alternatives. The combed wheat reed used in Compton was traditional in the wetter West Country. It is tougher than the puny wheat bending with the wind in today's fields, which with genetic modification and pesticide treatment is now too weak to use for roofing. While thatch is weather-resistant and effectively insulates buildings, a spark escaping from a chimney quickly sets it alight, and burning thatch is difficult to extinguish.

Although tiles and slate are practical for new buildings, converting a thatched roof to brace those different materials is expensive. The pitch has to be adapted, and new rafters and purlins of sawn timber substituted for their rough timber supports. A thatched covering was economical, and became known as the 'poor man's roofing' in the Victorian era. By contrast, during the last 30 years it has become a luxury. Today, four cottages still sport a straw roof

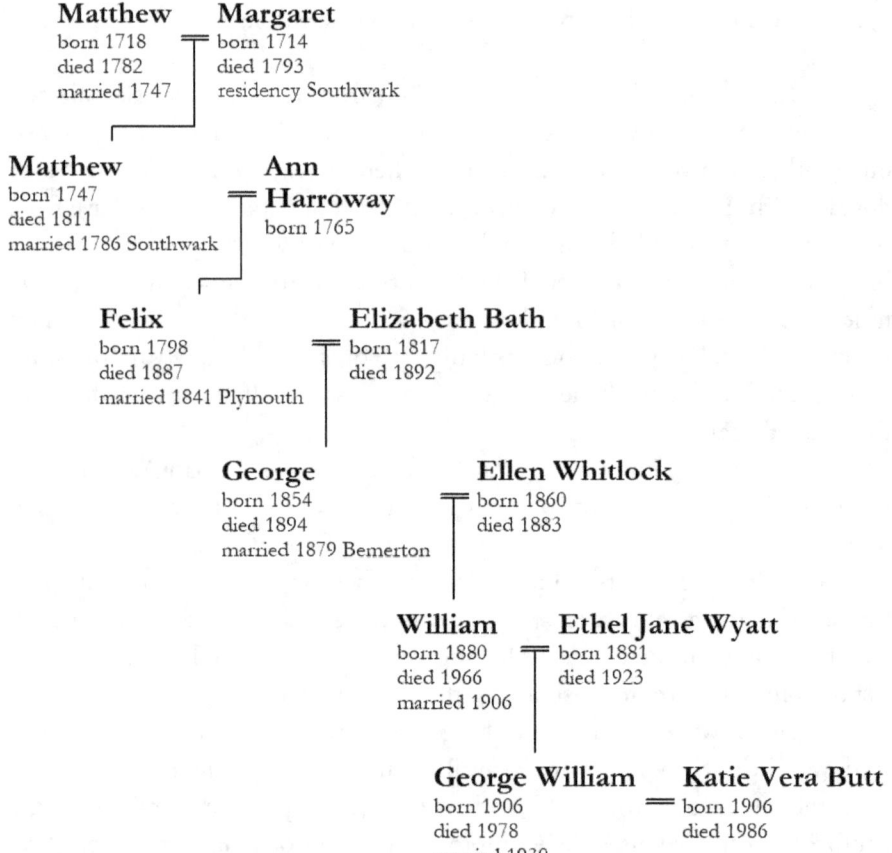

William Wyman.

in Compton: Turnpike Cottage, Forge Farmhouse, Piggotts, and Camel Cottage.

Thatching has changed very little over the centuries. The husbandman William Elliott, who we met up a ladder thatching Joan Oake's roof in 1600,* worked with the same mallet, shears, and leggett — a tool for tapping the thatch's ends flush — still used today, though leggetts were then made from wood rather than steel. Thatching cottages, barns, and ricks was a general skill enjoyed by self-sufficient Elizabethan husbandmen.

No thatcher was recorded at Compton in any census before George Wyatt's entry in 1901. That same year, John Ewence, Henrietta's illegitimate son, was a sexton and thatcher at Bemerton in Wilton. Before he left Compton in 1874, he had been employed by the squire as a 'labourer.' Either he was already a thatcher or he mastered that skill, which required at least five years of learning, on the job at Bemerton.

George William's father, William Wyman, was born at Bemerton in 1880 to parents George and Ellen. George had been baptised by Felix, described as a hawker, and his wife Elizabeth at Fisherton Anger in February 1856. Felix was an interesting chap in his own right, but we should first take his background into account. His grandparents, Matthew and Margaret, were non-conformists who married at Southwark in July 1747.† They were both interred at the Maze Pond Baptist Burial Ground there, which is now completely covered by Guy's Hospital. Matthew died in 1782 and Margaret in 1793. Their son Matthew was christened at Huntingdon in July 1747. In his early twenties, his father apprenticed him to the joiner William Cook of London, who was a carpenter.[381]

Matthew junior was 39 when in August 1786 he wed 21-year-old Ann Harroway of Camberwell, Southwark. They baptised six children in the

---

* See Chapter 12.

† Information from Desmond Wyman's notes.

George William in front of number 1 Post Office Cottages.

borough between 1789 and 1809, including Felix in 1798. Felix Wyman's unique name made him easy to trace. He was named in newspaper reports, for instance in *New Lloyds Evening Post* on 11 January 1832, as having been present at the infamous Bristol riots of 29-31 October 1831, and indicted together with Samuel Browning for stealing a pair of sheets and several items of wearing apparel belonging to a Mr Richardson during the fires in Queen Square on 30 October. The pair were also proved to have been active during the violent demonstrations. Their defence, also pled by others who had been tried earlier, was that they had found those articles in the streets. The jury returned a verdict of guilty, which condemned them to two years' imprisonment and hard labour.

Was Felix present to protest for electoral reform, or had he just fallen in with a mindless mob intent on looting and causing trouble? The Bristol riots sprang from calls for reform to curtail the influence of the Tory landowning class. Pro-reformers' demands climaxed in 1830 with the death of its strongest opponent, King George IV, and accession to the throne of the more moderate William IV. Meetings to tackle the general unfairness attached to voting rights were held throughout the land. Groups advocating change sought to extend voting rights, liberating them from the dominion of powerful landowners who bought votes for their candidates, and to eradicate rotten boroughs. While these constituencies with their tiny electorates could each return a representative to Parliament, others, such as Bristol, a rapidly expanding prosperous port, were restricted to only one MP in the government. The city's population had doubled during the previous 30 years, with only 6,000 of its 104,000 inhabitants allowed to vote. What's more, its local authority was notoriously corrupt.

The governing Whig Party managed to pass the Second Reform Bill in the House of Commons. However, the House of Lords, led by the Tories, rejected the bill in September 1831. An infuriated public erupted in violent protest, but nothing could equal the massive destruction wrought by the rioters, arsonists, and looters in Bristol.

Sir Charles Wetherell, a magistrate, opposed the bill and declared in Parliament that the city was against it, whereas 17,000 of its inhabitants had signed a petition in support. Wetherell was due to open the assizes on the 29th of October, and planned to celebrate the legislation's defeat with the bishop and other notaries, despite being warned about local grievances against him. Angry pro-reformists stoned his carriage as he made his way to Mansion House in Queen's Square — the seat of the mayor. The next day, a mob gathered and set fire to the houses of wealthy merchants, turning the square into a raging inferno. They burnt down over a hundred buildings in the city including three prisons, where they released hundreds of inmates.

The riots were suppressed after three days, on the 1st of November 1831. Rather than portraying the participants as drunken, debauched louts, the press primarily blamed the authority's mishandling of the crisis, and Wetherall in particular for provoking the populace. The city's mayor was tried for his negligence in failing to take efficient measures against the activists, and was acquitted. Military commander Lieutenant-Colonel Thomas Brereton was court-martialled. He was suspected of sympathising with the pro-reformers, and effectively allowing the riots to occur. Initially, he refused to order the dragoons to open fire, then, under pressure, gave the order to charge into the crowds in Queen's Square with swords drawn. It is thought a number of the rioters were killed, and many more wounded. Brereton shot himself through the heart before his trial was concluded.

The government feared the insurrection might spark a revolution resembling the suffrage mutiny that had forced the king of France to abdicate. There were only a few show-trials and floggings, possibly to avoid inciting the public to even more unrest. Nevertheless, Felix and his pal were lucky. Four insurgents were hanged, and eighty-eight transported or imprisoned. A Third Reform Bill passed both Houses of Parliament and received Royal Assent on 7 June 1832.

Felix married Elizabeth Bath at Plymouth in 1841. I have not found him in either the 1841 or 1851 census. They were living at Fisherton Anger, which now lies within the bounds of Salisbury, in 1861 and 1871, with their children George (born 1854), Henry (1856) and Felix (1860). In 1872, Felix junior also had a brush with the law. The *Salisbury and Winchester Journal* reported on 7 December that he and William Goodwood were cautioned for playing marbles on the pavement to the annoyance of the inhabitants of Butcher Row and Fish Market. In April 1877, young Felix, together with John Tilley and Herbert Coombs, was summoned for loitering on the platform at Fisherton station, interfering with luggage, and annoying passengers. According to the *Western Gazette,* an employee of the railway company had repeatedly told them to go away, but they only swore back at him. They pleaded guilty and were fined.

Felix's and Elizabeth's eldest son George was employed as a bricklayer's labourer in 1881. He had married a girl from Pitton, Ellen Whitlock, at Bemerton on 4 August 1879. The young couple lived on Wilton Road at Fugglestone St Peter with Ellen's widowed father William, her brother William, who also worked for a bricklayer, and their eight-month-old baby William.

Ellen died when William was just three years old. Soon after, George married a Compton girl, Barbara Anne Fry. They lived in Salisbury and had 5 more children before George died of pneumonia at the age of 40 in 1894. His occupation, as recorded in his death certificate, was stone sawyer. Consequently, Barbara had to find work to support herself and the children. She was entered in the 1901 census as a charwoman, still living in Salisbury, along with her three youngest children and a four-year-old illegitimate daughter. Her oldest two children had already moved out to work. Ethel, at age fifteen, was a house servant in a merchant's house in Wilton, and Charles, aged thirteen, was a shepherd's boy at Compton, living with his widowed grandmother Ann Fry.

Despite Anne's hard life* and the vicar's assessment of her as a very delicate woman, this generous soul also took in her step-grandson William Wyman. Thus, William's first appearance in Compton is as a twenty-year-old agricultural worker at Turnpike Cottage in the 1901 census. He was no doubt assisting his step-uncle James Fry, who was a shepherd living in the same cottage. Anne died at the age of 78 in 1909. William left to marry, and James and Charles were joined by Charles' younger brother Frank and sister Edith at the time of the 1911 census, which logged her as a 'General Servant (Domestic),' with the 'Employment' column left blank, indicating that she was housekeeping for the three unmarried shepherds.

---

* See Chapter 29.

Van Cottage, newly thatched: George Cross in his book Suffolk Punch, published in 1939, refers to Van Cottage as much-photographed and 'a proud example of Wyman, the village thatcher's, art.' It now has a slate roof.

William wed Ethel Jane Wyatt at Compton in 1906, and George William was born shortly afterwards. They were living at Well Cottage in 1911. William was a general labourer for George Aylward at Naishes Farm. He was not described as a thatcher in any census before the 1939 Register, when he and Ethel resided at number 1 Post Office Cottages. George William's occupation was entered as both farm labourer and thatcher. Unlike Compton's blacksmiths and shoemakers, neither father nor son is named as a trader in the Kelly's directories. George William Wyman died in 1978, and was the last village thatcher at Compton.

44
Naishes Farmyard

THE TWO YARDS at Naishes Farm appear to have been built in stages. An aerial photo taken around 1960 shows four buildings with thatched roofs. Three, which were timber-framed, formed the sides of the original oblong yard, bounded by a stone wall on its east side. Only the structure running across the north side was standing when the 1769 Compton estate map was drawn, which names it 'New Barn.' The buildings along the other two sides appear on the 1848 tithe map, which likewise depicts only one farmyard. A carthouse on this ground plan to the east of the yard, at the other end of the track that runs down to the A30, was no longer there when I was a child.

The buildings in the second (back) yard, constructed later, formed an L-shape. My father used them exclusively for his dairy cows and calves. On

Aerial view of the farmhouse and farmyard at Naishes, dating from the early 1960s.

Diagram of the farmyard. Credit Sophie Kari.

its north side, the fourth thatched building was made of stone and adjoined a barn with an open front, a linhay in local dialect — also stone-built — dating to about 1860. At its west end, a long low stone construction with a corrugated iron roof, used as a milking parlour and for calves, ran southwards. The thatched building with its two stable doors, split horizontally, also housed calves, but was probably originally subdivided into stables for horses, and the linhay used as a cart shed. The buildings shown in the aerial photo are all shown on the 1890 Ordnance Survey Map and were still standing when I was a child, but only the linhay survives today. Open on its north side, it has a slate roof supported by queen posts. I can vividly remember climbing into the hayloft located above one half to access the main loft that extended the length of the thatched calf shed. There, I would hide if I had been naughty, and wanted to cry with regret undisturbed. Another point of entry to the main hayloft ran up some steps on its south side. An open window on the north side provided irresistible opportunities for playing dare-I-jump-down.

The wood-framed buildings in the old yard were used for different purposes. The 'New Barn' had a large doorway at its centre on the north side, extending from the floor to its eaves. Farm machinery was kept there. The thatched barn and corrugated iron sheds on the west side housed animals, including a bull who had one end of a chain attached to a ring in its nose. The

The threshing and granary barn after it collapsed in the late 1960s. Note the staddle stones supporting the granary section.

other end hung from an overhead bar in the yard. This allowed it to pass in and out of its enclosure — but only in a straight line. Corn was processed and stored in the barn on the south side. One end was supported by mushroom-

View of the front of the 'New Barn.' Ray Kerley is seated on the tractor. Behind it, the end of the thatched barn that housed calves can be seen alongside the track leading to the Hollow which runs down to Compton village.

shaped staddle stones, and had originally been the granary. A door opened out onto a stone platform. The other end of the barn was built on a sandstone plinth, and had a central threshing floor with double doors on either side which had to be wide enough for packhorses, or wagons, bringing sheaves from the ricks to pass through. In our time, there was a corn drier here, which seemed dusty enough to us when operated. In past times, human threshers suffered more. They earned their wages during the winter by beating out grain with flails, while the chaff was blown away by a cross-draught, ingeniously created by opening the opposing doors on either side of the barn. The clouds of dust that engulfed the threshers, combined with the motes breathed in during haymaking and harvesting, lethally damaged the lungs of so many of those who were employed in agriculture.

Farmyard at Naishes, showing the roundhouse, c 1950.

A roundhouse, or gin gang, was tucked into a corner adjoining the threshing barn. Formerly, the gin (short for engine) in the threshing barn had been powered by a horse in the roundhouse ganging, or walking, around and around for hours on end. The fruits of its labour reached the threshing machine through a hole in the wall via a drive belt that linked a shaft, which was attached to its body by cogs and a spindle, to the gin. This system was followed until stationary steam engines known as 'barn engines' were developed during the first twenty years of the 19th century. They in turn gave way to portable engines fitted with shafts, with the horse's new task being to pull it to the harvest field where it would drive a thresher, and gin gangs fell out of use.

The lightning strike described earlier heralded the demise of the picturesque thatched wooden buildings encircling our farmyard. A few years later, the threshing and granary barn collapsed of its own accord. When we left Naishes in 1978, only the oldest of the four thatched barns — the one titled 'New Barn' on the 1769 Compton estate map — and the thatched calf shed were still standing. Sadly, all that remains of the New Barn that had so impressively survived for over 200 years are parts of the wall it once stood on. Our harmonious thatched outbuildings have been replaced by a jumble of iron-clad Dutch barns, makeshift sheds, and doors that close with a clang instead of a thump.

The barns of the other thatched farmyard in Compton, Manor Farm, endured longer. The last one was pulled down in July 1981. In his weekly letter to me, my father told me he had seen a sizeable load of beams being hauled away, and thought someone must have bought them: 'There is now a large heap of old thatch and broken wood, which I expect will be burnt on some one's washing day.'

45
The Wyatts: Sawyers and Hurdle Makers

WHY DID WILLIAM Wyman become a thatcher? This question set me on the trail of the Wyatt family. William's wife was the daughter of John Wyatt, whose brother George was the first man described as a house and rick thatcher at Compton — but not until the 1901 census. The Incumbent's Book tells us that he was employed by the squire. In the 1881 census, his occupation is recorded as general labourer, and sawyer in 1891. In 1911, aged 71, he was still practicing his craft, climbing long ladders, while lining up his nephew-in-law William Wyman, who was still labelled a general labourer, as his successor.

The Wyatt family came to Compton from Fovant. James Wiett (Wyatt) was baptised there in 1783. He married Hester Ames (Emm), sister of the unfortunate Charlotte (Ames (Emm)/Ewence/Wilkins), at Fifield Bavant in 1808. The bride and groom were both living at Fifield before they married, swelling its population to nineteen adults, just one more than noted in the Domesday Book. Today, the village is still the smallest in Wiltshire. Weddings were not comparable to our present extravaganzas, but a more magical rural location than the village's medieval church could hardly be imagined. This tiny stone and flint checkerboard gem stands alone, elevated above fields stretching as far as the eye can see. Access is gained by trudging through a farmyard. I regularly attended services there with my mother, who loved the drive up from Fovant to the crest of the hill. The single-track road was lined with thin fence posts, and carved a straight line through seas of sheep grazing on the open grassland as faintly as a thread of gossamer, summoning up an age of bygone tranquillity.

In the early years of their marriage, James and Hester baptised three children at Fovant: Hannah in 1808, Aaron in 1810, and James in 1811. They moved to Compton sometime before 1815, where they baptised five more, including Mary Ann in 1819 and John in 1825. The vicar noted that five adults and five children, including their grandchildren, lived in two rooms.

Aaron became a shepherd at Naishes Farm. His last child with his wife Elizabeth was baptised at Compton on 23 March 1851. Elizabeth, aged 36,

Fifield Bavant Church, June 2023.

and much weakened after bearing eight children in the space of ten years, was buried soon after on 1 June. Aaron then moved to Wilton, where he was living with three of their children in 1861. His situation deteriorated. By 1881, he was an inmate at Wilton Workhouse.

Fate also dealt harshly with his elder sister Hannah. She managed to give birth to only one child. Three ceremonies at Compton Church recount the story of her short life. She married Charles Frampton on 5 October 1829, baptised their daughter Elizabeth on 6 February 1830, and was buried at the age of 21 on 10 March. Charles deposited Elizabeth with her grandparents, James and Hester, and immediately remarried. He was living in Britford with his new family of five children at the time of the 1841 census. Both he and his wife died before the next population count, when their three youngest children were recorded as orphans at Alderbury Union Workhouse. These were hard times. Left alone, and without relatives like James and Hester or Ann Fry who were willing or able to take them in, young and old alike found themselves abandoned in the poorhouse.

James' and Hester's third child James had better luck. He married Elizabeth West at Compton in 1836. She was nineteen years old, and subsequently gave birth to three boys and nine girls. By the time the last was born, she was 47. This infant died after ten months. James' and Hester's eighth child John wed Elizabeth Ward, who was of a nervous disposition according to the vicar.

James senior died in 1852. His occupation was farm labourer according to the 1841 and 1851 censuses, as was that of his sons John and James until 1871. By then, John had decided he was really a sawyer. He initially worked in the squire's yard, but left, and was recorded at Wilton with the same occupation ten years later. James and his son John literally came out of the woodwork at Compton in the same census, when James reported himself a woodman and John a crib maker. A second son, George, was still a labourer, but likewise resurfaced as a sawyer in 1891. He had probably taken over his uncle John's job as he was employed by the squire, whereas his father and brother worked at Naishes Farm for William Targett. No doubt, while John Sansom was styled a sawyer in the 1841 census, joined by his sons in the two which followed, the Wyatts throughout this time had been serving the squire and farmer as employees, sawing wood, making hurdles for restraining sheep, and cribs for feeding them.

One of John Sansom's sons, James, spotted an opportunity. Coaches stopped at Compton every day, travelling three times to Salisbury, twice to Shaftesbury, once to Yeovil daily, and to Wincanton three times a week, and carriers also passed through every day, according to Kelly's Directory of 1855. Why not then offer a local transport service himself? James was listed as a carrier in Kelly's Directory of 1867, and in the two subsequent censuses. He took villagers to Salisbury market and back on Tuesdays and Saturdays, in direct competition with Lot Plowman who, according to the Post Office Directory, was already running such a service in 1859.

James and John Wyatt ultimately set up on their own. They might have taken advantage of an opening created when the Sansom family gave up their primary occupation of cutting wood. James Wyatt had become a wood merchant by 1891, and John was entered as a hurdle maker in Kelly's Directory of 1898. James' three youngest daughters, Jane, Sarah, and Eliza, also seized the chance to escape a life of domestic service and became dressmakers. Some years later, Sarah and Eliza, still spinsters at the ages of 44 and 46, ran a grocery shop in Salisbury.

John had married Sarah Card at Tisbury in 1868. Olive May, the youngest of their seven daughters, was still living at home at the time of the 1911 census, working as a post office assistant in Compton, while her only brother William was a sub-postmaster at Dinton. He had been the proprietor of Compton's post office and shop in 1889. The income from delivering the village's letters was probably quite meagre, since he logged himself as working with his father making sheep cribs in 1891. Due to a subsequent fall in demand for cribs, he had switched jobs to become a foreman at Naishes Farm by 1901, before moving on to Dinton with his wife Frances.

The Salisbury Times described William's marriage to Miss Frances Emma Pringle on Christmas Eve 1898:[382] 'The church was beautifully decorated for the double event of the marriage and Christmas day and as the newly married couple left the church a merry peel was rung on the bells.' Frances was a former mistress of the village's Church of England School, which Kelly's Directory of 1898 states had the capacity to educate 60 children, and an average attendance rate of 33. She received a handsome silver biscuit box as a wedding present from seventeen families whose children attended the school, including two of my great uncles. Biscuit boxes, invented by George Palmer of Huntley & Palmers, which today claims to be Britain's most famous biscuit company, had become fashionable with the rise in popularity of afternoon tea. William was the organist at Compton Church, but it was the vicar's wife Mrs Digges who played for this occasion.

Despite their ages — George then being 71 years old and John 67 — the brothers were still practicing their trades at the time of the 1911 census. George's occupation, as in 1901, was entered as thatcher, and John's as woodman. In her recollections of Compton dating to 1913, Hilda Kerley describes John as an adept craftsman when it came to making spars, hurdles, and sheep feeding cribs. She also brings to life cosy scenes at the winter services in St Michael's

The Wyatt family. From left to right: John Wyatt, his son John, his grandson, and Sarah Wyatt, his wife. Reproduced with kind permission from Alan Clayton.

Church. A large stove in the middle of the transept coddled the parishioners. At the back, William's successor Mr Fry played the harmonium, surrounded by his family who led the singing — except for one. Some unfortunate soul would have had to energetically work its wooden lever to pump air through the reed into the main bellow.

The Wyatts' story epitomises Compton life at the turn of the century — large families at a time when childbearing was still life-threatening for women, a social safety net limited to the workhouse, a farming community heavily centred on sheep, village thatchers gainfully employed, well-attended church services, a post office, village school, and weekly transport to Salisbury on market days. The village also boasted a shop, pub, and blacksmith's forge. For better or worse, none of these, except for a daily bus service to Salisbury, lives on in Compton today.

Hurdles

Wattle hurdles were mainly used as portable fencing panels for penning sheep in their folds at night, and when they were being dipped or sheared, additionally offering protection from wind and rain at lambing time. My grandfather's brothers discovered that they could also be adapted into a substitute stretcher when they carried him home after a shooting accident at Manor Farm that lost him his right thumb.

Hurdles were especially practical because the split (riven) hazel panels were light enough to be carried on one's shoulder four at a time. Their rods were harvested from coppiced trees, which were then cut back to ground level on a seven-year rotation system to stimulate regrowth of 'spring wood' from the stump, or stool. This fast-growing malleable timber was suitable for making posts, handles, thatching spars, baskets, furniture, and faggots, which were tight bundles of brushwood used to light fires and lay the bases for hay ricks. A number of copses, mainly bordering the Nadder, are recorded at Compton in the manorial rolls and 1597 survey. The need for them and a village hurdle marker evaporated with the demise of the sheep-and-corn farming system and industrialisation.

46
Annie Gets her Man

COMPTON CHAMBERLAYNE WAS at the centre of a court case which captivated the public's interest and was reported in several national newspapers in 1889.[383] Annie Bailey was charged with making a false declaration to the marriage registrar. Her uncle John Wyatt gave evidence for the prosecution. Annie was the daughter of his sister Maria. Maria, John, and another sibling named Mary were born one after another in 1844, 1845, and 1847. Annie Bailey was determined to get her man, whatever her uncle and the vicar had to say about it.

In July 1889, when she was Reverend Mangin's housemaid at East Knoyle, she told him that she had given notice of her intended marriage to the Registrar of Mere, and asked the vicar to conduct the wedding at his church. All was fine, until he heard indirectly that the reason she had gone to the registry office, rather than having the traditional banns published, was to avoid 'talk' in her home parish of Compton Chamberlayne. He contacted Reverend Digges there, who reported that her intended, his parishioner William Clapp, was her uncle-in-law. After hearing this alarming news, Reverend Mangin spoke to Annie on 11 August, this time with William in tow, and told them he could not marry them because their relationship fell within the prohibited degrees of affinity listed in the Book of Common Prayer. They agreed to give up all thought of a nuptial.

Why, you may ask, as William did of the vicar, could they not wed, when first cousins were married in church all the time? The discrepancy — highlighted by Annie's own parents being first cousins — could not have escaped him. A long list of forbidden marriages had been drawn up by the Church of England in 1560. Surprisingly, it did not include first cousins. The general public only became anxious about such unions after Charles Darwin criticised 'perpetual self-fertilization' in his 1862 book on orchid fertilization. Orchids would otherwise have been of little consequence, but Darwin, who had himself married his first cousin, added that 'marriage between near relations is likewise in some way injurious.' Cathy Day, in her study of first cousin marriages, found there is a very small increase in mortality and morbidity for the offspring. In her article 'Prevalence of Cousin Marriage,' published in October 2011 in the *Wiltshire Family History Society Journal*, she states that Wiltshire cousin marriage peaked during the middle of the 19th century. George Darwin, son of the naturalist Charles, estimated cousin marriage rates by counting the number of unions between people of the same surname, and concluded that 2.2% of marriages in rural districts were between first cousins.

Despite social unease at the time, the Church carried on unperturbed. First cousins continued to marry with impunity, and the list remained unchanged until the 20th century, when some relationships were removed by successive Acts. Marriage between a man and his deceased wife's sister was permitted by the first of these, in 1907. However, marrying a widowed uncle-in-law, a more remote non-blood tie, stayed on the list until 1921, with such forbidden unions treated as voidable, rather than invalid.

Sorting out exactly how William and Annie were related presented a challenge, but one that turned out to be less complicated than at first appeared. By the time they decided to wed, William had lost his second wife, and Annie her mother. These two deceased ladies were sisters — Mary and Maria Wyatt. William had first come to Compton in 1872 to take up a position as the farm bailiff of John Keevil. Only the year before, he had married Mary Dean at Wellington, Somerset. She died in 1882. William then married his second wife, Mary Wyatt, at Salisbury in 1883. She died four years later at Compton. Meanwhile, George Bailey had wed Maria Wyatt in 1865. Their union was registered at Wilton. They lived in Compton, where they baptised Annie in 1866. Maria died three years later, in 1869. The following year, George married again, with Elizabeth Wilds at Marnhull, Dorset.

Even before she heard the unwelcome news from the vicar, Annie must have been aware of loud mutterings — which might also account for her move to East Knoyle sometime between 1881 and 1889 — as on 1 August she and William attended the registrar's office in Wilton. William told the clerk to the Superintendent Registrar that he wished to give notice to be married to Annie Bailey at the parish church in East Knoyle. The clerk duly asked if they had the clergyman's consent, and gave them a form which they were required to sign by statute. In it, they declared that there was no kindred impediment to their union. On 19 September, Annie visited the office again, and explained that they wished to be married by licence at the registrar's office rather than in church, as there had been some unpleasantness. She signed a second declaration, and the ceremony was performed by the registrar on 21 September. Their age difference of 20 years was clearly not considered an obstacle for the then 23-year-old

Family Tree Illustrating how Maria Wyatt and George Bailey were First Cousins, & William Clapp was Annie Bailey's Uncle-in-law

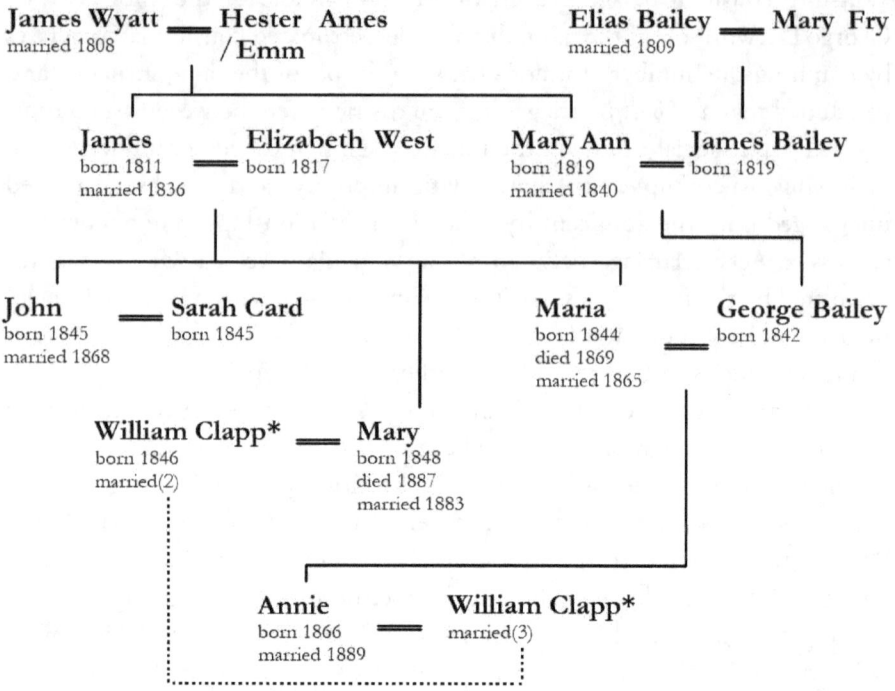

* Mary was William's second wife. He married his first wife Mary Dean in 1871. She died in 1882.

Annie. On 29 October, the clerk was informed of their relationship, and Annie was charged with having committed perjury in her declaration of 19 September. The case came before Salisbury Police Court on 22 November.

John confirmed that one of his deceased sisters had previously wed the groom, and another the bride's father. The defence attorney argued that the pair had thought marrying in the registrar's office was different to a church ceremony — a common belief at the time. The registrar's clerk could not remember whether he had cautioned them about relationships. However, Reverend Mangin testified that he had told them he could not marry them, and why. On being pressed as to whether he had said they could not be married at the registrar's office, his reply was: 'No, certainly not.' The defendant was granted bail, secured by her father and brother, and committed to trial at the assizes.

Reverend Mangin's statement in court became a talking point amongst the good folk of Salisbury, and such an embarrassment for the vicar that he wrote to the local newspaper. In his letter, published on 14 December, he expressed a wish to correct a wrong impression, which he had found existed in the city, relative to his evidence. He clarified that Annie had been charged with making her declaration knowingly and wilfully, fully understanding that the same was untrue, as she had been clearly informed of that fact. Therefore, the only evidence of value that he could give was that he had told her the proposed marriage was prohibited. As three months had elapsed between their meeting on 11 August and his summons to attend the hearing, and he had heard nothing more in the meantime, perhaps he could be excused for not remembering minutely every word that had passed between himself and the parties concerned.

The jury at Annie's trial believed she had not understood that the Church's rules also applied to marriages officiated by a registrar. Although she was found not guilty of perjury, the affair evidently caused the couple considerable consternation. They were living in Compton at the time of the 1891 census. William was head of their household, but Annie was recorded as his niece, rather than his wife. Her occupation was 'housekeeper.' Four of William's children were living with them. We will meet the eldest, William John, then aged sixteen, again in the future.

Either their standing in the village became intolerable or William lost his job, as he found a new post at Manor House Aldingbourn, Westhampnett, Sussex, where the 1901 census places him with his wife Annie. William's second son Francis was living with them, while his first son William John farmed at Northfield Farm in the same village. He was 26 years old and his wife, a little older at 28, was the daughter of his father's former employer at Compton, John Keevil. William and Emma Blanche Keevil wed at Putney in 1899.

Considering Annie's ancestry, her grit served her well in life. The girl's great-grandparents, Elias Bailey and Mary, née Fry, had baptised their son James in 1819. He became a carter, and married Mary Ann Wyatt, the daughter of James and Hester Wyatt. Annie Bailey's father George was the second of their nine sons. He and two of his brothers spent intervals as adults at Roundway Asylum in Devizes. William was a resident for two spells of five months each in 1881 and 1882. The teacher at the village's National School immediately removed six of his children from her register, noting that they had gone to the workhouse in Wilton.[384] He was again living in Compton with his wife and two sons at the 1891 census.

George was admitted in April 1882. The hopeless circumstances of his unfortunate family are poignantly revealed in a letter the *Salisbury and Winchester Journal* published on 28 October 1882. The author, Reverend

Frederick Courtenay Burrough, wrote that he could not stand by and see the poor 'hardly' dealt with. A most respectable man in his parish, for seventeen years a faithful servant to Charles Penruddocke, had been removed to the county asylum. He and his wife had for years kept the lodge at the entrance to the squire's park. The vicar did not name the couple but was clearly referring to Annie's father and stepmother, George and Elizabeth Bailey, who were listed at the Gatekeeper's lodge at Compton in the 1881 census. As Mary, George's grandmother, was recorded there when she died in 1856, the family had been living at the lodge for at least 25 years. Initially, the vicar explained, the man's wife had been told that she would not have to pay rent for the six months prior to her husband's departure. Now she was being asked for the arrears. Her pleadings of poverty and inability to find the money had been to no avail, and his on her behalf had only met with a request not to interfere between the squire and his tenants. Since her husband's removal, the poor woman has been in a very bad state of health produced by sorrow and by the terrible strain on her nerves through her husband's condition. The Board of Guardians refused to aid her because, the vicar believed, they felt she should not have to plead for relief. Rather, she should be paid for her continued attendance to the park gates. She was left with a young child to support, who was traumatised by the recent events, and the wages her older stepchildren earnt were too low for them to be able to help her. Her only income was a remittance from washing she took in for two small families. Her expression that she 'wanted for nothing' was noble proof of how often the poor were willing to keep quiet about the 'pinchings' of poverty. The vicar wanted to acquaint the public with Elizabeth's sad case and wrote he would be happy to receive anything on her behalf to apply to her relief. The journal's readers responded with generosity. Charles Penruddocke penned a letter to the editor rebuking the vicar for throwing mud at his patron and squire. He claimed the cleric had distorted the truth, considered he himself had lived in friendly intercourse with his private friends at Compton and had never been deficient in Christian charity towards them. Reverend Burrough resigned in July 1884, only 5 years after the squire had appointed him to the living. The squire had even less luck with his next vicar Dudley Digges, as detailed in Chapter 50. George was discharged from Roundway in April 1885 and readmitted in 1900, recorded there with the infirmity 'lunatic' attached to him in the 1901 census. He died while still incarcerated in 1904.

Thomas William entered the asylum in February 1918 and died there in August that year. All three brothers were described as paupers on admission.[385] Mary, their grandmother, was likewise listed as a pauper in Compton in the 1851 census. Given such a background, Annie scored a triumph with her marriage, eventually achieving the title poultry farmer's wife in the 1911 census.

A Trophy Wife?

The 20-year age gap between Annie and William was as nothing compared with the 45 years separating Joseph Scammel and Mary Foyle, reported in the *Salisbury and Winchester Journal* on 21 January 1788:

> Last Monday was married Mr Scammel, of Compton Chamberlain [*sic*], a healthy old oak of 66, to Miss Mary Foyle, of Wiley, a blooming belle of 21.

Joseph was indeed healthy, having lived until the grand old age of 89 by the time he was buried at Fovant in 1813.

47
The Keevils: Autocrats with a Sickening End

John Keevil came to Compton from a farm at Wimborne Minster in Dorset with his wife Anne and four children, William, Walter, Elizabeth, and Emma, at the end of 1861, possibly at the behest of Charles Penruddocke, whose family also owned a residence in Wimborne. He took over Manor Farm, while the Targett family was established at Naishes, the village's second biggest farmstead. The newcomer became immensely successful. By the time of the 1881 census, John held Naishes and was cultivating most of the land in the village. Although it was William Cull, one of his bailiffs, who occupied Naishes Farmhouse, Walter was registered there for voting purposes. Later, great-grandfather registered his sons as occupiers of furnished bedrooms at Manor Farm in order to secure their voting rights. John's eldest son William moved to a grange at Teffont. Later, he was the last-ever farmer to live in Swallowcliffe Manor, which he left in 1907.

John employed a substantial number of labourers — 50 in total — which is all the more surprising as mechanisation was already underway to boost cultivation. His employees included an engine driver. John's predecessor at Manor Farm, Thomas Patten Galpin, came to Compton between 1851 and 1855 and quit the tenancy at Michaelmas 1861, stating he would rather leave than be subject to the mean annoyances he continually received from Charles Penruddocke, who had not behaved towards him as a gentleman should behave.[386] Thomas might not have been an easy man himself. I would love to know what prompted George Jolliffe, George Wyatt, Thomas Raymond and William Lampard to up and leave his employ in September 1859. Thomas brought a charge against them for it.[387] Jolliffe was sentenced to sixteen, Raymond to fifteen and Lampard to fourteen days' hard labour. Wyatt had to forfeit two days' wages (5s).

Otherwise, we know little about Thomas except that he was an innovative farmer who made a tiny but consequential splash in the papers during his period of occupation. Brothers James and Frederick Howard were the proprietors of the Britannia Iron Works, Bedford, where they began to manufacture a portable steam engine used for threshing, pumping, and ploughing in about 1857. It featured a pair of winding drums, which enabled a single engine and an anchored return pulley to plough away from and back towards the motor. By contrast, the Fowler system needed a pair of engines, which stood at opposite ends of a field, each one alternately pulling the plough. My cousin Jean remembers the day she saw two large black traction engines still using the Fowler system in the 1000-acre field below the White Horse hill figure on Pewsey downs:

> This was a unique sight, I must have been aged 6 or 7 [c 1937]. Rupert [her father] stopped the car to have a look, as farmers do … We clearly saw two traction engines opposite each other, they were pulling the [six-furrow] plough through the heavy soil from each other, and as the opposite engine received the plough, so it was arranged to start the next row.

On the way back from their journey in the late afternoon, they stopped again and marvelled that so much had been tilled in the three hours that had passed. The following week, during a repeat trip, they saw that the whole field had been ploughed over.

Advertisements for Howard's steam cultivators regularly appeared in the *Salisbury and Winchester Journal* throughout the 1860s.

The brothers wrote a letter to its editor, which was published on 27 July 1861:

> Sir, —The farmers of your district will soon have an opportunity of forming an opinion of our New Patent Steam Cultivating Apparatus.
>
> Immediately after harvest we shall start two or three sets in your neighbourhood, one for Mr Galpin, of Compton Chamberlain [*sic*].

Farmers are a sceptical lot, and this new mode of ploughing met with some grumbles of discontent, prompting the pair to write a second letter in answer to their critics, published on 21 September:

> A few weeks since some correspondence was admitted into your journal condemnatory of our New Patent Steam Cultivating Apparatus.
>
> Your readers will perhaps remember that we then ventured to ask them to suspend their judgment until some sets we had on order from your district had been started.

Their cultivator, they proclaimed, had broken up one farmer's land to his entire satisfaction, and at the end of the week they would be starting a similar set on Mr Galpin's property. Development proceeded apace, with Howard traction engines able to plough and carry out numerous other tasks newly introduced during the 1870s.

While most of John Keevil's large assortment of implements were not detailed in the announcement of his farm sale in 1897, three items were highlighted to entice prospective buyers — a steam thrashing machine and tackle, viz. 8-HP engine and thresher by Clayton and Shuttleworth, and a four-wheel elevator by Titt.[388] Nathaniel Clayton and Joseph Shuttleworth had built their first portable steam engine in 1845, and first threshing machine in 1849.

Meanwhile, the Keevils were in cahoots with Charles Penruddocke and dominated Compton. Their standing in the village is exemplified by their joining forces with the squire in 1878 to contribute a bell to the church, which is inscribed 'Fear God C Penruddock J. Keevil Churchwardens.'[389] They conducted themselves in a manner that suited the squire. For instance, for the Jubilee celebrations in 1887, they provided a field and tent, and joined forces with Charles to give each person in the village one and a half pounds of best beef.[390] It was therefore against the Keevils that *The Salisbury Times* encouraged villagers to rise up in its article covering the recruitment efforts of Wiltshire Labourers' Union in 1893.[391] Although I have not found any family connection with them at Compton, the reporter, had he but known, might have considered the vicar of Stourton's amendment of Evil to Keevil in his parish's register[392] decorous, though not entirely fitting given the family's suppression of Compton's inhabitants. In any case, 'Keevil' actually derives from a combination of Old English words, which together mean hollow in a woodland clearing.[393]

The family's grip on the village remained absolute, until Charles Penruddocke came into direct conflict with the vicar and his churchwarden.* Something untoward must have happened, as Walter did not seize the opportunity to retain Manor Farm after his father's death in January 1896. One immediate reason that springs to mind is that the enterprise had become unprofitable. Arthur Street, a farmer, broadcaster, and writer, informs us in his fiction set at Manor Farm, Compton[394] that 1879 was a disastrous year which heralded two decades of depressed farming — the Great Depression of British Agriculture following the repeal of the Corn Laws. However, my great-

---

*   See Chapter 50.

grandfather writes in a letter that Manor Farm had continued to generate a good sum — £900 a year. Either Walter became disillusioned or, as I suspect was the case, his family was brought down by a plague of illnesses and associated stress.

There is undoubtedly more to the Keevil family than meets the eye. A nurse, Sarah Bunting, had visited their household much earlier, at the time of the 1881 census, and, curiously, she came from Matlock in Derbyshire — the very location of Anne's death, at Smedley's Matlock Bank, thirteen years later. During the interim, Anne's brother James Kendell had died, aged 62, at the same sanatorium in December 1885. He never married, and had been living at Teffont with William, John's and Anne's eldest son, before he became a patient. His death was caused by the rupture of an aortic aneurysm.

The sanatorium had been established by an unusual man, John Smedley, who astonishingly turned around his family's failing clothing business by experimenting tirelessly with the adaptation of cotton machinery to the manufacture of woollen goods. Their fortunes restored, a severe chill caught in a damp church in Switzerland while on honeymoon left this energetic and enterprising individual in a nervous and despondent condition for some years, from 1848 until 1851. Drugs alone were unable to cure him. Eventually, cold-water therapy provided him with a miraculous new lease of life, and he resolved to confer the benefit of this treatment on others, starting with the 1500 workers at his mills. Driven by an intense religious fervour, he proposed to combine physical healing with spiritual instruction. Henry Steer writes in his review of the philanthropic labours of John and his wife that the ordinary business of the mills was thrown into confusion while everything was made to give way 'to experiments with the dipping sheet, the wet pack, the douche, and so on; and everybody had to undergo some form of new treatment, whether he was ailing or not. Cattle, as well as human beings, were experimented on.'[395] John was not only eccentric, exhibiting characteristics that suggest he suffered from a bipolar disorder, but also exceptionally kind. He established a free hospital adjoining the mills, which over the years expanded into his mammoth sanatorium. This new champion of hydropathy believed he had a threefold mission: to promote his remedy, to expose the evils of the old allopathic system of bleeding, blistering, and cupping, instead administering preparations such as mercury, strychnine, and opium, and to reform the clergy. He thought that the latter could not truly believe in the doctrines of their prayer book if they imagined they could transform children into members of Christ through a mere rite, or bury an impenitent drunkard with the words 'in the sure and certain hope of the resurrection to eternal life.'

By the time Anne came to be a patient at Matlock, Smedley's was run by John's nephews, he and his wife having both passed away. According to Dr Evans, who signed her death certificate in January 1894, Anne's death was caused by gastroenteritis and exhaustion. An article by Richard Metcalfe, which appeared in *Hydropathic World* in January 1892, explains the rationale of hydropathy — a treatment for brain-fag, comparable to today's 'burnout,' and mental depression:

> The brain is ... the reservoir of nervous energy, and when this is exhausted there is a flagging of the whole system. The stomach is often the first organ to suffer. It loses tone and digestion goes on imperfectly ... so direct is the influence of the brain on the digestive organs that sickness and vomiting are among the earliest symptoms of many affections of the head.

But which came first for Anne? Was it her exhaustion or her stomach problems that compelled the Keevils in their misery to seek help for her from Smedley's establishment? The palatial sanatorium, with its Corinthian columns and pilasters, would have been a comfort to the sufferer of either condition. It was beautifully situated amongst trees on the River Derwent, where it enters a gorge with 'lofty heights, faced upon one side by precipitous walls of limestone, which gleam like marble when the sun strikes full upon them.'[187] The treatment Anne received was probably not unlike the one described in Henry Steer's book by another woman who became a patient while in a weakened state caused by overwork and worry, and in want of rest. Hers took the ordinary mild form: a tepid wet sheet before breakfast, warm wet pack in the forenoon, and tepid sitz-bath in the afternoon. She did not have powerful applications of mustard packs or steam boxes to cleanse the blood; she only needed gentle

Tombstone of John and Anne Keevil in Compton Chamberlayne Cemetery.

stimulants, plain diet, cheerful companionship, and rest.

But if Anne collapsed as a result of her gastric condition, the fall of the house of Keevil could have a more sinister explanation than clinical depression and burnout. John's death certificate informs us that his cause of death exactly two years later was 'Paralysis of upper extremities. Paralysis of deglutition. Incompetence of epiglottis.' He had either stiff or floppy paralysed arms, an inability to swallow, and his epiglottis failed to prevent anything from going down into his lungs. He was therefore at risk of aspirating and developing pneumonia. The two most common events that could have given rise to this type of infirmity are a stroke or a brain/brainstem tumour. Both would have caused stiff paralysis. Another possibility is botulism, which results in floppy paralysis as well as difficulty swallowing. Preserving one's own food is the biggest risk factor associated with botulism, but farmers, who habitually did so, were not aware of this danger in the 19th century. Did Anne and John Keevil poison themselves to death with their poor food handling practices?

They were laid to rest in Compton cemetery. Walter continued to farm at Naishes. He, too, suffered from stomach problems. But more about this in Chapter 53.

48
Great-Grandfather Moves Up-Country

GREAT-GRANDFATHER WILLIAM WAS still at Truscott in Cornwall in 1895 and, as ever, struggling to make ends meet. As we have seen, farming was shifting continually further towards mechanisation, with the purchase of machines, and more horses to pull them, bringing additional outlays. William used a reaper to cut hay and corn, while wheat sheaves were still bound by hand, and barley was carried loose. He also had access to a threshing machine. Even so, cutting down on labour meant that farmers had to work harder themselves. Physical toil sometimes brought William to the point of exhaustion.

He resolved to move up-country, which for a Cornishman meant anywhere in England except Cornwall, and to take on a bigger farm. Even at the end of the 20th century, most farms in Cornwall measured less than 100 acres. Was it a difficult decision? Some West-Country farmers were reluctant to take such a wrenching step. John Boaden, a tenant farmer who lived on the Lizard Peninsula, had pondered a move with his family in 1879. He later wrote in his memoirs: 'I decided not to send my sons up; I wished to keep them together as much as possible, and to sell all and go up was a very big job and I felt I should never be as happy again as in the neighbouroughhood [sic] of my birth.'[396] William's decision would have been made easier as his nephew-in-law, William Burrow, had already left, and was cultivating Manor Farm at Ashmore in Dorset, on its border with Wiltshire. The future would see my grandfather take over this farm in 1911, and my father born there in 1912.

The West Country had been left behind by Britain as a whole, and there was yet another reason to leave Cornwall at this time. William and his wife Emily had nine children: Mary, born 1874, Ada, 1876, Joseph, 1881, John, 1883 (my grandfather), Emily, 1885, William, 1887, Reginald, 1890, Cecil, 1892, and Rupert, 1894. William saw his boys' future as following on in his own footsteps. They were to become farmers. This was the only life William knew. For him, farmers were the most important people in the world, and, as Robin Stanes explains in his book about life on the land in Cornwall, farming

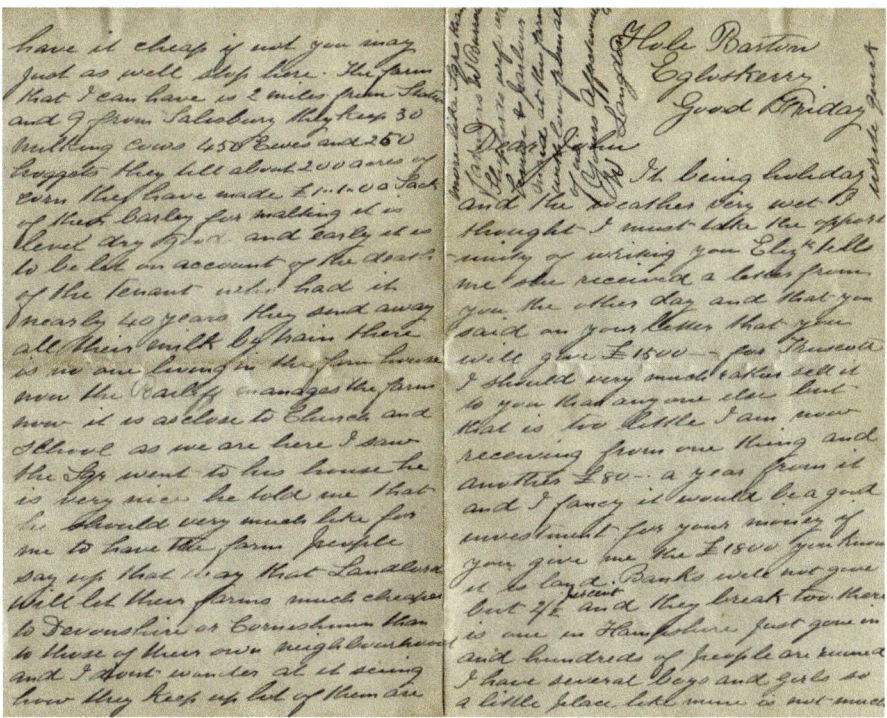

William's rainy-day letter to John, his nephew, written on Good Friday 1895.

was 'a man's life;' no other existence was considered 'a real life' in the way that farming was.[397] There was never a thought given to any other occupation and, with the exception of William junior, that is how the sons saw their future too.

The rain on Good Friday in 1895 kept William inside his house. He wrote to his nephew John in Australia, telling him why he wanted to leave Cornwall: 'It being holiday and the weather very wet I thought I would take the opportunity of writing to you ... I have several boys and girls so a little place like mine is not much divided besides I want to go upward and take a better farm and for less money than I am giving for this.' Not only were the farms bigger up-country, but also their rents were lower. Since the Napoleonic Wars, land fees in Cornwall had remained high despite the lean years that followed.[398]

Cornish landlords could charge such high rents because, the depression notwithstanding, competition for farms was keener than ever. Boaden supplies the reason: farmers wanted their sons nearby in order to share labour and resources, but they struggled to find land for them, as owners had amalgamated the small farms. While mixed farming had allowed Cornish agriculturalists to survive, tenants in other parts of Britain had been forced to give up their land.

Ex-landlords were experiencing difficulties replacing them with new lessees, especially on large farms, because so much capital was needed to run them. Owners had to reduce rents to stave off the risk of their land running wild and deteriorating.

Continuing his rainy-day despatch, William describes his visit to Wiltshire, where he viewed Manor Farm at Compton Chamberlayne:

> I was up a fortnight ago now to see some farms. I went over one that I should like very much ... I am certain with my family I can do much better up there. It is about 15 miles from W Burrows [at Ashmore]. The farm that I can have is 2 miles from a station and 9 from Salisbury ... It is level dry ground and early it is to be let on account of the death of the tenant who had it for nearly 40 years. They send away all their milk by train. There is no one living in the farmhouse now. The bailiff manages the farm now. It is as close to church and school as we are here. I saw the squire [Charles Penruddocke], went to his house. He is very nice. He told me that he should very much like for me to take the farm ... It is over 600 acres and it use to make £900 a year. And I can have it for £400 but it will take some cash so I want to clear out of everything hear.

Then, he adds a telling remark about Wiltshire farmers: 'People say up that way that landlords will let their farms much cheaper to Devonshire or Cornwall men than to those of their own neighbourhood and I don't wonder at it seeing how they keep up, lot of them are more like squires than farmers.'

Notably, the farm's main attractions for William were its proximity to a school and church, and that a railway station was nearby. It was further described in the *Western Gazette*'s announcement on 29 January 1897, which advertised it for let, as comprised of a house, farm buildings, and 6 cottages, together with just over 13 acres of pasture, 43 of water meadow, 403 of arable, 149 of down (arable and pasture), and 17 of copse and waste land. It was available from Michaelmas 1898, but with the possibility of a pre-entry. William had already moved into the farm by the time of publication.

His new squire was open to innovative agricultural practices. Farmers in Compton were among those selected for a sugar beet cultivation trial. This crop provided the main source of sugar in Continental Europe, but in Britain sugar was refined from cane imported from the country's colonies in the West Indies. Beet roots had, nevertheless, been introduced from Germany for cattle feed during the 1770s. This experiment was unsuccessful, since they proved to be no better than mangolds for fattening cattle. A quaint story tells us that the German mangold-wurzel (beet-root) was read as mangel-wurzel, popularly interpreted as 'scarcity root.' This mistranslation resulted in a belief that the vegetable could be useful for feeding the poor during periods of famine.[399]

Even before the abolition of slavery, the profitability and benefit of the West Indies plantations for the British nation had been questioned. Sigmund Stein was a German specialist in the manufacture of sugar who relocated to England to manage a sugar cane refinery in Liverpool. Despite his professional engagement with cane, he was convinced that the beets' large roots made them a potentially viable source for sugar in England. He sent seeds to 400 British farmers, and asked them to return samples of their yield to him for analysis. The saccharine content of the roots from Compton, especially those sent in by Miss Penruddocke in 1898, exceeded those of German-grown roots.[400] The area's clayey soil combined with a proportion of sand produced the best results, as was also found by W. F. Lawrence, a prominent advocate of producing sugar from beets, who himself grew experimental crops at Cowesfield in Salisbury. He was an MP, and served on the Sugar Committee in the House of Commons. However, as long as the British government continued to protect its vested interest in the West Indies by imposing higher levies on locally-produced beets, farmers saw no benefit to growing such crops. Later, in the 1920s, sugar beets were cultivated at East Farm, bordering Manor Farm to the west.

The former tenant reported to have died in William's rainy-day letter was John Keevil. As we already know, he gave up the ghost in January 1896, but had probably given up on his farm earlier, as he was already seriously ill in 1895. William had first moved to Compton with his second son, my grandfather John, leaving his eldest son Joseph to take charge in Cornwall. He told his nephew John how he brought his stock up to Compton:

> Me and John came up here the 1st October we brought up 12 horses with us 2 truck loads. I brought 2 in Lanson [dialect for Launceston] cattle market for £60, the rest I had before. I shall have to get some more, it will take 18 to work this farm properly. We left Lanson station about 6 pm the evening and arrived Dinton about 5 the next morning. We made up [slept] in the guards van.

Elsewhere, it is evident that he had had five horses for working Truscott, and later managed to build up that number to eighteen at Manor Farm.

The journey alone was quite an undertaking. First, the horses were walked about two miles to Egloskerry station, where there were pens to hold animals awaiting transportation. Conveniently for William, this station had opened just five years before. While hanging around, he had plenty of time to tell the stationmaster in painstaking detail about his new enterprise, and no doubt got a kick out of doing so. Later in his letter, he expounds: 'It has almost frightened some people down our way to think that I have taken such a farm for it so happened that there are two men in our neighbourhood that knowing it, one is the station master at Egloskerry and the other is Rogers the game keeper at squire William.' Neither would have kept mum. Chatter that William had crossed the Tamar, 'Ee's gone up north,' soon spread. For all his bravado, William was apprehensive too. Telling others must have bolstered his spirits to face the daunting task that he knew lay ahead of him.

Postcard showing the main street of Compton Chamberlayne as it was when William drove his horses from Dinton train station to Manor Farm at the end of the street. The house on the right later became the post office. Opposite, the steep thatched roof of Camel Cottage is visible.

After a night on the train, and unloading their horses at Dinton station, father and son only had a couple of miles to chivvy them along the grassy track to Compton. They soon reached the wooden bridge spanning the Nadder River at Dinton water mill. Latticed among willows, the mill still ponders its reflection in the green waters. It's a small building, standing picturesque and lonely. Further forward, on the village road, the entourage passed under a high wooden bridge supporting a bridleway leading to the Big House. From here, they paraded through Compton's main street. The villagers would surely have stepped out onto their front porches to watch such a spectacle, and become acquainted with the new arrivals. Mutterings of 'Lawk aw! if 'tean't the new Measter. I lot [reckon] ee be mad to take on sich a girt varm [big farm] wi' a gabborn [comfortless] owld house' might have been heard. Perhaps the beerhouse keeper, Arthur Roberts, who farmed several acres in the village, tossed them a greeting: ' 'Tis a main blooming [very sultry] marnin', izzent it?' A quick break at his establishment, the King's Elm, to quench their thirst would have been welcome, even if it ' 'twas a lang time afore ee could get un [the horses] to bide still enough,' while onlookers advised 'ee got a right sharper [dodgy, nervous horse] there.' The weather had been scorching dry. William undoubtedly heard tell of 'Tes a terr'ble bad harvest to-year [this year],' and picked up on the villagers' gossip and banter:

'Well, an' how be 'ee Tom today?'
'Pretty middling [well], Jack. I wur bad aal last wick wi' rheumatiz, but I be about agen now.'
'I zeed they weeds be a comin' up in yer garne as ever they can diggle [grow thick together].'
'Now dwoan't 'ee caddle [tease] I zo Jack, or I'll tell thee vather o' thee caddle! They tells I owld Bill got a new missis agen.'
'Ees, but her's no proper beauty. Her be sinful ordinary [plain to the last degree].'
'Arr, it be ben it,' agreed Tom.

Refreshed, William and John just had to pass twenty-five or so houses to reach Manor Farm 'yander,' at the far end of the village.

Later, Emily came up with 'Little' Emily. Her older sisters, Mary and Ada, and younger brothers, William, Reg, Cecil, and Rupert, were still with Joseph, Rupert being a mere three years of age. In a letter to me, my father gave an account of a journey from Cornwall that suggests William went down to collect his three youngest sons:

The other boys travelled up with grandfather, they were quite small [the eldest, Reg, was 7 years old]. The story goes that at one station in Devon where the train stopped, grandfather spotted a friend, got out and had a chat. So absorbing was the conversation [he was probably boasting again] that he did not realise the train was leaving until it was too late to get onto the same carriage as the boys. But he managed to jump into a carriage further towards the rear. The train consisted of the old carriages where there were no corridors.* So, the boys thought they had

---

* The first corridor train was run on the London to Penzance line in 1893. It was fitted with gas lights, and equipped with electric communication for passengers with the guard, plus steam-heaters, so no footwarmers were required.

lost their father (until the next stop) and in the meantime cried so much that there was a dispute in the family for many years as to who cried the most.

Manor Farmhouse, early 1900s. Note the monkey puzzle tree.

Postcard of Manor Farmhouse as I remember it. The clump of trees on the downs was planted in the shape of a pear.

Imagine William's feelings when he first surveyed Manor Farm — the exhilaration of the future he had dreamed of before his eyes, mixed with a sinking apprehension of the responsibility for such a huge enterprise, the stern square stone house standing tall and solid above his diminutive figure. Impassive casement windows, perfectly aligned between neatly trimmed ivy, condescendingly stared back at the new occupant. It was not an immediately welcoming home. How many acres William had at Truscott is no longer known. Regardless, Manor Farm, with its 632 acres, was at least five times larger. He trusted his ability to work hard, but he desperately needed capital to succeed. His nephew, who was generally believed to be making his fortune mining in Australia, seemed the obvious solution. The first hint of John's acceptance of his bankrolling function occurs in a letter written by Emily on 4 July 1896, in which she thanks him for sending money, assuring him it will be helpful because they have had much to pay since they came up to Compton. She elaborates, revealing her hopes and fears:

> [We] have not had much return yet, only the dairy but I hope it will be better when the corn and hay comes to sell but it takes such a lot to stock this farm and costs a lot in labour but the people around here say if the farm is well managed it will produce any amount of crops. We have a splendid lot of hay this year. They have harvested 70 acres in good order and today they commenced harvesting another piece 30 acres. Joe cuts all with the machinery, John rakes it [he was 12 years old]. They have about 8 acres of clover hay left to cut and several acres of meadow. The men are mowing that. The wheat and barley are looking well. All were in full ear a bit ago. I hope we have a good corn harvest we have had a splendid hay harvest.

As for the dairy:

> We are now milking 24 cows. They say there is grass enough here for 8 or 10 more. We send our milk to London twice a day in summer and once a day in winter. The cows are kept down in the water meadows nearly a mile from here nearer the station. They will not be brought [up] again before winter. [Where the] cows are there is a milk house. We have just a cow or two for our own use up here. The milk boy milks up here after they have finished. The dairyman goes to the station with the milk.

The track to Dinton Station leads directly from the milk house meadow. It was probably the one named as Milk Meadow in a lease to Joel Rowden, a

Milk House in the water meadows at Manor Farm in 2016.

former resident of Manor Farm, in 1795.[401] The dairyman's trip, passing by Dinton Mill, represented a distance of less than 2 miles, and took around 30-45 minutes. It was the way William and John had driven their horses along when they brought them up by train. Emily adds: 'The customs here are very different from what they are in Cornwall but I think we shall get into it after a little while.' Disappointingly, she does not explain what those differences were.

Until I came across this letter, the wooden-slatted structure that stands alone in the middle of a pasture had perplexed me. Milk House is an apt description, because it looks like a dwelling. It is U-shaped. Two identical sides face down river-wards, each with a large paned window at its end, and two more cut into the outer walls. There are another three on the rear side of the U. Altogether, they allowed light to stream into the milking parlour before the dawn of electric illumination.

William, writing in October 1897, requested another loan from John. The reason is not difficult to appreciate after reading how he had paid £1000 for cows and sheep:

> I will give you a little news about which I am sure you will be anxious to know. I have told you before the size of this farm and also the stock that was on it. Their sale was on 27 of September, their stock corn and everything on this farm hath and will make more than 6000- so you may think it is a good farm and a big thing for me to undertake. You will understand that I will have to go into it in a

smaller way than the late farmer has done. It is not going to cost me one half of the rent that it has been making. I have 5 carters, 2 shepherds, 2 dairymen and 3 labourers and they are costing me £5.14.0 a week and I must have more now we are milking 15 cows sending the milk to London. We are about 80 miles from there. Wm Burrows [from Ashmore] and his father [Thomas] came here to see us last Friday. Thomas said it is the cheapest farm that ever he saw but the worst of it is I want a £1000 more than I have got, I ought to have £5000 to work it like anything. If you or John [a cousin] have a few hundred to spare I will give you good interest and pay you every penny again. I have now a little over 300 ewes and I intend to buy another 100 as soon as I can get the money. I have bought 15 cows and 9 heifers in calf that will come in milk next spring. These cows, heifers and sheep cost me more than £1000 I believe. I could very well keep 40 cows and 600 sheep and till 200 acres of corn.

Only a year on, thanks to John's loans, William had managed to build up the number of his sheep to the size of his predecessor's flock.

49
Great-Grandfather's Good Fortune

THERE ARE NO signs that William ever regretted his move up-country or, as John Boaden would have done, yearned for the home of his youth. He was far from Wiltshire's only local migrant from the West Country. Soon after he arrived, he attended a dinner held at the County Hotel in Salisbury. *The Salisbury Times* characterised the event in its 1 April 1898 issue as the fruition of a long-expressed wish for a reunion between the very many Devonians and Cornubians residing in Salisbury and district. William was mentioned, along with 53 other guests — there were more present, but not mentioned by name. They were merely 'the ladies,' relegated to the balcony. The front of the gallery was decorated with shields bearing the arms of the attendees' respective counties. Speeches were made proclaiming the beauty of these shires, and their significant share in the history of the county. Special dishes were provided:

Carters with their shire horses in the farmyard at Manor Farm.

junket and cream for the Devonians, and pasties for the Cornishmen, sent specially from St Austell. My great-uncle Rupert said he longed for the pasties his mother had made when he was hungry in Palestine, while serving in World War I.

Farm workers at Manor Farm taking a break from harvesting with a mechanical reaper.

Emily talks about her charges on the farm in one of her exchanges: 'I am going in for more poultry this year. I have a goose, many hens and about 45 nice chickens and more ... There seems a demand for eggs around here. We do not keep many pigs, we killed two back in the winter and have two nice ones coming on now. We rear a few heifers.' Poultry, pigs, and heifers fell under the purview of the farmer's wife. Traditionally, only the back-breaking work of ploughing, mowing, and sheep-shearing were exclusively a man's work.

A couple of years passed, and William's brother-in-law visited from Cornwall. He sent a report describing the crops and sheep in a letter to his nephew John at the end of October 1899:

> I have been up to see Mrs Wm. I went out one week before we begun harvest. They were cutting wheat when I came up there. Harvest is a few days before ours. You like to know what I think of the farm. I think it a very decent farm. He had very good wheat, very good barley, oats middling. He got 25 acres of beans a total failure he said it was 100 pounds lost to him. I told him he must put more manure [a]nd get heavier crops for his sheep. The sheep are all

Farm workers at Manor Farm posing in front of a rick at harvesttime.

hurdled. One field is nearly 400 acres. I think he could do with 5 men lest [less] I will give you my reason. When I was up there Wm had 700 sheep. I went to see W Burrow [at Ashmore]. He had 14 hundred sheep and only keeps 12 men. W Burrow is the largest farm.

William's venture began to bear fruit. Ada writes in her first letter of the new century: 'Father has today sent off 3 waggon loads of barley to Salisbury, he sent 2 loads last Friday and I expect 3 loads will go again next week. We have a very good dairy now, last month's milk account was the biggest we have yet had, rather over £40.' However, later that year, in April 1900, the court in Salisbury heard William's claim against Messrs Main and Sons, corn merchants, for the price of the grain he had sold them.[402] The claim was admitted, but a counterclaim relating to William's failure to deliver the quantity contracted for was successful. The firm contended that William had agreed to sell 100 quarters of barley. He insisted the agreement was for 100 sacks. Could an increase in the price of corn between the contract and delivery dates possibly have influenced great-grandfather's argument?

In general, providence was on William's side. He was farming the right farm, in the right place, at the right time. South Wiltshire farmers prospered from the end of the Boer War in October 1899 until the First World War began during the summer of 1914.

Manor Farm had downs and land that were easy to plough, suited to both sheep and arable farming, but also to pasture, including a fair proportion of water meadow. Emphasis could simply be switched to follow the line of maximum income. Arable-sheep farming became less profitable after a succession of cold springs and summers resulted in poor harvests, which coincided with a dramatic drop in corn prices following the introduction of cheap corn from America. Between 1870 and 1890, corn on the chalklands shrank by over 25%, as a growing percentage of arable was laid down to grass. Dairy farming became increasingly lucrative, and Manor Farm had excellent access to trains for transporting its milk to London. Prices for farm products rose steadily and new machinery brought greater efficiency, while labour outgoings and rent both remained static. Rather than the highest possible rent, what landlords most wanted was a tenant who would accommodate their sporting activities, and adhere to their politics of maintaining the status quo.

William and Emily Langdon setting out from Manor Farm before World War I, perhaps on a visit to Emily's nephew at Ashmore. Note the head gear.

Yet the farm took its toll on William. A letter which he and Emily wrote together — one page each — reveals that William was mentally sustained in his determination to exploit the land's full potential, but also beset by gloom. It starts, 'I think I must put a few lines to you on E's letter ... To begin I will tell you just what crops we have put in.' He expands on these in detail, relaying how much he will earn that year — £700, of which £400 was to be paid in rent. It is worth remembering at this point that the previous tenant had been making £900. Finally, he tells John about the expense and burden:

I ought to have ten more cows and they will cost nearly £200, which I have not got to lay out but hope to in time. It takes more money to farm this farm than I thought. I have 18 horses, then there is the implements harness machinery carriages, runs into a lot but I hope to get over it, please god to spare me. Sometimes I feel almost cast down. It is a big lift for me and I am not first rate sometimes but if I can have a couple good years it will put me right.

Emily adds on her page: 'William has not been very well for sometime. He cannot sleep well at night. He gets out around every day and I hope as the summer comes he will be better. He has had a lot of hard work since we came here.'

William Langdon (1846-1923) on his horse.

William and Emily occasionally visited Emily's nephew William Burrow at Manor Farm, Ashmore. In his memoirs, my father recalls the momentous event when William Burrow introduced the first self-binder to the village around 1896. These machines were revolutionary, cutting the corn and binding it into sheaves in a single operation, but they were still horse-drawn. Later on, great-grandfather also had such a machine at Compton. My cousin Jean recollected her father Rupert telling her how excited he was when it arrived.

William and Emily Langdon and their children dressed in their Sunday best, are pictured in this meticulously posed photograph. From the left, the sons standing in the back row are Rupert, Joe, Will, Reg, Cecil, and John. Emily and William sit in the centre of the front row with, when looking at the photograph, 'little' Emily to their left, and Ada to their right. Mary was already in America. Her face has been inserted into the back row between her brothers by means of a primitive forerunner of Photoshop. This photograph was taken on the lawn in front of Manor Farmhouse, probably sometime between July 1907 and April 1911. The family exudes the impression of being gentle folk, rather than fatigued by their daily rough and ready lives working on the farm. Shoes sparkle with polish. Collars on the men and ruffles on the women stand stiff and high. The men's ties are done up tight. Watch chains hang down Rupert's and Cecil's chests, and Will has something curious dangling from his right wrist.

The trip down to Ashmore, Emily writes in her 4th-of-July letter, 'is a nice drive from here.' Nevertheless, it was still quite a journey. Emily's daughter Mary wrote during the winter four years later that the pony, who as a point of passing interest was called Jessie, was getting old 'for such a long and cold journey ... I hope to go out again soon if we get some nice bright days, it is a very cold drive to their place. Ashmore is so high.' Indeed, it is the highest village in Dorset at 689 feet above sea level, but not a great deal higher than the hill on Manor Farm in Compton at 624 feet.

Nonetheless, at a time when working people, tinkers, and gypsies were commonly seen on foot on the highways and byways, farm labourers drove cows and sheep along this route to market, or elsewhere. David Davidge, who worked for my grandfather as a boy, and later for my father at Naishes Farm, told tales of how he drove cattle from Ashmore to Compton. The twelve-mile trek, no more than a normal day's work, may have passed out of memory, but the cooked dinners — farmers have dinner at lunchtime — which Emily gave him in the kitchen at Manor Farm, stayed with him. After eating, the lad had to walk another twelve miles back to Ashmore. Sheep were driven to the sheep fair in Wilton, and livestock to market in Salisbury too. Later, farmers found themselves in competition with increasing volumes of traffic. Mr Coombs of Fovant wrote to Salisbury Council in 1931 to protest about the difficulty he had experienced in driving 70 head of cattle through the streets to market, on account of the congestion he encountered from motor traffic.[403]

William had made his move up-country to a bigger farm at a good time. Although he battled at first, the period from 1905 until shortly before he retired to Salisbury in 1921 was one of great prosperity for farmers. While wages and rent continued to remain stable, prices for farm produce rose steadily.

> **How I came by My Great-grandfather's Correspondence**
> Some of us are more programmed than others to write and treasure letters. Gwen Shute, who was married to my father's uncle Alfred on his mother's side, wrote to Willie from Cornwall in 1980, 'It is always a thrill to get a letter from one's distant family it seems a shame, when the older ones pass on, the next generation just drift apart for the sake of a letter.' A still greater thrill for future generations is produced by care having been taken to save correspondence that describes the past, when no one is left to orally tell their writers' stories.
>
> As soon as a generation of Langdons became literate, this achievement was seemingly encoded in a letter-writing gene which has been passed down through its descendent lines, surfacing in one or two individuals along the way. Sometime in or before 1882, great-grandfather William's nephew John left Cornwall for Australia, where he worked for about twenty years throughout his 20s and 30s. He wrote and kept letters. His daughter Audrey, my father's first cousin, exclaimed in a note to my father in 1981, 'What do you think!! Ena [her sister] and I have been turning out for the last seven weeks reading Daddy's letters sent home to the parents when he was at college and abroad.' Fifty of them reached Willie's hands at the beginning of 1989. They eventually found their way to me. Others that John had saved are among the files that Bond, Pearce, Eliot, and Knape, solicitors of Liskeard, deposited at the Cornwall Record Office.

50
A Heroic Vicar Leads the Villagers' Struggle for Autonomy

For umpteen generations, the head of the Penruddocke family was called 'the Squire' by his folk, while tugging their forelocks, one fancies. The Penruddockes were paternalists. They held Christmas parties for Compton's villagers, gave an annual summer 'treat' to their children, donated land for a new cemetery, and built the village school in 1855, continuing to finance it until it became a National School with a government grant. A paternalist is one who manages subordinates in the manner of a father, but the term also embraces the usurping of individual responsibility and liberty of choice.

At the end of the 19th century, village society was troubled. Charles Penruddocke, the five-times great-grandson of he who lost his head in 1655, supported the Tory Party, as might be expected. In November 1885, just before the first parliamentary election in which most adult men were allowed to vote, he held a meeting to promote the Conservative candidate, Sydney Herbert.[404] He begged parishioners to remember that the majority of Herbert's party were landowners, and that class produced, or assisted in producing, food for the people. It was sheer folly, he maintained, to suppose they would do anything that would negatively impinge on the prosperity of those who lived by the land. Signs of disturbance at the election itself can be gleaned from a reprimand issued by the manor court on Monday, 14 December 1885:[405]

> The jurors at the court also express their disapproval of the unseemly behaviour of certain parties in the Parish during the late Parliamentary election and hope that measures will be adopted to prevent its repetition on any future occasion.

The Liberal party, led by William Gladstone, won the most seats, but was short of an overall majority. Another election held the following year enabled the Conservatives to form a government through the support of the Irish Liberal Unionist party. Presumably this passed quietly, as the manorial records are silent on the subject. But make no mistake, discontent was still bubbling below the surface, with the Liberal Party increasingly making itself felt in the village.

A branch of the Labourers' Union had been established in Compton for at least a decade, but its influence was constrained by the Catch-22 situation members found themselves in when its ideals clashed with the pressing needs of a man on the breadline. In July 1876, Sanger, its secretary, and another member, Henry Davidge, were convicted of attempting to intimidate Stephen Young in order to prevent him from working for his master John Keevil.[406] Barnett was the great-nephew of his wealthy namesake* and lived at Compton Hut. The incident in question occurred when Davidge and Young, along with three other men, left off mowing Keevil's meadow after the farmer told them he would not pay more than 3s 6d per acre for their work. Young, who was also a Unionist, made some disparaging comments but, being penniless,† he returned to continue the following day. He was approached by Sanger and the mowing gang, who asked him if he was going to 'stick.' When he answered he would stay where he was, Sanger threatened him, saying 'If I were thy mate, I'd chuck thee into the water.' Young was told he wore the white feather and was a 'black-legged.'

The 'Red Van' of the English Land Restoration League, working on behalf of the Wiltshire Labourers' Union, turned up on a piece of green at the entrance to the village, opposite the driveway to Manor Farmhouse, in 1893. Nowadays, a brick bus shelter stands on the same patch. A meeting held there under a clump of trees, which almost everyone in Compton attended, ended with 28 villagers signing up to the Union. In reporting the event, *The Salisbury Times* raised its cudgel, pointing out that the parish was owned by one person who let out almost all the land to a single farmer and his son.[407] They were effectively its sole governors, together with the vicar as a sort of sleeping partner, and held an unchallenged sway over the lives of the villagers. This was no exaggeration. The lessee was none other than John Keevil. He held the position of bailiff in the manorial court for twenty years, from 1875 until 1895,[408] and sat on its two-man jury alongside the squire's steward, Benjamin Love. Until 1882, he was also the hayward. Earlier, each of these positions had been held by different men. *The Salisbury Times*' report concluded with the rallying cry, 'Oh! When shall we have the Parish Councils Bill at work with the power of the Labourers' Union behind it!'

* See Chapter 35.

† See Chapter 37.

Ben Riley of the English Land Restoration League addressed the Liberal Club in the Town Hall at Earlestown on 19 March 1894. The organisation's main objective was the abolition of landlordism. Riley had accompanied the Red Van on its travels through England's agricultural districts. His speech was published in several newspapers under the heading 'The Land Question.' In it, he mentioned Compton by name:[409]

> In a place called Compton Chamberlain [*sic*], where the land belonged to one man only, and was rented by one farmer [John Keevil], who paid his men 6s. 7s. and 10s. per week, and to a boy 14 years of age, acting as a shepherd boy, he was paying 2½d. per day — (shame) — a branch of the labourers' union was formed in the place and the farmer when he got to hear of it, sent out word to the first man who took up his card, [that he] would have to leave his house and clear out of the village, and this was the power that monopoly of the land gave the farmers.

The Local Government Act that *The Salisbury Times* so eagerly awaited had received Royal Assent exactly two weeks before, on the 5th of March. Its purpose was to engender greater democracy by enabling landowners, farmers, and labourers to have a voice in the decisions which impacted their communities. Reverend Digges hastily awakened from his slumbers to become an active ally for his parishioners. He applauded the Liberal Party's success in introducing district and parish councils by means of the Act. Compton unfortunately failed to qualify for a parish council, which is a body corporate, because its population totalled less than three hundred. Instead, from 1895, its former vestry meetings, attended by the squire, parson, and principal ratepayers, were superseded by parish meetings, which were open to all congregants.

Paradoxically, although another aim of the Act was to break the hold of the Church of England, many parishes, including Compton, elected their vicar as chairman of the first parish meeting. With his election to the chair, Digges' influence increased at the expense of the real power broker in this particular village, the squire. Penruddocke, to his undoubted chagrin, lost his hegemony, and the vicar emerged as no run-of-the-mill clergyman. Far from seeking to shore up the squire, he was keen for parishioners to express their free opinion. He was supported by market gardener William Thorne, an ardent member of the Liberal Party. Relations between himself and the landowner had already become strained in 1894. Reverend Digges' appointment by the Board of Guardians to the chaplaincy of the workhouse in Wilton had been vetoed by the bishop, without any grounds being given. When the dismayed guardians asked the bishop to put forward his reasons, he replied that he could not discuss them.[410] The post had fallen vacant because Reverend John Hungerford Penruddocke, Charles' uncle, had resigned to take up another position. Would it be farfetched to surmise that the good Reverend Penruddocke whispered a word into the bishop's ear on behalf of his vengeful nephew?

Another facet of the Act which irritated Penruddocke was the obligation imposed on parish councils, or meetings, to provide allotments for the labouring poor if requested. At its very first assembly, the squire informed parishioners that if they required allotments at a reasonable rate, they could reach a mutual arrangement directly with the owner or occupier — this being a far preferable and less costly plan than renting them through the County Council.[411]

An article in *Truth* published on 6 January 1898 declared, 'The facts seem worth reproducing as a proof of the unchecked despotism still wielded here and there in rural England by lords of the soil.' Its reporter was referring to recent events at Compton Chamberlayne. *Truth* was a national liberal periodical known for its investigative journalism. Charles Penruddocke, Reverend Dudley Digges, and William Thorne, his churchwarden, were the starring protagonists of these events. Digges had become the vicar of Compton under Penruddocke's patronage in July 1884 — a patronage the squire had now come to regret. Hilda Kerley described him as a kindly man, who cared for his parishioners, and every year paid one shilling for each household into the village shop, so they could have something extra for their tea on Christmas Day. Digges took the trouble to give his parishioner a reference of good character, when the shepherd Alfred Shute was convicted for killing game following a complaint brought by H F Pollock MP, who had shooting rights on Penruddockes' land.[412]

Open warfare broke out when Digges shifted the Sunday afternoon service to the evening and introduced music to accompany the choir. He pointed out in a sermon that both changes were made at the request of members of his congregation.[413] Some were unable to attend church in the afternoon because they were obliged to undertake chores, such as milking. Husbandry was sacrosanct, and always took priority. Even the Court Baron session on 24 March 1655 had adjourned early to allow tenants to bring their stock to pasture.[414] The choir had asked for music, as many people now had harmoniums in their cottages, where such instruments had not been known before. The vicar felt his parishioners would no longer put up with the monotonal world of the past. Without change, they would be enticed to attend other churches which were literally more in tune with the times.

Penruddocke vehemently opposed these proposals. When the vicar refused to yield, the squire resorted to other means of persuasion — or retaliation. He withheld payment of a stipend of £10 per annum, with which he had agreed to supplement Digges' yearly salary of £90, a sum described by *Truth* as a very poor living for a vicar in any case. He evicted the parson from his stables and coach house, as well as from the small patch of land where his wife kept chickens to bolster their income. In the same vein, Digges turned his graphology hobby into profit — not much, admittedly — he charged only one shilling for analysing handwriting to identify personality traits.[415] Penruddocke then locked the gate leading to the church, which stood within the walls of Compton Park, and posted a notice announcing that the key could be obtained from him on request. He even complained to the bishop that the vicarage was in a poor state of repair, but here he found himself foiled, because 'thanks to the generosity of numerous gentlemen [from the village] the necessary sum' was subscribed, and work was carried out to put the building back into good repair.

At some point after 1894, the Parish Meeting Chairmanship passed to Charles Penruddocke, who preferred to convene such gatherings in the servants' hall at Compton Park. This change of venue to within his own house caused friction. The only public meeting place in the village was its schoolroom, also owned by the squire, but let to the education authority. How it should be used outside of school hours, however, Penruddocke considered to be for himself alone to sanction. He refused permission for use of the capacious room for a parish church choir supper in December 1898. The vicar was constrained to hold the event at the vicarage, where attendees were cramped for space.[416]

The squire's preference for holding meetings in his home may well have been influenced by a factor not mentioned by newspapers in this context. The schoolroom only had oil light, whereas his abode was brilliantly lit with electricity, generated by chromozone batteries patented by Emmens, as was the church, where eight Swann's bulbs produced aluminescence equal to that of five candles.[417] It was, thought the 1886 traveller W. L., the only county church so lit.[418] A newspaper article published a couple of years earlier reports that a letter V was placed on the north side of the Big House for the Queen's Jubilee celebrations, 'brightly illuminated, and formed of electric lamps.[419] These were burning all through the summer night, and the light could be seen from a long distance.' When George Cross acquired the house in 1933, candles were still its only method of lighting. Compton was one of the last villages to be connected to the national electric grid system during the early 1950s.[420]

As reported in the *Salisbury Journal* on 26 June 1887, tensions between the squire and vicar caused 'a regrettable split in the parish.' This led to two programmes being arranged for the Queen's Jubilee celebrations. One was drawn up by the committee, of which the vicar was chairman, William Thorne secretary and Walter Keevil treasurer. Walter's brother William of Swallowcliffe was the vice chairman. The other was arranged by Charles Penruddocke. Both started at 1.30. Ninety guests sat down to a substantial repast in a barn on Manor Farm by courtesy of the late John Keevil's executors. While a large party of Mr Penruddocke's people marched into the deer park and sat down in a tent to a sumptuous dinner. The surprising revelation that both Walter and his brother sided with the vicar makes me wonder if all along they — as well as their sister who married the bailiff's son in London — had rejected their father's mode of conduct in the village.

The annual Parish Meeting held on 17 March 1898 in the schoolroom was the first to be reported in the papers after Penruddocke had become chairman. He was proposed for a second term by Walter Keevil, and was reappointed to the chair. Keevil and William Langdon were elected as overseers: Keevil proposed by Arthur Roberts, the keeper of the King's Elm Inn, and seconded by Henry Jarvis, a blacksmith, and William, by Penruddocke, seconded by George Barrett, his gamekeeper.[421] Where William's allegiances lay became apparent fairly early on. He was more than content to have a Tory landlord, and there can be little doubt he voted for his party at every election.

Another dispute between the squire and the vicar, aided by his churchwarden, centred on the sum of £3 per annum payable to the parish clerk. Charles Penruddocke held this position, as well as those of lay rector and people's churchwarden. He appointed hurdle maker John Wyatt as his deputy, and assigned the parish clerk's duties to him. Digges, who was of the opinion that the squire, rather than his working-class parishioners, should bear the cost, decided to hold back the clerk's payment until such time as funds were sufficient. Although the fee would be passed on to Wyatt, the appointment of a deputy was not considered common practice.

The Easter Parish Meeting of 1898 was held in the church on 15 April.[422] As Penruddocke had a cold, his youngest daughter Sybil took his place — somewhat innovatively, given only four years had passed since the Local Government Act allowed women to serve on district councils. Presumably, Charles' wife Flora, adhering to her husband's traditionalist views, shied away from the task, and Sybil was a last resort, their only son married by then and living in Somerset. The first part of the meeting was taken up by an argument between Miss Penruddocke and the vicar about how the organist's salary should be paid. Eventually, the deputy clerk and his own remuneration came into question. The sharp exchanges of words William heard came as a shock to him. He was very sorry to witness such unpleasantness at that kind of assembly, and thought things had been aired which ought not to have been said. The vicar pointed out that he was new to the village, and unacquainted with past events. Jarvis demanded that Digges lay out the accounts. He was cautioned by Walter Keevil, who appears to have been of a more diplomatic disposition than his fellows, to be careful about any comments that suggested the vicar's finances were not in order. Walter proposed that the balance of the church money should be paid to the clerk, and Thorne volunteered to undertake the parish clerk's tasks on a pro bono basis, an offer Walter highly commended. Thorne then wrote a letter to *The Salisbury Times* addressed to Mr Penruddocke, stating that he had not yet received a reply to his offer. His letter was published on 29 April, together with Penruddocke's refusal to step down. He maintained that considerable dissatisfaction had been expressed by parishioners at the last parish meeting concerning the vicar's accounts, and suggested they be posted on the church door.[423]

Photo of Sybil Penruddocke (1896-1968).

Letters playing out the dispute between Thorne and Penruddocke continued to appear in *The Salisbury Times* in June.[424] Penruddocke contended that monies had been collected and should be used to pay the parish clerk, namely himself. Thorne affirmed that it was for the vicar to decide how the money was spent. But there were other commitments to be fulfilled:

> Do you suppose that any of the clergy in the neighbouring parishes or elsewhere do allow such uncalled for, and intolerable interference, by any parishioner,

even if he happens to be the squire, and although you *never* attend church during the divine service, I am very sorry that you find time to attend to such petty affairs.

Reverend Digges took to the pulpit to appeal for donations to cover the parish clerk's outstanding salary of £2 and 6 shillings. His sermon was reported in full in *The Salisbury Times* on 1 July 1898. Between 50 and 60 parishioners had attended the service. After reading a passage from the Bible appropriate to the situation, the vicar recounted the facts: when he had accepted his position fourteen years earlier, it had been agreed that all ecclesiastic expenses, including the parish clerk's salary, would be paid by a voluntary rate contributed by the lay preacher and two farmers. As of the last parish meeting, only 14 shillings of the £3 needed had been raised for his salary, after deducting necessary expenses for running the building. While the churchwarden had offered to undertake the clerk's duties on a pro bono basis, Mr Penruddocke had refused to step down. The collection at the service raised a further £1 7s 9d and 3 farthings.

At the beginning of February 1899, a ridiculous sub-dispute involving cushions arose after Thorne removed one from the church for repair. A complaint made to the bishop elicited the response that he regretted a quarrel over such trumpery as a cushion, and could not intervene in trivial matters.[425]

Thorne and the Reverend both preferred the schoolroom as neutral ground for parish meetings but, when it suited him, the chairman continued to hold them in his servants' hall at Compton Park, as he did on the 20th of February. A reporter from *The Salisbury Times* tried to attend, but was ejected after a proposal by Thomas Sansome, the foreman of the squire's estate, that they did not require any 'stranger' amongst them, was carried. Little business was discussed on the day, except for the county rate.[426]

This became too much for Thorne, who four days later convened another meeting in one of his hothouses in the gardens at Compton Park to decide where they should be held in future.[427] Fifteen parishioners attended. A reporter from *The Salisbury Times* was welcomed. The ambience is vividly described in his article of 3 March: 'The dim light of a candle at one end of the house, and that of a lamp placed upon an impoverished table for the *Times* man, consisting of a board laid across a large water tank, was all there was to lighten the darkness.' But he was optimistic: 'For a long time past there have been progressives, and pretty vigorous ones, in the parish, but these have been practically alone, or if followed only by a number whose following had been done in secret. But "the worm will turn" at last, and it looks very much as if Compton people are beginning to assert themselves.' The need to urge the burial board to extend Compton's cemetery, as only one plot was left in its current ground, was also discussed at the meeting.

Penruddocke's fury boiled over when he read the report. He called yet another meeting in the schoolroom on 4 March, when he brought into question that those who had attended the hothouse were not on the voting register, as too old and infirm to sign, or having bankruptcies in their family.[428] Thorne immediately contested these allegations, whereupon the chairman used the time remaining to attack Thorne, arguing that he did not carry the support of the parishioners. Predictably, Thorne again resorted to the press, writing a letter to *The Salisbury Times* denying the accusations made against him.[429]

Votes at parish meetings were customarily registered by a show of hands. Thorne had proposed holding secret ballots following Penruddocke's election as chairman in 1897, but this had failed, as did his opposition to a counter-proposal in 1899 that the chairman be allowed to choose the venue, prompting Thorne to proclaim that parishioners who backed Penruddocke were 'on chain' to him.[430]

On 22 September 1899, *The Salisbury Times* reported that after a prolonged period of quiet in Compton, another dispute had arisen between Reverend Digges and Mr Penruddocke. The vicar, having discovered that the harvest festival decorations had not been taken down, gathered them together himself and left them in the porch. He sent a letter to the squire requesting to have them removed and, as was the norm, to arrange for the lights in the church to be turned on for the next service. Although it seems to have been Penruddocke's duty to do so, the decorations were not taken away, and only the altar was illuminated. When Digges complained to Mr Chalke, who had replaced Wyatt as his deputy clerk, he refused to carry out the vicar's instructions, maintaining that he only took orders from the squire.

Charles Penruddocke died on 30 October 1899. In reporting his death, *The Salisbury Times* journalist wrote tongue-in-cheek:[431]

> Our readers are well aware of the interest Mr Penruddocke took in parochial matters. He was a Chairman of the parish meeting and of the burial board. He was parish clerk as well. He never lost his hold on parochial matters, and however much we have felt it our duty to disagree with him, it is with much regret that we announce his sudden demise, and realise the fact that he will take no further part in the parish difficulties which had made Compton Chamberlayne notorious.

William's daughter Ada gave her own account in the letter she wrote on the first day of the new century: 'There are several people laid up here with influenza, our shepherd is home for one, Joe is also very poorly today, has not been out all day. I don't think any of us have written since the squire died, that was father's landlord, he died the last day of October [actually the day before], only ill a few days.'

The *Salisbury and Winchester Journal's* obituary informs us that he had been in feeble health for some time, and had had a paralytic seizure, which ended fatally on his return from sitting as a magistrate at the county court. Ada continued her letter by explaining Charles Penruddocke's background, as well as how there came to be a photograph of Sybil Penruddocke amongst our family papers:

> He was 72 years [actually 71] and had lived in Compton for 50 years, he inherited the property from his [great] uncle when he was only 14 [in 1843], he has one son and four five daughters, the son is married and has been living down in Somerset, where they own a good bit of property, but I suppose very soon now he will be coming to Compton to live, three of the daughters are married, and the other two [Sybil and Constance] with their mother are going to live at a place called Teffont, a few miles from here, the youngest (Miss Sybil) came up to say 'Good Bye' to us the day that Mary and I fetched John home from school [at Wilton, where he was a weekly boarder], I was sorry not to see her, but she is very nice, she brought mother her photograph ... Mary, Emily and I are going to Salisbury now.

The squire's family rewarded loyalty with a photograph. Penruddocke's son, who she says is to move up from Somerset to take over the estate from the deceased, was also called Charles.* Tensions in the village, at least between the vicar and squire, eased after old Penruddocke's death. However, his successor was soon to experience problems of another kind.

Once the old squire had departed this world, parish gatherings became excruciatingly dull affairs. Their pinnacle of excitement was the post office protest great-grandfather William initiated in his capacity as an officer of the Parish Meeting during the War.† The parish had joined the Wilton Poor Law Union in 1836, and came under the jurisdiction of Wilton Rural District Council in 1894. At a meeting of the Board of Guardians and Rural District

---

* Charles junior lived at Brinsome in Bratton Seymour, near Wincanton.

† See Chapter 54.

Council, reported by the *Salisbury and Winchester Journal* on 17 August 1907, William called for the county surveyor to trim the hedges to reduce the danger of a serious collision between motor cars and other conveyances at the junction of the Compton and Dinton roads. Only nine months later, the need to pay close attention to road safety became evident. An inquest was held at Manor Farmhouse concerning little Albert Noyce, a farm labourer's son who was knocked down and killed by a car in Compton, just short of his fifth birthday.[432] The driver's view had not been obstructed. He had had time to blow his horn several times. Nevertheless, he was exonerated. It makes one wonder about 'justice' favouring the richer members of society.

51
Turn of the Century Madness Repeats Itself

Just as we saw a glut of legal actions during the transition from the 16th into the 17th centuries, the citizens of Compton took up arms in the courts again at the dawn of the 20th.

Discomforting as it is to admit, my great-grandfather was the main protagonist. He teeters on the edge of living memory, half in sight, half falling away. Tantalisingly, my father, who knew his grandfather — he died when Willie was eleven — never spoke of him. Not only that, he did not pass down any sense of family feeling towards him. A sole exclamation mark in one of his letters to me hints at how he regarded his grandfather. In describing the contents of the correspondence between Mary and John, which I discuss in Chapter 53, he told me that Mary wanted to go to Australia, and then, referring to William, wrote 'Grandfather was being difficult!' From this, I surmise that it was not an unusual occurrence.

Oddly, there are virtually no family stories about him. An impression of his personality can only be gleaned by reading family letters and newspaper articles. These point to his not having been an easy person to deal with. His brother-in-law, perhaps with a pang of jealousy, claimed that William 'gets some way people take rather a dislike to him.' But he was certainly hardworking. There are accounts of him becoming ill with the unremitting burden of his labour, physical strength having been the essence of a farming life, and the source of its pride. It distinguished the admirable from the less worthy. William's sister Elizabeth disparagingly labelled many of her cousins 'delicate.' William's Cornish heritage instilled in him intensity and stubbornness — and he was ambitious too. He had to have possessed these qualities to take on Manor Farm, when perhaps his predominant motivation was to do his absolute best for his children. But there was something else as well, a fidelity to farming as the only real life, the one he was determined his sons should also embrace.

I have no doubt that William was a good farmer in the same way as Bill Petch — an agriculture-college-educated tractor driver who worked for my great-uncle Rupert between 1961 and 1965 — described his boss in his unpublished autobiography as 'one of the neatest and most careful farmers I have known.'[433] After reporting that his dairyman thought Rupert was a sweet old man, Petch admitted 'stubborn and bigoted' came more readily to his mind, but he admired Rupert regardless:

> The main reason that I liked him was that he cared for his stock ... His concern for his cattle was not because he loved them; he wanted to be proud of them. His stock must be at least equal to his neighbour's cattle and preferably be superior. His cattle on the down had to be checked, closely checked, every other day in summer and every day in winter.

My father also displayed a competitive streak. On drives through the countryside with him, his eyes were not so much on the road as over the hedge, examining crops and comparing them with his own.

An interesting aspect of William's personality was his attitude towards hierarchy. While I remain amused by his condemnation of some Wiltshire farmers who behaved like squires, this shows that he was conscious of his place within the social pecking order — and accepting of it. He had a convivial relationship with 'the Squire,' his landlord. He submitted to him, rather than joining fellow tenant Thorne, the market gardener, in challenging the village hegemony.

William belonged to a generation that considered a farmworker of low status, yet demanded his loyalty — a labourer taking employment with another farmer in the neighbourhood was viewed as treasonous. Little empathy towards workers, or appreciation of their need for a decent wage, impinged upon a farmer's consciousness. Neither were they concerned about what happened to labourers after they became too old to work, and impoverished. Like most farm toiling families, the Plowmans, starting with the stonemasons, had lived in Compton for generations. Joseph, the last of them, was an agricultural labourer. In 1904, he was 69, and in such a poor situation that his son William, who was a coal haulier earning £1 a week, was summonsed by Wilton Union for failing to support his father.[434] He could not afford financial help because he had an invalid wife. Earlier in the year, Joseph's wife Annie had advertised in *The Salisbury Times* for washing and needlework.[435] Fortunately, she was appointed as sub-postmistress at Compton during the following summer,[436] a happy turn of events of which Joseph was unaware, as he had died during the preceding winter.

Newspaper reports of court cases suggest that William had trouble with his farmworkers or, perhaps more accurately, they with him. They testify to the fact that he had a hot temper, which was especially vented on his workmen. He sued two of them in 1902, the first incident reported in *The Western Gazette* on 2 August. William alleged that Henry Fry (James' and Anne's son) had assaulted him. Fry had struck William in a moment of temper. William withdrew the summons after he apologised and promised to behave in future. On 19 December, *The Salisbury Times* reported a claim for £5 damages against George Thomas, who had left William's employment after a fortnight without giving notice. I have been unable to discover the outcome of this case.

Next, on 27 October 1905, *The Salisbury Times* reported that William had appeared before the Sarum County Sessions, himself summonsed for assaulting Annie Roberts, the wife of his dairyman Edward Roberts, who had left his service two years before to better himself. Edward subsequently returned at William's invitation, and had been with him for four or five months when he met with certain injuries, which were to be the subject of a civil action. He wrote a letter to his employer which his wife, accompanied by their daughter Mrs Ruddle, delivered to the farmhouse:

> Mr Langdon, just a line to you to tell you that owing to you driving a cow over me while I was doing my work I have to send for my doctor. I don't know what you intend to do. I am not able to work, therefore you must stand the consequences of it. I must tell you it has ruined me for life. You can please yourself what you do as I have shown it to different people and will show it to you if you come. I have three or four witnesses. — E. Roberts.

Annie's solicitor presented her version of what happened when she gave the letter to William:

> Mr Langdon said he must go in and put his glasses on, and after a lengthy absence he returned and said he knew nothing about what the letter referred to. Mrs Roberts then asked him for the boys' wages [due to her sons for leading horses during ploughing], whereupon Mr Langdon seized her by the dress, tore it, and catching her hold by the throat knocked her against the laurels, and threw her on the ground, stunning her. He then dragged her halfway across the yard, when she became unconscious. The husband, Mr Roberts, was sent for, and came near the scene, but he felt that perhaps his presence would only aggravate the situation, and so he remained outside and sent for the police.

William's take on events was somewhat different. He claimed that Roberts had refused to do his work and left. Three days later, Annie came to his house and handed him a note. He asked her what it meant, saying a cow had not stepped on her husband, the whole affair was a pack of lies, and she should go about her business. She refused to move until she received compensation, along with her husband's wages. Knowing she was a dangerous woman, William went indoors until his son Joe came, so that he would have a witness as to what transpired. He then ordered her to leave, or he would put her out. She attempted to strike him, he caught her by the wrists and pulled her five or six paces, whereupon she 'flopped' down. And there he left her, while her daughter walked up and down with a baby in her arms, laughing. She was not insensible. He never struck her in any way, and had never struck a woman in his life.

On cross-examination by William's solicitor, Annie denied that she had tried to strike the farmer in the face, although she admitted to putting up her hands when he attacked her. She could not remember whether, when her daughter came and whispered to her as she lay on the ground, she immediately got up and walked away. She had been in this court before, but it was nothing to do with the present proceedings.

Questioned by Annie's solicitor, William maintained that he was unaware of any opinion in the neighbourhood that he had a lot of trouble with his workpeople. He could always get plenty of labour. The bench dismissed the case and ordered each side to pay its own costs. It is worth noting that one of the eight magistrates was Charles Penruddocke, William's landlord.

The truth of this matter is illusive. Edward Roberts was a violent man. A report in *The Salisbury Times* on 14 August 1903 describes an incident during which he turned his family out of the house and went after his son with a knife. The son told Constable Perrett that his father had gone out of his mind. Although the prosecution requested the charge be dropped, Roberts was bound over to keep the peace. His tribe was altogether dubious. One of the two Annie Roberts in Compton was found guilty of stealing tobacco in Salisbury in April 1904.[437]

The Salisbury Times of 12 January 1906, under the heading 'Strange Conduct of a Farmer,' reported that Henry Ruddle of Compton had been summonsed for failing to send his son to school regularly. The school attendance officer said he believed the boy was being kept away against his parents' wishes, that a farmer was meeting him on his way to school and taking him off to work. The inspector had warned the farmer, but no notice had been taken. The child's mother, when questioned, agreed that this was true. She was asked to name the farmer: 'Mr Langdon, sir.' This report needs, however, to be considered in the context of the unsuccessful case Mrs Roberts, her mother, had initiated against William only three months before. Revenge might have prompted the accusation — although surely, if not true, William would have said so to the school inspector. More likely, William was influenced by the heated debates in Parliament with regard to Elementary Education Acts that made schooling compulsory up to the age of thirteen years. Opponents of state-provided education argued that the place to learn farm work was in the fields, and warned that once labourers became educated, they would not want to do manual work anymore. They would be seduced to better themselves. Learning would give them dangerous ideas above their station, and erode the social hierarchy. William was one of those ruthless farmers who ignored the provisions of the Acts which made employing a child under thirteen — before he or she had attained the minimum requirements for leaving school — illegal. He had no compunction in spiriting the boy away as cheap labour, all the while paying for his own children's private education. However, even his own children missed lessons to help with gathering in the harvest. The village school register, which is available for the years 1872-1899,[438] consistently records poor attendance from mid-June to mid-July, when the boys were in the fields haymaking, and for August and the first week in September, when they were harvesting. William's predecessor John Keevil employed children for these tasks, even though he was the school's manager and despite the school mistress' reports of the unlawfully hiring to the school inspector, who frequently visited to check on the children's attendance.

The last report I have uncovered where great-grandfather found himself in court was published by *The Salisbury Times* on 1 March 1912 and pointedly emphasises the impasse between the farmer's and labourer's view of their situations. James Henry Noyce, Albert's father, sued William for dismissal without notice. His boss claimed he was a slacker. Noyce's lawyer, Mr Trethowan, asked him, "If Noyce was so unsatisfactory I wonder you didn't get rid of him before?" William replied, "There are a good many wonders in this world. We employers of labour have got to put up with a good deal." Mr Trethowan countered, "Yes, so have agricultural labourers." William paid Noyce 12s a week, whereas the national average for a farmwork was around 16s.

The other Roberts couple in the village, Emmanuel and Annie, also found themselves in court. Emily Parsons brought a complaint against Emmanuel for using threatening language.[439] The case was heard at the Salisbury County Petty Sessions in March 1904, amid much hilarity in the public gallery. The parties and witnesses accused each other of swearing and using abominable language. They were neighbours, living next door to the post office, which was on the A30 to the east of Manor Farm at the time. Seemingly, the trouble

The old post office cottages on the A30 main road, where the warring neighbours, the Roberts and Parsons, lived next to the original post office.

started when a lodger moved from the Roberts' to the Parson's household. Emily deposed that Roberts had accused her of breaking into his house, and threatened to break her neck. Roberts countered that she had pinched his lodger, and stolen food from him: 'You taken eggs and fowls and buckets of milk to keep him with.' Emily denied this, insulting Roberts by calling him 'Ginger.' A second complaint, brought by Annie against Emily Parsons, was heard at the same time, also based on the use of threatening language, viz threatening to put her to bed for three years. Both of the accused were bound over to keep the peace in the sum of £5.

The upper crust was not exempt from legal troubles either, as we will shortly see in the next Chapter.

52
CRUELTY AT THE BIG HOUSE

THE PENRUDDOCKE NAME became infamous throughout Britain once again. At the instigation of the Royal Society for the Prevention of Cruelty to Children (RSPCC), an action was brought against Annie Penruddocke, the wife of the new squire Charles, for ill-treating their daughter Letitia Constance. Connie, as she was called, had just passed her sixth birthday. She was the fifth of six children. Flora, Charles, and twins George and Sybil, were older, and Thomas was younger than she. The case came before Mr Justice Bigham at the Old Bailey in November 1902, having been transferred from Wiltshire when it was deemed that local feeling against the defendant would prevent a fair trial.[440]

A letter sent by the senior housemaid and butler had alerted the RSPCC to the girl's plight. This was a brave move, which would not have been undertaken lightly. They knew they risked losing not only their employment, but also the home which came with their jobs. The Society obtained a warrant, and dispatched a surgeon to the house to examine Connie. He found multiple marks on her body, confirming that she had been beaten. He additionally noted that her face was swollen, consistent with the allegation that her mother had rubbed it with nettles.

The prosecution set out their contention that the mother had not just beaten her daughter, she also had a spiteful antipathy towards her, treating her differently from her other five children. Evidence was given by two former governesses and servants of the household. They testified that they had heard screams from the 'Justice Room,' and afterwards seen bruises on Connie's body. The mother had been seen with a whip in her hands, and was observed pushing her daughter off some mounting stones, whose purpose was to facilitate climbing onto the backs of horses. She had hit the girl with her fist, causing her to fall in the park and cry with pain. The child herself testified that her mother often kicked her, and had put a half-dead wasp down her neck.

One of the former governesses reported that Connie was given very little food compared with the other children. Once, her mother had asked if she would like some cake, which she was not usually allowed, and then gave her a piece with mustard inserted into it. Pepper had been put into the child's mouth. Connie was not allowed to go on walks with the other children. Instead, she was made to run between the house and lodge gates for two to three hours, or to stand in the fork of a tree for hours on end — this, in all weathers. She was clothed poorly, banished to a bedroom in the attic away from the rest of the children, and given fewer bedclothes. Upon hearing that the girl's hair had been admired, her mother cut it off and tied a piece of string to what remained, attaching the other end under her arm, claiming it would improve her deportment.

The sentiments Annie expressed towards Connie were alarming. One day the children had been riding a donkey. When they came in for dinner, the little boy Charlie told his mother that the groom had put Connie on the donkey. 'I wish she had fallen off and broken her neck,' said the mother to her children. 'But the groom held her on, mother,' Charlie explained. 'Then for the future the groom should not hold her on.' Mrs Penruddocke replied. She was overheard saying it would be very good if Connie ate poisonous berries, and made her sleep in the same room as a sibling with chickenpox, voicing her hope that she would become ill, and it would finish her off.

Most of the allegations were denied. For the rest, the substance of the defence was that the treatment Annie had meted out was intended to cure the girl of an infirmity or, as it was sometimes styled, 'bad habit.' The nature of that habit was not once identified. However, the defence lawyer provided a single clue: he referred to the book *Advice to a Mother on the Management of Her Children* by Pye Henry Chavasse in support of Annie's decision to reduce the quantity of Connie's meat and bedclothes. He asked, 'Does this habit occasionally arise from idleness in which case a little wholesome correction would be necessary?' Page 315 of the 15th edition, published in 1898, reads: 'Occasionally wetting the bed arises from idleness in which case a little wholesome correction will be necessary ... the child should sleep in a well-ventilated room and not too warmly covered with bedclothes ... it could be due to an over acid state of the urine or to some article of food,' under which circumstances the quantity of meat in the diet should be reduced. That a mother could become so malevolent over such a trivial thing as bedwetting is beyond unfathomable!

Annie Penruddocke was found guilty of neglect and causing bodily harm to her daughter, but cleared of causing her unnecessary suffering. Notwithstanding, Mr Justice Bigham expressed his extreme sorrow that the jury had felt themselves compelled to come to the conclusion at which they

Newspaper sketches of the trial of Annie Penruddocke at the Old Bailey in November 1902. A reporter observed that Mrs Penruddocke, clad in costly furs and wearing a fashionable black toque, looked strangely out of sympathy with her surroundings. Newspaper image © The British Library Board. All rights reserved. With thanks to The British Newspaper Archive (www.britishnewspaperarchive.co.uk).

had arrived. He thought the defendant had merely allowed her temper to get the better of her, and treated the child in an unkind way. The girl's health had not suffered, and she would be safe in future. He delivered Connie into the custody of Dr Charles Penruddocke, her father's cousin — despite the fact that he had deposed at the hearing that she seemed perfectly happy during his visits to Compton Park.

On the night of the verdict, people tramped miles into Salisbury to hear the result. An enormous crowd waited for a promised telegraphic message of the results of the trial outside the *Salisbury and Winchester Journal* office. While, the entrance to the Railway station was blocked by people buying the evening newspapers, until they sold out.

Even though the judge ruled that Connie would be safer away from her mother, it seems he could not bring himself to hand down a severe punishment.

The fine imposed on Mrs Penruddocke — £50, when the maximum penalty could have been £200 or two years' imprisonment — caused a national outcry. The *Daily Express* published a sensational report of riots in Salisbury after the verdict was announced, which its mayor dismissed as nonsense, but the news was emphatically received with surprise and indignation. Protests at one law for the rich, another for the poor, were heard. The *Western Gazette* compared the sentence to contemporary ones handed down under the same Act to two poor women. One was sent to prison for two months with hard labour for neglecting her two children and the other condemned to two months' hard labour for neglecting her six children. The media considered that Annie had been mollycoddled by the court. She was allowed to sit on a cushioned, maroon-coloured leather armchair in the dock, and escorted to luncheon each day in the under-sheriff's room. Members of the public, including some of the jurors, wrote angry letters to the press. Questions were raised in Parliament.

Murmurs regarding a Penruddocke mother's cruelty to her child still lurked under the surface in my day, but I only learnt the facts from reading old newspapers. My grandfather believed her malice had been exaggerated. The *Western Gazette* reporter who visited the village found that, although people in Compton were wary of disclosing their opinions, bitter feelings towards Mrs Penruddocke were palpable. Tenants felt detestation and horror at the revelations made at the Old Bailey. The reporter referred to past strife in the village: 'Now again the outlook is gloomy, and everything appears unsettled.' Locals, however, were less condemning of the lady's husband. In his testimony, he had claimed in, as the *Morning Leader* reported, 'a peculiarly thin voice for such a big man' not to have been aware of any ill treatment, but said he had known of, and indeed approved, the reduction of meat in their daughter's diet. He was removed from his role as magistrate — but fear not — he was later reappointed. Compton House was shut for a period, as it had once been two and a half centuries before. The Penruddockes returned to their home at Wimborne in Dorset. They considered selling up at Compton, and closing the family vault, but soon came back to the village.

The *Morning Leader* set up a fund for William Warr, the butler who had been a co-informant in the case. With the £39, 7s 6d raised, he was able to emigrate to California.[441] Reginald Sansome, an employee who gave evidence, was dismissed after the hearing, and served with a notice to quit his cottage on Christmas Day in 1903. He was a young man of 22, the only provider for his recently widowed mother according to a report in the *Dundee Evening Post*, which concluded with the commendation that Reginald 'is stated to be a good worker and bears an excellent character.'[442] He thankfully secured a job as a carpenter in Long Bredy, Devon. Reginald's father had been the foreman who proposed the motion that *The Salisbury Times* reporter be removed from the parish meeting in February 1899,[443] no doubt at the behest of Charles Penruddocke senior. So much for loyalty.

The medical practitioner Charles Penruddocke lived in Wylye House near Dinton. How long Connie stayed with him, and whether she ever lived with her parents again, is not known. At the time of the 1911 census, she was attending a boarding school in Bridport in Dorset. A Constance Penruddocke was one of the mourners listed at Charles' funeral at Compton on 5 October 1929.[444] A then 33-year-old Connie might have forgiven her parents, but this lady could equally well have been her spinster aunt Constance, who was 72, and also lived in Dinton.

Ultimately, Connie fared better than her siblings. The First World War and its effects cut short the lives of her three brothers, and her two sisters never married. Constance wedded Horace Edgar Bowle, a member of the Diplomatic Service, in 1917. They appear not to have had children. He lived to the age of 92. Connie not only survived him, but all her siblings. She died in 1989, at the age of 93.

53
Breach of Promise: Langdon vs Keevil

THE ATMOSPHERE WAS fraught, not only at Compton Park, but also at Manor Farm. Only Mary among William's nine children seems to have had the strength of character to challenge her dominant father. She grew up at a time when it was firmly believed that God had set out principles by which moral supremacy was committed into the hands of men. While women of Mary's social class were beginning to seek control of their lives, the stark practicality of their total financial dependence on their male 'benefactors' stood implacably in their way.

Mary was 25, with a younger sister about to marry, when in desperation she turned to her cousin John in Australia. She wrote to him on 8 October 1899:

> I am writing to ask you if you think there is a good prospect of such an one as me getting on well in Australia, and could I be of any service to you in looking after any of your concerns whilst you are home next year; Every thing seems to go wrong with me home here, so I feel determined to get away somewhere to Australia if you think there is a good prospect and I can get father to pay my passage out; I cannot go into the details of all the worries and bothers I have had here. I think father is responsible for a great many that is why I wish to get away from home, I know perfectly well it is no use to expect all sunshine anywhere but for a long time here it has been all clouds ... I have thought of writing you about my going to Australia for sometime past but have kept putting it off in the hope that matters would eventually brighten up here but it only seems to go worse and worse; will you be kind enough to send me your opinion on the matter by return if possible in the meantime I shall make all the enquiries I can about passage etc. Please do not say a word about this to anyone ... I have not been to Cornwall since I left and I feel now I would not go there for a holiday if I had the chance. Of course, I am sorry to write you such a sad letter and hope all things are prospering with you.

Compton Chamberlayne
Salisbury
Oct. 8. 99.

Dear John,

No doubt you will be a bit surprised to hear from me again seeing it was only a few weeks ago I wrote, I am writing to ask if you think there is a good prospect of such an one as me getting on well in Australia, and could I be of any service to you in looking after any of your concerns whilst you are home next year; Everything seems to go wrong with me home here, so I feel determined to get away somewhere to Australia if you think there is a good prospect and I can get father to pay my passage out; I cannot go into the details of all the worries and bothers I have had here but I think father is responsible for a great many that is why I wish to get away from home, I know perfectly well it is no use to expect all sunshine anywhere but for a long time here it has been all cloud. I think Mother told you that Ada was to be married next Lady day and go to Gutter Aunty will be glad to have her near Hendra Green again. I have thought of writing you about my going to Australia for a long time past but have kept putting it off in the hope that matters would eventually brighten up here but it only seems to go worse and worse, will you be kind enough to send me your opinion on the matter by return if possible in the meantime I shall make all the enquiries I can about passage etc. Please do not say a word about this to anyone I feel I can trust you to keep this a secret until it is decided also that you will give me your honest opinion. Of course I will not let my people think you slocked me out there, I have told no one I am writing you like this, when I get your reply I will tell them exactly what I have written

Mary's letter to John, her cousin in Australia, dated 8 October 1899.

John now faces a predicament. Being a kind man, he wants to help Mary, but not against her parents' wishes. He sends a letter, presumably by reply on 17 November, saying she might get on alright and do well, but there is 'a lot of chance about it. I will say this if you get your dear Mother and father and Elizabeth's* consent for you to come out here, I will promise, I will be faithful and kind to you, providing you give me the same respect, and do all I can for you.' He tells her he intends to leave Australia to return home to Cornwall on 1 April, but will stay on if she decides to come. Finally, he encloses a letter addressed to William and Emily, and asks Mary to show it to her parents, 'for I have written this in good faith.' At all costs, John wants to avoid conflict with William and Emily. It is intriguing that he thinks Mary also needs her aunt Elizabeth's consent. She must have been a significant person in all their lives, regarded as a matriarch perhaps, and family harmony was important to John. He writes in his next letter: 'It's one's duty to be kind to their parents.'

John surely agonised in trying to pitch his message to them in a tone that was conciliatory, yet supportive of his cousin:

> I hope Mary will show you the letter I have written in answer [to her letter]. I am very sorry to hear things are not going as they should and I must say I give you my heartfelt sympathy and what I have said I hope you will know that I am doing it in an act of kindness for I have very much respect for your family and I could not let Mary's letter go unnoticed so anything I can do for her I will with a good heart at home or out here.

After what must have been a tumultuous Christmas for her, Mary sent another missive on 2 January 1900:

> I hardly know how to reply to yours you will think I am very changeable but I have been considering ever since I wrote you and have come to the conclusion that perhaps after all it would be better to stay on here, at any rate I intend doing so, and to help Ada all I can for the next 3 months, or as long as she is here [before she marries], she is very industrious preparing for her new home ... to return to your reply to my letter, I thank you very much for your consideration. I hope you won't be angry with, or blame me when I tell you that I have not delivered what you wrote to my parents, as it was all about that one matter I

---

* Elizabeth was John's mother, my great-grandfather's only sister. John, who was illegitimate, was brought up by their parents. Elizabeth lived nearby with her husband, who was not John's father. Nevertheless, John had a close relationship with his mother and his uncle William.

thought perhaps as well saying nothing about it, if I did not intend to go, it would only be a disturbance for nothing, for I had not mentioned to them of going before, I have not known what to do.

This about-face crossed over with John's surprise proposal of marriage to his first cousin on 2 December 1899:

Dear Mary, No doubt before you get this letter you have answered my last and pretty well made up your mind what you intend doing, hoping you have the consent of your parents, they can see by my letter to you that I were not slocking [dialect for entice, lure] you out ... work is plentiful enough [here] but then it is so hot you would not like it. It's right enough to be your own mistress out here, and you know that generally takes time ... for my part I can-not see there should be any objection towards you and I getting married for I think we could be happy together.

He hesitates, "if you do not approve of my letter, burn it, and you and I will be good friends as ever." A matrimonial bond was not at all what Mary had in mind, for she was in love with another man. Her father opposed the relationship. Had she given up on trying to bring him around, or accepted the impossibility of standing up to him? Was this the source of such misery that all she wanted was to escape as far away as possible? In the next episode of the correspondence, dated 11 January, she takes flight, but also reveals the truth behind her despair:

I thank you very much for your kind letter, it is indeed kind of you to think so much of me, before you receive this letter you will I hope have received my letter in reply to yours of a week ago — your last letter I have and will keep secret [did she burn it? John kept a copy] and we shall I hope be as good friends as ever, but I do not at all see my way clear to getting married, although I am sure I have every respect for you, the fact is I have been corresponding etc. with a young fellow home here for two years, but my father and him do not get on at all well, consequently it has been very painful for me all along and I am afraid it is not over now, of course I cannot go into the details now in writing, but I have some time got very disheartened with everything home here, as I was when I wrote you asking about coming out; I am very sorry if by my writing in such a strain I have caused you any pain, I observe the very unselfish way you write, not scarcely studying your own self in this matter, well I hope you will come home and enjoy yourself too; perhaps you will meet with some one more worthy of you than I am. Do not say a word of anything I have told you in this to anyone, I shall not have written so much only I know I can safely confide in you.

I received your letter Sunday but was quite unable to reply by Tuesday's mail. I have had a cold in fact we all have and Ada and Will have a slight attack of influenza, Ada being unwell it has made Emily and I very busy, Joe and John have been poorly too they each had a stay indoors for two or three days, they get out now but are far from well, the last few days mother has had rheumalie or something in her hands so you see we have had a lot of sickness … well I hope you have good luck in clearing up your business to come home, and that you will have a pleasant journey.

With so much illness about, the household was in a frenzy before the first of William's and Emily's children was due to marry.

The path to true love continued to be rough for Mary. Seven years later, in 1906, she sued Walter Keevil of Naishes Farm for breach of promise. Newspaper reports, like the one published in the *Cheltenham Chronicle* on 19 January 1907, give an account of the case and a report of the settlement — for the sum of £500 — that Mary received from Walter Keevil. The court hearing took place before Mr Justice Grantham at the Wiltshire Assizes on Monday, 14 January. People jostled for the best places in the public gallery in the hope of sensational entertainment, only to be disappointed when the parties reached an agreement out of court at the last minute. Reporters avidly sprung upon such cases, because the amusement they provided was immensely popular, like our 'clickbait' of today — as the numerous contemporary melodramas and comedies centring on 'the trial' bear witness to. Charles Dickens' debut novel *The Pickwick Papers*, published in 1836, for example, includes a subplot in which widowed landlady Mrs Bardell sues the hapless Mr Pickwick for breach of promise, landing them both in prison for debt.

Mary's suit aroused particular excitement because some years before Lord Herschell had introduced a bill in Parliament to abolish such actions. Mr Justice Grantham was thought to support the bill. He suspected that the parties had settled in the belief he was biased, and set out his position to their advocates. While he accepted that the right to bring proceedings for breach of promise provided a necessary protection for women, he often did not agree with it, considering that a great deal of harm could be caused as a result.

The right to sue over a broken engagement evolved in the common law courts during the reign of Charles I, when a promise to marry was considered to be a contract, like any other. If one party failed to fulfil the bargain, the other was entitled to damages for the loss of the benefit that would have accrued to them if it had been honoured. In the 50 years before Mary filed her writ, around a thousand such actions saw juries awarding damages to the plaintiff, usually a woman, not counting those which were settled out of court. These were times when a woman was not only dependent on men for financial security, but those counted in the middle-classes had few opportunities for employment. Consequently, her chance of an assured future was slim if she had been cast-off by a man she was engaged to and had trusted.

Several bills seeking to abolish such actions were introduced by private members in the House of Commons during the late 19th century. The one proposed by Lord Herschell was debated on 6 May 1879.[445] He contended that numerous cases were brought simply for the purpose of extortion. A torrent of invective from Judge, prosecution counsel, and jury would be brought down on a man if, in trying to justify his refusal to marry, he suggested that the woman was anything but an angel, 'a very embodiment of all the female virtues.' Whereas, had the merits of the given case been fairly investigated, it would have been concluded that the man had not been the one who was to blame. While speaking in the debate, Mr Justice Grantham, adopted a more nuanced approach than newspapers later reported him to have adopted towards the advocates in Mary's action. Even though the law might occasionally be used for purposes of extortion, he believed it had historically worked well for the public. If a girl had been engaged for five or six years, and was then thrown over, she had lost almost three chances out of four of marrying, which would additionally be a great pecuniary loss to her, for which she was entitled to be compensated.

The pleadings in Mary's breach of promise case reveal that she was seeking £2000 in damages.[446] She claimed that on the 27th of June 1905 Walter had promised to marry her 'almost immediately,' and they subsequently fixed the date for the first week in October. But autumn came and went, with no marriage ceremony enacted. By 24 May 1906, she had had enough of his procrastination, and issued the writ. If he was the man she had told John she had been corresponding with for two years at the turn of the century, she had already wasted eight years of her life on him.

Walter's defence was not, as was commonplace, that Mary was a scheming, avaricious gold-digger and he had never made such a promise, but that there had been an implicit agreement not to marry if either of them became ill. In such a case, the nuptials would be postponed until he or she had recovered. He had suffered a severe attack of gastroenteritis and congestion of the liver in August, and was still suffering relapses of vomiting, pain, and insomnia. Consequently, he was in no fit state to marry, with a reasonable timeframe for performance of the contract not having elapsed, and it would not do so until he was fit again.

Walter appears to have been chronically ill. In fact, he was unwell, or had been, at the time he proposed. In March, a newspaper report concerning the Wilton Board of Guardians, of which he was a member, referred to Walter's continued absence from meetings, which was understood to be due to illness.[447] He had not attended for the past six months. What's more, apart from a cook and housemaid, there was a 'hospital trained nurse' recorded in his household at the time of the 1901 census, suggesting that he had been in poor health for some years. Might the presence of a nurse in the Keevil home in 1881 cast doubt on the well-being of the entire family?

In 1965, Parliament directed the English Law Commission to review outdated laws.[448] The Commission concentrated on those that concerned social assumptions which were no longer valid. Two World Wars had been fought since Mary's breach of promise action. Women had entered the workforce in droves after being called upon to help in the war efforts. The Commission concluded that Women's role in society had changed. Breach of promise actions had run their course, and become outdated for modern times. Consequently, they were abolished by Parliament in 1970, by which time Mary had been dead for over ten years.

On the day she attended court in 1907 she was 34, and still living with her parents. As a young woman she was trapped in an era of complete paternal control, without any financial means of her own and, as a farmer's daughter, she was also expected to assist her mother, leaving her with next to no possibility of finding outside employment. Mary's desperation to escape from her father's stifling grip had been writ large years before, in the letter she wrote to her cousin John in 1899. The courtship she revealed to him would have been joyous, had her father not disapproved of the match. Moving forward eight years, everything had changed for Mary. With all hope of marrying and running a happy family home of her own dashed, she seized the opportunity to gain financial independence from her father, and emigrated to America.

Walter was 52 at the time of the court hearing. The impression created by his contribution to parish meetings is that his was the most diplomatic and reasonable voice in the whole charade. Was Walter the 'young' man whom Mary said in her letter that she had been 'corresponding etc.' with for two years? Was the failure of the liaison the very same, or yet another of the 'worries and bothers' for which Mary held her father responsible? Might the two principal farmers in the village, the remnant of the old guard and the new wind, have clashed? Their temperaments were certainly markedly different.

Although Walter gave up Manor Farm after his father died, expansion of his agricultural activities remained his plan five years later, in 1901, when he secured the tenancy of Hurdcott, the farm neighbouring Naishes. Only four years had passed before a notice of auction for the sale of his stock and equipment at Naishes and Hurdcott stated in September 1905 that he was 'relinquishing' farming.[449] He left Compton at the end of that year. On 29 December, *The Salisbury Times* reported that after eleven years of occupation by Walter, and fourteen by his father before him, Naishes Farm had passed to Thomas Rivers, and Hurdcott to Mr J. C. Green. We cannot know if Walter fled because he wanted to escape Mary, her father, or farming. Mary waited months — until 24 May 1906 — before she lost hope and filed her breach of promise claim.

Walter's actions towards Mary were undoubtedly cruel. But, just possibly, his intentions were nobler. Could he have wanted to spare her the burden of an ailing husband? Or did he feel unable to marry because he was at odds with his prospective father-in-law? Or was he simply a confirmed bachelor, like his uncle James Kendell seems to have been, who got cold feet? We will never know.

At the time of the 1911 census, Walter was living in Christchurch, Bournemouth, a renowned retirement location; he was single, and employed a housekeeper and domestic servant. Aged 56, he described himself as a retired gentleman. His brother William and his wife Isabel had also retired and were living in Bournemouth, where Walter died in 1932, having remained a bachelor all his life though, interestingly, he was buried in the cemetery at Compton Chamberlayne. The cause of his death was carcinoma of the larynx.

Walter's two sisters left Compton, never to return. The eldest, Elizabeth Ann, known as Bessie, married a wealthy businessman at Compton Church in 1884. Her husband, Alfred Thomas Manger, was a widower of Putney. He retired from banking and entrepreneurial activities in Hong Kong and London in 1890, and bought Stock Hill House, an estate at Langham near Gillingham. Alfred died there in 1917, before his plan to build a church on the estate came to fruition. Elizabeth had him interred at the same location where he had wanted to erect his place of worship, and herself died in 1919. Their eldest son, Lieutenant Colonel Charles Manger, built a tiny, thatched church over their grave in 1921. It is dedicated to St George, the patron saint of soldiers, as a memorial to those from the estate and hamlet of Langham who had died in the First World War, amongst them his younger brother Lieutenant John Kenneth Manger. As we learned in Chapter 46, Elizabeth's younger sister Emma

Blanche married William John Clapp, the son of her father's scandalous bailiff.

Mary, finally, at the age of 59, married a widower, James Wait, at her home in Santa Barbara, California, in 1933. She never shed her emotional ties with home. Her wedding card and letters were kept amongst grandfather's papers. Without fail, she sent presents for Rupert's children on their birthdays and at Christmas. After the war, thinking they must be starving and suffering badly due to the rationing, she dispatched food parcels. A packet of prunes in one was particularly bemusing. Mary died childless in 1954, and is buried in a cemetery looking over the sea at Santa Barbara.*

Mary Langdon (1874-1954) in her mid-30s in America.

---

* Mary's story in America can be read in the January 2023 issue of the *Wiltshire Family History Society Journal.*

54
THE GREAT WAR COMES TO COMPTON

ON 4 AUGUST 1914, only three years after its joyous coronation celebrations, Britain declared war on Germany, beginning what came to be known as the First World War. In his letter of 4 August 1974, my father wrote:

> I reminded uncle [Rupert] that it was 60 years ago today that the First World War began, and he told me that he remembered the day well. Your grandfather had been to Salisbury and was returning to Shaftesbury on that very new-fangled mode of transport, the country omnibus. And as he passed Compton Chamberlayne he looked over the hedge and saw uncle Rupert cutting wheat with a self-binder.

As it would for many young men, the War was about to bring about a seismic change in Rupert's parochial life. Almost half a million men voluntarily enlisted within the first two months. Three of William's and Emily's sons joined the army: Reg, the Royal Wiltshire Yeomanry, Will, the Royal Army Ordnance Corps, and Rupert, the Royal Horse and Field Artillery. Reg was discharged as medically unfit for service in December 1914. Will enlisted on 21 May 1915 at Woolwich Arsenal, which was the headquarters of the Ordnance Corps. Rupert enlisted in February 1916. Ten months later, he learnt that Will had been among the 420,000 British soldiers slain at the Battle of the Somme, notorious as one of the bloodiest battles in military history. Will was killed on 9 November, only a week before the official end of combat, which ceased when the mud became too deep to undertake any more fighting until the spring. Rupert had been very fond of his older brother. He told his daughter Jean that the empty space left by Will created a profound sadness that the family carried with them ever after. He felt that loss throughout his life, and would refer to 'My brother Will' in such reverential tones as to spark off tittering amongst his children. My father recalled his parents talking at the time about his uncle Will's death on their way home from a visit to his grandparents

Rupert, back row, second from the right, with his fellow soldiers.

in Compton, just as the horse was slowly pulling their carriage up the steep hill by Win Green towards Ashmore. I located the grave of Armament Staff Sergeant William Langdon at the Bienvillers Military Cemetery near Arras on a visit there during the 1980s.

Rupert's son Robert wrote a brief account of his father's war experiences in response to an appeal for stories about life during the First World War by the Gold Hill Museum in Shaftesbury in 2014. He explained that his father had been quickly drafted into the Royal Field Artillery as a Driver because he had a way with animals, and was able to handle the teams of four horses used to manoeuvre heavy guns. He fought in the Palestine Campaign. My father told me that Rupert took part in the last cavalry charge of modern warfare. Rather than participating in it himself, he was present alongside the famous mounted charge of the 4th Light Brigade. Still, when the infantry had orders to go over the top, drivers like Rupert followed them through the terrifying gunfire, riding one of the horses in their team used to pull the gun carriage forward to its next position. Can one at the safe distance of today properly fathom the agonising adrenalin pumping through a young man's veins while sitting on his charge, himself a target high above the melée, bracing himself against the next blast that threatened to rip his body apart? Rupert was only 23 years old.

A card Rupert sent from the Front in France to his sister Mary at Christmas in 1918. It shows two scenes from the campaign in Palestine, and an estaminet (another word for café in French) in France, providing an insight into how Rupert spent his leisure time. They were a distraction from the unspeakable atrocities the young men witnessed, and typically had coloured lights, artificial flowers, and live music, and were ran by a proprietress.

During the War, farmers were encouraged to provide horses for the War Effort. Officers from the Army Remount Service visited farms and offered good money for them, but the farmers were reluctant to let go of those they were particularly fond of. To avoid appearing unpatriotic, they often concealed them in haystacks. Rupert, however, when he arrived to report for duty at Tidworth riding his own horse, led in two that belonged to his father. They both died during the rough voyage across the Bay of Biscay on their way to Egypt. The young man was broken-hearted, and must have deeply regretted taking them to war. With his singular empathy for horses, he noticed that tears rolled down their faces when they were frightened. Another distressing incident concerning them occurred while he was in Alexandria, watching a ship out at sea being bombed. It was carrying horses to replace those that had been shot by enemy fire. He could see the newcomers thrashing about in the water, drowning. The Germans were known to specifically target horses with their gunfire.

Robert recalls that Rupert told him about the mercy killing of (mainly) horses and mules, but also of extremely badly wounded men, both English and German, begging to be put out of their misery. This was strictly forbidden, but

Firearms Form 7.

FIREARMS ACT, 1920.
(10 & 11 Geo. V., c. 43, s. 13 (2).)

58

Intimation of dispensation with Firearm Certificate in respect of possession of

FIREARMS AS TROPHIES.

This is to signify that a Firearm Certificate can be dispensed with as regards the possession, by *Compton Rupert Langdon* (Name) of *Manor Farm Compton Chamberlayne* (Address), as trophies of the *Great 1914–18* (War), of Firearms as follows :—

One German Revolver N⁰ 8952

Hoel Llewellyn Lt Col: (Name)
Chief Constable (Rank)
Date *19th Nov 1920* *Wiltshire* (Police)

Firearms possessed as trophies may not be used or carried and no ammunition for them may be purchased. Breach of this provision renders liable to fine and imprisonment.

LONDON: Published by His Majesty's Stationery Office. To be purchased from H.M. Stationery Office at the following addresses: Imperial House, Kingsway, London, W.C. 2, and 28, Abingdon Street, London, S.W. 1; 37, Peter Street, Manchester; 1, St. Andrew's Crescent, Cardiff; 23, Forth Street, Edinburgh.

1920. *Price 6d. Net per 25 forms.*

(6668) Wt. 17082—C 437/154 6,200. 9/20. J. T. & S., Ltd. **162.**
(6668) Wt. 21019—305 50,000 10/20 J. T. & S., Ltd. **162**

Firearm Certificate for the German revolver Rupert took as a trophy during the First World War. He said that revolvers and ammunition were lying around there on the battlefield.

frequently done. On one fairly quiet Sunday morning Rupert was shooting horses, with his opposite number doing the same barely 50 yards away, when the latter waved to him and called something out, but Rupert did not understand German. He thought he said something along the lines of 'Well done mate.'

These visions, the huge number of bodies and overpowering stench on the battlefield, would return to haunt him. After the War, he was plagued with bouts of malaria, an infection for which he had been hospitalised in Cairo. Gradually, these ceased, but later in life he suffered a stroke, and began to speak more about his wartime experiences. Listening to these stories saddened his daughter Jean, because he kept crying as he related them. A less painful one concerned horses that were taken for exercise to the sea, probably the Mediterranean, at Deir el Belah. Those carers who could not swim were told to hang on to their horses' tails. An officer noticed that Rupert had lost his hold, and called for him to be rescued. My father described an outing with Rupert in November 1971:

> I went to Shaftesbury market on Thursday with uncle Rupert. I think he wanted company as he was taking his Fiat down to be serviced and it took over 4 hours … We had lunch in King Alfred's Kitchen. We kept off the cake in case he had burnt them again. But we charged with the Australian Light Cavalry over the soup, defended Beersheba over the plaice, and rode into Jerusalem over the ice-cream.

Compton morphed into a military megalopolis during the War. A series of camps was built along the A30 road, stretching about five miles from Barford to Fovant, and the railway line extended from Dinton to Compton, with its head on that main thoroughfare towards Fovant. I have no idea how great-grandfather avoided having his land commandeered, when neighbouring East Farm, despite protests from its tenant John Combes, and Naishes Farm, were taken over by the military.

Hilda Kerley describes the village's tranquil life when she was eleven, before the War changed it almost overnight. Life in 1913, as she recalled it, was little different from any of the centuries that came before. People worked, and spent their leisure time in the village. Many had never seen the sea, or travelled beyond Salisbury or Shaftesbury. During the day, men toiled with their horses in the fields. Cows going in for afternoon milking ambled quietly along the street with no traffic to worry them, not even when they crossed the A30. Entertainment for the men was a drink at the King's Elm in the evening, while women chatted at the door or gate about their children, and the day's

Hilda Kerley (left) with Dorcas Davidge, David Davidge's wife, in costume at a Victorian picnic in Compton Chamberlayne to mark the jubilee of the village's Women's Institute in June 1965.

work. The village store and post office, which sold everything from a packet of pins to men's heavy boots, paraffin, and coal, was another busy place to stop by and exchange gossip. Although still a post office with a rudimentary village store during my childhood, it was a far cry from the hive of activity Hilda described. The village bulletin, *C C Courier*, reported a sad day in its January 1996 issue: 'Just over a year ago Bob and Betty Logan took over the village shop and tried so hard to make a go of it — but to no avail. In the end the lethal combination of supermarket competition and a small population made it an impossible task.'

At the onset of the war, thousands of workmen arrived to build the camps. As Hilda related: 'All we could hear then were the huge traction engines along the main road tearing it up with their heavy loads of timber.' These monsters panted and wallowed in the mud in the fields. The village became such a mire that the newcomers called it Compton-Chamberlayne-in-the-mud. Soldiers soon swarmed everywhere. A good number of them brought along their families to live in the village, while squaddies from the London regiments, many of whom had never been to the countryside before, were particularly disruptive. They ruined the place by tearing up flowers to send home.

Australian forces arrived just before the bitter winter of 1916 to '17. Not having encountered such conditions before, many succumbed to respiratory disorders, and some died. Twenty-eight Australian soldiers are buried in Compton cemetery, and forty-four at Fovant. Most of them had only enlisted six months earlier, two of which were spent on the voyage from Australia — a testament to the senselessness of war.

The village was inevitably drawn into camp life. A special parish meeting was called at Compton in 1916, when a letter from the Salisbury postmaster was read out.[450] The village postman had handed in his notice, and the post office was to be closed for the duration of the War, or for as long as the post office at the military camp in Hurdcott remained open. Parishioners heard the news with dismay — at least, that is what Mr Langdon reported in a petition demanding that it remain open. It had served the village for nearly 70 years, and its closure would mean women and girls would have to walk two miles on a road full of soldiers on dark evenings to mail a parcel. This is what happened, though: villagers had to go to the camp post office at Hurdcott to conduct all their business, although stamps could still be bought at the village shop. Great-grandfather's concern was not without substance. An Australian soldier, Don Clarkson, wrote a letter to his wife dated 22 August 1915,[451] saying 'Things have been a bit hot here lately, there is a band of outlaws about here and they can't get them. They reckon they are about, hiding in the woods all day and they come out at night and steal, and it is not safe to be out at night in a lonely place.' Three Australian soldiers went AWOL from the Hurdcott camp and lived rough in the woods, stealing what they could to keep alive.

During the War, Mr Churchill inhabited a remote cottage in Compton woods near the boundary to Fovant. He delivered goods, newspapers and mail round the villages with his white pony. His cottage was so isolated that up until 1904 Wilton Rural District Council had used it to quarantine people suffering from smallpox. The Council probably first rented the cottage from Charles Penruddocke in 1896. A tramp admitted in the spring of 1903 was its last patient, and the lease expired in 1904.[452] The nurse obtained to care for him confided to the medical officer that she nearly bolted, owing to being shut up there for six weeks without anyone to speak to.[453] Mr Churchill feared the band of Australian soldiers and kept his pony in the kitchen in case they snatched him to feed themselves. He later committed suicide and the cottage has since been demolished.

Another soldier, Wilfred Denver Gallwey, wrote home to his mother in 1918:[454]

> You maybe surprised to hear that a few men in these camps are the worst animals I ever came in contact with. During the last few weeks quite a number of men have been murdered and stabbed in the main thoroughfares of the camp after dark. It is scandalous and the authorities seem powerless to arrest the perpetrators. It is not safe for anyone to go out alone at night ... all the civilians are too frightened to go out at night. Can you wonder why Australians get the name they do.

Cathy Sedgwick has undertaken the mammoth task of researching every Australian First World War soldier buried in Britain.[455] Not one of those buried in Compton and Fovant is recorded as murdered. Of the deaths which were due to causes other than pneumonia or bronchitis, one in Compton resulted from internal injuries received in a motor-car accident, and another from concussion of the brain after a fall from a horse. There were three suicides in Fovant: by a gunshot wound to the roof of the mouth, hanging, and a railway accident, the soldier having placed himself on the rails. Private Durkin was murdered at Sutton Veny Camp, near Warminster, twenty miles northwest of Compton. Private Asser, who shared a hut with him, shot Durkin through the head while he was asleep. Asser was executed at Shepton Mallet Prison, and his body buried within its precincts.[456] Efforts may well have been made to conceal awkward fatalities. Durkin's death, for instance, was originally described as a self-inflicted wound.

The War weighed heavily on Reverend Digges. Hilda recalled how he had tears in his eyes when he talked about the fallen in France. He broke down completely when, in 1915, Nurse Cavell was shot by a German firing squad for helping allied soldiers escape from occupied Belgium. Now an elderly man, the Reverend was failing fast, and died the following year. He had served the church and the village for 33 years. Services were then taken over by the padre from the military camp.

Great-grandfather William supplied the camps with milk, which his son Joe delivered in a churn loaded onto a horse-drawn cart. On one occasion, my father joined his uncle. He had a vivid memory of a nurse at a hospital giving him a kitten to hold. The hospital, he said, was inside Compton Parish bounds, and therefore must have been the Military Hospital in Fovant, rather than the Gropup Hospital at Hurdcott Camp.

At the end of the War, Fovant Camp became a demobilisation centre. Between two and three thousand soldiers travelled there every day, Rupert among them. He was discharged at the Dispersal Centre on 6 March 1919. As he was leaving the demobilisation hut after receiving his papers, he was called back by the sergeant, who reminded him that he had not taken his rail pass. Oh, but he didn't need a pass, he just had to walk a mile to his home in Compton.

A parish meeting was called there on 17 November 1919, to discuss the erection of a permanent memorial to the parishioners who had fallen.[457] Mr Penruddocke offered £5 to start a fund, and a house-to-house collection was made for a plaque with the names inscribed, which was placed in the nave of the church.

Either on the 11th or 12th of November 1918, as my father wrote in his memoirs, he hurried home from his school in Ashmore to tell his own

Joe Langdon with his milk cart at a First World War military camp in Compton Chamberlayne.

father what he probably already knew — that the War had ended — little realising himself what war really was. This was three months short of his eighth birthday, and it had begun two and a half years after his birth. Willie gives a young boy's impression of the camps in Compton, describing how they passed the large town of hutments on their way to visit his grandparents: 'Long rows of green corrugated-metal huts, marching soldiers. The camp cinema and post office I remember there, but the railway was what I most wished to see.' When he was lucky, they had to wait while the little narrow-gauge train that served the camps rumbled across the road. He remembered 'seeing Australian soldiers sweeping the road with mules and one side of their hats pinned up (the Australians', not the mules').' Once there were German prisoners standing in a group in Manor Farmyard. He often saw prisoners from the Blandford Camp on his travels through Iwerne Minster. He was told that some of them were picking food from the hedgerow for their rabbits. The prisoners made little animal figures out of silver paper, which the children bought at his school in Ashmore for a few pence.

The War finally ended. Farmers had profited from it. Great-grandfather had boosted his bank balance by supplying the camps with produce. Possibly, like John Combes at East Farm, he had also offered the soldiers his services by taking in wives visiting their husbands stationed at the camps as paying guests, and setting up a shop and canteen in one of his barns. Local girls, who had been employed at the camps as nurses, now saw new opportunities to escape domestic service. Life went on. The mood was optimistic. William cheerfully wrote to his sister in August 1919:

> We are getting on very well with the harvest, we have cut all our wheat and carried seven ricks, one rye rick and one winter oat rick and cut about 50 acres of oats our barley is late this year owing to such a very cold spring. I expect John is busy harvesting now [John at Ashmore] ... Rupert has been cutting with the binder every day since our return and Cecil has been carrying every day.

Hilda tells how village life changed once more in 1918:

> The troops went their way and our boys came home to settle down. But it did not have the same atmosphere in the village now. The old leisurely way of life had gone, most of the old people had left and those who were here now were more restless. We began to get a more social time with whist drives and dances and concerts ... It was now the thing for the children of the village to be taken by char-à-banc to the seaside for their outings. Many events were organised in our village for this purpose. One event was a football match between Compton and Barford ladies. Compton won 7 - 0. 30 shillings was collected on the field, we thought it was great. Mr Jarvis of Fovant now started a bus service to Salisbury 3 times a week. No more walking to Dinton station to get to Salisbury. Later another bus service was started ... we were able to go to Salisbury on Saturday evening to do our shopping, or the young people to go to the cinema. This was really the breaking up of village life.

Willie, in his capacity of church warden and member of the Fovant Home Guard Association, responsible for maintaining the map of Australia on the hill at Naishes Farm, was struck by a bright idea. He reported to me in a letter dated 20 September 1976 that the church bells were in a sorry state, and he intended to write to the primate of Australia and the archbishop of New South Wales to ask for a contribution towards their restoration, adding: 'We could get the bells to play Waltzing Mathilda every time the hour strikes.' His efforts met with success, after another begging message to the archbishop of Sydney, in which he logged 'a plea that Australian soldiers carved their map on our downs and some of them were left behind in the graveyard.' Although, at the time, the archbishop regretted not being able to help, my father heard from him again after almost a year: 'Guess my surprise when I received a letter from him this week enclosing a cheque for nearly £200 (not Australian dollars). It had been collected by the chaplains of three RAAF stations and three army depots.'

In a later letter dated 20 April 1977, he wrote that he and other churchwardens had been engaged that week in historical events. Over the course of two evenings, they had removed the church's six bells from their frames in the tower and lowered them by means of pulley blocks to ground level: 'Last evening the Press came out and took our photographs standing by the large bell.' All were then taken to Ted Brine's workshop for further transport to the Loughborough Bell foundry. They had last come down from their exalted positions 99 years before,[*] but at that time there had only been four. Of today's six bells, one is inscribed with the date 1614, another with 1616 and the motto 'Honour the King,' and a third with 1656.[†] The other three date from 1878.[458] One replaced an earlier bell. Two were donated by Charles Penruddocke, and the third, given by his wife Flora and their daughters, is emblazoned with 'Our voices shall with joyful sound make hill and valley echo around.' Bells rang out from the tower at the weddings of my sisters and myself. As brides, we walked through the porch to enter the

Churchwardens with a bell being transported to Ted Brine's workshop in 1977. Willie Langdon stands on the right, Ted Brine is the fourth man from the right. © Salisbury Museum.

---

* See Chapter 24.

† See Chapter 28.

church between the ringers. Nowadays, ringers are separated from the comings and goings of the congregation, following the construction of a chamber above the porch in 1982.

Compton's Banjo Band

Compton banjo band: Back row centre: John Coombs. End right: Hilda's 16-year-old son Ray. Front row, end left: Mr Dacre.

An article in the February 1948 issue of *Banjo Mandolin Guitar* magazine relates the story behind Compton's banjo band, which is one example of the increasing number of social activities in the village that Hilda spoke about. Less than a year before, a Mr J. B. Dacre and his partner had played a banjo and guitar duet at a social gathering in Compton. After their performance, he was asked if he would start a weekly banjo class. To his surprise, when he arrived the following week, he found that nearly all the young men in the village had bought banjos. The band made good progress during its first year, playing at public shows and making recordings. Mr Dacre predicted a grand future for this group of enthusiasts, who were led by John Coombs.

55
THE PENRUDDOCKES' FALL

WHILE WILLIAM AND Emily lost one son to the First World War, all three of the Penruddockes' sons were effectively sacrificed to it. Two, Thomas, aged 19, and Charles, 25, were killed in France in 1917 and 1918. Almost a year to the day before Charles was killed, *The Times* announced his engagement to Evelyn Lorna Russell, the youngest daughter of C. R. Shore, of Binfield, near Bracknell.[459] She subsequently married another, in 1929. In a story the *Frankston & Somerville Standard* published on 19 December 1923, an Australian soldier related how he took a stroll from the crowded camp at Fovant to Compton Church one snowy winter's day in 1918. There, he found himself alone, except for a white-haired lady in deep mourning, who was replacing wax candles on the altar. As he stood reading a brass plaque commemorating Thomas Penruddocke, he heard a soft sad voice over his shoulder saying 'That was my youngest son.' He tried to express the usual commonplace sympathy, recovered his hat, and tip-toed out of the church into the dusk and now fast-falling snow, past rows of thatched cottages and the King's Elm hostelry, where the sign 'sold out' was exhibited in the window. Their middle son, George, was placed on the

Plaque commemorating Thomas Penruddocke.

retirement list due to wounds sustained in 1918. He was awarded the Military Cross for his gallant actions at the Somme, where he led an attack on an enemy trench and killed six Germans. Their mothers grieved too. As we learn below, George's combat experiences never left him.

Flora, their eldest daughter, was engaged to Vivian Clay, the brother of our GP Dr Clay. Her fianceé did not returned to marry her. He was killed on his 24th birthday. Captain Clay has no known grave, but is commemorated on the Thiepval Memorial at the Somme. One of his men in the Wiltshire Regiment described him in a letter home: 'We have a splendid officer in Mr Clay and all the boys are very fond of him.'[460] He had been his father's favourite son: 'His loss hit the old man hard. He never got over it.'[461] Dr Clay described a vivid dream which he had on 18 October 1916. He woke up and noted by means of his watch that the time was 5. In that dream, he saw his brother Vivian lying in a bed in a large hospital ward:[462]

> I knew he was wounded that he was conscious and wanted to send a message to me, but was unable to do so, because he was wounded in the throat... This dream worried me very much for many days, and I hesitated to write to my parents to ask if Vivian was safe. He had gone back from leave only 2 weeks ago. To my great surprise my mother wrote to me soon afterwards to say that he had been killed on October the 18th. Sometime afterwards Sergeant Valentine, who was with him when he was killed, wrote to say that he had died at 5 a.m. from a wound in the throat.

The War — and falling land values — were the ruin of the Penruddocke family. They sold off their properties in Baverstock, followed by Manor Farm in Compton, which passed out of their hands in 1924. After Charles died, his son George put the rest of the village up for sale, and the family moved to Canford Magna in Dorset. In 1946, George's mother and twin sister Sybil returned from church to find his lifeless body lying outside their house. The cause of death was a 'gunshot wound inflicted through the mouth.' He took his own life at the age of 52.[463]

Charles' sister Constance noted in a postcard that the estate was sold because her nephew's trustees advised him that he could not afford to keep it up.[464] Constance was one of the unmarried daughters who, as Ada wrote, went to live with their mother at Teffont following the death of Charles Penruddocke senior in 1899. She devoted herself to caring for the Australian soldiers camped in the vicinity during the War, handing out baksheesh baskets of ration tickets, cards, and souvenirs at Dinton and Wilton railway stations,

War memorial in St Micheal's Church.

and providing hospitality at her house. Referring to herself as an 'old' woman at 62, Constance wrote a New Year's message in 1919 to the Australian soldiers who had passed through her 'Little Grey Home,' where she kept a visitors' book.[465] She declared that she had only ever received courtesy and kindness from the soldiers, and thanked them for their consideration and goodness to her, adding the inspirational words: 'Those whose lives were saved by God must take up the fight for Him as bravely as they did for King and Country.'

So ended the Penruddocke's reign over the village of my childhood. The last sentence of a newspaper article written in 1910, mainly about Compton House, provides an ironic twist in hindsight: 'As he [Charles Penruddocke] has sons to succeed him, we may well hope for a long continuity of the old connection between the Penruddockes and Compton Chamberlayne.'[466] None of those six children left descendants. People come and go.

George Cross, a London property developer and my father's landlord, bought the 'residential, agricultural and sporting estate,' to quote the particulars of sale published in 1930.[467] This blurb was largely taken up by a paean of praise for the house: its fine lounge-hall and magnificent panelled dining room, both with carvings attributed to Grinling Gibbons, and beautiful drawing room, richly decorated in the style of Robert Adam. By contrast, George writes in his autobiography: 'Before I took possession there was hardly a part on the bedroom floor without a leaky ceiling; in many, portable baths of the Victorian order stood in the centre and had, judging from the sediment at the bottom, collected the drippings for ages. The floor of the entrance hall was propped up by a forest of posts from the cellars.' The house was riddled with death-watch beetle, and its bulging cracked walls had not seen paint for 30 years. The arable and meadow land on the estate was in such a neglected condition that he was ashamed to own it. As he recounted, 'The greater part is let to small farmers who cannot afford to pay the wage bill which would be required to keep it clean.' Five derelict cottages and two in ruins are listed in the particulars of sale. The new owner's arrival was understandably greeted with enthusiasm. He provided employment and modernised the cottages, installing water closets and baths.

George was a nature lover, and observed the woods around him as a child might:[468]

> Of all my fourteen hundred acres my favourite haunt is Compton Wood — it is a mile or more from end to end ... Here for a couple of hours I will sit as still as I may on a fallen tree, and observe the teeming life around me ... A pair of red squirrels play touch on the lower branches of the trees, making the most amazing flying leaps. The Lord be praised, there are no grey ones yet to exterminate these dear little natives.

Alas, little more than twenty years later, I only ever saw grey squirrels. George watches as a molehill erupts:

> A bright shiny object on the top of the tiny mountain catches my eye, and quietly I get up to investigate. Full of excitement, I realize Mr. Mole has thrown up a flint arrow-head of the neolithic age ... I hope he didn't cut his soft little snout; having no eyes he couldn't see. What animal was the weapon aimed at, thousands of years ago?

It's springtime, and on his way home he spots a profusion of pale mauve rhododendron blossom, the same display that later caught my mother's fancy from a train she was travelling on between Barford and Dinton, before she lived at Naishes.

According to the 1939 register, George Cross, born in 1884, is listed at Compton Park as a married man. Also recorded is Blanche G. Ealand, a single lady, twenty years his junior. She was his stylish mistress. This unconventional couple were friendly with Dame Laura Knight, R.A., and her husband Harold Knight, R.A., who were frequent guests at the Big House. Harold's portrait of George was exhibited at the Royal Academy in 1932. Laura was one of

Britain's most successful female artists of the 20th century and, in 1936, the first woman to be elected as a Royal Academician. Her painting for George Cross of 'The Old Church' sold for £6,875 at Christie's in December 2010. She also painted Ealand's portrait, on which she clasps a shotgun. The painting was exhibited at the Academy in 1928. According to the *Royal Academy Illustrated,* it depicted a 'typical finely finished English Girl of today, with her short hair, passion for sport and clear-cut self-reliance.' During my time, Estella Norton Dawson, who lived in Rose Cottage, was generally known to be his mistress. In George's book,[469] his mistress is called Rosemary:

> I do not ask for everything of this life, and for the time am more than content to dally in the shade on the river side, and watch Rosemary cast a skilful fly and rejoice with her when she lands a one-pounder, or a very rare two-pounder, and commiserate when she loses her fly, and the biggest fish that was ever fool enough to take a synthetic black gnat.

George dropped dead in his 89th year from a heart attack following a day's shooting in November 1972. His obituary in *The Times* described him as a highly individual character. A butcher's son, he started work in a haberdasher's shop at the age of fifteen. In 1920, he bought 70 acres of the Edgeware Manor Estate and developed it, constructing houses and a shopping centre. With the accumulation of wealth, he acquired hotels and built more shopping parades. After making over trust funds of nearly £1 million for the benefit of relatives, friends, and staff, he made little effort to avoid death duties, which he considered a charitable donation. He once told my father that he was the richer of the two of them because, unlike my father, he had no children.

The whole village, aside from Manor Farm and the Big House, was put up for auction once again. George's family was unable to buy it, as they had wished. The particulars of sale extolled it as 'An Outstanding Residential, Sporting and Investment Estate.'[470] Note that its favourable income tax relief of £1,878, under Section 68 of the Capital Allowances Act 1968, was a key selling point, as opposed to its agricultural potential. The estate was sold at the Red Lion Hotel in Salisbury for £850,000 to an initially undisclosed purchaser, who subsequently also acquired the Big House, on the afternoon of 24 June 1974. The event was sufficiently newsworthy to feature on television that evening — also in *The Daily Telegraph* the following day, and it received a mention in *The Observer Review* on 7 July. Mary Locke,* a young nurse who

---

*   With many thanks to Mary Tomes, née Locke, for permission to quote extracts from her personal recollections.

grew up in the village, was on night duty making beds, and stopped in her tracks when she saw her village on the ward's television. She wrote up her anxious reaction: 'I felt a lump in my throat and tears well up. I remember my legs were shaking.' As the camera scans through the village, her memories of carefree days playing hide and seek and making camps in the woods come flooding back; the summers the village kids cycled to the mill with jam pots to fish for minnows and sticklebacks. She reflects on George Cross: 'Many people thought Cross was mean ... Each of us had different opinions of him ... Was he mean to let us walk through his woods and fish in his river?' She is sure he didn't want the village to change its character, 'He wanted to see country cottages and gardens, fields and meadows, and people happy.' Questions wrack her brain: 'Will we no longer be able to wander through the woods with all its wonders?' 'Will it change?' 'I hope not.' If the purchaser builds new homes, she hopes he 'will do it with kindness and think of us, and not of himself.' The new owner made an offer to tempt my father to leave. We considered it was not a fair offer, but he was keen to give up farming and retire to his books.

The final death throes of the small farms are made clear by a comparison of their historical sales details.

Acres recorded on the 1930 and 1974 particulars of sale

Farms	1930	1974
Naishes Farm	460 acres	510 acres
The Forge (still with a lean-to blacksmith's shop in 1930)	24 acres	32 acres
The King's Elm Inn	31 acres	1/3 acre
Piggotts	100 acres	(not listed)
Home Farm	221 acres	272 acres
Post office & adjoining cottage	21 acres	1.6 acres

Three houses were built on Forge Farmyard in 1994, and the farmhouse retains its status as a Grade II listed building to this day. Apart from Manor Farm, as sold by the Penruddockes in 1924, there are no farmers left in Compton. Naishes and Home Farms are run by the estate. A once thriving agricultural community has been annihilated.

References

1. *Salisbury and Winchester Journal*, 16 October 1886.
2. *Hedgerows*. Woodland Trust. Online at https://www.woodlandtrust.org.uk/trees-woods-and-wildlife/habitats/hedgerows/
3. Hudson, W. H. *A Shepherd's Life*. J.M. Dent & Sons Ltd., 1936.
4. Hall, Rachel. *The Industrial Revolution began in the 17th not 18th century, say academics*, 2024. Online at https://www.theguardian.com/education/2024/apr/05/industrial-revolution-began-in-17th-not-18th-century-say-academics?utm_term=660f774ae88c05cba149e3c1cobb6f6b&utm_campaign=GuardianTodayUK&utm_source=esp&utm_medium=Email&CMP=GTUK
5. *Agriculture*. Hansard. Online at https://api.parliament.uk/historic-hansard/commons/1960/may/16/agriculture
6. McKenzie, M.A. *We were here — remember us! The story of Fovant Camp*. Fovant History Interest Group. Online at http://www.fovanthistory.org
7. Cross, G. *Suffolk Punch: A Businessman's Autobiography*. Faber and Faber Limited, 1939.
8. Defoe, D. *A Tour Through England & Wales*. Everyman's Library, 1948.
9. Evans, Rob. Half of England is owned by less than 1% of the population. *The Guardian*. 17 April 2019. Online at https://www.theguardian.com/money/2019/apr/17/who-owns-england-thousand-secret-landowners-author
10. Farr, Brenda, ed. *Crown Pleas of the Wiltshire Eyre 1268*. Wiltshire Records Society 65, 2012.
11. *History of Parliament*. Online at https://www.historyofparliamentonline.org/volume/1509-1558/member/penruddock-george-1527-81
12. *The Wiltshire Archaeological and Natural History Magazine* 89, 1996.
13. WSHC 549/8.
14. Barker, Katherine. *The Medieval Deer Parks of the Cranborne and West Wiltshire Downs Area of Outstanding Natural Beauty*, 2006. Online at https://cranbornechase.org.uk
15. Shirley, Evelyn Phillip. *Some Account of English Deer Parks*. John Murray, 1867.
16. Sykes, Naomi. The Introduction of Fallow Deer to Britain: A Zooarchaeological Perspective. *Environmental Archaeology* 9(1) 2004.
17. WSHC 549/8.
18. WSHC 332/293.
19. WSHC D1/42/18.
20. Fenwick, Carolyn C. ed. *The Poll Taxes of 1377, 1379 and 1381. Part 3 Wiltshire-*

Yorkshire. Oxford University Press, 2005.
21 WSHC 549/5.
22 WSHC 549/6.
23 WSHC 549/7.
24 WSHC 549/10.
25 WSHC 332/250.
26 WSHC 549/7.
27 WSHC D1/42/17.
28 WSHC D1/42/18.
29 WSHC 549/7.
30 WSHC 549/10.
31 WSHC 332/250.
32 Grundy. Saxon Land Charters of Wiltshire. *Archaeological Journal*, 76, 1919.
33 Dr Clay's stories about highwaymen from his Notes on the History of Fovant. Online at http://www.fovanthistory.org
34 WSHC 332/119.
35 Langdon, Willie. Compton Hut. *C C Courier* (Compton Chamberlayne parish newsletter). February 1997.
36 *The Salisbury Times*, 4 May 1906.
37 Jeffries, Richard. *Greene Ferne Farm*. William Foster Ltd., 1947.
38 WSHC 332/293.
39 Ingram, M. *Church Courts, Sex and Marriage in England 1570-1640*. Cambridge University Press, 1988.
40 WSHC 549/8.
41 WSHC 549/5.
42 WSHC 549/8.
43 TNA C142/247/57.
44 WSHC 549/5.
45 WHSC D1/42/24.
46 WHSC D1/42/21.
47 WSHC 549/5.
48 Ingram, M. *Church Courts, Sex and Marriage in England 1570-1640*. Cambridge University Press, 1988.
49 Ibid.
50 Ibid.
51 Ibid.
52 WSHC 1641 subsidy book, bundle 163 (on p41 of NRA 2nd-stage report).
53 Hearth Tax Digital. Online at https://gams.uni-graz.at/context:htx
54 WSHC 549/8.
55 WSHC 549/10.
56 WSHC 549/8.
57 Ingram, M. *Church Courts, Sex and Marriage in England 1570-1640*. Cambridge University Press, 1988.
58 Ibid.
59 Ibid.
60 WSHC D1/42/23B f.43r.

61 WSHC 549/5.
62 WSHC 549/7.
63 Ibid.
64 WSHC 549/5.
65 WSHC 549/7.
66 Ibid.
67 Slack, Paul. *The Impact of the Plague in Tudor and Stuart England*. Clarendon Paperbacks, 1991.
68 WSHC 549/60.
69 WSHC 549/8.
70 Ibid.
71 Ibid.
72 WSHC 549/10.
73 WSHC 549/8.
74 WSHC 549/10.
75 A Dictionary of the Scots Language (up to 1700): Available online https://dsl.ac.uk/our-publications/a-dictionary-of-the-older-scottish-tongue-dost/
76 WSHC 549/5.
77 Ibid.
78 WSHC P2/E/14.
79 Craven, Alex. *Compton Chamberlayne – Local Government*. Online at https://www.history.ac.uk/research/victoria-county-history/county-histories-progress/wiltshire/xix
80 WSHC 549/6.
81 Ibid.
82 WSHC 549/8.
83 Ibid.
84 Ibid.
85 Ibid.
86 Ibid.
87 WSHC 549/7.
88 WSHC 549/8.
89 WSHC D1/54/6/4 f. 2r.
90 WSHC 549/5.
91 WSHC 549/10.
92 WSHC 549/8.
93 Ibid.
94 Ibid.
95 WSHC D1/42/18.
96 Ibid.
97 WSHC 549/10.
98 WSHC 549/8.
99 Ibid.
100 Ibid.
101 Ibid.
102 Ibid.

103 WSHC 1641 subsidy book, bundle 163 (on p41 of NRA 2nd-stage report).
104 Hearth Tax Digital. Online at https://gams.uni-graz.at/context:htx
105 WSHC 549/10.
106 Ibid.
107 WSHC 549/7.
108 WSHC 549/5.
109 WSHC 549/8.
110 Ibid.
111 Cunnington, Edward Benjamin Howard. *Records of the County of Wilts: Being Extracts from the Quarter Sessions Great Rolls of the Seventeenth Century*. G. Simpson & Company, 1932.
112 WSHC 549/8.
113 Ibid
114 Ibid
115 WSHC 549/10.
116 Ibid.
117 WSHC 549/8.
118 WSHC 549/10.
119 WSHC D1/54/6/4 f. 2r.
120 *The Salisbury Times*, 14 August 1908.
121 *The Salisbury Times*, 28 November 1902.
122 Wiltshire Notes and Queries. *The Wiltshire Archaeological and Natural History Magazine*, 1855.
123 Ravenhill, W.W. Records of the Rising in the West, A.D. 1655 (part 3). *The Wiltshire Archaeological and Natural History Magazine* 14, 1874.
124 WSHC 332/265/25.
125 Baker, T.H. Notes on the History of Mere. *Wiltshire Archaeological Magazine* 29, 1897.
126 WSHC 332/265/27.
127 *Tree symbolism*. Online at https://treesymbolism.com/elm-tree-symbolism-meaning.html
128 Jones, Eric L. *Small Earthquake in Wiltshire. Seventeenth-century conflict and its resolution*. The Hobnob Press, 2017.
129 Hampshire Archives 9M73/G539.
130 Hurley, Beryl, ed. *The Hair Powder Tax Wiltshire 1796 and 1797*. Wiltshire Family History Society, 1997.
131 WSHC 332/293.
132 Johnson, C. *Wiltshire County Records: minutes of proceedings in sessions, 1563 and 1574 to 1592*. Wiltshire Archaeological and Natural History Society Records Branch, 4, 1949 for 1948.
133 *An Act Touching Badgers of Corn, and Drovers of Cattle to be Licenced. 1562*. Printed by John Baskett, E. and R. Nutt, and R. Gosling, 1706.
134 WSHC 549/7.
135 WSHC 549/6.
136 WSHC 549/8.
137 Ibid.

138 *State Papers, 1655.* British History online. Online at https://www.british-history.ac.uk/thurloe-papers/vol3/pp295-310#highlight-first
139 WSHC 549/10.
140 WSHC 332/73.
141 Watson Greig *The anti-vaccination movement that gripped Victorian England.* 28 December 2019. Online at https://www.bbc.com/news/uk-england-leicestershire-50713991
142 *The Salisbury Times,* 7 October 1898.
143 WSHC 332/250.
144 Hobbs, Steven, ed. *Gleanings from Wiltshire Parish Registers.* Wiltshire Record Society 63, 2010.
145 WSHC 332/250.
146 Ibid.
147 Ibid.
148 WSHC 549/16.
149 WSHC A1/306.
150 Mattock, David, and Chilton, David. *Summary Convictions Minor Offences in Wiltshire 1698-1903.* Wiltshire Family History Society, 2019.
151 WSHC 332/250.
152 Ibid.
153 WHSC 345/123.
154 *Wiltshire Times and Trowbridge Advertiser,* 20 April 1907.
155 WSHC 332/250.
156 Dale, Christabel, ed. *Wiltshire Apprentices and their Masters 1710-1760.* Wiltshire Archaeological and Natural History Society Records Branch, 17, 1916.
157 *Poor Law in Wiltshire Removal orders, Settlement Certificates & Settlement Examinations 1670-1890.* Wiltshire Family History Society, 2015.
158 WSHC 1671/57/4-5.
159 WSHC 332/74.
160 WHSC D1/42/21.
161 WSHC 332/114.
162 WSHC 549/8.
163 WSHC 549/10.
164 WSHC 549/8.
165 WSHC 549/27/1.
166 WSHC 549/28.
167 WSHC 549/27/4.
168 Fry, George S, and Fry, Edw. Alex. eds. *Abstracts of the Inquisitions Post Mortem Relating to Wiltshire, returned to the Court of Chancery in the Reign of King Charles I.* British Records Society, 1901.
169 *Elizabeth Home, Countess of Home.* Online at https://en.wikipedia.org/wiki/Elizabeth_Home,_Countess_of_Home
170 Kerridge, Eric. ed. *Surveys of the Manors of Philip Earl of Pembroke and Montgomery 1631-2.* Wiltshire Archaeological and Natural History Society Records Branch 9, 1953.
171 WSHC 549/5.

172 Ibid.
173 WSHC 549/7.
174 WSHC 549/5.
175 WSHC/1306/33.
176 WHSC 345/123.
177 TNA G23/1/138/166.
178 WSHC 1168/1.
179 *Western Gazette,* 14 and 21 December 1894; *The Salisbury Times,* 14 and 21 December 1894; *Salisbury and Winchester Journal,* 15 December 1894.
180 WSHC 1168/1.
181 WSHC 332/250.
182 *The Wiltshire Archaeological and Natural History Magazine* 98, 2005.
183 WSHC 549/6.
184 WSHC 549/7.
185 WSHC 549/8.
186 Ibid.
187 Ibid.
188 Salaman, R. A. *Dictionary of Woodworking Tools c.1700-1970.* Astragal Press, 1997.
189 *Shoemaking Dictionary of Terms.* Online at https://shoemakersacademy.com/shoemaking-dictionary-terms/
190 Hobbs, Steven, ed. *Wiltshire Glebe Terriers 1588-1827.* Wiltshire Record Society 56, 2003.
191 WSHC 549/8.
192 Feather, Clive D. W. *Archery Laws of England.* Online at http://www.archery.mysaga.net/archlaws.html
193 WSHC 549/10.
194 WSHC 549/8.
195 WSHC 549/10.
196 WHSC D1/42/21.
197 Hurley, Beryl, ed. *Strangers in Salisbury 1675-1738 & Relief of poor 1757.* Wiltshire Family History Society, 1997.
198 WSHC 332/250.
199 WSHC 332/108.
200 WSHC 332/105.
201 WSHC 332/104.
202 WHSC 345/123.
203 WSHC 332/106.
204 WSHC 332/133.
205 Ibid.
206 WSHC 332/250.
207 Ibid.
208 Ibid.
209 Ibid.
210 Mattock, David, and Chilton, David. *Summary Convictions Minor Offences in Wiltshire 1698-1903.* Wiltshire Family History Society, 2019.

211 WSHC 332/250.
212 WSHC 1168/1.
213 Craven, Alex. *Compton Chamberlayne - Social History and Local Government.* Online at https://www.history.ac.uk/research/victoria-county-history/county-histories-progress/wiltshire/xix
214 WSHC A1/306.
215 WSHC 332/103.
216 WHSC 345/123.
217 *Salisbury and Winchester Journal,* 22 August 1914.
218 Mattock, David, and Chilton, David. *Summary Convictions Minor Offences in Wiltshire 1698-1903.* Wiltshire Family History Society, 2019.
219 *Devizes and Wiltshire Gazette,* 5 January 1846.
220 *Salisbury and Winchester Journal,* 23 July 1853.
221 Church, Rosemary (transcriber). *Bastardy Records Volume 3 Calne, Devizes, Salisbury and Tisbury 1835-1893.* Wiltshire Family History Society, 1998.
222 *Salisbury and Winchester Journal,* 27 July 1867.
223 WSHC 1168/1.
224 WSHC 549/5.
225 Ibid.
226 Ibid.
227 WSHC 549/6.
228 Ibid.
229 WSHC 549/8.
230 WSHC 549/6.
231 Ibid.
232 WSHC 549/8.
233 WSHC 332/109.
234 WSHC 332/127.
235 WSHC 332/109.
236 WSHC 332/250.
237 WSHC 332/76.
238 Hearth Tax Digital. Online at https://gams.uni-graz.at/context:htx
239 WSHC 549/13.
240 WSHC 332/100.
241 WSHC 332/250.
242 Ibid.
243 Ibid.
244 Ibid.
245 Ibid.
246 Ibid.
247 WSHC 549/10.
248 Calthrop, M. M. C. (ed.), *Recusant Roll No. 1., 1592–3. Exchequer Lord Treasurer's Remembrancer Pipe Office Series.* Catholic Record Society, 1916.
249 Lane, Michael David. *Of Whims and Fancies: A Study of English Recusants under Elizabeth, 1570-1595.* Louisiana State University and Agricultural and Mechanical College. Masters thesis, 2015.

250   WSHC 549/8.
251   WSHC 549/10.
252   Ibid.
253   Wiltshire Protestation Returns for Ebsborne (sic) in Salisbury Division - Chalke Hundred. *Wiltshire Notes & Queries*, 7, 1911-16; WSHC HOUSE/LORDS R.O.
254   Hobbs, Steven, ed. *Wiltshire Glebe Terriers 1588-1827*. Wiltshire Record Society 56, 2003.
255   WSHC 549/8.
256   Ibid.
257   WSHC 549/10.
258   Meers, Peter. *Ebbesbourne Wake through the Ages*. Dial Cottage Press, 2006. Online at https://www.southwilts.com
259   WSHC F8/500/81/1/1.
260   *Salisbury and Winchester Journal*, 22 February 1845.
261   Sawyer, Rex. *Collett's Farthing Newspaper*. The Hobnob Press, 2018.
262   Clay, R. C. C. Fifty Years of Practice. *Salisbury Medical Bulletin*, 1969.
263   Hunnisett, R.F. ed. *Wiltshire coroners' bills, 1752-1796*. Wiltshire Records Society, 36, 1981.
264   *West Country Mirror*, 30 July 1862.
265   *West Country Mirror*, 23 March 1873.
266   *The Salisbury Times*, 21 August 1886.
267   WSHC 549/10.
268   WSHC 549/8.
269   WSHC 1641 subsidy book, bundle 163 (on p41 of NRA 2nd-stage report).
270   WSHC 549/10.
271   SurnameDB. Online at https://www.surnamedb.com
272   WSHC 332/138.
273   WSHC 332/250.
274   WSHC 549/10.
275   WSHC 568/22.
276   WSHC 332/250.
277   WSHC 332/138.
278   WSHC 332/250.
279   WSHC 332/279.
280   WSHC 332/281.
281   Natives of Mere. *The Wiltshire Archaeological and Natural History Magazine*, 29, 1896-97.
282   Craven, Alex. *Compton Chamberlayne - Religious History*. Online at https://www.history.ac.uk/research/victoria-county-history/county-histories-progress/wiltshire/xix
283   WSHC 332/124.
284   WSHC 332/250.
285   WSHC 549/5.
286   WSHC 549/8.
287   WSHC 549/10.
288   TNA IR/1/27.

289 WHSC 345/123.
290 WSHC A1/306.
291 WSHC 332/126.
292 TNA IR/1/47.
293 WSHC 332/250.
294 WHSC 345/123.
295 TNA IR/1/64.
296 Hurley, Beryl, ed. *Wiltshire Pew Lists*. Wiltshire Family History Society, 1994.
297 WSHC 332/250.
298 *History of Smallpox*. Wikipedia. Online at https://en.wikipedia.org/wiki/History_of_smallpox
299 Mattock, David, and Chilton, David. *Summary Convictions Minor Offences in Wiltshire 1698-1903*. Wiltshire Family History Society, 2019.
300 *Salisbury and Winchester Journal*, 21 October 1871.
301 Mattock, David, and Chilton, David. *Summary Convictions Minor Offences in Wiltshire 1698-1903*. Wiltshire Family History Society, 2019.
302 WSHC 332/250.
303 Jeffries, Richard. *Field and Hedgerow*. Longmans, Green and Co., 1889.
304 Parker, Sophie. *Records reveal 'incredible' details about 17th Century*. 28 December 2024. Online at https://www.bbc.com/news/articles/cy9qj7n23r00
305 Hobbs, Steven, ed. *Wiltshire Glebe Terriers 1588-1827*. Wiltshire Record Society 56, 2003.
306 Clayton, Micheal. *Christie's Pictorial History of English and American Silver*. Phaidon, 1985.
307 WSHC 549/5.
308 Hobbs, Steven, ed. *Gleanings from Wiltshire Parish Registers*. Wiltshire Record Society 63, 2010.
309 WSHC 549/21.
310 Dale, Christabel, ed. *Wiltshire Apprentices and their Masters 1710-1760*. Wiltshire Archaeological and Natural History Society Records Branch, 17, 1916.
311 ibid.
312 TNA IR/1/55.
313 TNA IR/1/27.
314 TNA IR/1/47.
315 TNA IR/1/58.
316 TNA IR/1/64.
317 TNA IR/1/18.
318 WSHC 332/250.
319 Hurley, Beryl, ed. *Wiltshire Pew Lists*. Wiltshire Family History Society, 1994.
320 *Salisbury and Winchester Journal*, 16 October 1886.
321 *The Post Office Service*. Fovant History Interest Group. Online at https://fovanthistory.org/?s=post+office
322 SurnameDB. Online at https://www.surnamedb.com
323 TNA IR/1/59.
324 *Salisbury and Winchester Journal*, 6 June 1836.
325 WSHC 332/250.

326 *Western Gazette*, 19 October 1866.
327 WSHC 332/250.
328 *Salisbury and Winchester Journal*, 5 August 1882.
329 *Western Gazette*, 14 and 21 December 1894; *The Salisbury Times*, 14 and 21 December 1894; *Salisbury and Winchester Journal*, 15 December 1894.
330 TNA IR/1/28.
331 TNA IR/1/30.
332 TNA IR/1/33.
333 WSHC 332/290/12.
334 Craven, Alex. *Compton Chamberlayne - Local Government*. Online at https://www.history.ac.uk/research/victoria-county-history/county-histories-progress/wiltshire/xix
335 *Salisbury and Winchester Journal*, 11 September 1837.
336 *Salisbury and Winchester Journal*, 25 August 1860.
337 *Report on the Rates of Wages and Hours of Labour for ordinary labourers in agriculture* prepared by the Labour Department of the Board of Trade in 1908.
338 *The Salisbury Times*, 29 November 1879.
339 *Windsor & Eton Express*, 17 May 1884.
340 *Salisbury and Winchester Journal*, 28 December 1895.
341 *The Salisbury Times*, 17 March 1899.
342 *The Salisbury Times*, 22 May 1908.
343 *The Salisbury Times*, 13 July 1900.
344 *Salisbury and Winchester Journal*, 22 January 1848.
345 WSHC F8/500/81/1/1.
346 Sawyer, Rex. *Collett's Farthing Newspaper*. The Hobnob Press, 2018.
347 TNA IR/1/18.
348 WSHC 332/113.
349 Ibid
350 WSHC 332/77.
351 *Hampshire Chronicle*, 2 August 1819.
352 Raymond, Stuart A. *Stourton Before Stourhead*. Hobnob Press, 2019.
353 Hurley, Beryl, ed. *Wiltshire Pew Lists*. Wiltshire Family History Society, 1994.
354 *The Southampton Herald and Isle of White Gazette*, 22 December 1823.
355 WSHC A1/125.
356 *Winifred Johnson - Life in Sutton Mandeville before WW1*. Sutton Mandeville Parish Council 2022. Online at https://www.suttonmandevillepc.org/post/winifred-johnson-life-in-sutton-mandeville-before-ww1
357 Mattock, David, and Chilton, David. *Summary Convictions Minor Offences in Wiltshire 1698-1903*. Wiltshire Family History Society, 2019.
358 *Salisbury and Winchester Journal*, 15 July 1839.
359 Hamilton, Jenkin, A K. *Cornwall and its People*. J M Dent & Sons Ltd, 1945.
360 WSHC 549/5.
361 WSHC 549/8.
362 *Western Gazette*, 15 September 1905.
363 WSHC 332/290/12.
364 WSHC 332/250.

365 The Museum of English Rural Life and Special Collections University of Reading, FR WIL 15/1/2.
366 Sawyer, Rex. *Nadder: Tales of a Wiltshire Valley*. The Hobnob Press, 2006.
367 The Pigott Family of Queen's Country, Ireland; Some Ancestral Connections. Online at http://pigott-gorrie.blogspot.com/
368 WSHC 332/126.
369 WSHC 332/250.
370 *Morning Advertiser*, 24 August 1835; *London Evening Standard*, 24 August 1835; *Sun*, 24 August 1835 & 31 August 1835; *Bell's New Weekly Messenger*, 30 August 1835.
371 Convict Arrival Indent. Online at www.stors.tas.gov.au
372 State Archives of N.S.W., Kingswood; AO Reel 2423, Colonial Secretary, Musters and other papers relating to Convict Ships, 1817-1840; 'Lady Nugent,' 1836.
373 A Naval Biographical Dictionary. Online at https://en.wikisource.org/wiki/A_Naval_Biographical_Dictionary/King,_George_(a)
374 *Perry's Bankrupt Gazette*, 4 March 1837.
375 *The Albion and the Star*, 29 October 1835.
376 *Hobart Town Courier*, 16 January 1830.
377 *Colonial Times* (Hobart), 22 January 1830.
378 *Tasmanian* (Hobart Town), 4 June 1830.
379 Ticket-of-Leave Butts (NRS 1202). State Archives of N.S.W.
380 Freedom of the City Admission Papers, London, 1681-1925. Online at https://www.ancestry.com/search/collections/2052/?name=Matthew_Wyman&keyword=William+Cook&name_x=s_s&residence=_london-england-united+kingdom_5274
381 Freedom of the City Admission Papers, London, 1681-1925. Online at https://www.ancestry.com/search/collections/2052/?name=Matthew_Wyman&keyword=William+Cook&name_x=s_s&residence=_london-england-united+kingdom_5274
382 *The Salisbury Times*, 30 December 1898.
383 *Gloucester Citizen*, 23 November 1889; *Salisbury and Winchester Journal*, 23 November 1889 and 14 December 1889; *Exeter Flying Post*, 23 November 1889; *Bristol Mercury*, 23 November 1889.
384 WSHC F8/500/81/1/1.
385 *Wiltshire Asylum (Roundway) Admissions & Discharges 1851 – 1919*. Wiltshire Family History Society, 2020.
386 WSHC 332/277.
387 *West Country Mirror*, 14 September 1859.
388 *Warminster and Westbury Journal*, 18 September 1897.
389 Walters, H.B. The Bells of Wiltshire: Their Inscriptions and History. *Wiltshire Archaeological Magazine*, 1928.
390 *Salisbury and Winchester Journal*, 25 June 1887.
391 *The Salisbury Times*, 8 September 1893.
392 Raymond, Stuart A. *Stourton Before Stourhead*. Hobnob Press, 2019.
393 *Keevil Family History*. Online at https://www.ancestry.com/name-

origin?surname=keevil
394 Street, A. G. *Strawberry Roan*. Faber and Faber, 1932.
395 Steer, Henry. *The Smedleys of Matlock Bank*. Elliot Stock, 1897.
396 *Memoirs of John Boaden 1828-1904*. Cornwall Archives, X664.
397 Stanes, Robin. *Old Farming Days*. CPI, 2005.
398 Rowe, John. *Changing Times & Fortunes: A Cornish Farmers Life 1828-1904*. Shot Run Press Ltd, 1996.
399 Harveson, Robert M. *History of Sugarbeet*. Online at https://cropwatch.unl.edu/history-sugarbeets.
400 *Western Gazette*, 25 November 1898.
401 WSHC 332/59.
402 *The Salisbury Times*, 13 April 1900.
403 Soulsby, Carol. *The Heavy horse Experience. A "potted history" of some of the streets and buildings of Salisbury*. Wessex Horse Omnibuses. Published privately 2004.
404 *Salisbury and Winchester Journal*, 14 November 1885.
405 WSHC 1168/1.
406 *The Salisbury Times*, 8 September 1893.
407 *The Salisbury Times*, 8 September 1893.
408 WSHC 1168/1.
409 *Widnes Examiner*, 24 March 1894; *Runcorn Examiner*, 24 March 1894.
410 *The Salisbury Times*, 9 February 1894.
411 *The Salisbury Times*, 7 December 1894.
412 *The Salisbury Times*, 19 January 1900.
413 *The Salisbury Times*, 1 July 1898.
414 WSHC 549/10.
415 *The Salisbury Times*, 13 May 1898.
416 *The Salisbury Times*, 9 December 1898.
417 *Western Gazette*, 26 December 1884.
418 *Salisbury and Winchester Journal*, 16 October 1886.
419 *Salisbury and Winchester Journal*, 25 June 1887.
420 Langdon, Willie. Compton Chamberlayne – The Electric Light. *C C Courier* (Compton Chamberlayne parish newsletter). October 1997.
421 *The Salisbury Times*, 25 March 1898.
422 *The Salisbury Times*, 22 April 1898..
423 *The Salisbury Times*, 29 April 1898.
424 *The Salisbury Times*, 24 June 1898.
425 *The Salisbury Times*, 3 February 1899.
426 *The Salisbury Times*, 24 February 1899.
427 *The Salisbury Times*, 3 March 1899.
428 *The Salisbury Times*, 10 March 1899.
429 *The Salisbury Times*, 17 March 1899.
430 *The Salisbury Times*, 3 March 1899.
431 *The Salisbury Times*, 3 November 1899.
432 Wiltshire Coroner's Inquests 1801-1920. Online at https://salisburyinquests.wordpress.com/1908-2/noyce-albert/
433 *Autobiography of Bill Petch*. Museum of English Rural Life, Reading University,

DX1221/ SP1/1-3.
434   *The Salisbury Times*, 17 June 1904.
435   *The Salisbury Times*, 26 February 1904.
436   *The Salisbury Times*, 7 July 1905.
437   *Wiltshire Times and Trowbridge Advertiser*, 2 April 1904.
438   WSHC F8/500/81/1/1.
439   *The Salisbury Times*, 4 March 1904.
440   *The Salisbury Times*, 21 & 28 November 1902; *Salisbury and Winchester Journal*, 21 & 22 November 1902; *The Morning Leader*, 21 & 22 November 1902; *Daily Express*, 21 November 1902; *Manchester Courier*, 21 November 1902; *Daily Telegraph and Courier*, 21 November 1902; *The Wiltshire Chronicle*, 22 November 1902; *Daily Express*, 21, 22, 24, 25, 29 November 1902; *Western Gazette*, 28 November 1902; *The Wiltshire Times*, 29 November 1902; *Evening News* (London), 22 November 1902; *Bournemouth Daily Echo*, 20 November 1902; *Dundee Courier*, 22 November 1902.
441   *Morning Leader*, 6 February 1903.
442   *Dundee Evening Post*, 3 January 1903.
443   *The Salisbury Times*, 24 February 1899.
444   *Wiltshire Times and Trowbridge Advertiser*, 12 October 1929.
445   Breach of Promise. Hansard. Online at https://hansard.parliament.uk/Commons/1879-05-06/debates/4a6b87e6-e590-495a-8c0d-f5ce2de3b3d1/BreachOfPromisehs
446   TNA ASSI 28-16 f1r-f5v.
447   *Salisbury and Winchester Journal*, 18 March 1905.
448   The Law Commission Bill. Hansard. Online at https://hansard.parliament.uk/Lords/1965-04-01/debates/8a792889-771c-4b3a-a0b9-32c83d243264/LawCommissionsBill
449   *The Salisbury Times*, 8 September 1905.
450   WSHC 2897.
451   Mckenzie, M. *Fever (Isolation) Cottage*. Fovant History Interest Group, 2021. Online at https://www.fovantvillage.com/historicalinterest
452   *The Salisbury Times*, 13 March 1903, 14 October 1904.
453   *Salisbury and Winchester Journal*, 20 February 1904.
454   *Letters from Wilfred Denver Gallwey to his family, October to December 1918.* Denver Australian War Memorial. Online at https://www.awm.gov.au/collection/C2088232
455   Sedgwick, Cathy. *WW1 Australian Soldiers & Nurses who Rest in the United Kingdom*. Online at https://ww1austburialsuk.weebly.com/
456   *Taunton Courier and Western Advertiser*, 13 March 1918.
457   WSHC 2897.
458   Walters, H.B. The Bells of Wiltshire: Their Inscriptions and History. *Wiltshire Archaeological Magazine*, 1928.
459   *The Times*, 6 October 1917.
460   Hall, Neil G. M. *Salisbury in the Great War*. Pen and Sword Ltd, Barnsley, 2016.
461   *Autobiography of Bill Petch*. Museum of English Rural Life, Reading University,

DX1221/ SP1/1-3.
462   Snow R. *Strange Experiences*. Flying Disk Press, Pontefract, 2018.
463   *Poole and Dorset Herald*, 31 October 1946.
464   University of Nottingham. Manuscripts and Special Collections Reference number La H 48. Online at https://mss-cat.nottingham.ac.uk/Calmview/Record.aspx?src=CalmView.Catalog&id=La%2fH%2f47-73%2f48&pos=3
465   The Australian War Memorial archive. Online at https:// www.awm.gov.au/collection/C2088232?im- age=219.
466   *Salisbury and Winchester Journal,* 20 August 1910.
467   WSHC 2676/5.
468   Cross, G. *Suffolk Punch: A Businessman's Autobiography.* Faber and Faber Limited, 1939.
469   *The Times,* 30 November 1972.
470   WSHC 1844/45.

Sources & Bibliography

Parish records and the census returns 1841-1922 were accessed online via the commercial genealogical websites:
Findmypast: www.findmypast.co.uk
Ancestry: www.ancestry.co.uk

Wills and inventories were downloaded from Ancestry
https://www.ancestry.co.uk/search/collections/61333/

Other sites that were consulted
The Victoria County History of Wiltshire, Compton Chamberlayne pdfs by Alex Craven:
https://www.history.ac.uk/research/victoria-county-history/county-histories-progress/wiltshire/xix
Wiltshire OPC: https://wiltshire-opc.org.uk/genealogy/2003/04/29/compton-chamberlayne/
National Archives Discovery: https://discovery.nationalarchives.gov.uk
Wiki tree: https://www.wikitree.com/genealogy/
Family Search: https://familysearch.org

The following are the sources for the Field Book of 1597, Estate Map of 1769, Tithe Award, Tithe Map, Incumbent's Book or the vicar's notes referred to throughout the book:
Field Book 1597: WSHC 332/252.
Estate Map 1769: WSHC 332/284/2H.
Tithe Map 1848: TNA IR 30/38/87.
Ramsay, G. D. *Two Sixteenth Century Taxation Lists 1545 and 1576.* Wiltshire Archaeological and Natural History Society Records Branch 10, 1954.

Crowley, D. A. *The Wiltshire Tax List of 1332*. Wiltshire Record Society, vol XLV, 1989.
Fry Edw. Alex. ed. *Abstracts of the Inquisitions Post Mortem Relating to Wiltshire, returned to the Court of Chancery in the Reigns of King Henry III, Edward I and Edward III. A.D. 1242-1326*. British Records Society, 1908.
Abstracts of Wiltshire Inquisitions Post Mortem Edward III. Wiltshire Archaeological and Natural History Society, 1912.
Sandell, R. E. ed. *Abstracts of Wiltshire Tithe Apportionments*. Wiltshire Record Society, 1975.
Mattock, David (transcriber), Pope, Jenny, Chilton, David (indexer). *Wiltshire Tithe Awards*. Wiltshire Family History Society, 2020.
Hurley, Beryl, ed. *Compton Chamberlayne Incumbent's Visiting Book 1847-76*. Wiltshire Family History Society, 2005.

General background bibliography
Compton Chamberlayne is recorded in the Doomsday Book on page 163.
Williams, W. M. *A West Country Village Ashworthy*. Routledge & Kegan Paul, 1963.
Rogers-Davis, N. A. *Land Enclosure and its effects*, 2003. Online at http://www.angmeringvillage.co.uk/history/Articles/Enclosures.htm
Overton, Mark. *Agricultural Revolution in England 1500-1850*, 2011. Online at https://www.bbc.co.uk/history/british/empire_seapower/agricultural_revolution_01.shtml
Crittall, Elizabeth. ed. *Agriculture 1500-1793* in *A History of the County of Wiltshire*, 4, 1959. British History. Online http://www.british-history.ac.uk/vch/wilts/vol4/pp43-64
Wilkes, A. R. Adjustments in Arable Farming after the Napoleonic Wars. *Agricultural History Review*, 28 (2), 1980.
Thompson, Denys. *Change and Tradition in Rural England; An anthology of writings on country life*. Cambridge University Press, 1980.
Porter, Valerie. *Yesterday's Farm*. David and Charles Limited, 2006.
Hennell, Thomas. *Change in the Farm*. Cambridge at the University Press, 1936.
Hall, C J. *A Short History of English Agriculture and Rural Life*. A&C Clack Ltd, 1924.
Afton, Bethanie. The Great Agricultural Depression on the English Chalklands: The Hampshire Experience. *Agricultural History Review* 44 (2), 1996.
The Corn Laws. Britain Express. Online at http://www.britainexpress.com/History/victorian/corn-laws.htm
Hare, John. *A Prospering Society: Wiltshire in the later Middle Ages*. University of Hertfordshire Press Studies in Regional and Local History 10, 2011.
Fry Edw. Alex. ed. *Abstracts of the Inquisitions Post Mortem Relating to Wiltshire, returned to the Court of Chancery in the Reigns of King Henry III, Edward I and Edward III. A.D. 1242-1326*. British Records Society, 1908.
Slack, P. *The Impact of the Plague in Tudor and Stuart England*. Clarendon Press, 1991.
Ian, H. *My Ancestor was an Agricultural Labourer*. Society of Genealogists Enterprises Ltd., 2010.

Wormleighton, Tim. *Title Deeds for Family Historians*. The Family History Partnership, 2012.
Mayhew, A.L. and Skeat, Walter W. *A Concise Dictionary of Middle English*. Online at http://www.scribd.com
Clergy of the Church of England Database: http://db.theclergydatabase.org.uk

Background sources for specific chapters

Chapter 4: Compton's Manor Courts and Lords of the Manor &
Chapter 6: How Compton Manor Controlled its Inhabitants
Court rolls/books: WSHC 549/5-8, 10, 11-13, 15, 60; 332/50; 332/250; 549/15-16; 1161/1.
Forrest, Mark. *Manors and Manorial Documents after 1500*. British Association for Local History, 2022.
Types of manorial record. University of Nottingham. Online at https://www.nottingham.ac.uk/manuscriptsandspecialcollections/researchguidance/manorial/types.aspx

Chapter 9: Lost Love
WSHC D1/42/24.
WSHC D1/42/9 f.206 *v*, f. 207*r* and f.186*v*.
WSHC D1/42/25 f.56*r* + *v*.
Court Depositions of South West England, 1500-1700, University of Exeter, http://humanities-research.exeter.ac.uk/womenswork/courtdepositions

Chapter: 10 Salacious Rumours
WSHC D1/42/21.

Chapter 11: Much Ado about a Cake
WSHC D1/42/17; D1/42/18 f.29b*r* and f.29b*v*.

Chapter 12: Feisty Joan Elliott and the Troublemaker's Wife and Daughter
WSHC D1/42/18 f.22b*v* - f.28b*v*; f.30b*r* and f.62b*r*.
WSHC D1/42/17 f.74*v* - f.77*r*.

Chapter 13: The Unending Jeay-Elliott Wars
WSHC D1/42/17 f. 78*r* - f.80*r*.
WSHC D1/42/ 23 f.14*v* - f.15*v*.
WSHC D1/42/23B f.29*r* and f.43*r* - f.45*r*.
WSHC D1/42/18 f.43b*r* - f.45b*r* and f.54b*r*.

Chapter 16: Jeay Slanders Joan Penruddocke
WSHC D1/42/30 f.44*r* – f.53*r*.

Chapter 17: William Jeay's Children
Corderoy vs Francis Jeay: WSHC D1/42/38.
Edward Reade vs Alice Nicholas: WSHC D1/42/28 and D1/42/29.

Chapter 18: The Penruddockes' Chaotic 17th Century
Woolrych, A. H. *Penruddock's Rising 1655*. The Historical Association, 1973.
Ravenhill, W. W. Records of the Rising in the West A.D. 1655. *Wiltshire Archaeological Magazine* 13, 1872.
Butler R. *Penruddock's Rebellion – Wiltshire's Royalist uprising of 1655*, 2016. Wiltshire & Swindon History Centre blog: https://wshc.org.uk/blog/item/penruddock-rebellion-wiltshire-royalist-uprising-of-1655.html
Waddell B. *The Penruddock Petitions: The Aftermath of a Royalist Revolt, 1655-1660*, 2020. Online at https://petitioning.history.ac.uk/blog/2020/05/the-penruddock-petitions-the-aftermath-of-a-royalist-revolt-1655-1660/
Compton Park, Wiltshire. *Salisbury and Winchester Journal*, 20 August 1910.
Wiltshire Rebels. *Wiltshire Times and Trowbridge Advertiser*, 3 July 1909.
Trafalgar Park, Wiltshire. Wikipedia. Online at https://en.wikipedia.org/wiki/Trafalgar_Park,_Wiltshire

Chapter 20: The Elkins: A Yeoman Family
Deacon, Bernard. *The Surnames of Cornwall*. CoSERG, Redruth, Cornwall, 2019.

Chapter 22: Nicholas Lawes and his Slave-owning Namesake
Legacies of British Slavery. Sir Nicholas Lawes. Online at https://www.ucl.ac.uk/lbs/person/view/2146652865
Caribbean Volume Extracts. Laws of Jamaica. Online at http://www.jamaicanfamilysearch.com/Members/bcarib72.htm
Howard, Robert, Mowbray. *Records and letters of the family of the Longs of Longville, Jamaica, and Hampton lodge, Surrey*. Simpkin, Marshall, Hamilton, 1925.

Chapter 24: Watts: From Husbandmen to Craftsmen
Fox, Sarah et al. The regulation of midwives in England, c.1500–1902. *Medical Law International*. 2020. Online at https://journals.sagepub.com/doi/full/10.1177/0968533220976174

Chapter 32: A Co-operative of Blacksmiths, Wheelwrights, and the Cooper
Craft of the Wheelwright. Heritage Machines. Online at https://heritagemachines.com/nostalgia/craft-of-the-wheelwright/

Chapter 34: House Furnishings and Personal Effects (mid-16th to early 18th century)
Fussell, G.E. *The English Rural Labourer his home, furniture, clothing & food, from Tudor to Victorian times*. Batchworth Press, 1949.
Living in the 17th Century. Online at https://www.nationalarchives.gov.uk/currency-converter/living-in-the-17th-century/

Chapter 35: The Rise and Fall of the Village's Crafts and Trades
Kelly Directories 1855-1920. Online at Leicester university special collections: https://specialcollections.le.ac.uk/digital/collection/p16445coll4

Chapter 37: Vicars' Records of Parishioners: Poverty in the 19th Century
Crittall, Elizabeth. ed. *Economic history*, in *A History of the County of Wiltshire: Volume 4*, 1959. British History Online https://www.british-history.ac.uk/vch/wilts/vol4/pp1-6

Broad, John. Housing the rural poor in southern England, 1650-1850. *JSTOR* 2000. Online at https://www.jstor.org/

Baker, Mark. Aspects of the Life of the Wiltshire Agricultural Labourer, c.1850. *The Wiltshire Archaeological And Natural History Magazine*, 1980.

Chapter 38: The Kings and their Ironies
Collins, E. J. T. The latter-day history of the draught ox in England, 1770–1964. *Agricultural*
History Review, 2010.

Chapter 43: George William Wyman the Thatcher
The Thatcher's Craft, Rural Development Commission 1988. Online at https://cms.lowimpact.org

Mansell, Charmian and Hailwood, Mark ed. *Court Depositions of South West England, 1500-1700*,

The 1831 Bristol Riots: A History Told Through Sources. The Bristonian. Online at https://www.thebristonian.co.uk/publichistory/thebristolriotsprimarysourcesgale

Ball, Roger. *1831 And All That…* Online at https://www.brh.org.uk/site/articles/1831-and-all-that/

Revolting riots in Queen Square. BBC Home 2004. Online at https://www.bbc.co.uk/bristol/content/madeinbristol/2004/04/riot/riot.shtml

Slocombe, P M. *Wiltshire Farm Buildings 1500-1900*. Devizes Book Press, 1989.

Gin Gang. Wikipedia. Online at https://en.wikipedia.org/wiki/Gin_gang

Chapter 45: The Wyatts: Sawyers and Hurdle Makers
The first Huntley & Palmer tins. Reading Museum. Online at https://www.readingmuseum.org.uk/online-exhibitions/huntley-palmers-history/3-biscuit-tins/first-huntley-palmers-tins

Hurdle Making. Heritage Crafts. Online at https://www.heritagecrafts.org.uk/craft/hurdle-making/

Chapter 47: The Keevils: Autocrats with a Sickening End
Biering, Dave. *History Of Agricultural Equipment: Important Developments And Examples*. Online at https://www.tstar.com/blog/history-of-agriculture-equipment-important-developments-and-examples

Chapter 48: Great-Grandfather Moves Up-Country
Skeat, W. W. Agricultural Dialect Words. I. – Wiltshire. *The Archaeological Review,*

1888.
Dartnell, George Edward and Goddard, Rev. Edward Hunerford. *A Glossary of Words used in the County of Wiltshire.* Online at http://www.gutenberg.org

Chapter 49: Great-Grandfather's Good Fortune
Crittall, Elizabeth. ed. *Agriculture since 1870* in *A History of the County of Wiltshire.* 4, 1959. British History Online. Online at http://www.british-history.ac.uk/vch/wilts/vol4/pp43-64
Street, A. G. *The Gentleman of the Party.* Faber and Faber, 2009.

Chapter 53: Breach of Promise: Langdon vs Keevil
Wright, Harter, F. The Action for Breach of the Marriage Promise. *Virginia Law Review*, 10 (5), 1924.
St George's Church, Langham. Wikipedia. Online at https://en.wikipedia.org/wiki/St_George%27s_Church,_Langham
History of St George's Chapel. Online at https://www.achurchnearyou.com/church/9752/page/5318/view/
2nd Lieutenant John Kenneth Manger. Christchurch University of Oxford. Online at https://www.chch.ox.ac.uk/cathedral/war-memorials/2nd-lieutenant-john-kenneth-manger

Chapter 54: The Great War Comes to Compton
Crawford T.S. *Wiltshire and the Great War: Training the Empire's Soldiers.* The Crowood Press, 2012.
Combes, Lawrence. *"Badges in the Chalk" A Brief survey of the regimental crests, cut in the chalk hillside at Fovant, Compton Chamberlayne and Sutton Mandeville, near Salisbury, Wiltshire.* "Times" Printing Works.
Mckenzie. M. A. *We were here – remember us! (The story of Fovant Camp).* Wiltshire at War. Online at http://www.wiltshireatwar.org.uk/story/we-were-here-remember-us-the-story-of-fovant-camp/
Harden, Liz. *What effect did the World War 1 Military Training Camp established at Fovant in Wiltshire have on the village and its people?* Fovant History Interest Group. Online at https://fovanthistory.org
Camps around Fovant. Fovant History Interest Group. Online at https://fovanthistory.org/introduction/world-wars/camps-around-fovant/
Sedgwick, Cathy. *The Map in Letters and War Diaries.* Online at https://map-of-australia.com/the-badges/the-map-in-letters-and-war-diaries/

Place Name Index

Note that place names with no county designation are Wiltshire or overseas

Alderbury, 185, 248, 249, 280
Aldershot (Hampshire), 159, 183
Alvediston, 243
Ansty (Dorset), 230, 247
Ashmore (Dorset) 248, 296, 298, 305, 308-12, 351-53

Barford St Martin, 5, 29, 63, 193, 224, 235-37, 253, 254, 348, 353
   married at, 124, 141, 157, 225, 253
Baverstock, 5, 7, 15, 48, 88, 118, 132, 160, 163, 193, 208, 209, 253, 357
Bemerton, 208, 269, 272
Berkshire, 204, 205
Berwick St James, 227
Berwick St John, 174, 234
Bienvillers (France), 345
Bishopstone, 44, 180
Boldre (Hampshire), 133
Bowerchalke, 161
Breamore (Hampshire), 225
Bridport (Dorset), 334
Brighton (Sussex), 144
Broad Chalke, 13, 40, 49, 51, 118, 140, 143, 197, 207, 241, 243
Burcombe, 5, 67, 81, 86, 87, 93, 96, 122, 142, 191, 202, 215, 224, 249

California (USA), 333, 343
Canford (Dorset), 357
Cape of Good Hope (South Africa), 184, 241
Chicksgrove, 206
Chilmark, 208
Christchurch (Dorset), 240, 342

Compton Chamberlayne
  Admiral's House, 2, 42
  Baynton half-manor, 24, 34, 89-90
  Blacksmith's shop/forge, 92, 157, 199, 200-1, 204-5, 207, 230, 236, 283, 361
  Big House, 1, 4-6, 9, 48, 100, 111, 145, 196, 208, 231, 241, 300, 317, 333, 358, 359, 360
  Brook Lane, 6, 19, 103, 222
  Camel Cottage, 1, 269, 300
  Chiselbury, 44, 47, 85
  Church, 4, 5, 17, 109, 111, 112, 142, 173, 179, 185, 196, 197, 198, 223, 248-49, 317, 356, 358, 360
  Bells, 148-49, 177, 292, 353-54
  Churchyard, 40, 41, 119, 127, 130, 155, 256, 258,
  Coachway. See Ridgeway
  Compton Farm. See Manor Farm
  Compton House. See Big House
  Compton Ivers, 34
  Compton Park, 5, 15, 6, 19, 23, 32, 51, 111, 113, 359
  Copse Barn/Farm. See Home Farm
  Dower House/Priory Barn, 248
  East Farm, 299, 348, 353
  Edward Watts' Cottage, 42, 145, 159
  Forge Farm, 21, 199
  Hall, 6
  Haversham half-manor, 16-17, 24, 29, 89, 90, 134, 167, 251
  Hollow/Hollyhead/Hollow Head/, 46, 47, 151, 191, 253, 276
  Home/Old/Ancient Farm/Farm House, 6, 21, 134, 173, 189, 194, 227, 243, 244, 361
  Holmfield Cottage, 147
  Hurdcott Military Camp (WW1), 6-7, 348-53, 356
  Hut, 47-50, 227, 231, 239, 314,
  King's Elm Inn, 6, 111-13, 230, 318, 348, 356, 361
  Manor Farm
    description of, 7, 14, 21, 85, 173, 248, 278, 290, 292, 293, 298-312, 352
    owned/farmed/occupied by, 2, 16, 227, 247, 290, 292, 304, 342, 357, 360-61
    worked at, 159, 239
  Manor House. See Big House

Map of Australia, 2, 7-10, 50, 353
Martin's Meadow/Corner 32-33, 151
Naishes Farm
　description of, 2-3, 7-9, 13, 21, 32, 41,
　　46, 191, 213-214, 239, 252, 255, 353,
　　361
　farmhouse, 6, 191, 254, 255
　farmed/occupied by, 2, 7, 185, 189,
　　191, 195, 226-227, 244, 247, 248, 253-
　　255, 290, 295, 298, 342, 348, 361, 339
　worked at, 184, 186, 199, 273, 279,
　　281, 282, 312
Piggotts Cottage, 1, 5, 42, 185, 256, 269,
　361
Post Office, 6, 144, 230-32, 270, 273, 281,
　283, 300, 322, 328-29, 349, 350, 352,
　361
Ridgeway/Salisbury Highway, 41, 43, 47,
　48, 85, 229
School, 6, 42, 161, 182, 184, 229, 240,
　282-83, 287, 298, 313, 317-18, 320-22,
　327-28
Shop, 6, 202, 226, 229, 230-32, 281, 283,
　316, 349, 350
Smallpox Hospital, 350
Turner's Farm, 157
Turnpike Cottage, 185, 269, 272
Turnpike Road. See Ridgeway
Well Cottage, 142, 143, 273

Coombe Bissett, 134
Cornwall, 2, 296-99, 301, 304
Cranfield (Bedfordshire), 237
Cumberland, 18

Devizes, 194, 240
Dinder (Somerset), 138
Dinton, 5, 19, 29, 130, 159, 180, 199, 224,
　238, 249, 281, 282, 299, 300, 303, 323,
　334, 348, 353, 357
　baptised/born at 138, 253, 265
　Cole Mill, 138
　Dinton Mill, 5, 19, 32
　married at, 129, 134, 138, 201, 224, 253
Ditchampton, 148, 249
Donhead St Mary, 197, 205, 254
Dorset, 45
Dorsetshire, 208
Downton, 69, 141, 225, 243
Durnford, 173

East Stour (Dorset), 95
Ebbesbourne Wake, 154, 178-81

Fifhide. See Fifield Bavant

Fifield Bavant, 26, 181, 198, 205, 279, 280
Fisherton Anger, 82, 158, 208, 225, 269, 272
Fisherton Asylum, 143, 144, 288
Fordingbridge (Hampshire), 231
Fovant, 5, 7-9, 12, 22, 44, 49, 84, 88, 123,
　127, 128, 130, 144, 158, 164, 180, 181,
　183, 197, 209, 225, 231, 235, 247, 279,
　289, 312, 348-51, 353, 356
　baptised at 159, 279,
　buried at 118, 158, 258, 259, 289, 349,
　　351
　Gallows Hill, 48
　married at 92, 142, 158, 163, 173, 174,
　　181, 203
Fugglestone St Peter, 272
Fyfield Manor (Oxfordshire), 106

Gallipoli (Turkey), 185
Gloucestershire, 202
Gosport (Hampshire), 143
Great Wishford, 204
Grovely, 15, 227

Hampshire, 45
Hazeldon (Tisbury), 234, 244, 245
Hinton St Mary (Dorset), 173
Holt, 208
Homington, 181, 183
Hurdcott, 7, 41, 46, 71, 91, 234, 342

Idmiston, 255
Ireland, 225, 256, 372
Isle of White (Hampshire), 209
Iwerne Courtney (Dorset), 115

Keevil, 224
Kingston Deverill, 245, 247

Lanchester (Durham), 144
Langham (Dorset), 342, 380
Le Touret (France), 185
London, 4, 20, 77, 78, 83, 121, 161, 209,
　235, 249, 263, 269, 358
　died in 208
　Hampstead, 143
　Holborn, 263
　Isleworth 138
　married at 100, 145, 265, 318
　Putney, 287, 342
　sent milk to 303, 305, 309,
　Soho, 133,
　Trafalgar Square, 114,
　Uxbridge, 165
　Willesden, 249

Long Bredy (Dorset), 334
Longparish (Hampshire), 227
Luton (Bedfordshire), 259

Madras (India), 259
Marnhull (Dorset), 285
Martin, 15
Matlock (Derbyshire), 293-94
Mere, 130, 247, 284

Netheravon, 135
New Forest (Hampshire), 243
New Zealand, 241

Osmington (Dorset), 237

Pitton, 272
Portchester (Hampshire), 263
Portsea (Hampshire), 183, 249
Portsmouth (Hampshire), 143

Ringwood (Hampshire), 133
Roundway (Ryndway), 53, 54, 90,
  Roundway Asylum, 240, 287, 288

Salisbury/Sarum, 5, 10, 20, 34, 41, 46, 65,
  76, 91, 103, 108, 151, 154, 155, 225,
  228-29, 235, 239, 240, 252, 281, 283,
  298, 299, 306, 308, 312, 327, 332, 333,
  353
  baptised at, 106
  lived in, 99, 122, 132, 142, 154, 155, 165,
    184, 216, 254, 272, 312
  married at/marriage licence, 93, 95, 96,
    122, 123, 127, 130, 143, 154, 157, 158,
    180, 185, 202, 224, 260, 285
  died/buried at, 245, 272
Sebastopol (Ukraine), 242
Shaftesbury, 5, 20, 44, 47, 59, 136, 202, 241,
  281, 345
Shapwick (Somerset), 243
Shepton Mallet (Somerset), 138, 351

Silton (Dorset), 129
Somerset 45, 189, 318, 322
Southampton (Hampshire), 29, 164, 209,
South Newton, 39, 82
Standlynch, 114-16
Stapleford, 227
Stockton, 29
Stoke Farthing (Stoke Fardon), 140
Stoneham (Hampshire), 144, 260, 262-3
Stourton (Stourhead Estate), 245-7, 252, 292
Sutton Mandeville, 7, 8, 178, 243-48
Sutton Veny, 351
Swallowcliffe, 247, 290, 318
Swaythling (Hampshire) 260, 262, 263

Teffont Magna, 161, 290, 293, 322, 357
Tisbury, 110, 124, 161, 206, 234, 236, 244,
  245, 247, 248, 253, 254, 281, 368
Totton (Hampshire), 29
Trafalgar Park, 114, 115
Trowbridge, 191

Ugford, 164
Upper/Over Wallop (Hampshire), 136

Walcott St Swithin (Somerset), 228
Warwickshire, 20
Wellington (Somerset), 285
Westhampnett (Sussex), 287
West Indies, 183, 298, 299
West Lavington, 106
Wilton, 5, 47, 49, 110, 112, 148, 164, 191,
  193, 224, 231, 235, 237, 243, 245, 249,
  280, 281, 285, 312, 322, 341, 350, 357
  St John's Priory/Hospital, 80, 131, 132
  Workhouse, 164, 207, 208, 210, 240, 280,
    287, 315, 325
Wimborne Minster (Dorset), 290, 333
Winterbourne Stoke, 139
Wolverton (Buckinghamshire), 129
Woodlands (Dorset), 205
Wylye, 201, 334

Personal Name Index

Names of people who lived at Compton, married a native or were closely associated with the village or its inhabitants

Abraham/Abram, 226, 230, 231
Abrey/Abree, 123, 124, 125, 132, 201, 202, 225, 243
Adlam, 63-64
Aldredge, 120, 125
Allestree, 193
Allman, 149
Ambrose, 224
Ames. See Emm
Anderson, 202, 205
Andrews, 194
Antrum, 63, 92, 186
Armony/Armory/Armonell, 151, 201, 203
Atwaters, 154
Australian soldiers, 7, 8, 348-50, 352, 353, 356-58
Avery, 226,
Aylward, 185, 226, 273

Bacon, 63-64
Bailey/Bayley, 93, 94, 186, 187, 191, 212-16, 218, 224-26, 240, 284, 285, 286, 287, 288
Baker, 88, 92, 93, 228
Ball, 185
Banstame, 140
Barnes, 49
Barnett, 238
Barrett, 227, 318
Barter, 88, 92
Bartlett, 225
Bath, 268, 272
Baynton, 17, 18
Beach, 67, 68
Bechaut. See Brabraham
Bennet, 136
Bennett, 49, 257
Berry, 36, 152, 172, 173, 218
Bibblecombe, 167, 171
Bigg, 170, 173

Bignall, 191, 193, 195
Blake, 185
Boulter, 47
Bound/Bounde, 80, 148
Bower, 19
Bowle, 334
Bowles, 118, 224
Brabraham/Brabram, 118
Bracher, 226
Brassier, 191
Brine, 354
Browne, 238
Browning, 270
Brownsey, 240
Buckland, 114
Bunting, 293
Burden, 172
Burrough, 288
Bushell, 135, 136, 138
Butt, 268
Buttler, 26-28

Caldwell, 47
Card, 281, 286
Carpenter, 132, 223
Case, 86, 88, 92, 93, 97, 127, 181-188, 212, 213, 216, 217, 220, 221, 238, 358
Chalke, 321
Chamberlayne/Chamberlain/Chapelyne, 16
Churchill, 226, 350
Clapp, 284, 286, 343
Clarke, 100
Clay, Captain, 357
Clay, Doctor Chaloner 183, 184, 236
Clay, Doctor Richard Chaloner, 12, 44, 47-49, 181, 183, 252, 357
Clements, 183
Codrington/Cuddrington, 167, 177, 178, 251
Coffin, 19

FAMILIES PASSING THROUGH COMPTON CHAMBERLAYNE

Cole, 226
Comage/Commege/Comedge/Cumidge/
  Cumage, 30, 34, 94, 95, 97, 169, 170, 178
Combes, 59, 60, 96, 348, 353, 380
Cool/Coole, 206, 207, 210, 225
Coombs/Coombes, 89, 225, 226, 272, 312, 355, 358
Cooper, 60
Corderoy/Cordery, 101-3, 187
Corp, 49, 226, 227
Cross, George, 2, 9, 21, 25, 47, 49, 113, 182, 185, 273, 317, 358-61
Cull, 255, 290
Cunning Dick, 47
Curtys, 80

Dale, Sir Humphrey, 67, 68, 197
Daniell, 129
Davage, 235
Davidge, 311, 314, 349
Dawson, 360
Day, 47, 124, 125
Dean, 285
Digges, 198, 241, 282, 284, 288, 315-21, 351
Dodds, 160
Dorter, 129
Dryer, 245
Dugmore, 65-69, 72-74, 76, 82, 84, 95, 98, 178
Dunn, 226

Ealand, 359, 360
Elderton, 39
Elkins/Elkin/Elton, 119-25, 130-32, 152, 157, 167, 172, 180, 200, 202, 204, 212, 213, 217, 219, 220, 229
Elliott/Elyat, 30, 32-34, 38, 57, 66, 68, 70-97, 99, 102, 103, 136, 140, 148, 169, 177-79, 186, 212-18, 220, 221, 224, 251, 269
Emm/Emms, 156, 160, 165, 204, 209, 279, 286
Essence, 225
Estmeed, 150
Ewence/Ewens, 123-25, 156, 158, 160, 161, 164, 199-202, 204-210, 223, 225-30, 236, 237, 246, 269, 279

Figes, 260
Flexen, 226, 227
Foote, 243
Ford/Fford/Foard/Foord/Fowrd, 32, 34, 65, 68-69, 82, 84, 88, 91-93, 95, 97, 103, 119, 122-25, 150, 166-80, 186, 187, 224, 227, 228, 235
Forman, 88, 93
Foster, 208, 226, 227, 230, 231, 241
Foyle, 289
Frampton, 202, 206, 234, 280
Francis, 29, 30, 246-7
Frapwell, 156, 160
Fricker, 67, 68, 92, 150, 223
Fry, 34, 63-64, 134, 182-85, 239, 240, 272, 280, 283, 286, 287, 326

Galpin, 226, 290-92
Gawens, 55, 80, 81, 91
Gillingham, 142
Goffe, 253
Golden, 229
Goodfellow, 63, 122, 142, 143, 163
Goodwood, 272
Gosney, 200
Gould, 49
Grace, 135, 141, 175, 201, 202, 205, 225
Gray, 225
Green, 163, 342
Greene, 94
Grimstead, 16, 34
Gurd, 206
Gutters, 238
Gwilliams, 67-68, 82, 95

Hancock, 122, 191, 223
Hart, 238
Harvey, 239, 241
Harroway, 268
Harwood, 83, 86, 84, 90, 97, 152, 178
Haversham, 16, 17, 26, 223
Hawkins, 158
Hayter, 185
Hazlen/Haslen/Hazeling, 234, 235
Heasman/Haseman, 245
Hibberd, 88, 93, 94, 122, 123, 155, 174, 191, 202, 224
Hickes, 99, 100
Hickman, 123
Holloway, 124, 169
Hortington, 87
Howlett, 206, 207
Hunt, 184, 237

Ingram, 49, 197

Jarvis, 12, 121, 225, 226, 241, 318, 319, 353
Jeay/Jay/Jaye 30, 32, 36, 37, 45, 56-58, 60, 61, 67, 68, 70-72, 74-81, 93, 95-102, 104, 105, 136, 212, 213

Jefferys, 239
Jeffries, 170, 173
Jelliffe, 160, 156, 184
Jerrard, 118, 189
Jesse, 134
Johnson, 124, 225, 226, 239, 242, 247
Jonsson, 189
Joy. See Jeay

Keate, 22
Keevil, 7, 49, 184, 226, 238-40, 255, 285, 287, 290-95, 299, 314, 315, 318, 319, 328, 335-343
Kendell, 293, 342
Kerley, Hilda, 199, 223, 282, 316, 348, 349, 351, 353, 355
Kerley, Ray, 10, 13, 49, 51, 199, 276, 355
King/Kinge, 32, 208, 225-27, 243-50, 253, 258, 260-66
Knott, 202
Kynnett, 140

Lacy, 122, 123, 125
Lampard, 167, 172, 200, 223, 238, 249, 250, 290
Lane, 201
Langdon/my great-grandfather/grandfather/father, 2, 7, 8, 9, 10, 11, 13, 14, 21, 31, 35, 166, 189, 197, 199, 213, 225, 226, 241, 248, 274, 290, 296-305, 306-12, 318, 322, 324-328, 283, 292-93, 333, 335-43, 344, 345, 348, 350-52, 354, 358, 361
Larkham, 244, 246, 248
Laurence, 62
Lawes, 15, 19, 58-61, 63-4, 70, 76, 77, 98, 99, 119, 134-138, 197
Lawrence, 84, 224, 299
Leech, 89
Legg, 241
Le Rus, Walter, 16
Levet, 180
Lily, 161
Livelong, 127-33, 170, 174, 187, 197, 212, 214, 217, 224
Lodge, 130
Logan, 349
Long, 145, 225, 245
Love, 314
Loveless, 49
Lovell, 185, 226
Lucy, 18, 139
Lush, 63-64, 130
Lynwood, 34, 102

Maidment, 206
Main, 226
Major, 238
Manger, 342
Mangin, 284, 286
Marchant, 132, 157, 229, 231
Marshe, 28
Marshman/Marcheman, 36, 70, 72-74, 76, 83, 151, 166, 167, 251
Martin, 38, 87, 88, 94, 110-11, 149, 191, 196
Mason, 223, 226
Massey/Maffeys/Mathey, 47, 195
Masters, 158, 238
Matthew, 134
Maxwell, 2, 12
Mayhew/Mayow, 148, 217
Mead, 225
Meadan, 234
Middlewick, 165
Miles, 223
Miller/Millward/Mylward/Melward, 54, 61, 68, 86, 89, 95-97, 167
Mills, 134
Moore, 191
Morgan, 122
Mountigewe, 87
Moxon, 242

Naish, 122, 189-95, 212-17, 219-21, 224
Nelson, Admiral, 115-16
Newman, 117-18, 182, 183
Nicholas/Nycholas, 18, 24, 29, 30, 32-35, 37, 38, 52-62, 63-64, 68, 70, 75, 76, 78-80, 89-91, 95, 102, 105, 119, 139, 141, 167, 172, 177
Nightingale, 170, 173, 174
North, 187
Northeast, 122, 223
Noyce, 323, 328

Oake/Oakes, 30, 33, 34, 70-75, 102, 103, 190, 216, 269
Osbourne, 27
Ovens, 243

Palmer, 72-74, 150, 224
Panye, 87
Parck, 76
Parker, 37, 54, 91, 95, 102, 139-44, 150, 156, 157, 184, 220, 225-29, 237
Parsons, 328-29
Pearce, 191
Pembrooke, Earl of/Lady, 18, 49, 138, 227
Penne, 180

FAMILIES PASSING THROUGH COMPTON CHAMBERLAYNE 387

Penny, 239

Penruddocke
Annie, 330-33
Arundel, 24, 108-12, 121, 218
Charles, 2, 8, 19, 25, 48, 104, 123, 124, 132, 146, 155, 157, 160, 163, 174, 200, 236, 239, 241, 243, 244, 288, 290, 292, 298, 313-322, 327, 330-34, 350, 351, 354, 356-58
Charles, Doctor, 332, 334
Connie 330-33
Constance Henrietta Lowther, 118, 334, 357, 358
Edward, Sir, 18, 19, 20, 24, 25, 77, 90, 97, 98, 106, 168, 177
Edward 104, 108, 120
Family, 6, 8, 16, 18, 20-21, 22, 25, 53, 80, 100, 106, 109, 114, 116, 117, 131, 136, 145, 146, 178, 191, 194, 195, 197, 229, 230, 313, 333, 356-58, 361,
Flora, 239, 330, 354
George, 18, 24, 25, 89, 177, 330, 356, 357
Henrietta Stafford, 53
Henry, 106
Joan, 70, 98-100, 106, 114-15
John, Colonel, 22, 25, 95, 100, 104, 106-112, 114, 117, 118, 120, 121
John Hungerford, 25, 118, 157, 163, 227, 236
John Hungerford, Reverend, 316
John, Sir, 20, 24, 25, 61, 92, 96, 99, 106, 111, 134-35, 136, 189, 196
Letitia Constance. See Connie
Mary, Lady, 98, 195
Mary, 99
Robert, 19, 119, 171
Sybil, 299, 318-19, 322, 330
Thomas, 25, 112, 113, 117-18, 123, 129, 157, 172, 174, 189, 194, 356, 341, 356, 358

Perrett, 327
Petty, 225, 226
Phelps, 238
Pigott, 256-59 260, 265-66
Pilchard, 167, 178
Pinchard, 243
Pinnel, 155
Plaunche, 17, 18
Plowman, 144, 156, 175, 184, 208, 224, 226, 227, 229, 230, 234-37, 245, 246, 281, 325
Pope, 102
Porter, 154, 177, 262

Powell, 100, 234
Pringle, 282
Puget, 259
Purver, 231
Pyle, 136
Pyper, 28

Rattenbury, 47
Rawlings/Rawlyns, 150, 180, 201
Raymond, 164, 225, 226, 236, 290
Read/Reade, 19, 32, 34, 36, 39, 77-79, 82, 102, 103, 156, 159, 160, 184, 206, 209
Reginald of Frome, 16
Richardson, 270
Rivers, 185, 226, 342
Roberts, 41, 49, 207, 225, 226, 231, 301, 318, 326-29
Rose, 226, 231
Rowden, 159, 182, 209, 226-28, 236, 239, 247, 303
Rowley, 72
Ruddle, 326, 327
Rumball, 229
Russell, 356

Sadler, 265
Sandall, 48
Sanger, 49, 144, 163, 201, 206, 226-28, 231, 238, 314
Sansom/Sansome, 20, 156, 157, 160, 162, 182, 226, 248, 281, 320, 333
Saunders, 20, 76
Scammel, 289
Seagrim, 49
Seymor, 99
Seymour, Sir Thomas, 17, 18
Shean, 132
Shepherd, 138
Shuger, 34
Shute, 312, 316
Sidley/Sibell, 20, 28, 72-74, 77, 102
Sidling, 222
Singer, 61
Skidmore/Skidemore/Skydemor/Scudamore/ Scudemer, 26-30, 71-74
Smith, 21, 61, 154, 156
Snook, 174, 200, 202
Snow, 220
Sopar, 149
Southern, 226
Steel, 184, 240
Stevens, 49
Stone, 63-64, 134, 136
Strong, 181
Sturgis, 167

Summers, 123
Targett, 184, 191, 195, 197, 226, 227, 239, 248, 253-55, 281, 290
Taylor, 127
Ted. See Smith
Thomas, 33, 96, 326
Thorne, 315, 316, 318-21, 325
Thresher, 191
Thring, 48
Tilley, 272
Toomer/Tomer, 92, 167, 171, 182
Toppe, 54
Trig/Trigg, 167, 178
Trowbridge, 90
Turner, 157, 203
Tutt, 167, 171

Venice, 224
Vincente, 149

Walker, 122
Ward
  Bishop of Salisbury, 128
  Elizabeth, 280
Warr, 333
Waterman, 56-58, 63, 136, 226
Watts/Wattes, 15, 41, 42, 63, 67, 68, 80, 82, 90, 141, 145-65, 178-80, 202-4, 212-18, 220, 221, 224-28, 235, 238
Webb, 151, 152
Webbe, 99
Weeks, 124, 225, 226, 229
Welch, 183
Wells, 63, 82
West, 156, 159, 227, 229, 280, 286
Wheeler, 86, 94, 97
Whitemarsh, 92, 102
Whitlock, 183, 268, 272
Whityere, 82
Wild, 226
Wilds, 285
Wilkins, 208, 209, 226, 227, 279
Wilmot, 124, 143
Witt, 144
Wood, 238
Worth, 54-55, 123
Wyatt/Wiett, 223, 226, 268, 269, 273, 279-83, 284, 285, 286, 287, 290, 318, 321
Wyman, 183, 185, 267-73, 279
Wyndham, 191, 265

Young, 240, 314

Zachariah/ Zaccarye/ Zacary. See Elkins